Called to Account

Accounting fraud and how it has affected business practices both in the United States and internationally has never been of greater importance than it is now. *Called to Account* describes fourteen financial frauds that influenced the American public accounting profession and directly led to the development of accounting standards and legislation as practiced in the United States today. This entertaining and educational look at these historic frauds helps enliven and increase understanding of auditing and forensic accounting for students.

Chapters describe the tricks fraudsters such as "Crazy Eddie" Antar and "Chainsaw Al" Dunlap used to fool their auditors. Readers will learn how MiniScribe employees disguised packages of bricks as inventory, how Equity Funding personnel programmed the company's computer to generate 64,000 phony life insurance policies, and how Enron inflated its profits by selling and then repurchasing money-losing assets.

Complementing these chapters on high-profile crimes and criminals are chapters that trace the development of the public accounting profession and explain how each scandal shaped current accounting practices. Designed to complement dry, uninvolving auditing and advanced accounting texts with an engaging narrative, *Called to Account* also includes discussion questions and a useful chart which shows instructors and students how each chapter illustrates topics in leading accounting and auditing textbooks.

Paul M. Clikeman is Associate Professor of Accounting at the E. Claiborne Robins School of Business at the University of Richmond.

Called to Account

Fourteen Financial Frauds that Shaped the American Accounting Profession

Paul M. Clikeman

NEW YORK AND LONDON

First published 2009
by Routledge
270 Madison Ave, New York, NY 10016

Simultaneously published in the UK
by Routledge
2 Park Square, Milton Park, Abingdon, Oxon OX14 4RN

Routledge is an imprint of the Taylor & Francis Group, an informa business

Typeset in Sabon by Wearset Ltd, Boldon, Tyne and Wear
Printed and bound in the United States of America on acid-free paper by Edwards Brothers, Inc.

Library of Congress Cataloging-in-Publication Data
Clikeman, Paul M.
Called to account : fourteen financial frauds that shaped the American accounting profession / Paul M. Clikeman.
p. cm.
Includes bibliographical references and index.
1. Accounting fraud–United States. 2. Corporations–Corrupt practices–United States–Accounting. 3. Accounting–Standards–United States. 4. Fraud. I. Title.
HF5616.U5C575 2009
364.16'30973–dc22 2008028151

ISBN10: 0-415-99697-X (hbk)
ISBN10: 0-415-99698-8 (pbk)
ISBN10: 0-203-88448-5 (ebk)

ISBN13: 978-0-415-99697-6 (hbk)
ISBN13: 978-0-415-99698-3 (pbk)
ISBN13: 978-0-203-88448-5 (ebk)

To my parents, Jan and Frank Clikeman

Contents

Acknowledgments

The inspiration for this book, like the ideas for many of my writings, came from my students. Members of the class of 2002, who spent their senior year watching Enron implode and Arthur Andersen disintegrate, asked for my opinion about the future of the public accounting profession. Many were worried about the status of their future employers and some had begun to regret majoring in accounting. "Don't worry," I tried to assure them. "Enron is nothing new. There was a bigger scandal than this while you all were in grade school, a bigger scandal than that before you were born, and a bigger scandal than that before I was born. The world will always need good accountants and auditors."

Although I outlined this book in a morning, it took more than three years to write. I could never have completed it without the research help of Kevin Rouba and Adam Cram, who spent many hours in the library, often with no more instructions than, "Go read fifty articles about such-and-such and give me a list of the five articles I should read."

Thanks to my friend and colleague Joe Hoyle, who listened to my plans for the book and encouraged me to stop planning and start writing.

Thanks, most of all, to my wife Margaret and my children John, Kathryn, and Miles who reminded me daily that this book was not the most important thing in the world.

P.M.C.

Introduction

> Double-entry bookkeeping is one of the most beautiful discoveries of the human spirit...
>
> (Johann Wolfgang von Goethe, 1796[1])

Accountants and auditors are the offensive linemen of the business world—underappreciated and seldom even noticed unless they give up a sack or get called for holding. While superstar CEOs collect huge salaries for quarterbacking their companies to victory, and Wall Street analysts earn accolades for forecasting winners and losers, accountants and auditors rarely get the credit they deserve for gathering and verifying the financial information essential to a modern economy.

The accountant's role is to provide useful information to economic decision makers. Accountants summarize millions of transactions into a few pages of financial statements, enabling managers, stockbrokers, portfolio managers, bank lending officers, bond traders, private investors, and government regulators to evaluate each company's performance.

Auditors protect decision makers from erroneous or fraudulent information. By examining samples of recorded transactions and verifying the existence of assets, auditors provide reasonable (but not absolute) assurance that the financial statements have been prepared fairly in accordance with generally accepted accounting principles.

Every day in the United States, investors trade millions of shares based on companies' reported earnings and creditors extend billion-dollar loans based on borrowers' balance sheets. Capital markets could not function efficiently without accurate financial statements prepared by accountants and verified by auditors.

Public Accountants and Fraud

The public accounting profession was born in Great Britain during the mid-1800s. The English Companies Act of 1845 required corporations to submit to an annual audit by a committee of shareholders and permitted the shareholders to hire, at company expense, outside accountants to help perform the audit. English and Scottish accountants established firms of "public accountants" to provide audit services. Notable among them were S.H. Price and Edwin Waterhouse, who established their famous partnership in London in 1860.

Throughout history, a handful of accountants and auditors earned praise for their success in fighting financial crime. William W. Deloitte, founder of today's Deloitte & Touche, helped unravel accounting frauds at the Great Northern Railway and the Great Eastern Steamship Company in England during the 1850s. Elmer Irey, head of the IRS Special Investigation Unit during the 1920s, played a key role in sending mobster Al Capone to Alcatraz. The *Wall Street Journal* (May 19, 1995) praised accounting professor Albert J. Meyer for exposing a $200 million investment scam at the Foundation for New Era Philanthropy. Auditor Cynthia Cooper was named one of *Time* magazine's 2002 "Persons of the Year" for her role in uncovering the $11 billion accounting fraud at WorldCom.

But throughout the twentieth century, American public accountants failed to detect many audacious frauds perpetrated by their clients. Accounting problems at companies such as McKesson & Robbins, National Student Marketing, Lincoln Savings & Loan, ZZZZ Best, MiniScribe, Sunbeam, Cendant, Rite Aid, Phar-Mor, MicroStrategy, HealthSouth, and Parmalat cost investors tens of billions of dollars. Each scandal was followed closely by angry cries of "Where were the accountants?"

Although auditors often responded with denials and excuses, many of these scandals eventually led to significant improvements in auditing procedures and financial reporting practices. This book describes 14 accounting scandals that significantly influenced the American public accounting profession. The scandals are listed in Table 1. Many of the scandals occurred because accountants and auditors violated existing professional standards. Other scandals revealed deficiencies in the standards of the time.

Table 1 also lists the most important reforms that followed each pair of related scandals. Some reforms were adopted voluntarily by the public accounting profession. Other reforms were mandated by federal legislation.

Frauds are certainly not the sole source of progress within the public accounting profession. Thousands of men and women worked diligently during the last 150 years to improve corporate disclosures, establish meaningful accounting principles, and develop effective auditing procedures. But change is often painful, especially for "conservative" accountants. A well publicized accounting scandal has often been necessary for the profession to admit its shortcomings and adopt improvements. Few politicians pay much attention to accounting until angry constituents demand reform.

Table 1 Scandals and Related Reforms

Scandals	*Reforms*
1. Ivar Kreuger (1932)	Federal Securities Acts (1933 and 1934)
2. McKesson & Robbins (1938)	Formation of the Special Committee on Auditing Procedure (1939)
3. National Student Marketing (1970)	Formation of the Financial Accounting Standards Board (1973)
4. Equity Funding (1973)	Metcalf Committee Report on the Accounting Establishment (1975) Cohen Commission Report on Auditors' Responsibilities (1978)
5. ESM Government Securities (1985)	Financial Institutions Reform, Recovery and Enforcement Act (1989)
6. Lincoln Savings & Loan (1989)	Federal Deposit Insurance Corporation Improvement Act (1991)
7. ZZZZ Best (1987)	Treadway Commission Report on Fraudulent Financial Reporting (1987)
8. Crazy Eddie (1987)	Nine "Expectation Gap" Auditing Standards (1988)
9. Fund of Funds (1970)	Organization of accounting firms as limited liability partnerships (1994)
10. MiniScribe (1989)	Private Securities Litigation Reform Act (1995)
11. Waste Management (1998)	Formation of the Independence Standards Board (1997)
12. Sunbeam (1998)	Revision of the SEC's Auditor Independence Requirements (2000)
13. Enron (2001)	Sarbanes–Oxley Act (2002)
14. WorldCom (2002)	SAS No. 99—Consideration of Fraud in a Financial Statement Audit (2003)

In spite of recent headlines, today's public accountants have much to be proud of. American capital markets operate more efficiently than any other markets in the world. And although highly publicized accounting frauds periodically raise doubts about the competence or integrity of American auditors, audit failures are really quite rare. Fewer than 1 percent of corporate audits are ever questioned by regulators or in civil litigation. But it is impossible to understand the American public accounting profession without understanding the scandals and failures that influenced so many of today's practices. Much of today's success is the result of reforms adopted in the wake of past scandals. And many of today's problems come from failing to resolve controversies that have plagued accountants for decades.

1 Scandal and Reform

Mistakes are the portals of discovery.

(James Joyce)

American public accountants faced a crisis in the spring of 2002. More than 300 earnings restatements in 2000 and 2001 revealed just how illusory profits reported during the 1990s had been. Enron's bankruptcy in December 2001 shattered investors' confidence, launching a 2,000 point decline in the Dow Jones Industrial Average. Soon after the Justice Department indicted Arthur Andersen for shredding 20 boxes of Enron-related documents, internal auditors uncovered an even more audacious accounting fraud at WorldCom. CPAs, once held in high esteem by the American public, fell below politicians and journalists in public opinion polls.

By the end of 2002, American financial reporting had been dramatically transformed. Congress responded to the accounting scandals at Enron and WorldCom by passing the Public Company Accounting Reform and Investor Protection Act, better known as the Sarbanes–Oxley Act of 2002. The legislation limited the nonaudit services accountants could perform for their audit clients and established the Public Company Accounting Oversight Board (PCAOB) to regulate public accounting firms. The AICPA's Auditing Standards Board hurriedly issued a new auditing standard requiring auditors to perform more procedures specifically designed to detect fraud. The Financial Accounting Standards Board (FASB) tightened accounting rules for special purpose entities, and the Securities and Exchange Commission (SEC) demanded more extensive disclosures of off-balance sheet financing.

But the events of 2002 were not without precedent. Seventy years earlier, Ivar Kreuger's investment scam at Swedish Match Company inspired Congress to pass the U.S. Securities Acts of 1933 and 1934. These landmark Bills required corporations to publish annual audited financial statements and established the Securities and Exchange Commission to regulate financial reporting.

Between 1932 and 2002, the cycle of scandal and reform repeated itself many times. Auditors' failure in 1938 to detect $19 million of fictitious assets at McKesson & Robbins prompted the American Institute of Accountants to issue the first authoritative standards specifying procedures for appointing auditors and conducting audits. The Equity Funding scandal of 1973 led auditors to develop new procedures for testing computerized accounting records. The savings and loan crisis of the 1980s resulted in new legislation requiring more thorough audits of financial institutions. Arthur Andersen's audit failures at Sunbeam and Waste Management during the 1990s influenced the SEC to revise its auditor independence requirements. In fact, the history of public accounting in the United States can be described as a series of scandals followed by voluntary or mandated reforms.

Birth of a Profession

America's fascination with the stock market began during the early 1900s. The number of Americans owning corporate stock tripled between 1900 and 1925 as new companies in capital-intensive industries such as broadcasting and automobile manufacturing sought funds for growth. But American investors did not enjoy the same protections as their British counterparts. Although British corporations began publishing annual audited financial statements in the 1840s, American corporations were far more secretive. Neither the U.S. government nor the American stock exchanges required industrial corporations to distribute audited financial statements to their shareholders.

During the 1920s, a Swedish financier named Ivar Kreuger raised more than $250 million from American investors by promising to pay dividends as high as 20 percent per year. News of Kreuger's suicide in March 1932 was followed closely by the revelation that $115 million of investors' money could not be located. Senators George Norris of Nebraska and Huey Long of Louisiana demanded federal legislation to protect investors from "scoundrels who peddle blue-sky securities."[1]

President Franklin Delano Roosevelt responded to investors' concerns by signing the Securities Act of 1933. The 1933 Act required corporations to publish a registration statement containing audited financial statements before selling securities to the public. One year later, Congress passed the Securities Exchange Act of 1934, which required public corporations to file an annual report containing audited financial statements. The 1934 Act also established the Securities and Commission to administer and enforce federal securities laws.

Although the Securities Acts of 1933 and 1934 required public companies to open their books to auditors, audit procedures of the time provided little protection against fraud. Auditors in the early 1930s were not required to physically examine their clients' assets or communicate with the clients' purported customers. A twice-convicted fraudster named Philip Musica exploited these loopholes to commit a multimillion-dollar fraud at McKesson & Robbins. With the help of his three brothers, Musica forged sales invoices, shipping documents, and inventory records to inflate McKesson's profits and assets.

The discovery of the McKesson & Robbins fraud in 1938 sparked extensive debate about the adequacy of auditors' testing procedures. The SEC interviewed 46 witnesses trying to determine whether McKesson's auditors had complied with generally accepted auditing standards and whether those auditing standards were adequate to ensure the reliability and accuracy of financial statements. Within six months of the McKesson & Robbins scandal, the Institute of Public Accountants published its first Statement on Auditing Procedure requiring auditors to observe their clients' physical inventory counts and confirm receivables via direct communication with debtors.

Generally Accepted Accounting Principles

The Securities Exchange Act of 1934 granted the SEC authority to write financial accounting standards for public companies. But the early SEC commissioners delegated the task of writing detailed accounting rules to the Committee on Accounting Procedure and its successor, the Accounting Principles Board (APB).

National Student Marketing Corporation (NSMC) used a controversial accounting technique called "pooling of interests" to increase its revenues from $723,000 in 1967 to $68 million in 1969. A subsequent SEC investigation concluded that NSMC had overstated its revenues and improperly recognized profit on the sale of two subsidiaries.

When the APB tried to abolish pooling-of-interests accounting in 1969, angry financial managers and investment bankers bombarded the Board with hundreds of protest letters. IT&T threatened to sue the APB to block the proposed rule change. Representatives from three of the Big Eight accounting firms questioned the APB's ability to write accounting standards. The AICPA was forced to replace the APB with a smaller Financial Accounting Standards Board (FASB) and grant voting rights to representatives from industry and the investment community.

Within weeks of the FASB's establishment in 1973, an accounting scandal at Equity Funding Corporation of America (EFCA) threatened the new Board's existence. Whistleblower Ron Secrist revealed that EFCA employees had programmed the company's computers to generate 64,000 phony life insurance policies. Ten young women were employed solely for the purpose of forging policy applications, doctors' reports, and other documents to fill fictitious policyholder files. Twenty EFCA employees and two auditors were indicted for participating in the EFCA fraud.

Representative John Moss (D, California) and Senator Lee Metcalf (D, Montana) held a series of hearings in 1977 and 1978 to evaluate current procedures for writing accounting standards and performing audits. Several witnesses recommended abolishing the FASB and letting Congress, the SEC, or the General Accounting Office write accounting and auditing standards. Other witnesses complained that the SEC had no procedures for checking the quality of independent auditors' work. Federal legislation was averted only after accountants adopted significant reforms. Accounting firms auditing public companies agreed to undergo a peer review every three years to determine their compliance with GAAS. And the firms promised to assign a concurring partner to each SEC client and to rotate the engagement partner every five years.

The Savings and Loan Crisis

The savings and loan crisis of the 1980s was the biggest financial debacle since the Great Depression of the 1930s. Dishonest savings and loan operators squandered billions of dollars on junk bonds and unsuccessful business ventures while manipulating their accounting records to hide their losses from depositors and government regulators. The U.S. federal government spent nearly $500 billion during the late 1980s and early 1990s to close more than 700 failed financial institutions.

The savings and loan crisis originated with the volatile interest rates of the 1970s. Interest rate fluctuations caused sharp changes in the prices of investment securities. Managers at ESM Government Securities began buying and selling millions of dollars of treasury bonds, gambling that they could predict when interest rates would rise and fall. When ESM's luck turned bad, CEO Alan Novick concealed $300 million of losses by recording fictitious transactions with an affiliated company. ESM's bankruptcy in March 1985 led to the near collapse of the Ohio savings and loan system. After Cincinnati-based Home State Savings & Loan lost $145 million on deposit at ESM, Ohio Governor Richard Celeste closed the state's 70 privately insured thrifts until emergency legislation could be passed to shore up the state's insurance fund. The most shocking aspect of the ESM story is that the company's auditor, Jose Gomez, learned of the fraud in 1979 but allowed it to continue for five years while accepting $200,000 of "loans" from ESM executives. Gomez was sentenced to 12 years in prison for his role in covering up the ESM fraud.

Lincoln Savings & Loan's bankruptcy cost U.S. taxpayers $2.3 billion. Charles H. Keating Jr. purchased Lincoln Savings & Loan (LS&L) in 1983 for $51 million. During the next six years, Keating and his family withdrew $34 million from Lincoln while investing more than $2 billion of the thrift's assets in junk bonds, undeveloped land, and unsecured loans. When government regulators tried to seize LS&L

in 1987, five U.S. senators—recipients of hundreds of thousands of dollars of Keating campaign contributions—intervened on Keating's behalf. LS&L's auditors did little to constrain Keating's reckless investment practices. Arthur Young partner Jack Atchison accepted a $930,000 per year position with LS&L's parent company shortly after permitting the thrift to report $80 million of profits on dubious land sales.

The House and Senate Banking Committees held hearings in early 1989 to investigate why so many savings and loans needed intervention. During the hearings, several government regulators accused the nation's auditors of abetting their clients' crimes. A representative from the Office of Thrift Supervision testified that the deficient 1986 and 1987 audits of Lincoln Savings & Loan were "proof positive that any thrift in America could obtain a clean audit opinion despite being grossly insolvent."[2] A GAO representative cited multiple examples of auditors failing to identify or report clients' internal control problems. Representative Henry Gonzalez, chairman of the House Banking Committee, concluded at the end of the hearings that public accountants had been "derelict in their duty to sound alarms about impending disasters in the [thrift] industry."[3]

Congress tightened regulation of savings and loans through the Financial Institutions Reform, Recovery and Enforcement Act of 1989 (FIRREA). FIRREA doubled the minimum net worth requirements of savings and loans and restricted the amounts they could invest in risky assets. Two years later, Congress addressed a similar crisis in the nation's banking system. The Federal Deposit Insurance Corporation Improvement Act of 1991 (FDICIA) raised banks' minimum capital requirements, prescribed standards for loan documentation, and prohibited "excessive" executive compensation.

Two other provisions of the FDICIA significantly affected the accounting profession. The FDICIA required auditors to examine and report on each bank's internal accounting controls. Eleven years later, the Sarbanes–Oxley Act of 2002 extended the FDICIA's internal control reporting and auditing requirements to all public companies. Furthermore, the FDICIA required banks to disclose the fair market values of their monetary assets and liabilities. Since 1991, the FASB has moved slowly but steadily away from historical cost accounting toward mark-to-market accounting.

Auditors and Fraud

Investors have always believed that the auditor's primarily job is to prevent and detect corporate fraud. But throughout the twentieth century, American auditors tried to disclaim responsibility for their clients' deceitful accounting practices. *Verification of Financial State-*

ments, published by the American Institute of Accountants in 1929, warned that the recommended auditing procedures would "not necessarily disclose defalcations nor every understatement of assets concealed in the records by operating transactions or by manipulation of accounts."[4] The 1957 edition of Robert Montgomery's influential *Auditing Theory and Practice* text described fraud detection as a "responsibility not assumed."[5]

A series of well publicized accounting frauds during the 1970s and 1980s forced auditors to accept more responsibility for detecting and reporting corporate wrongdoing. Two of the most audacious frauds occurred at ZZZZ Best and Crazy Eddie, Inc. ZZZZ Best was founded in 1982 by a 16-year-old high school student named Barry Minkow. Within five years, ZZZZ Best had a market capitalization of $200 million. But when ZZZZ Best collapsed in 1987, investigators learned that most of the company's purported revenues were fictitious. Minkow, who was barely out of his teens, was sentenced to 25 years in prison. Eddie Antar, the founder of Crazy Eddie's Ultra Linear Sound Experience, realized more than $60 million from sales of Crazy Eddie stock while recording false sales and altering inventory records to inflate the company's stock price. After the Crazy Eddie fraud was discovered, Antar fled the country and eluded police for more than two years while living off money stashed in secret bank accounts. Antar was eventually captured in Israel and sentenced to seven years in prison.

In 1988, the Auditing Standards Board issued nine new auditing standards designed to reduce the incidence of fraudulent financial reporting. SAS No. 53 required auditors to design their audits to "provide reasonable assurance of detecting errors and irregularities that are material to the financial statements." And the standard required auditors to treat management representations with professional skepticism. No longer could auditors simply assume that management was honest, barring evidence to the contrary. Other standards sought to enhance audit quality by improving auditors' procedures for evaluating internal controls, performing analytical procedures, and evaluating accounting estimates. The auditor's report was also revised to communicate more clearly the procedures performed and responsibility assumed by the auditor.

Auditors' Legal Liability

Auditors can be held liable under common and statutory law to their clients and to third parties, such as creditors and investors, who suffer losses after relying on false financial statements. Public accountants actually welcomed legal liability early in the twentieth century as a means of promoting higher-quality audits and disciplining negligent or dishonest auditors.

In 1968, Arthur Andersen auditors discovered, but failed to report, that King Resources overcharged Fund of Funds (FoF) millions of dollars on land transactions. FoF's subsequent lawsuit against Arthur Andersen for breach of contract resulted in an $81 million judgment against the accounting firm. Afraid that future plaintiffs would use the FoF case as a precedent to seek higher damages from auditors, the general counsel of a rival Big Eight firm called the FoF verdict "the single worst thing that has ever happened to the accounting profession."[6]

But the worst was yet to come. In 1992, a Texas jury ordered Coopers & Lybrand to pay $220 million for its deficient audits of MiniScribe. Senior managers at computer disk-drive maker MiniScribe had materially misrepresented the company's financial status by overstating revenues, understating expenses, and counting boxes of bricks as inventory. Although Coopers & Lybrand eventually settled the MiniScribe suit for "only" $45 million, the prospect that a single audit failure could bankrupt an international public accounting firm focused auditors' minds on the need for litigation reform.

Accountants' first priority was to protect their personal assets by reorganizing their firms from general partnerships into limited liability partnerships (LLPs). Laventhol & Horwath (L&H), the seventh largest public accounting firm in the United States, was forced to liquidate in 1990 after losing several civil lawsuits. Because L&H was a general partnership, L&H partners had to contribute $47 million of personal assets to satisfy the firm's obligations. After L&H's bankruptcy, accountants embarked on a multi-year campaign to convince state legislatures and boards of accountancy to permit accounting firms to reorganize as LLPs. In August 1994, Hawaii became the fiftieth state to allow out-of-state LLPs to practice accounting within its jurisdiction. Within weeks, all of the Big Six accounting firms had reorganized as LLPs.

Accountants' second desire was to reform the nation's tort liability system. Accountants objected strongly to the doctrine of joint and several liability, under which one defendant could be required to pay another defendant's share of the total judgment. Because accounting firms were often the only solvent defendant following a client's bankruptcy, auditors sometimes had to pay 100 percent of the damages caused by a client's willful wrongdoing. Accountants also complained that punitive damages were unjust and wanted plaintiffs to reimburse the defendant's legal fees if the court decided a suit was without merit.

When Newt Gingrich endorsed tort reform in his 1994 "Contract With America," accounting-related political action committees showered $3.6 million of donations on sympathetic congressional candidates. The Private Securities Litigation Reform Act of 1995, enacted through a congressional override of President Clinton's veto, contained several provisions that accountants hoped would limit their liability to shareholders and creditors.

Auditor Independence

Independence is the cornerstone of auditing. Investors and creditors demand audits out of fear that management-prepared financial statements might be biased. The auditor's role is to render an impartial and objective opinion on the financial statements. As U.S. Supreme Court Justice Warren Burger explained in a 1984 decision, "If investors were to view the auditor as an advocate for the corporate client, the value of the audit function itself might well be lost."[7]

Accounting restatements by two Arthur Andersen audit clients in 1998 raised serious questions about whether the auditors were truly independent of the companies they were supposed to be policing. Trash collector Waste Management recorded $3.5 billion of charges in February to correct prior year misstatements of depreciation expense, capitalized interest, environmental cleanup liabilities, and asset impairment losses. Eight months later, home appliance maker Sunbeam fired CEO "Chainsaw Al" Dunlap and recalled its 1996 and 1997 financial statements, saying they were materially misstated.

SEC investigators discovered that auditors at both Waste Management and Sunbeam had uncovered, but failed to report, millions of dollars of accounting violations. Waste Management's auditors waived $128 million of proposed adjustments at the end of the 1993 audit based on company executives' promise to correct the misstatements in the future. The partner in charge of Sunbeam's audit decided that known misstatements totaling 16 percent of Sunbeam's reported 1997 income were immaterial.

SEC chairman Arthur Levitt concluded from the Sunbeam and Waste Management scandals that auditors had lost their independence. Rather than providing an objective opinion on the financial statements, auditors were simply rubber-stamping management's desired results. Levitt, who had frequently questioned the propriety of accountants performing management advisory services for their audit clients, spent much of 2000 trying to revise the SEC's auditor independence requirements. Levitt wanted to limit the nonaudit services public accounting firms could provide to their audit clients.

The big public accounting firms strenuously opposed Levitt's efforts to restrict their service lines. Management consulting services, at that time, comprised more than 50 percent of their total revenue and an even larger share of their profits. The AICPA and the Big Five accounting firms spent more than $12 million lobbying congressional leaders to thwart Levitt's plans. Forty-six members of Congress wrote to Levitt urging him to withdraw or amend the independence proposal. Senator

Richard Shelby (R, Alabama) even prepared an appropriations rider that would have barred the SEC from spending any of its funds to implement or enforce the proposed rules.

In a last minute compromise, the SEC commissioners adopted new rules that permitted public accounting firms to continue performing information systems design work for their audit clients on the condition that companies disclose in their annual proxy statements the amounts paid to their accountants for nonaudit work. Auditors were also permitted to continue performing up to 40 percent of their clients' internal audit work. It would be another two years, until the Sarbanes–Oxley Act of 2002, before auditors were banned from performing information systems design and internal audit work for audit clients.

Professionalism

Public service distinguishes a profession from a business. In return for receiving an exclusive franchise to sign audit reports, CPAs are expected to protect the public from erroneous or fraudulent financial information. Article II of the AICPA *Code of Professional Conduct* requires members to "accept the obligation to act in a way that will serve the public interest, honor the public trust, and demonstrate commitment to professionalism."

For the first 70 years of the twentieth century, most CPAs managed to earn a comfortable living while fulfilling their obligations to the public. The growth in the U.S. economy and the increase in the number of publicly traded companies ensured a steady increase in public accounting firms' revenues. AICPA rules prohibiting advertising, direct solicitation and competitive bidding kept competition low and audit fees high.

But the market for audit services changed dramatically during the 1970s after the Federal Trade Commission forced the AICPA to rescind its rules against competitive bidding, advertising, and direct solicitation. Public accounting firms slashed audit fees in an attempt to gain market share. As auditing profits fell, accounting firms turned more of their resources and energies toward management advisory services (MAS). By 1998, MAS provided more than half of the major accounting firms' total revenue while accounting and auditing brought in only 30 percent. A special committee of the AICPA predicted that accountants could double or triple their revenues by performing new services such as certifying Web sites and evaluating the quality of health care. Critics wondered whether public accounting firms, which were promoting themselves as "multidisciplinary professional services firms," had abandoned public service in favor of profit maximization.

Enron and WorldCom convinced the American people and their representatives in Congress that certified *public* accountants had forgotten their responsibility to the public. Arthur Andersen collected $52 million of fees from Enron in 2001 while permitting their lucrative client to report improper gains from selling assets to special purpose entities (SPEs) at inflated prices. Enron's bankruptcy cost thousands of employees their jobs and pensions. Investors lost an estimated $60 billion as Enron's stock price dropped from $90 per share in August 2000 to just pennies a share in December 2001. WorldCom was an even more egregious audit failure. Somehow the auditors failed to notice that WorldCom accountants had capitalized $3.8 billion of line costs as additions to property and equipment instead of recording the costs as operating expenses.

Enron's bankruptcy led directly to Arthur Andersen's collapse. Even before the Justice Department charged Andersen with obstruction of justice for shredding Enron-related documents, dozens of Andersen's premier clients fired the firm, having lost faith in the reliability of its audit opinions. An auditor's only real product is his or her credibility. Nobody had any use for an accounting firm that was the butt of nightly jokes by David Letterman and Jay Leno.

One day after WorldCom announced that it would record a record-breaking earnings restatement, Senator majority leader Tom Daschle (D, South Dakota) decided to expedite a financial reform Bill drafted months earlier by Senator Paul Sarbanes (D, Maryland). Thanks to public uproar over WorldCom, the Sarbanes–Oxley Act of 2002 (S–Ox) passed the Senate by a vote of 97 to 0.

S–Ox was the most dramatic overhaul of the nation's financial reporting system since the Securities Acts of 1933 and 1934. The Bill tightened auditor independence requirements, assigned new responsibilities to corporate audit committees, required more disclosure of off-balance sheet financing, and increased the maximum prison sentences for fraud. Most embarrassing to public accountants, S–Ox established a governmental oversight board with authority to write auditing standards and inspect public accounting firms to evaluate the quality of their audits. Of most concern to corporate executives was a provision requiring companies to assess their internal accounting controls every year and disclose any material weaknesses in their annual reports. Some multinational companies reported spending 70,000 man hours—the equivalent of 35 full-time employees—to comply with S–Ox's internal control requirements.

Conclusion

Throughout the twentieth and into the early twenty-first century, clever fraudsters exposed flaws in the nation's financial reporting system. Some scandals led accountants to write new accounting standards to close perceived loopholes. Other frauds prompted auditors to adopt more rigorous testing procedures. When Congress or the SEC concluded that accountants were not responding adequately to protect investors, new safeguards were sometimes mandated.

The following chapters describe 14 financial frauds that shaped the American public accounting profession. Each pair of related frauds is followed by a description of the ways in which accountants, politicians, and regulators reacted to the frauds. Many of today's accounting and auditing practices can be traced directly to financial scandals of the past.

Part I

Birth of a Profession

2 Out of Darkness

Men loved the darkness rather than light, for their deeds were evil.
(John 3:19)

Charles Waldo Haskins, founding partner of Haskins & Sells and dean of New York University's School of Commerce, cited the above verse in a 1901 editorial urging U.S. corporations to voluntarily publish annual audited financial statements.[1] Although British corporations began publishing audited balance sheets in the 1840s, American investors were still living in the Dark Ages. Neither the U.S. government nor the American stock exchanges required industrial corporations to include audited financial statements in their annual reports. Few corporations voluntarily disclosed their financial condition.

Many corporate officers in the early 1900s argued that revealing their companies' revenues and profit margins would aid their competitors. Some complained about the cost of compiling, auditing, and distributing consolidated financial statements. Others questioned the benefits of financial reporting, claiming that few members of the general public had sufficient training to understand financial statements. The following statement by Westinghouse Electric's chairman in 1901 typifies the prevailing thinking of the time.

> the Directors as well as the Stockholders who own the largest amounts of stock, [believe] that in view of the existing keen competition and the general attitude towards industrial enterprises, the interests of all would be served by avoiding, to as great an extent as possible, giving undue publicity to the affairs of the Company.[2]

In reality, many business leaders probably resisted financial reporting because they didn't want their transactions and the results of their decisions exposed for public scrutiny.

U.S. Steel defied convention when it published its first set of audited financial statements in 1903. The company's president explained the path-breaking decision saying, "Corporations cannot work on a principle of locked doors and shut lips."[3] Other companies eventually followed U.S. Steel's example until, by 1930, almost 90 percent of the companies listed on the New York Stock Exchange regularly published audited balance sheets. Factors contributing to the spread of public financial reporting included: (1) heavy reliance on outside sources of capital, (2) the growing influence of the public accounting profession, (3) criticism from reformers, and (4) government prodding.

Capital Markets

The number of publicly owned corporations operating in the United States increased dramatically during the first 30 years of the twentieth century. New York issued almost 25,000 new corporate charters in 1925 alone. The number of companies traded on the New York Stock Exchange increased 50 percent from 1921 to 1928. Many of the new corporations were in industries such as mining, steel production, automobile manufacturing, and radio broadcasting that required huge amounts of capital.

The number of Americans owning corporate stock tripled between 1900 and 1925. At the turn of the century, most people kept their savings in a local bank or building and loan. Only 4.4 million Americans owned corporate stock. But during World War I, the U.S. government raised millions of dollars selling Liberty Loan bonds to the public. These bonds introduced middle-income Americans to the idea of buying securities. After the war, many novice investors were attracted to the financial opportunities available in the stock markets. Rising wages gave people more money to invest. An estimated 3.4 million Americans became first-time stockholders during the three years after 1917. By 1923, the number of shareholders had grown to 14.4 million.

In spite of this increase in public stock ownership, the United States still faced a capital shortage. Great Britain, through the early years of the twentieth century, was the wealthiest country in the world and had the most efficient capital markets. British financiers invested heavily in American ranching, mining, and railroad enterprises during the westward expansion of the mid- to late 1800s. The flow of capital from England to the United States continued until World War I.

U.S. corporations' demand for capital created a corresponding demand for financial reporting. British bankers were accustomed to receiving audited balance sheets from their borrowers. The banks began sending teams of English and Scottish accountants to the United States to keep track of their investments. British accounting firms opened U.S. offices to serve their British clients.

As U.S. corporations competed to attract capital, they gradually began disclosing more financial information. Famed hat maker John B.

Stetson Company was the first American corporation to furnish an auditor's certificate when it offered its shares to the public. Other companies eventually figured out that an auditor's certificate made their securities more marketable. J.E. Sterrett commented in 1909:

> Corporations of a better class here are of their own volition ... retaining public accountants to make periodic audits. Within very recent years this practice has made such headway that the present rate of increase will shortly place in an apologetic position those corporations that do not adopt the practice.[4]

The Public Accounting Profession

New York passed legislation in 1896 coining the title "Certified Public Accountant" and restricting its use to those who passed the state's entrance exam. Few people, at the time, knew exactly what public accountants did. Accounting pioneer Robert H. Montgomery was fond of joking, "The public thinks a public accountant is a bookkeeper out of a job—who drinks."[5] But public accountants gradually earned recognition for their expertise in preparing and auditing financial statements. By 1921, all 48 states had passed CPA legislation similar to New York's. There were approximately 12,000 CPAs in the United States by 1932.

As businesses grew larger and more complex, more companies sought an outside expert's help in summarizing their transactions and preparing financial statements. Corporate accounting records, maintained manually by often poorly-trained bookkeepers, frequently did not even balance at the end of the year. Auditors spent hundreds of hours locating and correcting errors. Auditors also helped top management deter and detect frauds committed by lower-level employees.

Public accountants practiced in firms ranging from sole practitioners to several hundred employees. In 1932, *Fortune* magazine listed the largest public accounting firms in the United States.[6] The top eight firms measured by number of NYSE members audited were:

1. Price Waterhouse & Co.
2. Haskins & Sells (forerunner of Deloitte Haskins & Sells)
3. Ernst & Ernst (forerunner of Ernst & Whinney)
4. Peat Marwick Mitchell & Co. (forerunner of KPMG)
5. Arthur Young & Co.
6. Lybrand Ross Bros. & Montgomery (forerunner of Coopers & Lybrand)
7. Touche Niven & Co. (forerunner of Touche Ross & Co.)
8. Arthur Andersen & Co.

Collectively, the top eight firms audited half the companies traded on the New York Stock Exchange. These firms, later dubbed the "Big Eight," dominated American auditing for the remainder of the twentieth century.

Public accountants used their growing influence to promote more complete financial reporting. The *Journal of Accountancy* regularly published articles and editorials encouraging companies to distribute audited financial statements to their stockholders. A January 1906 editorial praised the Equitable Life Assurance Society for hiring Price Waterhouse & Co. to audit its accounts.[7] The editors predicted that competing companies would be forced to adopt a similar policy to retain the confidence of the public. Another editorial credited the British Companies Acts with keeping England relatively free from corporate scandal, and lamented the fact that the United States recognized no duty for corporate managers to provide investors adequate information to evaluate the managers' performance.[8] In January 1919, the *Journal's* editors urged Congress to mandate audits of corporate accounts.[9]

Outside Critics

Harvard economist William Z. Ripley was an outspoken advocate of improved financial reporting. Ripley published an article in the September 1926 issue of *The Atlantic Monthly* decrying the sorry state of corporate financial reporting.[10] He chided International Business Machines (IBM) for jumbling most of its assets into a single account called "Plant, Property, Equipment, Machines, Patents, and Goodwill" without revealing the amounts of tangible versus intangible assets. Few companies recorded depreciation systematically. American Can doubled its reported net earnings in 1913 by recording only $1 million of depreciation expense after recording $2.5 million in the previous year. Many companies set up arbitrary reserves during good years and reversed them when they needed an earnings boost. Few holding companies published consolidated financial statements.

Ripley's 1927 book *Main Street and Wall Street* described the problems caused by inadequate financial reporting. Ripley argued that the lack of reliable financial information encouraged market speculation: "Speculation germinates in and thrives upon mystery."[11] Because investors were unable to evaluate the performance of individual companies, they resorted to trying to time swings in the overall market, buying indiscriminately when stock prices were rising and dumping their holdings when prices began to fall. Inadequate public information left average investors at a great disadvantage vis-à-vis corporate insiders who used their knowledge of companies' operations to make advantageous trades. Finally, Ripley believed that corporate secrecy contributed to labor disputes. Rumors of obscene profits enraged workers who had no reliable information with which to judge employers' true ability to pay higher wages.

Citing the proverb "Nothing kills bacteria like sunlight," Ripley recommended "publicity" (i.e., improved financial reporting) as the path to better corporate governance and more stable capital markets.[12] He argued that requiring companies to publish periodic financial statements would discourage managers from over-expanding, borrowing too heavily, or entering into imprudent transactions. Ripley asserted that periodic financial reporting would lead to fairer stock prices, thus benefiting even the investors who never opened their copy of the annual report.

Columbia law professor Adolf A. Berle, Jr. was another influential advocate of improved financial reporting. His 1932 book *The Modern Corporation and Private Property*, coauthored with Gardiner C. Means, criticized the inadequacy of information given to investors. Berle and Means described accounting manipulations such as overvaluing assets, deducting expenses directly from retained earnings, and crowding sales into the last period through which companies reported abnormal profits. Berle later became a member of President Franklin D. Roosevelt's "brain trust" and helped draft the federal Securities Acts of 1933 and 1934.

Government Regulation

At the beginning of the twentieth century, the U.S. federal government played an insignificant role in regulating industrial corporations. Corporations were regulated (or not) by the states. In the *laissez-faire* environment of the early 1900s, few states monitored corporations closely. States were eager to collect corporate registration fees and competed with each other to offer the most business friendly (i.e., least restrictive) terms. National publications such as *Collier's* and *Scientific American* regularly contained advertisements aimed at corporate organizers. Arizona promised one day approval of applications. Delaware offered the "Best, Quickest, Cheapest, Most Liberal" corporate charters. An ad promoting incorporation in South Dakota boasted, "This beats New Jersey."[13]

Professor Ripley termed the states' behavior "scandalous prostitution."[14] He accused states of pandering to corporate executives by issuing corporate charters granting broad powers to managers and few rights to shareholders. In *Main Street and Wall Street*, Ripley cited examples of charters that limited the rights of shareholders to participate in future issues of securities; granted management authority to issue new securities having priority over those already existing; permitted management to sell assets or enter into new corporate relationships without hindrance; and exempted officers and directors from liability arising from transactions contrary to the interests of the shareholders.[15]

Several U.S. Presidents flirted with the idea of requiring industrial corporations to publish annual financial statements. Theodore "Trust Buster" Roosevelt proposed in 1905 requiring full disclosure of the accounts of corporations doing interstate business. Roosevelt's successor, William Howard Taft, strengthened the Interstate Commerce Commission, which set up a uniform system of accounting for railroads. But Taft stopped short of requiring financial reporting by all companies.

The Federal Reserve Act of 1913 established the Federal Reserve Board (the "Board") to oversee the country's banking system. The Board, in an effort to help banks reduce their default rates, began encouraging banks to ask borrowers for audited financial statements. Thus, the federal government promoted auditing while not yet requiring it.

The Clayton Antitrust Act of 1914 established the Federal Trade Commission (FTC) and authorized it to investigate deceptive and unfair trade practices. FTC vice-chairman Edwin Hurley proposed establishing a uniform system of bookkeeping and cost accounting for all the principal businesses of the country. Hurley never succeeded in establishing uniform accounting standards, but under his prodding, accountants made their first serious attempt to codify acceptable accounting procedures.

Conclusion

Such was the state of financial reporting at the beginning of the 1930s. Audited financial statements were common, but not mandated. And the financial statements left much to be desired. Companies had wide leeway in valuing and classifying their assets. Cash flow statements were unheard of. Footnote disclosures were minimal.

In 1932 and 1938, respectively, accounting scandals at Swedish Match Company and McKesson & Robbins drew attention to inadequacies in the country's accounting system. Swedish Match's bankruptcy cost American investors $250 million—a huge sum at the time. Newly elected President Franklin D. Roosevelt acted swiftly to prevent future accounting frauds. But five years later, auditors' failure to detect a $19 million fraud at McKesson & Robbins revealed that accepted auditing procedures of the time were not sufficient to protect investors from management fraud. The McKesson & Robbins scandal prompted public accountants to overhaul their auditing procedures to improve audit quality.

3 Ivar Kreuger

> Someday people will realize that every balance sheet is wrong because it doesn't contain anything but figures. The real strengths and weaknesses of an enterprise lie in the plans.
>
> (Ivar Kreuger[1])

Ivar Kreuger earned the nickname, "Savior of Europe" by lending European governments nearly $400 million after World War I to rebuild their shattered economies. Greece used its $5 million loan to repatriate refugees from Turkey and Macedonia. Latvia and Estonia used Kreuger's money to build railroads and purchase seed grain. Poland was able to aid flood victims. Kreuger's $75 million loan to France helped stabilize the country's currency. A grateful French Parliament awarded Kreuger the Grand Cross of the Legion of Honor, the country's highest civilian medal. During the late 1920s, Kreuger was even mentioned as a candidate for the Nobel Peace Prize.

Ivar Kreuger's fortune was not built on oil, steel, shipping, or minerals. He made his money selling matches for one-half penny per box. During the early part of the twentieth century, when people still cooked with wood or gas and before the invention of the pocket lighter, the world's population consumed 40 billion boxes of matches per year. Kreuger's 250 factories produced 80 percent of those matches. His business was built on the philosophy "It doesn't matter what you make. Just so you make lots of them. And you control every one."[2] Ironically, Kreuger never carried matches himself, citing a "petty superstition" to anyone bold enough to inquire the reason.

After Kreuger's death in 1932, $115 million of purported assets could not be located. Kreuger had attracted investors by paying dividends as high as 20 percent annually. Although his match factories earned millions of dollars of legitimate profits, they did not earn enough to sustain such generous payouts. Kreuger's plan to dominate the world match market had deteriorated into an enormous "pyramid" or "Ponzi" scheme. Dividends had been paid out of capital, and the company relied on subsequent loans and stock issuances to repay initial investors.

Ivar Kreuger

Ivar Kreuger was born in 1880 in the small town of Kalmar, Sweden. His father Ernst was a wealthy businessman whose ventures included textile operations, papermaking facilities, and two small match factories. Young Ivar possessed an amazing memory. Family members claim that when Ivar was five years old he recited verbatim a sermon he had just heard. Then, as an encore, he repeated the sermon backwards. As a student, Ivar found he could recall whole chapters of books he had read days before. Kreuger used this gift in later years to impress business associates with his mastery of facts and statistics about almost any subject.

Kreuger was an indifferent student but, with the help of his memory and some suspected cheating, he earned a degree in civil engineering from the Tekniska Högskolen (Technical College) in Stockholm. After his graduation in 1899, Kreuger opted to seek his own fortune in America rather than join his father's business.

The 19-year-old Kreuger struggled in America. When his youth and accent prevented him from finding work as an engineer in New York, he traveled to the Midwest, where Swedish natives were more numerous. Kreuger worked briefly as a lineman for the Illinois Central Railroad and failed miserably trying to sell real estate in Chicago. He traveled to Denver and New Orleans before signing on with 10 other engineers to help build a bridge in Veracruz, Mexico. Within months, nine of the young men died of yellow fever and the tenth was murdered. Ivar returned to Sweden in 1901 to recover from his own mild case of yellow fever.

Kreuger arrived in New York for the second time in 1903 and found work with the Fuller Construction Company. For 50 cents an hour, Kreuger verified calculations in structural plans. At Fuller, Kreuger worked on a number of future landmarks, including Macy's department store, the Plaza Hotel, and the Metropolitan Life building.

Kreuger learned how to build with reinforced, or trussed, concrete while constructing the football stadium at Syracuse University. This notable innovation used iron bars inside the concrete forms to strengthen the building's foundation. Kreuger convinced Julius Kahn, the inventor of trussed concrete, to let him introduce Kahn Iron to Europe.

Kreuger returned to Sweden in 1907 and met a fellow engineer named Paul Toll who was also interested in opening a European agency for Kahn Iron. Their partnership, Kreuger & Toll, was an immediate success. With Kreuger bringing in contracts and Toll supervising construction, the firm tackled ever expanding projects such as a viaduct outside Stockholm, a switchback railroad, and a six-story "skyscraper" in downtown Gullspang. Stockholm hosted the 1912 Olympic games in a massive new stadium constructed by Kreuger & Toll.

The Match King

In 1913, Kreuger left the thriving construction company in the hands of his partner and devoted his full attention to his father's two small match factories. Sweden, at that time, produced the finest matches in the world thanks to an abundant supply of aspen wood and Gustaf Erik Pasch's invention of the safety match. It was Pasch's idea to remove the flammable phosphorus component from the matchhead and add it to the striking surface of the matchbox.

Swedish match production was dominated by the Jönköping Trust—a network of factories that produced billions of matches a year. To compete with Jönköping, Kreuger began acquiring the remaining match factories not controlled by the Trust. By 1915, Kreuger controlled ten factories consolidated in a company named United Match Factories. Kreuger's company earned $500,000 in profits and paid a dividend of 17 percent in only its third year of operations.

World War I, which devastated Europe between 1914 and 1918, was a blessing for Ivar Kreuger. With submarines prowling the North and Baltic Seas, the Jönköping Trust struggled to obtain raw materials. Kreuger produced his own potash and phosphorus, ensuring his match factories a steady supply. By late 1917, Jönköping's phosphorus inventory was nearly exhausted. Kreuger had just purchased Hamilton & Hansell, Sweden's leading phosphorus producer, putting him in control of Jönköping's fate. In December, Kreuger's larger, but weaker, rival agreed to a merger that united virtually the entire Swedish match industry under the name Swedish Match Company.

After the war, Swedish Match exported billions of matches to Western Europe, Russia, and Asia. The company's growth was hampered, however, by trade barriers. Many countries charged high tariffs on imported goods. To avoid the excessive duties charged on Swedish matches, Kreuger began buying match factories within his target markets. His agents used threats and bribery to convince reluctant owners to sell. When Kreuger gained control of enough small factories in a country, he closed them down and replaced them with a large, modern factory employing Swedish machinery and technicians.

By 1922, Kreuger controlled most of the match market in northern Europe and the Baltic region. But there were still large sections of Europe he could not penetrate. Several large countries including France, Germany, Spain and Poland produced their own matches through state monopolies. No imported matches were allowed and there were no privately owned domestic match factories to buy.

Kreuger eventually found a way to take over the state monopolies. Many European countries were deeply in debt and were desperate for funds to rebuild their war-torn economies. Kreuger offered loans of up to $125 million to governments in return for receiving the exclusive right to sell matches within the countries' borders. Prices were set by contract and the loans were repaid through an excise tax on Kreuger's matches. This strategy enabled Kreuger to obtain absolute monopolies in 15 countries and dominate the match market in 19 others.

Kreuger's wealth and political connections allowed him to live like a king. He maintained apartments in Stockholm, Berlin, Warsaw, Paris, and New York. The New York apartment—a penthouse on Park Avenue—was decorated with paintings by Rembrandt and Reubens and featured a rooftop garden with soil imported from France. Although luxurious, each apartment had one sparsely furnished "Silence Room" into which Kreuger retreated for hours of solitary thought. He was fond of the Swedish proverb, "Great things happen in silence."

Kreuger appeared to live a charmed life. He never married, but supported a mistress in most of the cities in which he had a residence. Society pages speculated about a possible relationship with Swedish actress Greta Garbo.

Even the great stock market crash of 1929 did not seem to bother Kreuger. He visited the White House in January 1930 at the invitation of Herbert Hoover and advised the President not to panic. That spring, Kreuger returned to Syracuse University to receive an honorary Doctor of Business Administration degree. New York Governor Franklin D. Roosevelt received an honorary doctorate at the same ceremony.

The Kreuger & Toll Fraud

Kreuger's method of taking over state match monopolies required huge amounts of capital. Between 1923 and 1931, Swedish Match paid an estimated $384 million for match concessions lasting 20 to 50 years.

When Kreuger had exhausted nearly all the sources of capital in Europe, he turned to America. Kreuger incorporated an American subsidiary, International Match Company (IMC), in 1923. IMC's common stock was held by Swedish Match, but its debentures and preferred stock were peddled to U.S. investors by the New York investment banking firm of Lee Higginson & Co. (LHC). Major institutional investors included Continental Illinois Bank, Chase National Bank, and the endowment funds of Harvard, Yale, and Brown Universities. IMC securities were also popular among small investors eager to share in the booming stock market of the roaring twenties.

IMC raised more than $250 million from American investors. The funds were transferred to Europe and loaned to various governments in return for match monopolies. IMC's money often passed through several of Swedish Match's 400 subsidiaries before reaching its final destination. Kreuger claimed the intercompany transfers shifted income from high-tax to low-tax jurisdictions. In reality, the transfers concealed the company's true financial condition. Swedish Match did not prepare consolidated financial statements and Kreuger took care that no one could see the entire picture. The employees who worked at Swedish Match's Stockholm headquarters had very segregated jobs. Rarely was one employee able to see both sides of a transaction.

After the worldwide stock market crash in October 1929, most companies contracted their operations and tried to reduce their outstanding debt. But Kreuger continued expanding. In 1930, he stubbornly proceeded with plans to acquire Germany's state-owned match monopoly. He did so in spite of the fact that Swedish Match was already overextended, new capital was difficult to obtain due to the deepening worldwide depression, and Germany's political and economic future looked uncertain. Kreuger advanced $50 million to Germany on August 30, 1930 and an additional $75 million on May 29, 1931.

At the same time Kreuger was lending $125 million to Germany, governments in central Europe began defaulting on their earlier loans. And unemployed individuals stopped buying new shares of Kreuger securities. Kreuger borrowed as much as he could from banks, often pledging the same assets as collateral for multiple loans, but he eventually exceeded his credit limit. As Kreuger grew more desperate for cash, he resorted to increasingly audacious schemes to obtain financing.

In one of his lesser frauds, Kreuger dropped a thick stack of currency on a Brussels bank manager's desk and demanded a receipt for 400 million francs. Kreuger departed with the receipt before the startled manager could count the money and determine that the bundle contained only 5 million francs. When summoned to return to the bank, Kreuger apologized, blamed the mistake on his stupid accountant, and returned the receipt. But in the intervening two hours, Kreuger had used the receipt to obtain a multi-million franc loan from another bank.

Kreuger's largest fraud involved $140 million of forged bonds. Kreuger traveled to Italy in October 1930 to negotiate for control of the country's match market. Benito Mussolini sought money to expand his military. Although the deal was never consummated, Kreuger pretended he had made the loan. He ordered his printer to produce 42 bonds, each with a face value of £500,000 sterling. The bonds were embossed with the Italian coat of arms and bore the names of Italy's General Director and Minister of Finance. Kreuger provided the signatures with his own hand. Then he reported the bonds as assets on his balance sheet and pledged the counterfeit bonds as collateral to borrow more money from Swedish banks.

Kreuger had little trouble keeping his auditors, underwriters, and directors in the dark. IMC's financial statements were audited by the public accounting firm Ernst & Ernst. Because IMC simply forwarded money to and received money from Swedish Match and its various subsidiaries, Ernst & Ernst's audit procedures consisted primarily of confirming transactions with employees at Swedish Match's headquarters via transatlantic cable. There were no contracts, vouchers, or statements that needed to be produced.

Donald Durant, principal underwriter with LHC, traveled once to Stockholm to visit Swedish Match's headquarters. Kreuger hosted a lavish party and introduced Durant to several distinguished-looking "ambassadors" and their wives. Durant, who spoke only English and could not converse with any of the guests, was awed by the pomp and elegance of the affair. He never suspected that the well dressed men and beautiful women were movie actors hired for his benefit.

On another occasion, Percy A. Rockefeller, the most distinguished member of IMC's board of directors, visited Kreuger's Stockholm office. Kreuger's desk contained two telephones. One telephone was real. The second was a dummy phone that rang when Kreuger pushed a secret button under his desk. Rockefeller's brief meeting with Kreuger was interrupted by "incoming calls" from Benito Mussolini and Josef Stalin. Rockefeller left the interview suitably impressed.

The King is Dethroned

After fooling his auditors for 15 years, Kreuger's luck finally ran out. IMC provided the $50 million for the initial loan to Germany in 1930. A.D. Berning, the Ernst & Ernst partner in charge of IMC's audit, could not understand why the German bonds were not deposited in the United States. He pestered Kreuger with questions, receiving one unlikely explanation after another. Tired of Kreuger's excuses, Berning informed Kreuger that he would travel to Europe in early 1932 to examine the bonds personally. In reality, the bonds were no longer in Kreuger's possession, having been pledged as collateral for yet another loan.

Needing money to pay his dividends, Kreuger offered to sell a Swedish telephone company he owned to International Telephone & Telegraph (IT&T). Based on IT&T's preliminary agreement to pay $11 million, Kreuger was able to borrow $4 million from various American banks. But IT&T's managers insisted on an audit of Ericsson Telephone's books before completing the purchase. When auditors from the London office of Price Waterhouse & Co. arrived in Stockholm, they discovered that Kreuger's company had a $7 million cash shortage. IT&T withdrew from negotiations in February 1932, leaving Kreuger more deeply in debt than ever.

Kreuger's last chance for financing was the Swedish government. While in New York, Kreuger negotiated a $2 million loan from the Riksbank. The agreement stipulated that Swedish government accountants would be permitted to examine Swedish Match's accounts. Kreuger agreed to the terms only because he believed the auditors would not begin their examination before he returned to Stockholm.

Kreuger was confident he could dominate any face-to-face discussion with the auditors.

Kreuger sailed from New York to Paris, arriving during the first week of March 1932. While staying in Paris, Kreuger learned that the Swedish accountants had begun their examination and were asking pointed questions about the Italian bonds. The accountants wanted to know, among other things, why the bonds had never been stamped and why the General Director's name was spelled three different ways.

Unable to pay his debts and under pressure from two sets of auditors, Kreuger realized his fraud would soon be discovered. Ivar Kreuger fired a bullet into his own heart on March 12, 1932, choosing death over public disgrace. Although his body was found within an hour, Kreuger's board of directors persuaded the French government to withhold news of his death until after the New York Stock Exchange closed for the weekend.

The Exchange opened in turmoil on Monday morning. The opening trade of Kreuger & Toll stock was at less than half of Friday's closing price. Trades of Kreuger's securities comprised one-third of the day's volume. The price of Kreuger securities also fell sharply in heavy trading in Berlin, Paris, and London. The Stockholm Stock Exchange closed for several days to prevent a feared crash.

Although news of Kreuger's death was a shock, the bigger surprise came three weeks later when investors learned the truth about his company and the reason for his suicide. The Swedish government engaged Price Waterhouse in late March to unravel Kreuger's financial affairs. Their preliminary report, issued April 5, concluded that Kreuger & Toll's last published balance sheet had been a "gross misrepresentation."[3] The December 31, 1930 balance sheet showed assets of $405 million, but the auditors concluded that many of the assets were reported at inflated values, were entirely fictitious, or were duplications of assets reported on the books of affiliated companies. The auditors estimated that Kreuger's companies' true earnings for 1918 through 1932 were approximately $40 million rather than the $316 million originally reported.[4]

The auditors' final report showed that Kreuger had paid far more in interest and dividends than his companies had ever really earned. For 15 years, Kreuger had relied on new loans and stock issuances to pay dividends and repay old loans. More than $100 million of investors' money could not even be accounted for and was presumed lost. The Match King and Savior of Europe was really the greatest swindler of his generation.

4 McKesson & Robbins

> Oh, what a tangled web we weave,
> When first we practice to deceive.
>
> (Sir Walter Scott[1])

F. Donald Coster, M.D., Ph.D. was the president and largest shareholder of McKesson & Robbins, a 100-year-old pharmaceutical company with annual revenues exceeding $170 million. The 1937 edition of *Who's Who in America* listed Coster as a graduate of Heidelberg University, a director of the Bridgeport City Trust Company, and a member of the exclusive Black Rock Yacht Club.

Philip Musica was the son of poor Italian immigrants. He grew up in a crowded tenement on Manhattan's Lower East Side and quit school at age 14 to work in his family's small grocery. Musica was an alumnus of the New York State Reformatory at Elmira and The Tombs prison in New York City, having been convicted of fraud twice before his thirtieth birthday.

On December 15, 1938, federal agents learned that F. Donald Coster and Philip Musica were the same man. Marshals arrived at Coster's mansion early the next morning to take him into custody on suspicion of committing fraud at McKesson & Robbins. But Musica would not be convicted a third time. Like Ivar Kreuger six years earlier, Coster picked up a revolver and took his own life.

Coster *né* Costa *né* Johnson *né* Musica

Philip Musica was conceived in Naples, but born in New York City in 1884. His parents came to America shortly after their wedding at the insistence of Philip's mother. The couple eventually had eight children, four boys and four girls. Philip's three younger brothers played active roles in the McKesson & Robbins fraud.

As a boy, Musica idolized Teddy Roosevelt, New York's brash young police commissioner. Musica followed Roosevelt's exploits in the newspapers, attended his speeches, and copied the future President's speech and mannerisms.

Musica was a business prodigy. By age 16, he was running the family's small store. Musica taught himself the import-export business while still in his teens so he could import olive oil, spices, and cheese from Italy. His direct importing eliminated the wholesaler's profit, enabling him to underprice his competitors.

Unfortunately, Musica was also a crook. In 1909, investigators discovered that Musica had been avoiding import tariffs by bribing customs officials to record incoming shipments at a fraction of their true weight. Musica pleaded guilty and was sentenced to one year in the New York State Reformatory at Elmira. He returned home less than six months later when his sentence was commuted by President William Howard Taft. It is still a mystery exactly how Musica was able to win the President's favor.

Musica's second business venture was also a fraud. Shortly after his release from Elmira in 1910, Musica founded the U.S. Hair Company. Wealthy ladies of the time used hairpieces to create elaborate hairstyles. Good-quality hair in lengths of 12 in. to 20 in. sold for up to $80 per pound. Musica borrowed large sums of money using forged documents indicating that he held large inventories of valuable hair. The company's stock traded briefly on the New York Curb Exchange. Musica's scheme collapsed in 1913 when an alert clerk at Bank of Manhattan Company noticed that a bill of lading had been altered. Bank employees opened containers purported to hold $370,000 of marketable-length hair and found only $250 worth of inferior hair, barbershop sweepings, and old newspapers.

After his second arrest, Musica was sent to The Tombs, New York's infamous city jail. While in The Tombs, Musica helped the District Attorney by informing on fellow inmates. Although he should have been transferred to a state penitentiary, local prosecutors kept Musica in the city jail where they could benefit from his information. Musica's cooperation earned his release after only three years.

Having been caught twice, Musica decided to work with the legal authorities rather than against them. Through friends he made in The Tombs, he got a job in 1916 as a special deputy of the New York Attorney General's office. He spent much of World War I chasing draft dodgers and investigating suspected German collaborators. During those years, he used the alias William Johnson to conceal his criminal past.

Prohibition was a godsend for people who possessed business skills and lacked scruples. Shortly after the Eighteenth Amendment was ratified in 1919, Musica/Johnson adopted a new alias, Frank D. Costa, and founded the Adelphi Pharmaceutical Manufacturing Company. Adelphi produced high alcohol-content products such as hair tonic and cosmetics. Bootleggers bought Adelphi's products in huge quantities and distilled out the alcohol to make booze.

Musica/Costa was as devious in his personal affairs as he was in business. While operating Adelphi, he fell in love with Carol Hubbard, the wife of a former business associate. Costa began plotting to break up the couple's marriage. First, he destroyed Edward Hubbard's business by using forged documents and a false audio recording to convince Hubbard that his partner was embezzling. Then, he sent an anonymous letter to a member of Hubbard's church, claiming that Hubbard was sleeping with the man's teenage daughter. Finally, he sent evidence of a two-year-old business dispute to prosecutors who arrested Hubbard for cheating a customer. Carol divorced her traumatized husband and married Frank Costa.

Late in 1923, Musica assumed his final identity. He changed his name to F. Donald Coster, M.D., Ph.D. and founded Girard & Co. Like Adelphi, Girard produced legitimate pharmaceuticals that were sold to drugstores at normal prices, but also sold bulk quantities of alcohol-laden products to bootleggers at extremely high prices. Musica/Coster hired two of his brothers to work in Girard's treasury and shipping departments under the aliases George and Robert Dietrich. The three Musica brothers altered the shipping documents and sales invoices to make it look as if all the products were shipped to respectable customers at reasonable prices.

In 1926, Musica/Coster used his bootlegging profits to purchase McKesson & Robbins, a struggling but respected 90-year-old company that sold milk of magnesia, cough syrup, and quinine. During the next 12 years, Coster built a pharmaceutical distribution network that rivaled national chains such as Liggett, Rexall and Walgreen's.

By 1937, F. Donald Coster was a nationally recognized leader. McKesson & Robbins had survived the Great Depression while so many others had failed. It operated 66 distribution centers in 35 states and Hawaii. The company's financial statements, audited by Price Waterhouse & Co., boasted $174 million of revenues and $87 million of total assets. In December 1937, a committee of congressmen, financiers, and leaders of the Republican Party visited Coster's home and urged him to run for President. Coster shared their disdain for "that other Roosevelt," but declined their invitation to seek the Republican nomination.[2]

The McKesson & Robbins Fraud

Most of the McKesson & Robbins fraud occurred at a Canadian subsidiary, McKesson & Robbins, Ltd. (M&R, Ltd.). Coster organized M&R, Ltd. for the stated purpose of entering the international wholesale drug trade. Ostensibly, the company sold crude drugs, the raw materials used to manufacture retail pharmaceuticals. In reality, M&R, Ltd. was a shell company that held little inventory and engaged in few real transactions.

To create "customers" for M&R, Ltd., Coster established W.W. Smith & Co. The president of W.W. Smith was the fourth Musica brother, living under the assumed name of George Vernard. The W.W. Smith office was actually a "letter-writing plant" containing seven typewriters, each with a distinct typeface and a unique supply of British-manufactured stationery. Under the direction of Musica/ Vernard, a clerk wrote purchase orders bearing the names of fictitious companies and mailed them to McKesson & Robbins. Robert (Musica) Dietrich, who supervised M&R Ltd.'s shipments, forged documents to make it appear that inventory had been shipped to the customers. George (Musica) Dietrich, McKesson & Robbins' assistant treasurer, transferred money between bank accounts to create the appearance of cash payments for purchases and cash receipts from customers.

M&R Ltd.'s primary purpose was to enable the Musica brothers to skim profits from McKesson & Robbins. M&R Ltd. paid W.W. Smith a commission of 0.75 percent for each alleged sale. The four brothers shared the commission, with Philip, the oldest brother and mastermind, getting the largest share.

Price Waterhouse & Co. audited McKesson & Robbins' financial statements during each year that Musica/Coster owned the company. Auditors in those days were not required to examine inventory or observe the client's physical count. Instead, auditors reviewed the vendor invoices, receiving reports, and shipping documents that supported the company's recorded inventory transactions. Nor were auditors required to confirm accounts receivable balances with debtors. They reviewed correspondence between McKesson & Robbins and its "customers" and relied on Dunn & Bradstreet credit reports for evidence that the customers were legitimate. With one Musica brother writing forged purchase orders on W.W. Smith letterhead, a second Musica brother recording false shipments, and a third Musica brother recording fictitious cash receipts and payments, it was easy to make the auditors believe that millions of dollars of inventory were flowing through the Canadian warehouses.

The Fraud is Discovered

The man most responsible for uncovering the McKesson & Robbins fraud was the company's treasurer, Julian Thompson. Thompson was a Princeton grad, a gentleman farmer, and an amateur playwright. One of his plays, *The Warrior's Husband*, opened on Broadway in 1932 with a cast that included Katharine Hepburn.

Thompson was working as an investment banker in 1925 when Coster sought his firm's help selling shares of Girard & Co. Thompson was so enamored with Coster, whom he described as "charming, knowledgeable, intuitive, and efficient," that he eventually joined McKesson & Robbins as the company's treasurer.[3] Thompson was wholly unaware of the fraud being carried out under his nose. He was more interested in raising prize dairy cattle and writing plays than in pharmaceuticals. He delegated most of his responsibilities to the assistant treasurer, George (Musica) Dietrich.

But in 1937, Thompson began wondering why the company's fabulously profitable Canadian subsidiary never returned any profits to its parent. The accounting records indicated that M&R, Ltd. held $18 million of drug inventory. Thompson proposed, and the board of directors agreed, that $1 million of the Canadian inventory should be liquidated and the proceeds returned to the parent. Coster was unable to comply with the board's directive—there was no Canadian inventory to liquidate—so he argued that it was important that all the subsidiary's profits be reinvested to expand its operations. Thompson found the argument unconvincing.

Thompson's suspicions were aroused even more in 1938 when he discovered that the commission to W.W. Smith & Co. was being paid by the parent organization, not by M&R, Ltd. Not only was the subsidiary withholding its profits from the parent, but the parent was actually subsidizing the subsidiary's operations. Curious to learn more about W.W. Smith & Co., Thompson obtained copies of the Dun & Bradstreet (D&B) credit reports that had been used to satisfy the auditors of W.W. Smith's viability. When he showed the credit reports to a D&B representative, he learned that D&B had never heard of W.W. Smith & Co. and that the credit reports in his possession were forgeries.

Thompson confronted Coster in late November 1938. Coster denied wrongdoing and accused Thompson of joining in a conspiracy to take over control of the company. Convinced that Coster was involved in some sort of fraud, Thompson reported the forged D&B reports and the suspicious W.W. Smith payments to McKesson & Robbins' board of directors.

On December 6, 1938, the New York Stock Exchange suspended trading of McKesson & Robbins' shares and the SEC opened an investigation. Early the next week, McKesson & Robbins' board fired Coster and George Dietrich. On December 13, the SEC asked for the arrest of Coster, Dietrich, and Vernard. Federal agents arrested Coster, fingerprinted him, and released him on bond. They soon discovered that the fingerprints of respected businessman F. Donald Coster M.D., Ph.D. matched those of twice-convicted fraudster Philip Musica.

5 Into the Spotlight

> From the record of falsehood and betrayal with which Kreuger besmirched the very pillars of finance in the leading countries of the world has come, particularly in the United States, the erection of new safeguards for investors. In our Securities Act are to be found preventatives whose origin is to be traced definitively to the Kreuger experiences.
>
> (K.L. Austin, *New York Times*, March 7, 1937[1])

News of Ivar Kreuger's suicide in March 1932 attracted great interest in the United States and Europe. Earlier profiles in publications such as *Time* and the *Saturday Evening Post* had made Kreuger a household name. People naturally wondered why one of the richest and most influential men in the world had taken his own life. Rumors of blackmail or syphilis abounded. One "witness" claimed that a letter from a famous actress had been found crumpled in Kreuger's hand.

But four weeks later, when Price Waterhouse reported that $115 million of purported assets could not be accounted for, curiosity and pity turned to outrage. American investors held more than $250 million of securities issued by Kreuger's companies. The price of Kreuger & Toll stock dropped from $5 to 5¢ within weeks. Kreuger's American victims ranged from Rockefellers to widows and orphans.

Congressional Action

More than two years passed after the stock market crash of 1929 without substantive action from Congress. The factors that led to the crash were not easy for the general public to understand. Nor were they easy for Congress to address—especially with investment bankers, securities brokers, and other powerful business executives exerting their considerable political influence to stifle reform.

But Kreuger's fraud captured the public's attention. Everyone wanted to know how his scheme worked. The *New York Times* published more than 300 articles about Kreuger's fraud during 1932 and 1933. Articles in *Fortune*, *Business Week* and *The Nation* described the fraud and blamed accountants, investment bankers, directors, the stock exchanges, and ultimately the government for failing to protect the public.[2] Millions of readers, attracted by the sensational aspects of the Kreuger fraud, received their first tutorial in the workings (and failings) of the American securities market. Pressure mounted for government action.

On April 18, 1932, less than two weeks after Price Waterhouse issued its preliminary report on Kreuger's finances, Congressman Fiorello LaGuardia denounced on the floor of the House the "carelessness, indifference, or connivance of the New York Stock Exchange."[3] Senators George Norris of Nebraska and Huey Long of Louisiana led a discussion of the Kreuger case in July and called for legislation to protect investors from "scoundrels who peddle blue-sky securities."[4]

Franklin Delano Roosevelt was campaigning for the U.S. presidency in 1932. F.D.R. believed that securities regulation was a moral, as well as economic, issue. He often told the apocryphal story of a small village in New York that was devastated by the 1929 stock market crash. One hundred and nine of 125 families lost their savings and half of them lost their homes. Roosevelt blamed the New York Stock Exchange and the investment bankers for the villagers' misfortune. He promised federal legislation to require greater disclosure in the marketing of securities and to supervise stock exchanges.

On March 29, 1933, shortly after his inauguration, Roosevelt outlined his intentions in a speech to Congress.

> Of course, the Federal Government cannot and should not take any action which might be construed as approving or guaranteeing that newly issued securities are sound in the sense that their value will be maintained or that the properties which they represent will earn profit.
>
> There is, however, an obligation upon us to insist that every issue of new securities to be sold in interstate commerce shall be accompanied by full publicity and information, and that no essentially important element attending the issue shall be concealed from the buying public.[5]

The Securities Act of 1933

The Securities Act of 1933, often called the "truth in securities" law, was one of 15 major pieces of legislation signed by F.D.R. during his first 100 days in office. With Congress passing an average of one major Bill per week, few senators or representatives completely understood what they were enacting. Legislators relied heavily on committees to draft legislation and trusted the committee chairmen to produce Bills worth voting for. Sam Rayburn of Texas, the powerful leader of the

House Interstate Commerce Committee, was the man most responsible for guiding the Bill through Congress.

The 1933 Act, which was modeled loosely on the British Companies Act, regulated the initial offering and sale of stocks and bonds to the public. The Act's primary goal was to ensure that investors received complete and truthful information about the securities offered for sale. To that end, it required corporations to register securities before offering them for sale to the public. Further, it required corporations to provide purchasers with a prospectus containing, among other things, an audited balance sheet and income statement.

Congress adopted a "preventative" rather than "punitive" approach to regulation in drafting the 1933 Act. That is, Congress sought to *prevent* fraud by requiring *all* companies to publish a registration statement and prospectus before offering securities to the public. Such an approach burdened all companies in the hope of dissuading the (few) swindlers.

Price Waterhouse partner George O. May testified at the Senate hearings and cautioned the senators against imposing overly burdensome regulations. "This is an absolutely unique thing," May testified,

> and therefore I see danger in legislating against it. The public should always be protected, but there is always the question of balancing risks against the cost. If you erect machinery of protection that is too expensive you will kill industry. There is no use legislating when dealing with a super-crook.[6]

But May's description of Kreuger as a "super-crook" was at odds with his own firm's investigative report. The Price Waterhouse auditors who examined Kreuger's accounting records in Stockholm reported that "the manipulations were so childish that anyone with but a rudimentary knowledge of bookkeeping could see the books were falsified."[7] The report went on to state that "entries in [the] general books were palpably false, few entries even looking reasonable on the surface...."[8]

Unfortunately, no independent party had ever been granted access to Kreuger & Toll's accounting records. Congress concluded that requiring public corporations to open their books to auditors was a reasonable safeguard against future frauds. The vital question remaining was whether public accountants would continue performing corporate audits or whether Congress would establish a corps of government auditors to examine corporations' financial statements. Colonel Arthur H. Carter, a West Point graduate and a senior partner at Haskins & Sells, testified at the Senate hearings and urged the senators not to usurp the public accountants' role.[9]

SENATOR BARKLEY: Do you not think it is more in the interest of the public that is to buy these securities, if there is to be any checkup or any guarantee as to the correctness, that it be done by some government agency rather than by some private association of accountants?

COL. CARTER: I think it is an impractical thing for the government agency to do it effectively.

SENATOR REYNOLDS: Why?

COL. CARTER: Because it involves such a large force. It involves the question of time.

SENATOR REYNOLDS: Suppose that we decide in the final passage of this bill here to employ five or six hundred auditors from your organization, that would be all right, then, would it not?

COL. CARTER: I do not think the type of men that are in the public practice of accountancy would leave their present practice to go in the government employ....

In the end, Congress decided to rely on private firms of accountants as the first line of defense against fraudsters such as Ivar Kreuger.

The Securities Exchange Act of 1934

Within a year of passing the 1933 Act, Congress began drafting a far more extensive piece of legislation to regulate securities trading. The Securities Exchange Act of 1934 sought to end many abusive practices that had been common during the 1920s. For example, the Act forbid "wash sales" (i.e., successive buy and sell orders) which had been used to give the impression of active trading. The Act also regulated insider trading and limited the amount of credit a broker could extend to a customer to finance securities purchases.

The provision having the greatest impact on accountants was a requirement that public corporations file an annual report (Form 10-K) containing audited financial statements. Thus, the 1934 Act ensured a steady stream of revenue to the public accounting profession. All public corporations had to be audited annually and only CPAs were authorized to sign audit reports.

The 1934 Act also established a new federal agency, the Securities and Exchange Commission, to administer and enforce federal securities laws. The SEC's Division of Corporate Finance reviews the annual, quarterly, and special reports filed by corporations as well as the registration statements for public offerings. The Division of Market Regulation oversees securities exchanges. The Division of Investment Management regulates securities brokers and dealers. The Division of Enforcement investigates suspected violations of securities laws and has the authority to levy fines, delist securities, and ban brokers or accountants from working in the securities market.

The SEC is governed by five commissioners appointed by the U.S. President with the advice and consent of the Senate. To ensure bipartisan representation, not more than three commissioners may belong to the same political party. Joseph P. Kennedy, father of future President John F. Kennedy, served as the Commission's first chairman from 1934 to 1935.

McKesson & Robbins

The media frenzy surrounding Ivar Kreuger's fraud eventually died down and the public's interest in accounting waned. But the discovery of a $19 million fraud at McKesson & Robbins in late 1938 put accountants and auditors back in the spotlight. Banner headlines announced F. Donald Coster's suicide. The Musica/Coster story was a newspaperman's dream—bribery, bootlegging, blackmail, and bloodshed. There were even allegations (later determined to be false) that Coster had illegally smuggled thousands of rifles to Generalissimo Franco's fascist troops in Spain.

After the more prurient aspects of the scandal had been exhausted, journalists turned their attention to the auditors' failure to detect the massive fraud. *Newsweek* said the McKesson & Robbins fraud raised "the question of whether ... present accounting methods are adequate," and later opined that "existing laws and practices are not adequate to protect the public and stockholders of giant U.S. industries if the top officials are not honest."[10] *Business Week* predicted in January 1939 that Coster's "misdeeds" were "bound to accelerate reforms in American corporate and accounting procedure."[11]

An editorial in the February 1939 *Journal of Accountancy* bemoaned the news media's renewed interest in accounting.

> Like a torrent of cold water, the wave of publicity raised by the McKesson & Robbins case has shocked the accountancy profession into breathlessness. Accustomed to relative obscurity in the public prints, accountants have been startled to find their procedures, their principles, and their professional standards the subject of sensational and generally unsympathetic headlines.[12]

The SEC Investigates

The McKesson & Robbins scandal threatened to destroy the public's fragile faith in the securities markets less than five years after Congress shored up the public's confidence with the Securities Acts. Quick action was needed to avoid another stock market crash. The SEC commenced an investigation on December 29, 1938 with the dual objectives of determining whether the Price Waterhouse auditors had complied with accepted auditing standards of the time and whether those standards were adequate to ensure the reliability and accuracy of financial statements.

The SEC convened hearings from January 5 through April 25, 1939. Forty-six witnesses provided 4,587 pages of testimony and an additional 3,000 pages of exhibits. The topics discussed at the hearings ranged from the basic responsibilities of auditors and the meaning of the auditor's report to the ratio of accounting firm partners to staff and the specific procedures used to test various balance sheet accounts.

While the SEC conducted its investigation, auditors frantically reviewed their own procedures with the goal of adopting improvements before the SEC mandated more draconian changes. The most authoritative compilation of auditing procedures at the time was a brochure entitled *Examination of Financial Statements by Independent Public Accountants*, published by the Institute of Public Accountants (the "Institute") in 1936. In early 1939, the Institute appointed a committee, chaired by Patrick Glover, to consider whether auditing procedures should be amended in light of the failures at McKesson & Robbins.

By May 1939, Glover's committee had completed the first draft of its recommendations. The report recommended that auditors observe clients' physical inventory counts and confirm receivables via direct communications with debtors. Both procedures were recommended as best practices in the Institute's 1936 compilation of auditing procedures, but were not mandatory. The report also suggested that auditors be engaged or nominated by the board of directors rather than by company management. The recommendations were approved, with only minor revisions, by the members of the Institute at their 1939 annual meeting, and the substance of the report was published in Statements on Auditing Procedure No. 1, *Extensions of Auditing Practice*.

The SEC's final report on the McKesson & Robbins fraud, released in 1940, recommended reforms of auditor engagement and reporting practices.[13] Noting that Coster had hired Price Waterhouse without input from McKesson & Robbins' board and that board members did not receive copies of the engagement letter or long-form audit report, the SEC recommended:

1. Election of auditors for the current year by a vote of the stockholders at the annual meeting.
2. Establishment of a committee, selected from non-officer members of the board of directors, to nominate auditors and arrange the details of the engagement.
3. The short-form audit report (or opinion) should be addressed to the stockholders and copies of all other reports should be delivered by the auditors to each board member.
4. Auditors should attend stockholder meetings to answer questions and should report whether they were given access to all the information they required.

The SEC also recommended that auditors spend more time independently verifying assets rather than simply testing the accuracy of the client's accounting records. The SEC concluded, "The time has long since passed, if it ever existed, when the basis of an audit was restricted to the material appearing in the books and records."[14] The report called for "a material advance in the development of auditing procedures whereby the facts disclosed by the records and documents of the firm being examined are to a greater extent checked by the auditors through physical examination or independent confirmation."[15]

Other SEC recommendations included more thorough assessments of internal controls and more extensive background investigations of new clients.

Conclusion

The Kreuger & Toll and McKesson & Robbins frauds were the most significant accounting scandals of the first half of the twentieth century. During the first 30 years after New York passed the first CPA legislation in 1896, more than 12,000 accountants earned the CPA designation and investors came to expect corporations to provide audited balance sheets. But the future of the public accounting profession hung by a thread in 1933 as Congress contemplated establishing a corps of government auditors to perform corporate audits.

Ultimately, accountants and auditors benefited from Ivar Kreuger's chicanery. The Securities Acts of 1933 and 1934 increased the demand for public accountants' services by mandating that all public corporations file audited financial statements. Public accountants were perceived as watchdogs protecting innocent investors from swindlers such as Kreuger.

Five years later, faith in the public accounting profession was almost destroyed by the revelation that a twice-convicted fraudster had deceived the most respected public accounting firm in the world. Powerful voices in government and the media questioned auditors' procedures and demanded reform.

But once again, public accountants escaped relatively unscathed. The SEC declined to prescribe detailed audit procedures. The Commission commended Patrick Glover's committee for drafting new audit requirements in the wake of the McKesson & Robbins crisis. The American Institute of Accountants established the first permanent committee to write auditing standards in 1939. The Committee on Auditing Standards and its successors, the Auditing Standards Executive Committee and the Auditing Standards Board, were permitted to write auditing standards for the next six decades.

The February 1939 *Journal of Accountancy* editorial concluded:

> We feel that in the long run this publicity will not be entirely harmful to the profession. On no other occasion has there been as much public discussion about accounting simultaneously in all parts of the country. The importance of independent audits and of accounting procedure will not be forgotten. We predict that in the future auditors will encounter less resistance to examinations of wider scope and less effort to place limitations on their work than in the past.[16]

While this might have sounded like wishful thinking during the depths of the McKesson & Robbins scandal, audits did expand in scope and frequency in subsequent years. The next 60 years were a time of growth and prosperity for the public accounting profession.

Part II

The Profession's Principle Problem

6 Generally Accepted Accounting Principles

> Accounting is the universal language of business. The prime requisite of a language is that it be understandable. In order to be understandable, a language must possess a clearly defined terminology, and the lack of this is the chief defect of accounting. Accounting, however, needs something more than a definite nomenclature. It needs above all else the formulation of sound theories.
>
> (Henry Rand Hatfield, 1927[1])

Double-entry bookkeeping originated in Italy during the fifteenth century. Luca Pacioli, a Franciscan monk and renowned mathematician, published the first complete description of double-entry bookkeeping in 1494. Pacioli's treatise was translated into English, Dutch, Russian, and German. Merchants throughout the world soon adopted the "Venetian" or double-entry method of recording transactions. Double-entry bookkeeping remains the foundation of accounting and financial reporting today.

Few accounting principles were needed in the mercantile economy of Pacioli's time. Common sense was sufficient to record purchases and sales of inventory. And consistency between enterprises was not vital because there were few situations in which investors or creditors needed to compare the accounting records of two or more companies.

But in a modern economy, transactions are more complex and the need for sound accounting principles is far greater. The industrial revolution necessitated figuring out how to depreciate long-lived assets such as railroad lines and steel mills. Changing prices led to debates about whether assets should be reported at historical cost or current value. Complex financial instruments, such as preferred stock and convertible bonds, blurred the line between liabilities and stockholders' equity.

When U.S. corporations began publishing financial statements in the early years of the twentieth century, there were vast disparities in the methods used to value assets and allocate costs. William Z. Ripley documented many of these variances in *Main Street and Wall Street*. Accounting educator Henry Rand Hatfield complained that accountants did not even have universally accepted definitions for common terms such as net income.

Contrary to the modern stereotype of accountants as being obsessed with rules, accountants of the early 1900s fiercely resisted efforts to impose strict accounting standards. Accountants resented having restrictions placed on their professional judgment. Clients liked having flexibility to record transactions as they wished.

The American Institute of Accountants (AIA) responded to Professor Hatfield's criticism by publishing *Accounting Terminology*, a book of definitions of common accounting terms. But this glossary, published in 1931, was about as far as the AIA wanted to go in setting accounting standards. The AIA's Special Committee on the Development of Accounting Principles, chaired by Price Waterhouse partner George O. May, concluded in 1934 that it was neither feasible nor desirable to prescribe a uniform set of accounting rules for all corporations to follow. May advocated allowing accountants wide latitude to use whatever accounting methods they deemed appropriate as long as the methods were disclosed. He wrote:

> Within quite wide limits, it is relatively unimportant to the investor what precise rules or conventions are adopted by a corporation in reporting its earnings if he knows what method is being followed and is assured that it is followed consistently from year to year.[2]

Demand for Standards

Carman G. Blough was appointed the SEC's first chief accountant in 1935. One of the SEC's primary duties was reviewing the registration statements and annual reports filed by corporations and determining whether the financial statements fairly reflected the companies' profits and financial position. Blough soon became frustrated by the lack of uniformity among financial statements filed with the Commission.

In 1937, Blough published an article in the *Accounting Review* bemoaning the absence of a generally recognized body of accounting principles.

> In the course of our day to day work, it is necessary for us to decide whether accounting procedures followed by registrants are in accordance with principles that are accepted. It is almost unbelievable how many times questions are presented upon which it is impossible to find uniformity of opinion among text-book writers or among practicing accountants.
>
> Almost daily, principles that for years I had thought were definitely accepted among the members of the profession are violated in a registration statement prepared by some accountant in whom I

> have high confidence. Indeed, an examination of hundreds of statements filed with our Commission almost leads one to the conclusion that aside from the simple rules of double entry bookkeeping, there are very few principles of accounting upon which the accountants of this country are in agreement.[3]

Congress, in the Securities Exchange Act of 1934, gave the SEC authority to write financial accounting and reporting standards for publicly held companies. Blough expressed hope that the profession *itself* would develop more uniform accounting standards. But the last paragraph of his article contained the thinly veiled threat that the SEC would begin prescribing accounting principles if the profession failed to do so.

Committee on Accounting Procedure

Faced with the prospect of having standards imposed by the government, the AIA established the Committee on Accounting Procedure (CAP) in 1938 and authorized it to issue pronouncements on specific accounting issues. Accounting Research Bulletin (ARB) No. 1 explained the CAP's goal of providing investors with useful financial data. The CAP issued a total of 51 ARBs during the next 20 years advising companies how to account for transactions such as long-term construction contracts, pensions, contingencies, and business combinations.

The CAP decided at its inception to address specific accounting problems rather than try to write a comprehensive set of accounting principles. This early decision not to develop a conceptual framework probably doomed the CAP to failure. One of the major complaints about accounting in the 1930s was that there were multiple "accepted" methods for valuing inventories, calculating depreciation, recognizing income, and accounting for pensions. Alternative accounting treatments made it difficult for investors to compare the reported net incomes of two or more companies. But without agreed-upon principles for valuing assets and measuring profits the CAP had no basis upon which to judge one accounting method superior to another.

In fact, ARBs derived their authority solely from acceptance by the accounting profession. The SEC never granted the CAP official authority to write accounting standards, nor did the AIA require its members to follow CAP pronouncements. There was even disagreement over whether the CAP had authority to disallow widely used methods. Thus, financial statements came to be prepared according to "generally accepted" accounting principles, but not necessarily "logically consistent," "theoretically sound," or "economically relevant" accounting principles.

During the late 1950s, a number of factors led to the CAP's dissolution. The Committee tackled a number of contentious accounting issues for which no consensus existed as to the proper accounting. Committee members struggled to write standards that would garner the two-thirds majority needed for adoption. Also, members of the Controllers Institute of America (CIoA) complained about their lack of representation on the CAP. The AIA appointed only academics and representatives from public accounting firms to the CAP. CIoA members claimed they were not being given sufficient opportunity to comment on proposed bulletins before their issuance. Finally, Arthur Andersen partner Leonard Spacek accused the CAP of yielding to industry pressure on a proposed pronouncement. Although AIA leaders defended the CAP vigorously, Spacek's allegations damaged the Committee's reputation.

Accounting Principles Board

The Accounting Principles Board (APB) succeeded the CAP in 1959. The composition of the APB was similar to that of the CAP. The 21 members served on a volunteer basis while retaining their full-time jobs. A two-thirds majority was required to enact a new standard.

At the same time it commissioned the APB to issue pronouncements (called Opinions), the AIA also expanded its research division. Not wanting to repeat the fateful error of the CAP, the research division immediately took on the task of developing a set of basic postulates and principles to guide APB Opinions.

Accounting Research Study (ARS) No. 1, *The Basic Postulates of Accounting*, was published in 1961 without controversy. But ARS No. 3, *A Tentative Set of Broad Accounting Principles for Business Enterprises*, inspired heated debate.

The most controversial component of ARS No. 3 was its suggestion that inventories and fixed assets be reported at current values. In fact, the question of whether assets should be reported at historical cost or at current value had dogged the accounting profession for decades. Professor Hatfield noted in his 1927 essay that accounting deals primarily with imputed values and changes therein, yet accountants had never formulated a compelling theory as to what value is proper for accounting purposes.[4]

During the 1920s, some corporations experimented with revaluing certain assets to their current replacement costs at year-end. But the SEC, fearing that companies would report arbitrary values to manipulate their earnings, insisted that all assets be valued at historical cost. Professors W.A. Paton and A.C. Littleton defended historical cost accounting in their landmark monograph, *An Introduction to Corporate Accounting Standards*. Paton and Littleton's book, published in 1940, was distributed to all members of the AIA and became the most widely read book in college accounting courses during the 1940s and 1950s. Their book helped convince an entire generation of accountants that assets should be reported at historical cost.

Consequently, when ARS No. 3 was released in 1962, few APB members were open to deviating from historical cost accounting. The Board announced that ARS No. 3 was "too radically different from present generally accepted accounting principles for acceptance at this time."[5] It would be another 12 years after the rejection of ARS No. 3 before an accounting standard-setting organization made another serious attempt to develop a conceptual framework for accounting.

Without a set of basic principles to guide it, the APB continued the CAP's practice of addressing individual accounting problems on an *ad hoc* basis. Although the APB's approach to standard-setting has been described as "topic-by-topic firefighting," the Board did issue several important pronouncements. APB Opinion No. 3 added a third basic financial statement—the Statement of Sources and Applications of Funds—to companies' annual reports.[6] The APB also provided much needed guidance on how corporations should account for income taxes and calculate earnings per share.

The SEC's Influence on Accounting Standards

The Securities Exchange Act of 1934 granted the SEC authority to prescribe accounting standards for publicly traded corporations. Almost immediately, there was disagreement among the five commissioners over whether the SEC should write standards directly or allow accountants to take the lead in developing standards. Commissioners Robert Healy and William O. Douglas did not trust accountants to serve the public interest. Douglas, who was later appointed to the Supreme Court by Franklin Roosevelt, believed that auditors sometimes favored clients to the detriment of investors. But Chairman James Landis was reluctant to take on the task of writing accounting standards. Landis was not an accountant (nor were any of the other four commissioners) and did not feel qualified to make accounting decisions. In a 3–2 vote, Commissioners J.D. Ross and Robert Healy joined Landis in deciding to allow the private sector to take the lead in writing corporate standards accounting. The SEC announced in April 1938 that it would accept financial statements prepared according to accounting standards for which there was "substantial authoritative support."[7]

In spite of its decision to let accountants take the lead in writing their own standards, the SEC began issuing Accounting Series Releases (ASRs) in 1938. Most of the early ASRs supplemented CAP pronouncements or described disclosures the SEC wanted companies to include in their filings. Occasionally, however, the Commission grew impatient waiting for the CAP or APB to deal with a particular accounting issue and issued its own peremptory guidance.

The first serious conflict between the SEC and the APB occurred in 1962 when Congress established an investment tax credit for companies who purchased long-term assets such as vehicles and factory equipment. Companies were allowed to subtract a percentage of a qualifying asset's cost from their tax liability in the year the asset was purchased. After much debate, the APB concluded that companies should report the tax benefit on a piecemeal basis over the life of the asset.[8]

The APB's decision infuriated many members of the business community. They wanted to report the entire tax credit as a reduction of expense in the first year. Business lobbyists appealed to the SEC and Congress to overturn the APB's decision. Under pressure from the Kennedy administration and several powerful members of Congress, the SEC issued ASR No. 96 stating that it would accept financial statements prepared using either the APB's "deferral" method or the alternative "flow-through" method.[9]

In spite of AICPA president Robert E. Witschey's plea for auditors to enforce the APB's standard, many accounting firms issued clean audit reports to their clients who accounted for the investment tax credit using the flow-through method. Three of the Big Eight accounting firms announced that they would not follow the APB's guidance. The APB capitulated in 1964 by issuing a new Opinion allowing companies to account for the investment tax credit using use either of the two methods.[10]

Although the APB functioned for another 10 years, the SEC's failure to back the Board in 1962 seriously impaired the APB's effectiveness. One of the APB's original purposes was to narrow the areas of difference and inconsistency in accounting practice. But because of the SEC's lack of support, APB Opinion No. 4 ended up creating yet another opportunity for corporations to choose between two "generally accepted" accounting treatments.

The controversy over the investment tax credit also emboldened business groups to resist APB proposals and to appeal to the SEC and/or Congress if necessary. The APB had to defend many of its subsequent proposals from attacks by the business community. Members of the Financial Executives Institute wrote nearly 1,000 letters opposing a draft proposal regarding accounting for income taxes. The American Bankers Association fought a proposed rule regarding accounting for losses on sales of securities. Members of the leasing industry organized a letter-writing campaign aimed at convincing 50 influential members of Congress that American companies would be prevented from raising capital for expansion and modernization if they were required to report long-term leases as liabilities on their balance sheets. The SEC advised the APB to postpone its proposed action after hearing from several concerned senators and representatives.

Merger Mania

The frequency and size of corporate mergers increased dramatically during the 1960s. *Fortune* magazine attributed the increased merger activity to a "new breed" of managers who viewed corporations as portfolios (i.e., collections of businesses).[11] Such managers built diversified conglomerates with subsidiaries operating in many industries. Growth-oriented companies increased their earnings per share by acquiring companies trading at low price-earnings ratios. At the height of merger mania, some corporations began acquiring other companies simply to avoid being taken over themselves.

Most of the mergers in the late 1960s were stock deals. The acquiring company issued shares of its common stock to the target company's shareholders in exchange for their stock. Cash rarely changed hands.

The CAP, in 1957, authorized companies to account for certain stock-for-stock trades using an accounting procedure known as "pooling of interests." After a pooling, the two companies essentially added their financial statements together. The combined company's balance sheet showed both companies' assets at their original historical costs. The consolidated income statement showed both companies' revenues and expenses from all previous periods as if the two companies had always been one.

Under the alternative method of accounting for acquisitions—purchase accounting—the subsidiary's assets were added to the parent's balance sheet at their fair market values and only the earnings *since the acquisition date* were included in consolidated net income.

Pooling-of-interests accounting was originally intended to be used in situations wherein the merging companies were approximately the same size and the management team of the merged entity included representatives from both firms. Under such circumstances, it was difficult to say who had taken over whom. The business combination was recorded as if the two companies had simply combined their resources to form a more perfect union.

But by the mid-1960s, virtually all stock financed mergers were being accounted for as poolings-of-interests. The restrictions on pooling expressed by the CAP in ASR No. 48 were ambiguous and were rarely enforced by auditors. The primary attraction of pooling was permission to include the acquired company's entire annual net income in the acquiring company's profits even if the merger was consummated on December 31. Companies increased their earnings by acquiring other companies and it was difficult, if not impossible, for investors to determine how much of the earnings were generated by the original company and how much by the newly acquired subsidiaries. *Business Week* observed in October 1968, "This stratagem can help create a beautiful, parabolic earnings curve that mesmerizes investors...."[12]

Several prominent accountants such as J.S. Seidman and Abraham Briloff spoke out against pooling-of-interests accounting.[13] SEC chairman Manuel Cohen worried aloud that pooling was being used "to create an appearance of earnings and growth where they are not really present" and "to increase a company's reported sales and earnings without improving performance."[14] Some members of Congress called for the end of poolings, not so much because they really understood or cared about the accounting implications, but because they hoped to slow the growth of "rogue" conglomerates who were gobbling up small companies.

But when the APB debated abolishing pooling-of-interests accounting in 1969, angry financial managers and investment bankers bombarded the Board with hundreds of protest letters. Many claimed that forcing companies to use purchase accounting would thwart desirable mergers and ultimately hurt the economy. IT&T Corporation even threatened to sue the APB to block the rule change. In the end, the APB retained pooling-of-interests accounting, but placed more stringent restrictions on its use.

The Next Crisis in Accounting

The 1960s were much like the 1920s, but with hippies and marijuana in place of flappers and bathtub gin. The economy was generally healthy. Unemployment was relatively low. Rising stock prices and investor-friendly mutual funds attracted millions of new investors to the securities markets.

There were 71,000 CPAs in the United States in 1960. And life was good for most of them. Computers had removed much of the drudgery from bookkeeping and reduced the frequency of clerical errors. The growth of the economy and the increasing complexity of the tax code increased the demand for public accountants' services. The eight largest public accounting firms had separated themselves from the rest of the pack. Collectively, the Big Eight audited 80 percent of the corporations registered with the SEC. Accounting scandals at companies such as Westec, Yale Express, and Continental Vending had, thus far, failed to seriously diminish the public's faith in audited financial statements.

But audit failures at National Student Marketing Corporation (NSMC) and Equity Funding Corporation of America (EFCA) would soon reveal latent flaws in the nation's financial reporting system. Corporate takeover artists were using pooling-of-interests accounting to create misleading impressions of earnings growth. Fraudsters were using computers to perpetrate bigger and badder schemes.

NSMC was the quintessential 1960s growth company. Its revenues increased from $723,000 in 1967 to more than $68 million in 1969 thanks to 23 mergers, most accounted for as poolings-of-interests.

NSMC's stock price plunged from $144 to $6 in 1970 after a journalist revealed just how illusory the company's profits really were.

EFCA was recognized by *Fortune* magazine as the fastest-growing financial services conglomerate in America after acquiring three life insurance companies, three mutual funds, a savings and loan, and a cattle ranch within four years. But the California Insurance Commissioner seized the company in 1973 after discovering that EFCA employees had programmed the company's computers to generate 64,000 phony life insurance policies.

7 National Student Marketing

Being an entrepreneur is dangerous.

(Cort Randell[1])

Cortes (Cort) Randell founded at least five companies and purchased two dozen more. He also inspired several government investigations, defended himself against numerous civil lawsuits, and endured two stints in federal prison. Of course his path might have been less difficult if he hadn't taken so many ethical shortcuts.

If at First you Don't Succeed…

Randell's master's thesis at the University of Virginia was entitled "The Factors for Success in Starting a Business in the Youth Market." Shortly after graduation, Randell tried putting his theories into practice. He incorporated the National Scholastic Achievement Society (NSAS) as a nonprofit organization in the summer of 1964 for the stated purpose of helping high school students obtain financial aid for college. As NSAS's president, Randell wrote to high schools and collected the names of 35,000 top students. Then he sent letters offering the students membership in the National Scholastic Honor Society (NSHS). In return for their $5 application fee, students were promised counseling services and information on college admissions and scholarships. The fraud branch of the Postal Inspection Service questioned Randell after receiving numerous inquiries about NSHS from parents, teachers, and principals. Investigators discovered that NSHS performed no counseling services and had no paid staff. The Postal Service referred the case to the U.S. attorney for the District of Columbia, who decided not to press charges after Randell refunded the $8,000 he had collected from 1,600 students.

Randell's next venture was more successful, albeit short-lived. Randell earned $160,000 of total revenue in 1966 selling summer job guides, magazine subscriptions and airline discount cards to college students. Three years later, Randell's company—National Student Marketing Corp. (NSMC)—earned $68 million of total revenues. Randell lived near Washington, DC in a $600,000 *faux* "castle" complete with turrets and a mock dungeon. From his back lawn he could sail his hydrofoil and his fleet of radio-controlled model boats on the Potomac river. But Randell soon learned what a real dungeon looked like. He was forced to resign from NSMC in February 1970 and in 1975 began serving an 18-month prison sentence after pleading guilty to four counts of conspiracy and fraud.

Randell returned to prison in 1981 when a federal jury convicted him of mail fraud, interstate transportation of stolen funds, and submitting a false loan application to the Veterans Administration. The charges stemmed from his involvement with National Commercial Credit Corporation a real estate investment firm whose collapse cost 100 investors more than $1 million.

Randell helped found the Federal News Service (FNS) in 1984. FNS sold transcripts of governmental proceedings, such as congressional hearings and press conferences, to newspapers, lobbying agencies, and law firms. Although the company was successful, Randell's partner Richard Boyd filed suit in 1986, claiming that Randell had improperly issued all the shares of stock to himself and was withholding Boyd's share of the profits. Later, the Federal Trade Commission brought an antitrust case against FNS, alleging that the company had entered into an illegal agreement with a competitor. FNS settled the case without admitting guilt but agreed not to seek agreements to divide markets with any news transcript provider in the future. Finally, after being ousted as president of FNS, Randell sued the company, claiming he had been wrongfully discharged. Delaware Judge William Chandler concluded that the employment contract submitted into evidence by Randell was a forgery and scheduled a separate hearing to decide whether to charge Randell with contempt and perpetrating a fraud on the court.[2]

National Student Marketing Corporation

Randell's second venture, National Student Marketing Corporation (NSMC), had the greatest impact on the accounting profession. Randell founded NSMC in 1966 to sell goods and services to students between the ages of 14 and 25. That segment of the population was expected to grow 30 percent by 1975 as the postwar baby boomers came of age.

Randell's legion of 600 college students earned up to $4,000 per year tacking posters with tear-off response cards to campus bulletin boards. Clients included magazine publishers, phonograph record clubs, class ring manufacturers, and computer dating services. Some companies paid NSMC a flat fee to print and distribute their posters. Others gave NSMC a commission for each response card mailed in.

In 1968 and 1969, NSMC expanded its advertising media to include calendar desk pads, textbook covers, spiral notebook inserts, and campus telephone directories. NSMC helped promote several popular fad items of the late 1960s, including paper dresses and "Sock It to Me, Baby" sweatshirts.

NSMC's revenues grew from $723,000 during the fiscal year ended August 31, 1967 to $5 million in fiscal 1968 and $68 million in fiscal 1969. This extraordinary growth was achieved by purchasing many of the companies that employed NSMC to market their products and services. NSMC acquired six companies during fiscal 1968 including a computerized job placement service and a ceramic beer mug manufacturer. The next year, NSMC acquired 17 companies. The best known acquisition was probably Arthur Frommer's company, publisher of "Five Dollar a Day" travel guides.

NSMC's rapid growth created organizational chaos. The company undertook eight major reorganizations between August 1968 and April 1970. But regardless of what the organization chart *du jour* said, Randell remained in charge. He retained responsibility for all major decisions even after NSMC became a conglomerate with more than 20 operating units spread from coast to coast. Randell received little oversight from NSMC's board of directors. Only two directors did not report to Randell as employees of NSMC and one of those was Randell's father.

"Cort"ing Wall Street

Although NSMC's declared business was selling youth-oriented products to high school and college students, its real business was selling Cort Randell's dreams to Wall Street. Randell placed high priority on public relations. He spared no expense entertaining analysts and investment bankers, sometimes taking them for cruises on his 55 ft yacht. NSMC paid stock to several securities houses in return for investment banking services. Two such brokerages later issued favorable reports on NSMC.

Randell spoke to investor organizations at every opportunity, constantly repeating his promise to triple NSMC's revenues and earnings every year into the foreseeable future. Enough people believed Randell that NSMC's stock price rose from $6 when it was first offered to the public in April 1968 to $70 six months later. The price jumped an additional $20 per share in November 1969 when Randell predicted at a meeting of the New York Society of Security Analysts that NSMC would earn $4.00 per share during fiscal 1970 after earning $1.54 in 1969. NSMC's stock eventually reached a split-adjusted high of $144 per share in December 1969, nearly 100 times the previous year's earnings.

Randell depended on his company's appreciating share price to fuel its growth. Almost all of NSMC's 20-some acquisitions were stock trades. NSMC issued shares of its common stock in return for ownership of the target companies. A NSMC vice-president later described the company's business model as follows:

> Randell's earning prophecies were self-fulfilling. By announcing phenomenal earnings projections he got a phenomenal valuation of NSMC stock, which then allowed him to buy enough earnings to meet his projections. Then, to keep the momentum high, as all glamour stocks must, he would make another round of phenomenal projections. As long as he bought companies for a lower multiple of their earnings than the multiple at which NSMC stock was valued, earnings would increase more than equity would be diluted—so earnings per share would increase.[3]

The rising value of NSMC stock also enabled Randell to expand his corporate staff. NSMC salaries were low by New York City standards, but all new employees received stock options when they joined the company. Employment contracts were sometimes backdated and the option exercise price pegged to the earlier (lower) stock value. This increased the value of the options to employees without requiring them to pay income taxes on the options received.

Shortly after reaching its peak, NSMC's stock price collapsed even faster than it had risen. Alan Abelson published an article in the December 22, 1969 issue of *Barron's* questioning the quality of NSMC's reported earnings.[4] The stock price fell $20 the next day. It fell even farther in February 1970 when NSMC disclosed that it had suffered a loss during the quarter ended November 30, 1969. The original announcement reported a net loss of $573,000 on sales of $18 million. Two days later, NSMC revised the amount of the loss to $860,000 on sales of $14.4 million, citing a "mechanical error in transferring figures from one set of books to another."[5]

Institutional investors demanded to know why NSMC had lost money during the first quarter of a fiscal year for which Randell continued to predict record high profits. His explanations were evasive and contradictory. In reality, the losses occurred because NSMC's bloated corporate overhead exceeded the profits generated by the operating units. Randell, whose ownership of NSMC had been reduced to little more than 10 percent by the stock-financed mergers, was forced to resign on February 20. By July 1970 the stock was back down to its original issue price of $6 per share.

NSMC's Accounting

NSMC's preliminary trial balance for the fiscal year ended August 31, 1968 showed a net loss of $220,000. Then came the adjustments. With their auditors' approval, NSMC recorded an additional $1.7 million of revenue for fixed-fee marketing agreements allegedly entered into before August 31. A fixed-fee contract was one in which a client agreed to pay NSMC a predetermined amount to market the client's product. NSMC accounted for fixed-fee contracts using the "percentage of completion" method. That is, they recorded revenue prior to collecting their fee and before they had even fulfilled the contract. Each period, NSMC *estimated* the proportion of work they thought they had completed on each engagement and recorded revenue equal to a like percentage of the total contract amount. Although they lacked written contracts, NSMC claimed that the marketing agreements had been finalized before August 31. They also claimed that the majority of the work had already been completed, entitling them to include most of the revenue in the fiscal 1968 financial statements. The contracts recorded after year-end represented one-third of the $5 million of revenue ultimately reported for the year and transformed NSMC's preliminary loss into a $388,000 net income.

NSMC's financial statements for the year ended August 31, 1969 reported revenues of $67.0 million, a 13-fold increase over the previous fiscal year. This astounding growth was achieved by recording nearly all of the 17 acquisitions as poolings-of-interests. When NSMC merged with another company through an exchange of stock, the acquired company's revenues and profits were added into NSMC's consolidated income statement as if they had operated as one entity throughout the entire year. But NSMC took pooling-of-interests one step farther. NSMC included in its fiscal 1969 financial statements the revenues and earnings of eight companies whose acquisitions were not completed until *after* August 31, 1969. The earnings of those eight companies totaled $3.8 million, more than the entire $3.2 net income reported on NSMC's income statement.

In addition to reporting the earnings of companies it did not even own during 1969, NSMC recognized a $370,000 profit on the "sale" of two money-losing subsidiaries. In October 1969, NSMC's board of directors approved the sales of Collegiate Advertising, Ltd. and Compu-Job, Inc. to employees of the respective companies. The contracts were backdated to August 31 so NSMC could record the transactions during fiscal 1969. NSMC collected no cash and the $450,000 of nonrecourse promissory notes it received clearly stated that the purchasers were not personally liable for their payment. In addition, a side agreement obligated NSMC to absorb any losses suffered by CompuJob during the next year. The SEC later concluded that the sales of both subsidiaries were, in fact, "sham transactions."[6]

NSMC's fiscal 1969 financial statements included $2.8 million of revenues related to fixed-fee marketing contracts. Many of the contracts were recorded after year-end as NSMC's managers looked for ways to boost the company's reported earnings. In his guilty plea, Cort Randell confessed having personally altered a letter from the Pontiac Division of General Motors in an attempt to convince the auditors to let him record more revenue. The letter contained a sentence stating that Pontiac had decided to "not enter into an agreement with NSMC." Randell had typed over the last letter in "not" to make it read "now."

NSMC's Auditors

Arthur Andersen audited the financial statements included in NSMC's April 1968 registration statement. Andersen resigned in July of that year along with NSMC's outside legal counsel, Covington & Burling. Years later, Andersen told the SEC they had resigned after a series of events led them to question the reliability of the information NSMC's management was giving them. On the advice of counsel, Andersen did not volunteer the reason for their resignation to their successor Peat Marwick Mitchell & Co. (PMM). PMM did ask Andersen if there were any professional reasons why they should not accept the NSMC audit, but the SEC concluded that PMM's inquiries were inadequate given the unusual circumstances of the simultaneous auditor and attorney resignations.[7]

PMM issued a clean audit opinion on NSMC's August 31, 1968 financial statements. Although they were skeptical of the $1.7 million of revenues accrued after year end and bothered by Randell's insistence that they not seek written confirmations from NSMC's clients, they finally accepted the accounting after reviewing what documents there were and making a limited number of telephone inquiries.

During the summer of 1969, NSMC negotiated a merger with an insurance company, Interstate National Corporation (INC). Completing the merger required a favorable vote from the shareholders of both companies. So in August, NSMC mailed a proxy statement to its shareholders seeking their approval. The proxy statement contained financial statements for the year ended August 31, 1968 and for the nine months ended May 31, 1969.

By the time the proxy statement was being prepared, the PMM auditors knew that $1.4 million of the $1.7 million of revenue accrued at the end of fiscal 1968 had been written off during the first three quarters of fiscal 1969. In fact, four contracts totaling $750,000 had been fabricated by an employee trying to increase his commission. But rather than disclosing that the prior year's financial statements were materially misstated and requiring NSMC to record a prior period adjustment, the auditors allowed the company to bury the write-offs among the earnings of the subsidiaries acquired during 1969.

In October 1969, PMM was asked to provide a comfort letter to the directors of NSMC and INC. Although PMM had not audited the financial statements for the nine months ended May 31, 1969, the directors wanted to know whether the auditors were aware of any material errors in the statements. PMM wrote a letter on October 31 stating that the May 31 financial statements required adjustments that, if recorded, would reduce NSMC's net income from the $700,000 profit reported in the proxy statement to an $80,000 net loss. PMM also recommended that a revised proxy be sent to both sets of shareholders.

But upon delivering their letter to NSMC's legal counsel late in the afternoon of October 31, PMM learned that the two companies' directors had not waited for the auditor's comfort letter and had approved the merger earlier in the day. Not knowing exactly how to proceed, PMM mailed copies of their letter to each member of NSMC's and INC's board of directors. They took no further action, however, fearing that additional disclosure would violate state laws and professional standards protecting client confidentiality.

The SEC issued a civil injunction against PMM in February 1972 criticizing the auditors for (1) inadequate communication with the predecessor auditor, (2) not properly testing NSMC's accounting for fixed-fee marketing contracts, (3) not disclosing the errors in the fiscal 1968 financial statements, and (4) not notifying the SEC when NSMC refused to issue a revised proxy statement to its shareholders. The case was settled in 1975. Without admitting or denying wrongdoing in their audits of NSMC and four other companies, PMM agreed to undergo a review of their firm-wide audit procedures by an independent committee and to refrain from accepting new publicly traded audit clients for six months.

The SEC also referred the actions of PMM's engagement partner and audit supervisor to the Department of Justice. Anthony Natelli and Joseph Scansaroli were indicted in January 1974 on charges of making false and misleading statements with respect to material facts contained in NSMC's 1969 proxy statement. Regarding the auditors' failure to disclose and correct the errors in the fiscal 1968 financial statements, the Assistant U.S. Attorney told the jury, "This is a simple case … the two PMM auditors made a bad mistake (which is not a crime) and then buried it (which is a crime)."[8] The prosecutors argued that the auditors covered up the 1968 misstatements because they feared losing their CPA certificates if the errors became known.

After the jury found both auditors guilty, the sympathetic judge issued light sentences. Natelli was fined $10,000 and sentenced to 60 days in jail. Scansaroli received a 10-day sentence and a $2,500 fine. Scansaroli's conviction was overturned on appeal and he was never retried.

The civil litigation dragged out for 12 years. Shareholders filed a class action lawsuit against PMM in the summer of 1970. After legal jousting that reached all the way to the U.S. Supreme Court, PMM paid $6.4 million in 1982 to settle the shareholders' claims.

Postscript

Given Cort Randell's knack for identifying business opportunities, it was perhaps inevitable that he would attempt an Internet start-up company. In 2000, Randell founded eModel.com, a company that posted pictures of aspiring models on its website for modeling agents to peruse. The company's clients—primarily young women—paid $395 to have their pictures and vital statistics added to the site plus $20 per month to keep the information posted. The 64-year-old Randell had not lost his entrepreneurial touch. A newspaper reporter estimated in 2001 that eModel.com had collected $2.3 million in initiation fees and continued to collect $116,000 per month from the nearly 6,000 models on the website.[9]

But like Randell's other enterprises, the cash was followed closely by controversy. Company scouts earned commission by convincing women to post their photos. Although an eModel.com spokesman stated that the company screened applicants closely and accepted only those who showed potential as professional models, several former scouts claimed that anybody with $400 was accepted and the interviews were used merely to instill prospective clients with fantasies of high-fashion modeling. The Los Angeles Better Business Bureau rated the company's performance unsatisfactory and its president stated, "The whole thing fundamentally, from beginning to end, is a scam."[10]

8 Equity Funding

> If routine auditing procedures can't detect 64,000 phony insurance policies, $25 million in counterfeit bonds, and $100 million in missing assets, what is the purpose of audits?
>
> (Ray Dirks[1])

Ray Dirks stood out on Wall Street. Nicknamed the "hippie analyst" for his long sideburns and bangs that reached the top of his glasses, Dirks entered the securities business only after his theater company failed. Though unconventional, Dirks had an impressive list of clients. He developed a reputation for insight into the insurance industry by criticizing the proposed merger of ITT and Hartford Fire Insurance in 1970.

In March 1973, Dirks received a tip from a former employee of Equity Funding Corporation of America (EFCA). The informant claimed that senior managers at EFCA were inflating the company's assets by recording thousands of fictitious life insurance policies. The man's story was believable enough that Dirks advised several large clients to reconsider their holdings of EFCA stock.

During the next two weeks, Dirks interviewed dozens of EFCA employees, including CEO Stanley Goldblum, trying to either verify or disprove the allegations. While Dirks sought answers, his clients dumped several hundred thousand shares of EFCA stock, causing the price to drop 50 percent and prompting an investigation by the SEC. The authorities eventually discovered that 64,000 of EFCA's 99,000 alleged life insurance policies were phony and $62 million of the reported $117 million of loan receivables did not exist.

The first indictment issued by the SEC went to—Ray Dirks, for insider trading. Although he helped uncover the most significant accounting fraud since McKesson & Robbins 35 years earlier, the SEC believed he acted improperly by informing his clients of the suspected fraud. Dirks was convicted and lost the first several rounds of appeals. It was not until 10 years and $100,000 of lawyers' fees later that the U.S. Supreme Court overturned Dirks's conviction.

Equity Funding Corporation of America

Gordon McCormick had the idea of a lifetime in 1958. He combined the protection of life insurance with the growth potential of mutual funds. At that time, most Americans bought whole-life insurance policies. The insurance policies provided benefits at the time of death, but were poor vehicles for investing. The cash value of the policy grew by only approximately 3 percent per year, barely enough to keep pace with inflation. McCormick taught his salesmen to sell customers both a life insurance policy and a mutual fund. Customers invested, say $500 per year, in a mutual fund. Then they borrowed against their investment to pay the premiums on the life insurance policy. The customers paid perhaps 5 percent interest on the loan while hoping to earn an average of 8–10 percent on the mutual fund. As long as the mutual fund earned more than the interest rate on the loan, the customers could repay the loan out of their fund and have money left over, all the while providing for their beneficiaries in case of an untimely death.

Of course there was some risk. If the mutual fund lost money or earned less than the borrowing rate, the customer would not have sufficient money in the fund to repay the loan. But McCormick's salesmen downplayed the risk. No matter what happened to the customers, the salesmen came out ahead. They earned one commission on the sale of the insurance policy and a second commission on the sale of the mutual fund.

McCormick founded the Equity Funding Corporation of America (EFCA) on March 31, 1960 and began assembling a sales force to push his big idea. Six months later, four of his most trusted employees staged a coup. Ray Platt, Eugene Cuthbertson, Stanley Goldblum, and Mike Riordan bought out McCormick's share of the company and assumed control. Platt sold his share of EFCA in 1963 and died of a heart attack shortly thereafter. Cuthbertson quit in 1966, leaving Goldblum and Riordan in charge of the company.

Stanley Goldblum was EFCA's "Mr. Inside." After working for five years as a butcher in his father-in-law's meatpacking plant the insurance business seemed like paradise. It was clean and offered plenty of opportunity for growth. Goldblum liked making deals and giving orders. He just didn't like dealing with customers or the public. Goldblum was a neatness freak and a fitness fanatic. His office desktop held nothing but one small memo pad and a $15,000 Mont Blanc fountain pen. His home, located next door to Paul Newman and Joanne Woodward in Beverly Hills, contained $100,000 of exercise equipment.

Mike Riordan was "Mr. Outside." He loved talking to people and had been a top mutual fund salesman in New York before moving to California to join Gordon McCormick's Equity Funding. His celebrity friends included comedian Jonathan Winters, actor Ray Bolger, singer

Dennis Day, and football coach Vince Lombardi. Riordan loved night life and tipped generously. Lounge pianists at his favorite Irish pubs played *The Impossible Dream*, Riordan's favorite song, whenever he entered the bar.

Riordan's dream ended on January 25, 1969 when several tons of mud crashed through the sliding glass doors of his hillside mansion in the Mandeville Canyon area of Brentwood. It had been raining heavily for two weeks and more than 40 people had already been killed by mudslides. The first wave of mud pinned Riordan to his bed. While rescue workers struggled to free his legs, a second wave slammed into the house and buried him. Riordan's death left Goldblum in sole command of EFCA.

Originally, EFCA was merely a sales organization. Its army of 4,000 licensed agents sold life insurance policies written by companies such as Pennsylvania Life and mutual funds managed by companies such as Keystone Custodian Funds. But in 1967, EFCA began acquiring life insurance companies and mutual funds so it could sell its own products. EFCA bought the Presidential Life Insurance Company of America in December 1967. Later, it acquired two other life insurance companies, three mutual funds, a savings and loan, and a cattle ranch. In May 1972, *Fortune* magazine named EFCA the fastest-growing financial services conglomerate in America.[2]

The Equity Funding Fraud

The Equity Funding fraud consisted primarily of creating phony life insurance policies and selling them to other companies. Selling policies, which is called "reinsurance," is common in the insurance industry. One insurance company sells a policy to a customer who promises to pay premiums of, say $800 per year, for the next ten years. A second insurance company pays the first company maybe $2,000 to buy the policy. Then the second company receives the customer's premiums and bears the risk should the policyholder die. Often, the first company continues to collect the premiums from the customer and remits the money to the company that bought the customer's policy.

EFCA engaged heavily in reinsurance. Its agents sold life insurance policies to customers and EFCA sold ("reinsured") many of the policies to other companies. Sometime during 1970, EFCA began selling phony life insurance policies to its reinsurers. EFCA employees made up a name, address, age, medical information and so forth for each fictitious policyholder.

Each phony policy provided EFCA with cash. The cash receipts from selling the policies inflated EFCA's earnings. But each phony policy also created an obligation. In the example above, EFCA would receive $2,000 up front, but then it would have to pay $800 per year for the next ten years, ostensibly collected from the policyholder. The result was a giant pyramid scheme. EFCA had to sell more phony policies each year to collect enough cash to pay the premiums on the previous years' phony policies. The only way to break the cycle was to "kill" the policyholder. Each year, EFCA employees forged a likely number of death certificates in relation to the number of phony policies outstanding. The death benefits collected for these fictitious deaths provided more cash to fund the remaining policies.

Goldblum's primary role in the fraud was to set the earnings targets. EFCA's stock price dropped substantially during 1969. Goldblum was desperate to increase EFCA's stock price so he could make more stock-financed acquisitions. Each quarter, Goldblum told his subordinates what he wanted the earnings per share number to be. They did whatever was necessary to meet the numbers.

Goldblum's two top lieutenants were supremely qualified to carry out and conceal the fraud. Fred Levin was in charge of EFCA's life insurance subsidiary, Equity Funding Life. Levin had been an investigator for the Illinois Department of Insurance from 1961 to 1964. He knew what state regulators looked for and what evidence they would accept. Sam Lowell, EFCA's chief financial officer, had worked previously as an auditor for Haskins & Sells. He had even participated in EFCA's early audits. Levin and Lowell were well paid for their efforts. Each received a $250,000 salary plus $1,000 per month for local entertainment expenses.

Secrist Reveals Secret

Ron Secrist held a variety of positions within EFCA, eventually ending up as an assistant vice-president at Equity Funding Life. Secrist learned of the phony policies in 1971 when he was invited to help forge documents to create files for fictitious policyholders. Secrist did not approve of the fraud and planned to resign. Nevertheless, he was outraged in February 1972 when Fred Levin fired him.

Secrist decided to blow the whistle on his former employers but didn't know who would believe his story. Pat Hopper, who had resigned from one of EFCA's life insurance subsidiaries several months earlier because Levin had asked him to funnel insurance company assets to EFCA, suggested that Secrist talk to Ray Dirks, a Wall Street maverick interested in the insurance industry.

Secrist called Dirks on March 6, 1973. He told Dirks that EFCA had been selling fake insurance policies for at least three years and that one-third of the policies on Equity Funding Life's books were phony. Secrist also told Dirks that EFCA was trying to take cash out of its life insurance subsidiaries and replace the money with corporate bonds. What Secrist did not know at the time was that the bonds, with face values totaling $25 million and bearing the names of blue-chip companies such as Dow Chemical, Firestone Tire & Rubber, and Southwestern Bell, were forgeries.

Pat Hopper and former Equity Life controller Frank Majerus corroborated much of Secrist's story. Dirks warned several large clients that EFCA was "the Watergate of Wall Street" and flew to California to interview Stanley Goldblum. Goldblum talked to Dirks at length and granted him access to EFCA's senior executives, including Fred Levin and Sam Lowell. They dismissed Hopper and Secrist as disgruntled former employees and scoffed at the idea that the ninth largest insurance company in the United States was nothing more than a house of cards. Dirks didn't have access to the documents or computer records necessary to prove Secrist's allegations, but the large stock sales by his clients attracted the attention of the SEC and the New York Stock Exchange.

On the same day Secrist called Dirks, he also called the New York Insurance Commission. They took Secrist's complaint seriously, and two days later, notified the California Insurance Commission. Maurice D. Rouble, one of the California department's toughest and most experienced investigators, was assigned to the case. He was joined by two investigators from the Illinois Insurance Department. The Illinois Insurance Commissioner had heard disturbing allegations about EFCA and had decided to conduct a surprise audit.

On the morning of March 27, 1973, Ray Dirks, Pat Hopper, and Frank Majerus told an SEC representative what they knew about EFCA. The SEC halted trading of EFCA stock that afternoon. Three days later, the California Insurance Commissioner seized Equity Funding Life. The Illinois examiners had discovered that $25 million of corporate bonds were not in a Chicago bank as claimed, and Rouble had learned that computer tapes were being erased at EFCA's headquarters.

EFCA's board held an emergency meeting on April 1 and demanded resignations from Goldblum, Levin, and Lowell. The meeting was held in an attorney's office, rather than in the EFCA boardroom, because sound recording equipment had been discovered in the EFCA executive suite. Fred Levin had been using hidden microphones to eavesdrop on the state insurance examiners. He couldn't have liked what he heard.

Equity Funding's Auditors

Wolfson Weiner Ratoff & Lapin (WWR&L) began auditing EFCA's financial statements in 1964, the year EFCA went public. As EFCA grew, it eventually provided 60 percent of the accounting firm's Los Angeles office revenue. Although investors and board members occasionally suggested hiring a more prominent auditing firm to replace

WWR&L, Stanley Goldblum personally defended the small firm, citing their loyalty and service.

It is unlikely that Goldblum could have found more cooperative auditors. The SEC later concluded that:

> the audit practices employed by WWR&L's Los Angeles office were far below professional standards and employees of that office engaged in acts and practices in flagrant violation of rules of the Commission and standards of the accounting profession relating to independence.[3]

Specific criticisms included WWR&L partners spending most of their time on marketing and rarely reviewing audit workpapers; audit managers, some of whom were not even CPAs, being allowed to sign audit reports; and auditors not obtaining sufficient evidence to support their conclusions. Solomon Block, the lead auditor on the EFCA engagement, was one of the WWR&L managers who was not certified. Ironically, the 44-year-old Block finally passed the CPA exam in 1973, only to be barred from public practice several months later.

Seidman & Seidman inherited EFCA as a client when it merged with WWR&L in February 1972. The merger took place just as WWR&L was completing EFCA's 1971 audit. Without reviewing WWR&L's workpapers, Seidman & Seidman issued an unqualified audit opinion. The SEC later criticized Seidman & Seidman for signing EFCA's audit report without determining whether a proper audit had been conducted.

> The WWR&L audit work … is so obviously deficient that elaboration seems superfluous. With respect to Seidman & Seidman's conduct, it should be noted that a comparison of the recorded assets to the workpapers makes the total inadequacy of the audit evidence conspicuously clear. Yet Seidman & Seidman substituted its imprimatur for that of the WWR&L firm on EFCA's 1971 financial statements, without review of the WWR&L audit workpapers.[4]

Seidman & Seidman had nearly finished EFCA's 1972 audit when Ray Dirks contacted audit partner Bob Spencer to warn him about the alleged fraud at EFCA. The auditors had seen nothing suspicious during their testing and had given EFCA permission to announce its 1972 earnings. Dirks described the allegations and even gave Spencer a photocopy of his extensive notes. Spencer gave the notes to Stanley Goldblum. When Dirks asked why he had done it, Spencer replied, "They're clients of mine."[5]

"Aren't you independent auditors?" Dirks asked.

"Sure we're independent," Spencer said, "but we have an obligation to our clients."

As punishment for four deficient audits, including EFCA, the SEC ordered Seidman & Seidman to undergo a review of its audit practices by a committee of consultants approved by the Commission. Seidman & Seidman also agreed not to accept any audit engagements for new SEC clients for a period of six months.

Haskins & Sells (H&S) was the third accounting firm duped by Goldblum's fraud team. H&S audited EFCA's insurance subsidiary, Equity Funding Life, from 1968 to 1971. As part of their audit procedures, the H&S staff reviewed customer files to verify the existence of EFCA's alleged policies. Auditing standards at that time did not require auditors to confirm insurance policies with policyholders.

To supply the auditors with the necessary documentation, EFCA hired 10 young women and set them up in an office removed from EFCA's premises. For much of the year, the women had nothing to do. They spent their days listening to the radio, talking on the telephone, and cooking elaborate lunches. But when the auditors or a reinsurer asked to see the file of one of the fictitious policyholders, the women quickly created the necessary paperwork. They forged policy applications, doctors' reports, and other documents normally contained in a policyholder's file. The women worked assembly-line fashion so that the documents in each folder were prepared using a variety of handwriting styles and inks. To the auditors, the fictitious files looked just like the real ones.

Aftermath

Twenty former EFCA employees and two auditors were named in a 105-count indictment handed down on November 1, 1973. The charges included conspiracy to commit securities fraud, filing false documents with the SEC, bank fraud, interstate transport of counterfeit securities, and electronic eavesdropping. Stanley Goldblum was named in 45 of the counts. Auditors Julian Weiner and Solomon Block of WWR&L were charged with having intentionally conducted incomplete audits. Ron Secrist and Frank Majerus were named as unindicted co-conspirators.

Goldblum's trial commenced in October 1974. The prosecution planned to call 90 witnesses in a trial that was expected to last three months. One week after testimony began, Goldblum pleaded guilty to five counts of conspiracy and fraud. He admitted under oath that he had directed his subordinates to inflate EFCA's assets and earnings.

Goldblum served a total of three years in a California prison. It was quite a light sentence for the man who once chaired the ethics committee of the Los Angeles chapter of the National Association of Securities Dealers, where he was known for administering unusually harsh penalties to rules violators.

9 Déjà Vu

> This is like déjà vu all over again.
>
> (Yogi Berra)

For accountants and auditors, the 1970s were much like the 1930s. Newspapers and magazines lambasted auditors for failing to detect fraud. Accountants debated among themselves how best to write accounting standards. Congressional committees held lengthy hearings seeking proposals to make accounting firms serve the public interest.

The Financial Accounting Standards Board

Thirty years after establishing the Committee on Accounting Procedure (CAP), accountants still had not devised a workable system for writing accounting standards. The Accounting Principles Board (APB) was only marginally more successful at improving financial reporting than its predecessor had been. As of 1970, no conceptual framework had been established; alternative accounting practices still existed for items such as inventories, depreciation, income taxes, pensions and business combinations; and several contentious accounting issues such as leases and research and development costs still needed to be addressed.

From the mid-1960s forward, the APB endured harsh criticism from a host of sources. SEC chairman Manuel Cohen noted in several speeches that the APB had failed to reduce the variety of accounting principles permitted for recording similar transactions. Stock analysts complained that it was impossible to compare the earnings of different companies. An editorial in *Forbes* magazine opined that "generally accepted accounting principles mean damn little."[1]

While the SEC, the investment community and the financial press complained that accounting standards were too lax, financial executives and investment bankers complained that the APB's pronouncements were too strict. Members of the American Banking Association protested a proposal that banks be required to include loan losses in net income. Leasing companies claimed they would lose customers if lessees were required to record lease obligations as liabilities. Investment bankers said corporations' ability to raise capital would be impaired if the APB rewrote its rules for calculating earnings per share.

Finally, leading members of the public accounting profession turned against their own standard-setting body. After an especially rancorous debate in 1970 over whether to eliminate pooling-of-interests accounting, representatives from three of the Big Eight accounting firms sent letters to AICPA president Marshall S. Armstrong saying they had lost confidence in the APB's ability to write accounting standards. Ralph E. Kent, managing partner of Arthur Young, wrote, "A number of developments over the past several months have raised some doubts in my mind as to whether the present APB organization is the most appropriate ongoing mechanism for the establishment of accounting principles." Arthur Andersen chairman Harvey E. Kapnick wrote, "The APB, in our view, has not successfully carried out its mission nor does it currently give promise of doing so." Robert M. Trueblood of Touche Ross wrote that his firm was "presently reconsidering our entire participation in the affairs of the Board."[2]

Faced with pressure from without and mutiny within, the AICPA governing council appointed a special committee in March 1971 to study the organization and operations of the APB and to recommend improvements to the standard-setting process. Francis M. Wheat, an attorney and former SEC commissioner, chaired the committee. Other members included three CPAs, a securities analyst, an accounting professor, and Roger B. Smith (the future chairman and CEO of General Motors).

The "Wheat" committee released its recommendations in March 1972. In answer to the question of who should set accounting standards, the committee concluded that standard setting should continue to be performed in the private sector, subject to SEC oversight. But in order to keep standard setting in the private sector, the AICPA would have to relinquish some of its control over the standard-setting process. One of the most serious threats to private sector standard setting was the practice of industry groups running to Congress and the SEC whenever they didn't like an APB proposal. If the SEC had to keep arbitrating disputes between the APB and the business community, the commissioners might just as well write the standards themselves.

As to the question of how accounting standards should be set, the committee concluded that "while the procedures devised at the end of the 1950s for formulating financial accounting principles were probably appropriate at the time ... the time has come for a change."[3]

The CAP and APB each consisted of 18 to 21 members who served on a volunteer, part-time basis while retaining their regular jobs. Both boards were hampered by their members having limited time available to set standards. This problem was exacerbated during the APB's early years by a policy that permitted only firm-wide managing partners to represent accounting firms on the Board. The policy was enacted to increase the authority of APB pronouncements, but an unintended consequence was that most APB members were extremely busy men responsible for running huge organizations. Too few members devoted sufficient time to the APB's standard-setting activities.

A second problem with part-time volunteer members was that their votes were sometimes influenced by self-interest. Corporate executives pressured their auditors to support the client's position during deliberations. And few auditors enjoyed enforcing unpopular rules. Critics complained that the APB watered down its pronouncements to avoid angering corporate clients. One mutual fund analyst claimed that "accountants are so tied to the corporations whose financial statements they audit that they are unable to bite the hand that feeds them."[4]

The Wheat committee recommended replacing the APB with a Financial Accounting Standards Board (FASB) composed of seven full-time paid members. The committee believed that the complexity of accounting problems required full-time devotion to standard setting and hoped that separating Board members from their former employers would encourage them to vote according to the public interest.

A more controversial recommendation was that the FASB include members from outside public accounting. CAP and APB members were all CPAs drawn from academia or public practice. The Wheat committee recommended forming a Financial Accounting Foundation (FAF) whose trustees would select FASB members. FAF trustees would be nominated by five organizations interested in financial reporting. Initially, the AICPA, American Accounting Association (composed primarily of accounting educators), Financial Executives Institute, National Association of Accountants, and Financial Analysts Federation nominated FAF trustees.

The Wheat committee also recommended that the FASB follow an extensive "due process" in writing its pronouncements in order to win support from (or at least placate) as many constituencies as possible. The specific procedures have evolved over time, but current practices include: (1) all Board meetings are announced in advance and are open to the public; (2) proposed standards are circulated as Exposure Drafts and interested parties are invited to write comment letters; and (3) the Board votes on new pronouncements only after reviewing all comment letters and holding at least one public hearing.

Not all public accountants welcomed the Wheat committee's recommendations. Many CPAs believed their profession had a God-given right to set accounting standards; they vehemently opposed abdicating the standard-setting role. APB chairman Philip L. Defliese expressed concern that the new board "would be comprised of people withdrawn from practice and out of touch with day-to-day problems."[5]

In spite of these objections, the AICPA governing council endorsed the Wheat committee's recommendations in May 1972. The APB disbanded on June 30, 1973 and the FASB commenced operations the next day.

Both the AICPA and the SEC were determined to help this third standard-setting body succeed. The AICPA adopted a new *Code of Professional Conduct* in early 1973 containing a rule that required members to follow FASB pronouncements in determining whether financial statements complied with generally accepted accounting principles.[6] The SEC issued ASR No. 150 in late 1973 stating that "principles, standards and practices promulgated by the FASB in its Statements and Interpretations will be considered by the Commission as having substantial authoritative support and those contrary to such FASB promulgations will be considered to have no such support."[7]

But the SEC's vote of confidence did not prevent the Commission from overturning a FASB pronouncement only a few years later. The FASB issued a Financial Accounting Statement in 1977 requiring oil and gas companies to account for exploration costs using the so-called "successful efforts" method.[8] Several months later, the SEC issued an Accounting Series Release announcing that it would accept financial statements prepared using the alternative "full costing" method.[9] Although the SEC claimed to desire more uniform accounting standards, this was yet another example of the Commission permitting corporations to choose between alternative accounting treatments after the FASB tried to standardize accounting practice.

The FASB's Influence

The most substantial difference between the FASB and its predecessors has been the more active involvement of corporate managers and financial statement users in the standard-setting process. Although FASB members are supposed to be independent and must sever all ties with previous employers, the Board usually includes members with backgrounds in public accounting, corporate accounting, the securities industry, and academia. Thus, the FASB includes members who understand the often contradictory perspectives of financial statement preparers, users, and auditors. A Financial Accounting Standards Advisory Council, composed of between 20 and 30 economists, attorneys, accountants, auditors, securities analysts, bankers, and educators, ensures the FASB hears a variety of viewpoints.

The FASB finally accomplished the decades-long goal of writing a conceptual framework for financial accounting. Between 1978 and 1984, the FASB issued five Statements of Financial Accounting Concepts (SFACs) describing the objectives of financial reporting, defining basic financial statements components, and discussing recognition and measurement issues. A sixth Concepts Statement, released in 1985, replaced SFAC No. 3. Fifteen years later, the FASB released SFAC No. 7, which discussed cash flows and present value measurements.

Unfortunately, the conceptual framework has not helped the FASB eliminate disputes over how income should be measured. Industry groups continue to resist accounting reforms. And Congress continues meddling in the standard-setting process. An example is the debate over accounting for stock options, during which corporate lobbyists convinced members of the U.S. House of Representatives in 2004 to pass a Bill overriding a FASB pronouncement.

But the FASB has endured such pressure and criticism for more than 30 years. Had the AICPA not decided in 1972 to share standard-setting authority with other interest groups and make its due process more open to the public, it is unlikely the FASB would have survived the congressional challenges of its first five years.

The Moss and Metcalf Investigations

Watergate, the Arab oil embargo, and the ensuing energy crisis occupied Congress during much of the early and mid-1970s. But accounting frauds such as National Student Marketing and Equity Funding were too big to be ignored. Congressman John Moss (D, California), chairman of the House Subcommittee on Oversight and Investigations, was among the first to call for tighter government regulation of financial reporting. Congressman Moss explained his interest in accounting as follows:

> Congressional interest in accounting has built up over the better part of a decade. It began with the great scandals that have shaken our country over the past few years—Equity Funding; Penn Central; Four Seasons Nursing Homes; and National Student Marketing readily leap to mind. In all of those situations publicly-owned companies went bankrupt and caused substantial harm to investors with no prior warning from their independent auditors that anything was amiss. Those of us in Congress began to wonder where the auditors were during the period those companies were headed for their falls.[10]

Both Watergate and the oil embargo helped heighten politicians' interest in accounting. Maurice Stans, a former president of the AICPA, pled guilty to violating campaign financing laws while serving as finance chairman for President Nixon's 1972 reelection campaign. The financial press questioned why auditors failed to discover or report illegal campaign contributions, unrecorded slush funds, secret bank accounts, bribes and kickbacks by more than 200 major corporations. And

Congressman Moss discovered during his investigation of domestic oil companies that it was virtually impossible to evaluate their profits because of the variety of methods used to account for inventories and exploration costs.

Senator Lee Metcalf (D, Montana), chairman of the Senate Subcommittee on Reports, Accounting and Management, instructed his staff in late 1975 to study the accounting profession. His staff's 1,760-page report, entitled *The Accounting Establishment*, stated in its introduction:

> Historically, Congress and the public have regarded accounting as an arcane subject better left to accountants themselves. Continual revelations of wrongdoing by publicly-owned corporations have caused a new awareness of the importance of accounting practices in permitting such abuses to occur.... Accounting issues are too important to be left to accountants alone.[11]

The "Metcalf" report claimed that the Big Eight accounting firms controlled the standard-setting process through their financial support of the FAF and their membership on key AICPA committees. The report criticized the laxity of both accounting and auditing standards and concluded,

> It appears that the Big Eight firms are more concerned with serving the interests of corporate managements who select them and authorize their fees than with protecting the interests of the public, for whose benefit Congress established the position of independent auditor.[12]

The report was equally critical of the SEC. The Commission's decision to allow the FASB and its predecessors to write accounting standards was described as "an extraordinary delegation of public authority and responsibility to narrow private interests."[13] The report also complained that the SEC had no procedures for checking the quality of independent auditors' work. And it accused the SEC of not punishing large accounting firms sufficiently for known audit failures.

The report recommended that the federal government assume responsibility for setting standards and ensuring compliance. It recommended that accounting and auditing standards be set by the General Accounting Office (GAO), the SEC, or by federal statute. It also recommended that the GAO, the SEC, or a special federal audit inspection agency periodically inspect public accountants' audits of publicly owned corporations.

In addition to proposing reforms that would lessen accountants' professional autonomy, the report included proposals that might have substantially affected public accountants' incomes. It recommended that Congress consider methods of increasing competition among accounting firms, and it proposed prohibiting accounting firms from performing management advisory services for their audit clients.

Senator Metcalf's subcommittee held hearings during April, May and June 1977 to discuss the staff report and its recommendations. More than 40 witnesses offered suggestions ranging from dissolving the FASB and breaking up the Big Eight to improving accounting education and requiring corporations to establish independent audit committees.

Admiral H.G. Rickover, father of the "Nuclear Navy," strongly advocated having the SEC assume the FASB's role of writing accounting standards. Admiral Rickover became interested in accounting standards after observing that defense contractors, working on cost-plus contracts with the Navy, appeared to be allowed to account for costs in almost any manner they chose. He told the senators:

> The accountants and their associations have had many years to show they could do a responsible job without Government control. Have they performed their job responsibly? Is it not obvious that they have failed to live up to their responsibilities to the public? Yet their spokesmen would have us believe that somehow they will all of a sudden rise above their own interests; that they have repented and will henceforth devote themselves to the public well-being.
>
> To believe the accountants as they once more promise to take the necessary corrective action would be a triumph of hope over experience. No man can serve two masters. Under the present system the interests of the so-called public accounting firms do not coincide with the interests of the public. Accountants should not be in the position of having to reconcile the equity of the public with the needs of their clients. To expect a vested interest group to set its own standards is to expect them to be God-like.[14]

Representatives from the public accounting profession also testified at the Senate subcommittee hearings. Most expressed regret for past failures, promised to do better in the future, and urged Congress not to do anything drastic. But Price Waterhouse partner John Biegler stunned members of the other accounting firms by suggesting that firms auditing public-traded companies be required to register with the SEC and have their work reviewed periodically. Many CPAs considered Biegler's suggestion nothing less than high treason.

After considering the testimony, Senator Metcalf's subcommittee released a final report in November 1977. Surprisingly, the report proposed no new federal legislation and suggested reforms that were far more moderate than those contained in the original staff report. To increase auditors' independence, the report urged that accounting firms not place their employees with clients and stop performing certain management advisory services such as executive recruiting. It recommended that a new board with more diverse membership be established to write auditing standards. The standard auditor's report should be improved, and audit personnel should be rotated from year to year. Overall, the proposals permitted accountants and auditors to continue policing themselves, subject to more rigorous SEC oversight. The subcommittee members warned, however, that they were prepared to introduce legislation if the profession failed to enact meaningful reforms.

After Senator Metcalf passed away in January 1978, only two months after his subcommittee's final report was released, Representative John Moss launched his own investigation of the accounting profession. Moss's House Subcommittee on Oversight and Investigations discussed potential accounting and auditing reforms during January, February, and March 1978.

In June, Moss and four cosponsors introduced the Public Accounting Regulatory Bill (H.R. 13175), which proposed the establishment of a National Organization of Securities and Exchange Commission Accountancy (NOSECA). All CPA firms auditing publicly traded corporations would be required to join the NOSECA. Member firms would have to submit annual reports containing firm financial statements and lists of their SEC clients. NOSECA staff would perform quality reviews of member firms every three years, investigate allegations of substandard auditing, and impose necessary sanctions. To the relief of many accountants, Moss's Bill stalled in the House Committee on Interstate and Foreign Commerce and never reached the House floor. Moss did not stand for reelection in 1978 and the Bill was never reintroduced.

The Commission on Auditors' Responsibilities

Events of the early 1970s caused many auditors to believe they were being unfairly persecuted. Newspaper and magazine articles about National Student Marketing and Equity Funding assigned as much blame to the auditors as to the perpetrators. Juries ordered accounting firms to pay for their clients' frauds. And authorities filed criminal charges against auditors for actions their lawyers claimed were, at worst, errors of judgment. Public accountants feared that journalists, jurors, regulators, and members of the general public expected more from auditors than auditors could realistically deliver.

In November 1974, the AICPA appointed a special Commission on Auditors' Responsibilities to investigate whether a gap existed between what the public expected and what auditors could reasonably accomplish. Former SEC chairman Manuel Cohen headed the seven-member commission.

The "Cohen" commission's final report, published in 1978, concluded that an "expectation gap" did exist—and that auditors bore most of the responsibility. The report stated that users' expectations of the assurances auditors could provide were generally reasonable, but that auditors had failed to keep pace with the changing American business environment.[15]

The most significant problem involved auditors' responsibility for detecting and reporting management fraud. Auditors had claimed for the previous 50 years that routine financial statement audits were not designed to detect fraud and should not be relied upon to do so. But the profession's caveats sounded hollow to the thousands of investors who lost money at Westec, Continental Vending, National Student Marketing, and Equity Funding. According to the report, "Significant percentages of those who use and rely on the auditor's work rank the detection of fraud among the most important objectives of an audit."[16] The Cohen commission recommended that auditors accept responsibility for providing reasonable assurance that the financial statements are not affected by material fraud.

Another difference of opinion existed concerning the propriety of accounting firms providing management advisory services to their audit clients. By the late 1970s, accounting firms were offering services as diverse as executive recruiting, plant layout design, tax planning, and market analysis. Many accounting firms considered such services essential to their future growth and profitability. But a "significant minority" of financial statement users perceived a potential conflict between management advisory services and the audit function.[17] The commission stopped short of recommending that management advisory services be banned, but did propose that corporations disclose in their annual reports all services provided by their auditors.

The commission also concluded that the auditor's standard report was "unsatisfactory."[18] Auditors had been issuing the same boilerplate two-paragraph report for 20 years. The audit report did not distinguish the responsibilities of corporate management from those of the auditor. Nor did it describe in any detail the procedures performed in conducting an audit. The commission recommended that corporate managers begin issuing a separate report acknowledging their primary responsibility for the financial statements. The commission suggested that the auditor's report be expanded to include a "scope paragraph" and an opinion on the adequacy of the client's internal accounting controls.

Chairman Cohen and four other members of the commission described their preliminary recommendations to Senator Metcalf's subcommittee in the spring of 1977. Their testimony may have helped persuade the senator to give the profession one more chance to reform itself before Congress imposed radical changes.

Monitoring Accounting Firms

One of the chief concerns expressed by many witnesses at the Metcalf and Moss subcommittee hearings was that public accounting firms were largely unregulated. The AICPA could discipline members who violated professional standards but had no means of punishing the firms for which the members worked. The AICPA governing council decided that bringing accounting firms under its authority might stave off demands for government oversight of accounting firms.

In September 1977, the AICPA established a division for CPA firms. To qualify for membership, all of a firm's partners had to be members of the AICPA and a majority of its employees had to be certified. Member firms agreed to undergo a peer review every three years to determine their compliance with AICPA quality control standards. Firms auditing SEC clients also had to assign a concurring partner to each SEC client and rotate the engagement partner every five years.

Peer review was not a new idea. When an AICPA long-range planning committee floated the idea of peer reviews in 1967, opponents denounced the suggestion as unnecessary and burdensome. But during the 1970s, the SEC began ordering outside reviews for accounting firms charged with negligent auditing. Peat Marwick Mitchell & Co. had to have its firm-wide audit procedures reviewed by a team of outsiders as part of its settlement of the National Student Marketing case. Then, in 1976, the Metcalf report proposed that a federal agency periodically inspect all public accounting firms. Suddenly, firm-on-firm reviews appeared attractive if they could help avert government inspections. Price Waterhouse was the first Big Eight firm to undergo a voluntary peer review when it hired Deloitte Haskins & Sells to evaluate its quality control procedures for the fiscal year ended June 30, 1976.

Partner rotation was another reform public accountants adopted in an effort to avoid a more severe alternative—firm rotation. Consumer advocate Ralph Nader recommended to Congressman Moss's Oversight and Investigations subcommittee that publicly traded corporations be required to change audit firms every five years. Nader believed that prolonged auditor–client relationships caused auditors to relax their skepticism and identify too closely with the client. AICPA representatives argued during their testimony that partner rotation would mitigate Nader's concerns without being nearly as disruptive. Requiring a second audit partner to perform a concurring review provided additional protection against lax or permissive auditing by the engagement partner.

Computerized Accounting Systems

Computers were a godsend for accountants. Ever since Arthur Andersen consultants helped General Electric automate its payroll in the early

1950s, accountants have been devising new and better ways to use computers in the accounting process. But accounting frauds such as Equity Funding demonstrated that computers could also be used to commit fraud. Several articles appeared in accounting trade magazines in 1974 and 1975 advising auditors how to evaluate computerized controls and test electronic data.[19]

The AICPA Auditing Standards Executive Committee issued Statement on Auditing Standards (SAS) No. 3, *The Effects of EDP on the Auditor's Study and Evaluation of Internal Control*, in 1974. The standard identified risks posed by computerized accounting systems. Data processing was often concentrated in a single department without the traditional separation of duties. There was less human supervision of transactions. Computers lacked the judgment to recognize errors.

Large corporate accounting departments, which sometimes processed millions of transactions per year, stopped printing paper copies of all their journals and ledgers. This eliminated the traditional audit trail that auditors followed to track transactions from source documents through to the financial statements. Many files such as property ledgers and customer master files were available only in machine-readable formats. SAS No. 3 directed auditors to use computer-assisted audit techniques to perform procedures such as recomputing totals and scanning files for unusual or duplicate entries. Accounting firms spent millions of dollars in the 1970s developing specialized audit software.

Most college accounting departments taught their students little about electronic data processing prior to the early 1970s. But SAS No. 3 required that *all* auditors understand electronic data processing well enough to identify key internal controls and plan appropriate substantive tests. Public accounting firms had to train thousands of auditors in the basics of computerized data processing and controls. SAS No. 3 also stated that many audits would require the participation of a computer audit specialist. Accounting firms began hiring hundreds of (non-CPA) computer experts to analyze their clients' sophisticated systems.

Conclusion

The 1970s were a tumultuous time for accountants and auditors. The bitter debate over pooling-of-interests accounting destroyed faith in the APB's ability to set accounting standards. And well publicized accounting scandals such as National Student Marketing and Equity Funding raised doubts about auditors' ability to protect the public from fraud. Powerful members of Congress seriously considered directing the SEC or GAO to write accounting standards and regulate auditors.

But voluntary reforms such as accounting firm peer review, partner rotation, and seating non-CPAs on the FASB convinced Congress to back off. Congressional interest in the accounting profession waned after Senator Lee Metcalf's death in January 1978 and Representative John Moss's retirement later that year. Ronald Reagan's election to the presidency in 1980 effectively ended the possibility that significant federal legislation would be enacted to regulate the accounting profession. President Reagan was a strong proponent of deregulation. Unfortunately, the high monetary inflation of the late 1970s and the deregulation of the early 1980s set the stage for the next accounting crisis.

Part III

The Savings and Loan Crisis

10 It's a Wonderful Life?

A penny saved is a penny earned.

(Benjamin Franklin)

Actor Jimmy Stewart portrayed the quintessential building and loan operator in the classic movie, *It's a Wonderful Life*. Stewart's character, George Bailey, devoted his life to helping the working class members of his community—police officers, taxi drivers, tavern operators—purchase their own homes.

Building and Loan Associations[1]

Building and loan associations operated similarly to banks. Both accepted money from depositors and lent it to borrowers. But until the early 1980s, banks and building and loans served distinct markets. Commercial banks accepted primarily demand (checking) deposits and issued business loans. Building and loans accepted primarily time (savings) deposits and granted home mortgage loans.

Early building and loan operators portrayed themselves not as businessmen but as leaders of a progressive social movement. The first of their two primary goals was to promote savings. In 1919, the U.S. Treasury Department sponsored a National Thrift Week touting the virtue of paying bills on time and encouraging citizens to open savings accounts rather than fritter away their earnings on "wasteful" items such as cigarettes, gum, and alcohol. New Jersey Governor Woodrow Wilson praised his state's building and loan associations for their "moral influence on members."[2]

Building and loans' second goal was promoting home ownership. Social reformers believed that home owners were more responsible citizens. Socialists advocated home ownership as a means of emancipating workers from capitalist landlords. Commerce Secretary Herbert Hoover proclaimed a Better Homes Week in 1922 to encourage home ownership among lower-income people.

With such lofty goals, many building and loan operators believed they were answering a "calling" to serve their communities. Building and loan industry leaders described their associations more like religious than financial institutions. *Business Week* commented in 1930 that "the 'movement'—they still call it that—is imbued with a tinge of evangelism."[3]

Government Regulation

Until the early 1930s, building and loans were regulated by states. The state issuing the thrift's charter set restrictions on who could own and operate the institution, the types of deposits it could accept, the types of assets it could hold, and the number and location of branches it could operate.

The stock market crash of 1929 and the ensuing economic depression wreaked havoc on America's financial institutions. Between 1931 and 1932, almost 20 percent of the country's commercial banks went out of business. Building and loans fared better because they suffered fewer defaults on their relatively safe home mortgages. But many thrift organizations did experience severe liquidity problems. Banks called their loans, forcing them to turn over much of their available cash. Unemployed customers stopped making deposits and started making withdrawals.

In July 1932, President Herbert Hoover signed legislation establishing the Federal Home Loan Bank Board (FHLBB). The FHLBB's primary purpose was to lend money to thrift organizations, enabling them to make loans to their customers and/or meet their depositors' withdrawal requests.

Two years later, President Franklin Roosevelt signed a Bill establishing the Federal Savings and Loan Insurance Corporation (FSLIC) to insure customer deposits in the event of a thrift organization's collapse. Participation in the FSLIC was voluntary. Member savings and loans had to pay insurance premiums and maintain owners' equity equal to at least 5 percent of insured deposits. But institutions quickly discovered that FSLIC membership was crucial in attracting depositors. By 1960, 94 percent of the nation's savings and loans participated in the FSLIC. Notable exceptions were thrifts chartered in Ohio and Maryland, which insured their depositors through state-run organizations.

The Postwar Boom

For three decades after World War II, savings and loan executives thrived by following the simple "3/6/3 rule"—take in deposits at 3 percent interest, make loans at 6 percent interest, and be on the golf course by 3:00 every afternoon. Rising income levels enabled people to make larger deposits to their savings accounts. Improving transportation made it possible for people to build homes in the suburbs. The postwar baby boom motivated young couples to purchase bigger houses. Under these favorable conditions, the assets controlled by savings and loans increased from less than $10 billion in 1945 to nearly $600 billion in 1979.

Savings and loans faced very low default risk. Their loans were secured by liens on the borrower's land and house. And borrowers had to either pay a substantial down payment or obtain insurance through a government agency such as the Federal Housing Administration or the Veterans Administration. Real estate prices rose consistently during the postwar years ensuring that, even in situations where a borrower defaulted on a loan, the property could almost always be sold for an amount sufficient to pay the outstanding loan balance.

But savings and loans faced substantial interest rate risks. Savings and loans, by their nature, engaged in a risky practice known as "borrowing short and investing long." That is, they took in money through passbook savings accounts and invested in 30-year fixed rate loans. As long as interest rates remained stable, the thrifts earned profits by charging a higher rate to their borrowers than they paid to their depositors. But if interest rates rose unexpectedly, a savings and loan might find itself paying higher rates on its deposits than it earned on its loans. To shield savings and loans from unexpected interest rate fluctuations, the Interest Rate Control Act of 1966 capped the rates banks and thrifts were permitted to pay to their depositors.

Disaster

Between January 1978 and December 1980, the interest rate on three-month treasury bills increased from 6.5 percent to 15.6 percent. Meanwhile, the interest rate ceiling on passbook savings accounts was 5.2 percent. Savings and loan depositors understandably began looking for other places to invest their money. Money market mutual funds, which invested in short-term securities such as commercial paper and government notes, provided an attractive alternative. Money market accounts were not guaranteed by the federal government, but their higher yields more than compensated for the extra risk.

The total assets invested in money market mutual funds skyrocketed from $9.5 billion in 1978 to $236 billion four years later. Much of the money deposited in money market accounts was withdrawn from savings and loans. The rapid disintermediation created a liquidity crisis in the savings and loan industry. Many institutions had to sell large portions of their loan portfolios to satisfy the demands of customers withdrawing funds from their accounts. Losses recognized on the loan sales reduced institutions' net assets below regulatory minimums.

The only way to stop the flow of funds out of savings and loans was to allow them to pay interest rates competitive with money market mutual funds. So in April 1980, President Jimmy Carter signed the Depository Institutions Deregulation and Monetary Control Act (DIDMCA). The key provision of the legislation was the phaseout of interest rate ceilings. To help savings and loans attract deposits, DIDMCA authorized thrift institutions to offer NOW accounts[4] and increased the FSLIC deposit insurance from $40,000 to $100,000 per account. DIDMCA also allowed savings and loans to partially diversify their portfolios by investing up to 20 percent of their assets in consumer loans, commercial paper, and corporate bonds.

Although DIDMCA helped stop the flow of funds out of savings and loans, it did little to improve their operating profits. Institutions' interest expense increased with the higher rates paid on deposits. By 1982, the average rate savings and loans paid on their deposits was 11.2 percent. But the majority of thrifts' interest income was fixed at the rates that were in effect when the loans were granted. Many loans in their portfolios had been issued in the 1960s and early 1970s when rates were below 8 percent.

President Ronald Reagan and many members of Congress believed the best way to help savings and loans was to free them from government regulation. The Depository Institutions Act of 1982, cosponsored by Senator Jake Garn (R, Utah) and Representative Ferdinand J. St. Germain (D, Rhode Island), greatly expanded the types of assets savings and loans were permitted to own. The Garn–St. Germain Bill finally permitted savings and loans to issue adjustable-rate mortgages, reducing thrifts' exposure to interest rate fluctuations. Garn–St. Germain also allowed savings and loans to issue unsecured commercial loans, purchase corporate junk bonds, and even make direct equity investments in businesses.

Savings and Loan Accounting

One of the most momentous decisions made by the first group of SEC commissioners was to require companies to value assets at historical cost rather than at current market value. The SEC's decision, reinforced by Paton and Littleton's famous 1940 monograph *An Introduction to Corporate Accounting Standards*, firmly established historical cost as the only generally accepted method of valuing assets. Although the APB's Accounting Research Study No. 3 recommended valuing assets at current market value, and prominent academics such as Robert Sterling, Lawrence Revsine, Edgar O. Edwards and Philip Bell advocated current value accounting, historical cost accounting remained the rule.

The value of a loan (to the lender) varies inversely with prevailing interest rates. For example, if a savings and loan issues a $100,000 loan to a borrower at a fixed interest rate of 6 percent and the interest rate on similar loans increases subsequently to 10 percent, the market value of the loan decreases. If the savings and loan sells the loan to a third party, it will have to accept a price far below $100,000. But under the rules of historical cost accounting, as long as the savings and loan holds the loan in its portfolio, it can report the loan at its face value of $100,000.

When interest rates soared in the late 1970s, the market value of savings and loans' assets plunged. No losses were reported, however, unless the savings and loans sold their loans. If depositors withdrew too much money, a savings and loan would be forced to liquidate part of its loan portfolio and recognize a loss. So in 1980, savings and loans raised the rates they paid to depositors sufficiently to avoid large net withdrawals. Such a strategy was unsustainable in the long run because the higher interest payments, combined with the fixed interest income, created operating losses. But the balance sheets, which showed the thrifts' assets at face value, failed to reveal the true extent of the thrift industry's problems.

During the late 1970s and early 1980s, as interest rates rose and operating profits fell, savings and loans employed a number of accounting tricks to inflate their reported earnings. One scheme involved advancing borrowers more money than they actually needed for their projects. If a real estate developer needed $10 million, for example, the savings and loan might write the loan for $12 million and the borrower would leave the excess $2 million on deposit at the thrift. As early payments came due, the savings and loan would debit the developer's account and record interest income for the amounts "received." This practice enabled savings and loans to grant loans for speculative, long-term projects without worrying whether they would produce income in their early years. Even if the project never turned a profit, it could be several years before the initial deposit was exhausted and the loan had to be classified as nonperforming.

A second accounting gimmick involved charging borrowers large up-front loan origination fees. If the prevailing interest rate was, say 12 percent, a savings and loan might grant a loan at 10 percent if the borrower agreed to pay a large loan application fee. The savings and loan recorded the up-front fee immediately as income while reporting the below-market loan as an asset at its full face value.

To make matters worse, the FHLBB permitted savings and loans in 1982 to begin using Regulatory Accounting Principles (RAP) to prepare their financial statements for regulators. RAP permitted savings and loans to defer losses on sales of loans. For example, Guaranty Federal Savings (GFS) of Galveston, Texas sold its entire $280 million loan portfolio for $180 million. But instead of reporting a $100 million loss in 1982 when the loans were sold, GFS was permitted to amortize the loss over the next 23 years. The FHLBB authorized this odd accounting in order to encourage savings and loans to diversify their assets. Institutions would have been loath to sell their loans if they had been required to report large losses. In reality, the accounting rule encouraged savings and loans to dispose of relatively safe assets and replace them with riskier investments.

RAP also permitted savings and loans to revalue their land and buildings to current market value. This selective deviation from historical cost accounting resulted in buildings (which generally appreciated in value) being reported at current market value while loan portfolios (which had depreciated due to rising interest rates) were reported at historical cost.

RAP inflated savings and loans' assets and hid the severity of the industry's problems. But that was really their purpose. According to GAAP, 449 savings and loans were insolvent in 1984. Neither the FHLBB nor the FSLIC had the resources to deal with that many insolvent institutions. So the FHLBB changed the accounting rules used to measure solvency. Using RAP, only 73 savings and loans were insolvent in 1984. The FHLBB gambled that the majority of savings and loans would recover their losses and survive without government intervention if they were given enough time for the 1982 Garn–St. Germain reforms to take effect.

To its credit, the FASB warned that the savings and loans' FHLBB-authorized, non-GAAP financial statements could be misleading. FASB chairman Donald Kirk stated, "Revising the financial statements so that the [net worth] tests are not violated, in my opinion, does little for the credibility of the savings and loans or financial reporting in general."[5]

Gamblers' Paradise

Economists use the phrase "moral hazard" to describe a situation in which a person has an incentive to engage in abnormally risky behavior because the real or perceived potential costs of the behavior have been alleviated. Insurance policies provide a simple example. A driver with comprehensive automobile insurance might be tempted to drive more aggressively or leave the car doors unlocked knowing that the cost of an accident or theft will be borne by somebody else—the insurance company. For this reason, most insurance policies require the policyholder to pay a specified deductible with each claim. The deductible provision reduces moral hazard by giving the policyholder an incentive to avoid irresponsible behavior.

Before 1980, the FSLIC required member institutions to maintain owner's equity equal to at least 5 percent of insured deposits. This "net worth" requirement acted like an insurance policy deductible provision.

In the event of a savings and loan's failure, the owners would lose their investment before the FSLIC would have to pay the remaining depositors' claims. But the large losses suffered in the late 1970s placed many savings and loans in violation of the 5 percent net worth requirement. Rather than close the noncomplying institutions, the FSLIC lowered the net worth requirement to 4 percent of deposits in 1980 and then to 3 percent in 1982.

The conditions of the thrift industry in 1983 practically begged savings and loan operators to gamble. Because the FSLIC required members to maintain a net worth of only 3 percent, it was possible to purchase a savings and loan having $100 million of assets for as little as $3 million. And because of Garn–St. Germain, the savings and loan owner could invest the $100 million of assets in a wide variety of high-risk/high-return assets. If the assets were profitable, the owner, through the magic of financial leverage, could earn a substantial return on the initial $3 million investment. But if reckless investing caused the savings and loan to lose all $100 million of its assets, the owner could simply forfeit his $3 million and walk away. The FSLIC would have to reimburse depositors for their losses.

Under these conditions, it is almost surprising that so many savings and loan managers continued to operate their institutions safely and conservatively. But an important minority of thrift operators exploited the opportunities. The combined assets of thrifts in California, Florida, and Texas—states with the most permissive regulations—tripled between 1982 and 1985. Aggressive savings and loan managers advertised high interest rates to attract deposits from all over the country. Most of the new funds were invested not in home loans but in high-yield junk bonds, commercial real estate development projects, and raw (undeveloped) land.

As savings and loan officers diversified their portfolios, they began buying assets with which they had little expertise. Unscrupulous securities dealers began taking advantage of the thrift operators' naivety. A Florida-based securities dealer, ESM Government Securities (ESM), "sold" the same securities to numerous investors, promising to repurchase the securities later for a higher price. After Cincinnati-based Home State Savings & Loan lost $145 million on deposit at ESM, depositors scrambled to withdraw their funds. Ohio's governor had to close the state's 70 privately insured thrifts until emergency legislation could be passed to shore up the state's insurance fund.

And a new breed of savings and loan owners recognized the potential profits that could be earned in the deregulated, highly leveraged industry. Charles H. Keating, Jr. purchased Lincoln Savings & Loan in 1983 for $51 million. During the next six years, Keating and his family withdrew $34 million from Lincoln while investing more than $2 billion of the thrift's assets in junk bonds, undeveloped land, and unsecured loans. After Lincoln was seized in 1989, regulators had to pay approximately $2.5 billion to satisfy insured depositors.

In both cases, auditors bore some responsibility for the losses. The partner in charge of ESM's audit learned of the fraud in 1978 but issued clean audit reports during each of the next six years while accepting $200,000 of "loans" from the company's officers. Lincoln's auditors gullibly accepted Keating's assertion that Lincoln earned $80 million in profit on real estate sales at a time when the Phoenix real estate market was stagnant.

11 ESM Government Securities

> As for the ESM matter, I swear now that I did not know anything about the adverse financial condition or even suspect that there might be problems until January 21, [1985]. I am innocent of any wrongdoing in that case. So are my partners and Marvin Warner.
>
> (Stephen Arky's suicide note,[1] July 22, 1985)

Steve Arky began his law career in 1968 at the Securities and Exchange Commission in Washington. Stanley Sporkin, former Director of Enforcement at the SEC, called Arky one of his "finest young men."[2] Arky eventually transferred to the SEC's Miami office, where he investigated and prosecuted unscrupulous securities dealers until entering private practice in 1971.

On July 22, 1985, Arky closed his bathroom door and fired a bullet into his right temple. In his suicide note, addressed "To the world at large," Arky swore that he was wholly unaware of the massive accounting fraud committed at ESM Government Securities, Inc. (ESM). Between 1977 and 1981, Arky had defended his friends at ESM in a ferocious battle with the SEC. Arky blocked the agency's subpoenas and frustrated its investigators, eventually prompting the SEC to drop its investigation without filing charges. But in March 1985, a fraud was discovered at ESM that far exceeded anything the SEC had ever suspected. Although little evidence tied Arky directly to the fraud, the rumors and damage to his reputation were apparently more than he could bear.

ESM Government Securities, Inc.

Ronnie Ewton, Bob Seneca, and George Mead founded ESM in November 1975. The company acted primarily as a broker, buying bonds issued by the U.S. government and reselling them to municipalities and financial institutions. Seneca ran ESM's trading operations. Ewton and Mead were salesmen. The trio hired Alan Novick, a New York investment banker, to supervise ESM's financial and accounting work. Ewton's army buddy Steve Arky provided legal advice.

The U.S. government securities market is the largest financial market in the world. During the 1970s and early 1980s, the U.S. Treasury needed to sell more than $300 billion in bonds per year to fund the national deficit and refinance older bonds coming due. In addition, quasi-government organizations such as the Federal National Mortgage Association (FNMA or Fannie Mae) had billions of dollars of mortgage-backed bonds outstanding. The volume of government securities traded each year exceeded the volume of trades on the New York Stock Exchange by a factor of twenty to one.

Until the mid-1970s, the Treasury department sold most of its securities to a handful of large investment houses ("primary dealers") such as Merrill Lynch and Goldman Sachs who, in turn, sold the securities to banks, insurance companies, and pension funds. As the amount of Treasury debt outstanding increased from $400 billion in 1970 to more than $1 trillion in 1981, new investors had to be found to buy the securities. This provided an opportunity for smaller ("secondary") dealers like ESM to enter the market. While primary dealers sold bonds in $100 million bundles to huge customers such as Metropolitan Life and Chemical Bank, Ronnie Ewton and George Mead attended city manager conventions and entertained small-town bankers at the Kentucky Derby. ESM's customers/victims included Clallam County, Washington and the city of Beaumont, Texas.

Legalized Gambling

In addition to buying government bonds for resale, ESM also engaged in speculative trades—buying securities with the hope that their value would increase. In regulated equities markets, such as the New York Stock Exchange, investors must pay a substantial down payment to buy corporate stock. But in the government bond market before 1986, highly leveraged purchases were permitted. Securities traders could purchase government bonds with as little as 1 percent down. For example, a trader might purchase $100 million of securities with $1 million of his own money and $99 million of borrowed money. If the securities appreciated 3 percent to $103 million, the trader could sell the securities, repay the $99 million loan and be left with $4 million—four times his original investment. On the other hand, if the securities' value decreased only 1 percent from $100 million to $99 million, the entire $1 million investment would be lost.

The value of government bonds varies inversely with interest rates. A bond's price rises when interest rates fall and drops when interest rates rise. During the late 1970s, when the federal deficit was ballooning and inflation rates were in the double digits, interest rates fluctuated frequently. Enormous fortunes could be gained or lost overnight.

Bobby Seneca bought $29 million of Treasury bonds on ESM's behalf in September 1977, gambling that interest rates would drop in the near future. Instead, rates rose. By the time Seneca unloaded the securities, ESM had lost $2.3 million. With one bad trade, Seneca lost more than ESM's entire invested capital and accumulated earnings.

Ronnie Ewton sought Alan Novick's advice on whether ESM should declare bankruptcy. Novick replied, "If you get rid of Seneca, I'll get rid of the losses."[3] Seneca, who was going through a messy divorce, agreed to sell his stake in ESM and leave town. Seneca's shares were distributed to Ewton, Mead, Novick, and two other ESM officers.

Novick assumed control of ESM's trading operations after Seneca's departure. He believed that with skillful trading he could recover Seneca's losses in a matter of months. Unfortunately, Novick's trading skills did not match his confidence. Novick lost $5 million during 1978, leaving ESM with a negative net worth of more than $6 million. But this was only the beginning.

After losing another $14.4 million in 1979, Novick came up with a bold plan to erase ESM's red ink. In 1980, he used $100 million of customers' securities as collateral to purchase $1 billion of Treasury bonds. But when interest rates rose unexpectedly, the value of Novick's $1 billion portfolio plummeted. Novick lost $80 million of money that did not even belong to him because the securities used as the down payment really belonged to ESM's customers. By the time ESM went out of business in March 1985, its cumulative losses approximated $300 million.

The ESM Fraud

ESM's ability to continue in business (and continue losing money) depended on Novick's ability to hide the losses. Novick made ESM look profitable by recording fictitious transactions with a related entity, ESM Financial Group, Inc. (ESMFG). In reality, ESMFG was nothing more than a shell corporation controlled by Ronnie Ewton. ESM's December 31, 1984 financial statements disclosed $1.6 billion of transactions with an "affiliated company." The net result of the transactions was a $300 million receivable on ESM's balance sheet from ESMFG. The statements failed to disclose, however, that ESM had no hope of ever collecting the receivable because ESMFG had no significant assets and a negative net worth.

ESMFG also served as a conduit for channeling money from ESM to Ewton, Mead, and Novick. ESM transferred funds to ESMFG who then granted "loans" to ESM's senior managers. Between 1978 and 1985, ESM officers withdrew approximately $60 million in salaries, bonuses and loans from their money-losing enterprise. Ronnie Ewton spent more than $1.5 million in December 1984 alone on an Aston Martin Lagonda sports car, two polo ponies, and a yacht.

To achieve a positive cash flow in spite of heavy trading losses and the owners' generous withdrawals, ESM entered into securities repurchase agreements, commonly referred to as "repos." In a repo transaction, investors bought securities from ESM and ESM promised to repurchase the securities at a later date for a higher price. Repos are a popular way for counties and small towns to invest idle cash. When performed properly, repos are very safe investments because the purchaser/investor holds the securities as collateral in case the other party fails to honor the repurchase agreement. Unfortunately, many of the municipalities that dealt with ESM did not take physical possession of the securities they purchased. In fact, ESM offered a higher interest rate to customers who allowed ESM to retain possession of the securities. This enabled ESM to "sell" the same securities to multiple customers. ESM continued in business for seven money-losing years by entering into increasing volumes of repurchase agreements and using the cash receipts from subsequent repos to pay its obligations from prior repos.

Discovery of the Fraud

Alan Novick became ESM's de facto leader in 1980. Ronnie Ewton, ostensibly ESM's chairman, slipped into an alcoholic depression following his 1979 divorce. Ewton spent most of his time at his pony ranch in South Carolina, visiting ESM's headquarters only a couple of times each month. George Mead, the other remaining cofounder, had never been more than a salesman.

On November 23, 1984, Novick suffered a massive heart attack while seated at his desk and never awoke. Ewton and Mead didn't know what to do. Neither was capable of continuing the intricate transactions Novick used to hide ESM's losses.

Ewton confessed to a bankruptcy attorney on January 14, 1985 that ESM was insolvent by approximately $180 million. The true cumulative losses were far greater, but not even Ewton knew the full extent of Novick's manipulations. A week later, Ewton met with a criminal lawyer who agreed to represent Ewton in any suits relating to the fraud. Ewton paid himself a $710,000 bonus and then resigned on February 11, leaving Mead in charge of the company.

Mead, who understood little other than that he was in deep trouble, sought help from securities lawyer Tom Tew. Tew engaged accountant Laurie Holtz to help him unravel the true state of ESM's finances. Within three hours of arriving at ESM's headquarters, Holtz informed Tew that ESM was insolvent by at least $300 million. Holtz uncovered the seven-year fraud simply by comparing ESM's published financial statements to its federal tax returns. ESM's income statements showed healthy (fictitious) profits for each year from 1978 through 1984. But Novick, not wanting to pay taxes on profits he had not really earned, had reported the company's actual losses to the IRS.

Home State Savings & Loan

ESM's collapse led directly to the failure of Cincinnati-based Home State Savings & Loan. Home State was owned by Marvin Warner, who purchased the thrift in 1958. During the next 20 years, Home State grew to become the largest savings and loan in southern Ohio.

By the mid-1970s, Warner had become more interested in politics than business. He was a member of the Democratic National Committee and a leading fundraiser for Jimmy Carter's successful presidential campaign. President Carter rewarded Warner by naming him ambassador to Switzerland in 1977. When Warner returned from Zürich in 1980, he refocused his attention on his struggling savings and loan.

Steve Arky, who had married Warner's daughter Marlin in 1967, thought he was helping both his father-in-law and his friend when he introduced Warner to Ronnie Ewton in 1977. Warner was attracted to the high potential profits that could be earned in the government securities market. Home State soon became ESM's largest customer.

Arky telephoned Warner shortly upon learning the truth about ESM's dire financial condition in January 1985. At the time, Home State had $145 million of assets on deposit at ESM. Home State's CEO called ESM on March 1 to close the thrift's account and demand the return of its securities. But it was too late. ESM did not have sufficient assets to pay Home State what it was owed. The SEC closed ESM on March 3 and a federal judge appointed Tom Tew to act as bankruptcy receiver.

On Wednesday, March 6, the *Cincinnati Enquirer* ran a front-page article disclosing that Home State faced "a loss of undetermined proportion" as a result of ESM's bankruptcy.[4] Worried depositors began withdrawing their funds. By Friday, $154 million of Home State's $525 million of deposits had been withdrawn. The Federal Reserve Bank did what it could to support Home State, granting emergency loans and dispatching more than 150 truckloads of cash to Home State's branch offices. But Ohio regulators finally had to step in. A conservator was appointed on March 9 to close Home State and sell it to a healthy financial institution.

Panic in Ohio

Home State was one of 70 Ohio savings and loans that were not members of the FSLIC. The Ohio thrifts who opted out of the federal program obtained private insurance through the Ohio Deposit Guarantee Fund (ODGF). In early 1985, the ODGF had $136 million of assets available to protect the depositors of its member institutions. But Home State's potential losses approximated $145 million.

When depositors learned that Home State's claims might bankrupt the state insurance fund, panic spread to other Ohio savings and loans. Depositors withdrew more than $200 million from other privately insured thrifts on March 13 and 14. Hundreds of customers spent the night of March 14 in tents and sleeping bags outside savings and loan offices waiting to close their accounts the next morning.

Their wait was for naught. Ohio Governor Richard Celeste declared a bank holiday for all 70 of the state's privately insured thrifts before they opened on the 15th. It was the most extensive such action in the United States since President Franklin Delano Roosevelt shut all the nation's banks in 1933. More than 500,000 Ohioans were separated from their assets as ATMs stopped dispensing money and banks refused to honor checks drawn on shuttered savings and loans. Most of the thrifts remained closed for six days while regulators worked to expedite their acceptance into the federal insurance program. The Ohio legislature had to appropriate $200 million to bail out Home State and the other privately insured savings and loans.

Alexander Grant

One of the most disturbing aspects of the ESM story is that most of the fraud was conducted with the full knowledge and consent of the company's auditor. Ronnie Ewton hired Alexander Grant & Co. to perform ESM's first audit in January 1976. Grant was then the eleventh largest accounting firm in the country, third behind the Big Eight.

The man most culpable for Alexander Grant's failure was a young partner named Jose Gomez. Gomez's mother fled Cuba in 1961 and settled in Miami with her 13-year-old son. Jose helped support his mother by bagging groceries at a local supermarket. He eventually worked his way through the University of Miami, earning a degree in accounting. On August 1, 1979, Gomez's dreams were fulfilled when he was offered a partnership in Alexander Grant.

Before the month was over, Gomez's dream became a nightmare. Alan Novick confided at a luncheon meeting that ESM was secretly insolvent. Gomez had supervised ESM's 1977 and 1978 audits and was scheduled to serve as engagement partner on the upcoming 1979 audit. Novick explained ESM's losses and the journal entries he had used to conceal them from Gomez's audit team. Gomez wanted to recall ESM's 1977 and 1978 financial statements, but Novick kept repeating, "How's it going to look? It's going to look terrible for you, and you just got promoted to partner."[5] Novick outlined his plans to recoup the earlier years' losses and urged that if given a little more time, he could replace the money and nobody would ever know. In the end, Gomez remained silent because he didn't want to face the consequences of admitting he had missed an $8 million fraud in 1977 and 1978. By the time the cumulative losses surpassed $100 million in 1980, Gomez was too deeply entwined with the fraud to consider backing out.

Novick further ensured his auditor's cooperation by lending Gomez thousands of dollars during the next five years. After Novick's death in 1984, Ewton and Mead tried to hire Gomez to replace their deceased comrade. They knew that Gomez was the only person capable of maintaining the fraud. Gomez declined their offer, but accepted an additional $50,000 loan from each of them.

Alexander Grant & Co. paid heavily for Gomez's cowardice. Tom Tew sued Grant on behalf of ESM's customers, creditors, and the state of Ohio. After Grant agreed to pay $72 million to several large plaintiffs, Tew offered to settle $85 million of remaining claims for $10 million. The accountants foolishly declined Tew's offer, choosing to battle the claims in court. In November 1986, a six-member jury awarded Tew's clients $70.9 million. Grant and its insurers ultimately paid a total of $173 million in damages and legal fees.

The SEC took the unusual step of charging the entire Alexander Grant accounting firm with fraud. In spite of Grant's protestations that the firm should not be punished for the actions of a single rogue partner, the SEC concluded that Gomez was not the only Grant employee who neglected his duties. Kenneth Ortner, a Grant tax accountant, learned of Novick's loans to Gomez while preparing Novick's personal income tax return. Ornter asked Gomez about the loans, but did not report this clear violation of firm policy and professional independence standards to Gomez's superiors. Robert Hersh, another Grant tax accountant, reviewed and signed ESM's corporate tax returns. The tax returns showed that ESM had been insolvent since 1977, but Hersh never questioned his firm's clean audit opinions on ESM's financial statements. The SEC also found Grant's quality control review procedures to be woefully inadequate. Gomez testified that a concurring review partner had stated at the end of one audit, "I don't understand this sh.., so please tell me it's okay and I'll sign it."[6] In addition to disciplining five Grant employees, the SEC barred the accounting firm from accepting new public audit clients for 60 days.

Aftermath

Jose Gomez credits Steve Arky with saving his life. Gomez fell into deep depression after the fraud's discovery and refused to cooperate with investigators. But after hearing of Arky's suicide in July 1985, Gomez realized he had to take positive steps or he would sink to the same fate.

Gomez began cooperating with Tom Tew and the SEC. He claimed later that leading the investigators through the fraud had a "tremendous therapeutic effect" on him.[7] Gomez pleaded guilty to federal charges of fraud and conspiracy, and was sentenced to 12 years in a Tallahassee prison. An Ohio judge sentenced Gomez to 18 months for violations of state law, but rewarded Gomez's cooperation by allowing him to serve his Ohio sentence concurrently with his federal sentence.

Ronnie Ewton and George Mead were not so lucky. After a federal judge sentenced them to 15 and 14 years respectively, they traveled to Cincinnati to be sentenced on nine Ohio criminal charges. Although Tom Tew testified that Ewton and Mead had saved the government hundreds of thousands of dollars through their cooperation and had expedited restitution to the victims, Judge Fred Cartolano rejected their pleas for leniency. The judge, who was still outraged by the memory of hundreds of Ohioans shivering in queues outside closed savings and loans, ordered Ewton to serve nine years in an Ohio prison *before* commencing his federal sentence. Mead received a six-year Ohio sentence.

Sadly, Steve Arky's life was not the only one cut short by the ESM scandal. Henry Earl Riddel, ESM's controller and Alan Novick's right-hand man, committed suicide in November 1986, one month before he was to begin serving a three-year prison sentence.

12 Lincoln Savings & Loan

> Why do you look at the speck of sawdust in your brother's eye and pay no attention to the plank in your own eye?
>
> (Matthew 7:3)

Charles H. Keating, Jr. loathed smut-peddler Larry Flynt. Keating crusaded against pornography for 30 years and it galled him that Flynt's *Hustler* magazine had been founded in Keating's home town of Cincinnati, Ohio. Citizens for Decent Literature (CDL), which Keating founded in 1958, grew to become the largest antipornography organization in the United States with 300 chapters and 100,000 members. In 1970 alone, Keating traveled 200,000 miles giving dozens of speeches against pornography. Keating testified before several congressional committees and was appointed by President Richard Nixon to serve on the federal Commission on Obscenity and Pornography.

The battle between Keating and Flynt was long, personal, bitter, and—if the rumors are true—violent. Keating and CDL filed numerous lawsuits against Flynt and were instrumental in Flynt's 1977 conviction for distributing obscenity and engaging in organized crime. Shortly after Flynt's conviction, one of Keating's daughters was raped on the University of Cincinnati campus. Keating later came to believe that Flynt had offered a monetary reward for the girl's assault. A year later, an unidentified gunman shot Larry Flynt, leaving him paralyzed from the waist down. Keating's colleagues noticed that he was uncharacteristically silent on the subject of Flynt's shooting.[1]

Keating projected the image of the all-American boy—Navy fighter pilot, national breaststroke champion, defender of decency. He donated millions of dollars to charities, including Mother Theresa's hospital in Calcutta, and loaned millions more for the construction of homeless shelters. Yet Keating was as corrupt, albeit in different ways, as his nemesis Larry Flynt. Between 1984 and 1989, Keating and his family looted $34 million from Lincoln Savings & Loan (LS&L). They used land swaps and circular transactions to overstate the thrift's earnings.

Twenty thousand investors lost more than $250 million on Keating's worthless securities. The federal bailout of LS&L cost U.S. taxpayers approximately $2.5 billion.

Keating served four and one-half years in prison after being convicted of racketeering and securities fraud. But perhaps the cruelest blow to the fervent pornography foe came in April 1992 when *Playboy* magazine published a feature article describing how Keating "flimflammed investors, bribed senators, and rained ruin on every taxpayer."[2]

Keating's Early Career

Charles Keating and his brother William opened a law office in Cincinnati in 1952. The brothers specialized in corporate law and soon began performing services for Carl Lindner's American Financial Corporation (AFC). Lindner started in the grocery business, but began buying small savings and loans in 1959. AFC eventually evolved into a "financial department store." The holding company owned banks, savings and loans, insurance companies, and leasing companies.

In 1972, after William was elected to Congress, Charles Keating gave up his private law practice and joined AFC as a full-time employee. It was at AFC that Keating had his first encounter with the Securities and Exchange Commission. The SEC charged Lindner and Keating with issuing $14 million of sweetheart loans to AFC insiders through Provident Bank. In the most egregious alleged violation, the SEC charged that Keating borrowed $500,000 and then ordered the loan written off. AFC settled the charges in 1979, assigning most of the blame to Keating. Keating was fined $1.4 million and banned from the securities markets for three months.

American Continental Corporation

Keating's second career began in 1978 when he purchased American Continental Corporation (ACC), a former AFC subsidiary. ACC was a home building company operating primarily in Arizona, Utah, Wyoming, and Colorado. The population of the southwestern United States swelled substantially during the late 1970s and early 1980s as retirees escaped the bitter winters of the north. ACC built 18,000 homes during the first six years of Keating's ownership.

By 1983, Keating had grown bored with building houses. He was 60 years old and a multimillionaire. Keating should have either retired to his luxurious home in the Bahamas or devoted his full-time energies to his favorite charities. Instead, he bought Lincoln Savings & Loan.

LS&L was a federally insured institution chartered in California. Its $1.2 billion of total assets consisted primarily of home mortgages and government bonds. In the Change of Control Application filed with federal regulators, Keating promised to retain LS&L's top managers, continue issuing residential home loans, and not use brokered deposits to expand the thrift's assets.

Within weeks of acquiring LS&L, Keating fired its top executives and installed his son, Charles Keating III (known as "C3"), as the thrift's president. C3 was then a 24-year-old college dropout whose only work experience outside his father's companies was clearing tables in a country club restaurant. One of Keating's daughters and three of his sons-in-law held four of the other eight highest positions at LS&L. LS&L's board of directors was composed entirely of ACC employees.

LS&L's total assets doubled to $2.5 billion by the end of 1984. Much of the growth came from brokered deposits. Money brokers pooled the assets of small investors and searched for the savings institutions offering the highest interest rates. To obtain the deposits, Keating had to meet or beat the interest paid by every other savings and loan in the country.

LS&L's heavy reliance on brokered deposits caused the average interest rate paid on its deposits to be substantially higher than the average rate paid by most other institutions. LS&L could hope to earn a profit only by investing in high-yield—and high-risk—securities. Charles Keating became one of Michael Milken's largest junk bond customers. By 1988, 77 percent of the bonds in LS&L's portfolio were unrated junk.

Under Keating, LS&L also purchased large tracts of raw land (i.e., undeveloped real estate). Estrella was a 26-square-mile patch of desert 20 miles southwest of downtown Phoenix on which Keating planned to build a 200,000-person community. It would require more than $100 million of expenditures for roads, lakes, sewers, and other development before any of its 73,000 plots could be sold.

Because of LS&L's large investments in non-income-producing real estate, its interest-bearing liabilities exceeded its interest-earning assets by $1 billion by the end of 1987. LS&L's interest income barely exceeded its interest expense. Its ability to report profits and pay dividends depended entirely on its ability to report gains on land transactions. Without the $153 million of gains on real estate sales reported during 1986 and 1987, LS&L would have reported pretax losses totaling $8 million.

The Lincoln Savings & Loan Fraud

Keating's accounting shenanigans began the day he purchased LS&L. Keating allocated an improperly small amount of the $51 million purchase price to LS&L's loan portfolio and inflated the amounts allocated to other assets. When LS&L subsequently sold the loans at their true value, it reported a gain for the difference between the selling price and the understated carrying values.

The majority of the LS&L accounting fraud involved recording improper gains on bogus real estate transactions. Kenneth Leventhal & Co. investigated LS&L's accounting practices after the thrift's collapse. Leventhal examined a sample of 15 large real estate transactions and concluded that not one of them had been accounted for properly. One of the Leventhal partners stated in his testimony, "Seldom in our experience have we encountered a more egregious example of misapplication of generally accepted accounting principles."[3]

Hidden Valley consisted of 8,500 acres of undeveloped land so remotely located that it was accessible only by off-road vehicle. LS&L acquired Hidden Valley during 1985 and 1986 at an average price of $3,100 per acre. During 1987 and 1988, LS&L recognized more than $80 million of profits on "sales" of Hidden Valley land at prices as high as $17,500 per acre.

In one illustrative Hidden Valley transaction, LS&L sold 1,000 acres of land costing $3 million to a company called Wescon for $3.5 million cash plus a nonrecourse note for $10.5 million. The terms of the note restricted LS&L to simply taking back the land if Wescon failed to pay. One day before selling the land to Wescon, LS&L loaned $20 million to Ernie Garcia. Garcia, in turn, loaned $3.5 million to Wescon. Wescon had less than $100,000 of total assets prior to receiving the loan from Garcia. Thus, LS&L recorded an $11 million profit on a transaction in which it received only $3.5 million of its own money and a note it had little hope of collecting.

This type of seller-financed deal was common for LS&L during 1987. Most of the parties who purchased Hidden Valley land at inflated prices received direct or indirect loans from LS&L.

While LS&L was recording sham profits on dubious land sales, ACC switched from constructing single-family homes to building luxury hotels. Keating decided to build the most opulent hotel on earth in Phoenix, Arizona. Originally budgeted at $150 million, the Phoenician eventually cost $300 million or about $500,000 for each of its 600 rooms. Its ballroom, health club, swimming pools, and golf facilities were second to none. The Phoenician's construction was financed chiefly through ACC subordinated debentures (i.e., junk bonds). The most disturbing aspect of the financing was that the ACC bonds were sold through LS&L branches. Tellers informed wealthy customers of the higher yields offered by the ACC bonds. Many customers assumed that, because the bonds were sold through a savings and loan, they were federally insured like the certificates of deposit. They learned the sad truth after ACC declared bankruptcy in 1989.

Keating and his family reaped $34 million from salaries, bonuses, and sales of stock between 1985 and 1988. Former busboy C3 received

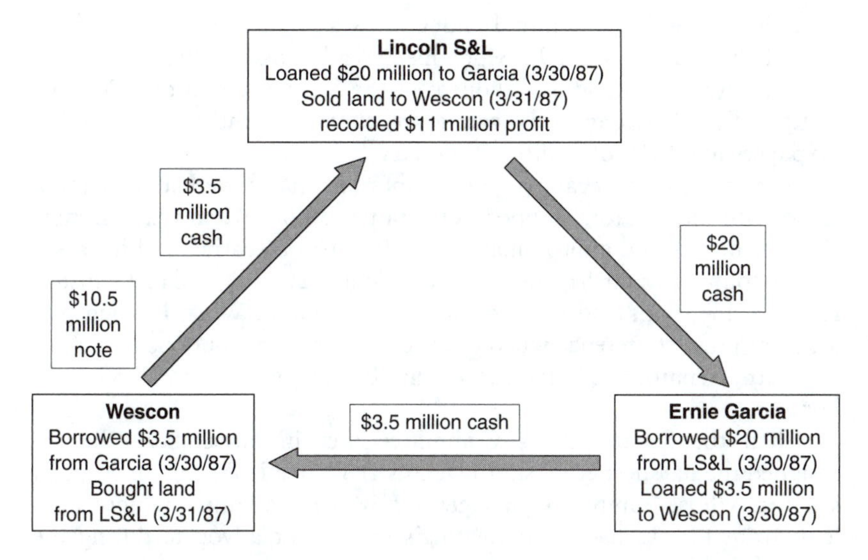

Figure 12.1 Illustrative Hidden Valley Transaction.

an annual salary of $1 million for serving as LS&L's president. Keating's daughter and sons-in-law each collected salaries as high as $500,000 per year. They also traveled extensively at company expense, received unsecured loans, and sold shares directly to ACC and its Employee Stock Ownership Plan.

The Keating Five

The Federal Home Loan Bank Board (FHLBB) seized control of LS&L in April 1989. At that time, 2 percent of LS&L's $5.3 billion reported assets consisted of home loans and 63 percent were risk assets (i.e., junk bonds, undeveloped land, unsecured loans). Newly inaugurated U.S. President George H.W. Bush was beginning to address the growing savings and loan crisis. Closing LS&L was a good place to start.

LS&L would probably have been seized much sooner but for the intervention of U.S. Senators John Glenn (D, Ohio), John McCain (R, Arizona), Alan Cranston (D, California), Dennis DeConcini (D, Arizona) and Donald Riegle (D, Michigan). Investigators from the San Francisco office of the FHLBB recommended closing LS&L in the spring of 1987. Among the unsafe operating practices described in the investigators' report were investing millions of dollars in unrated junk bonds, extending land development loans without appraisals, and back-dating loan applications. The senators, later dubbed the "Keating Five," met with FHLBB commissioner Ed Gray twice during April and urged him to leave LS&L alone. Gray took no action against LS&L during the next three months. On July 1, Ed Gray was replaced as head of the FHLBB by Danny Wall. In September, Wall took the highly unusual step of removing the LS&L audit from the San Francisco office's jurisdiction. The change gained Keating an extra 18 months and cost U.S. taxpayers hundreds of millions of dollars.

Keating's generous campaign contributions may have had something to do with the senators' support. Over a period of several years, Dennis DeConcini received approximately $40,000 from Keating and his associates; John McCain $110,000; John Glenn $200,000. Alan Cranston received donations and loans of almost $1 million. When Keating was asked at press conference whether his campaign contributions had influenced the senators to intercede on his behalf he replied, "I certainly hope so."[4]

When the Senate Ethics Committee met in November 1990, it assigned the harshest criticism to Dennis DeConcini. The senior Arizona senator, whose campaign manager received a $40 million unsecured loan from LS&L, had been Keating's staunchest advocate during the meetings with Commissioner Gray. The episode was especially embarrassing for John McCain, the future champion of campaign finance reform. In addition to accepting large campaign contributions from Keating, McCain and his family had taken at least nine trips at Keating's expense, sometimes traveling in ACC's corporate jet and vacationing at Keating's mansion in the Bahamas.

Keating's political influence extended beyond the U.S. Senate. He was even able to briefly influence the membership of the federal agency that regulated the savings and loan industry. In 1986, Keating recommended to Ronald Reagan's Chief of Staff, Donald Regan, that Lee Henkel be appointed to fill a vacant seat on the FHLBB. Henkel received a presidential appointment to the FHLBB in November 1986. But he resigned only four months later when the *Wall Street Journal* disclosed that LS&L had advanced more than $60 million in loans to corporations and partnerships in which Henkel had an ownership interest.[5]

Lincoln Savings & Loan's Auditors

Arthur Andersen audited LS&L during the first two years of Keating's ownership. Andersen resigned the engagement during October 1986 while LS&L was undergoing an extensive investigation by the FHLBB. Andersen told inquirers that it had no reservations about Keating's integrity and that it was resigning merely to reduce its exposure to risk of liability from savings and loan audits.

Although the majority of the fraud occurred after Andersen's resignation, the firm did not escape criticism. FHLBB regulators testified during congressional hearings that Arthur Andersen auditors had helped LS&L personnel create and backdate loan documents. LS&L allegedly issued loans without proper documentation and employed a "SWAT team" to review files and prepare necessary documents prior to the 1986 FHLBB audit. Andersen representatives denied the charge, stating that Andersen employees had merely assisted LS&L personnel in "organizing certain files."[6]

Several accounting firms bid on the LS&L engagement following Arthur Andersen's resignation, and Arthur Young was delighted to be selected. The $2.5 million fee for the ACC and LS&L audits comprised 20 percent of Arthur Young's Phoenix office revenue.

Researchers Merle Erickson, Brian Mayhew, and William Felix, Jr. from the University of Arizona reviewed the deposition transcripts and associated audit working papers from Arthur Young's 1987 audit of LS&L. Their article in the *Journal of Accounting Research* concluded that the auditors failed to obtain a sufficient knowledge of LS&L's business and the prevailing economic conditions.[7] LS&L reported $80 million in profit on real estate sales during a year in which construction employment and the number of single-family housing starts in Phoenix were declining, residential lot prices were flat, and millions of acres of similar undeveloped land were on the market. Under those economic conditions, it is unimaginable that LS&L could sell Hidden Valley land it had purchased only 18 months earlier for 4.7 times its acquisition cost. According to Erickson, Mayhew, and Felix: "If the auditors had compared LS&L's wholesale sales of undeveloped land to trends in Arizona's retail residential real estate market, it would have been apparent that the reported profit margins were too good to be true."[8] The Arthur Young audit principal stated in her deposition, however, that the auditors had not considered the condition of the Arizona real estate market nor did she think it was necessary for auditors to obtain and use such knowledge.

Jack Atchison served as the engagement partner during the 1986 and 1987 audits. While supervising the audits, Atchison wrote several letters to the FHLBB defending LS&L's operating practices. He also wrote to and met with senators urging them to intervene on LS&L's behalf. Atchison was richly rewarded for his advocacy. In the spring of 1988, shortly after the completion of the 1987 audit, Atchison resigned his $225,000 per year partnership at Arthur Young and accepted an executive position with ACC at an annual salary of $930,000.

Atchison's successor was not as compliant. In October 1988, Arthur Young engagement partner Janice Vincent refused to allow LS&L to recognize a gain on an exchange of assets with international financier Sir James Goldsmith. Keating, who had grown accustomed to accounting for transactions as he pleased when Atchison supervised the audit, demanded that Vincent be replaced. In a heated exchange, Keating shouted, "Lady, you have just lost a job."[9] Instead, Keating lost an accounting firm. Arthur Young resigned the audit engagement one week later.

Touche Ross & Co. succeeded Arthur Young. Fortunately for Touche Ross, federal regulators seized LS&L before the auditors issued their report on LS&L's 1988 financial statements. Touche Ross was nevertheless sued by investors who bought $170 million of ACC bonds during November and December of 1988. The bondholders claimed they would never have purchased the bonds if Touche Ross had not accepted the engagement.

All three audit firms were named as plaintiffs in civil litigation filed by LS&L's investors and creditors. Arthur Andersen settled the claims against it for $23 million. Ernst & Young, the successor of Arthur Young, paid $63 million. Touche Ross, who never even issued an audit opinion on LS&L, agreed to pay $7.5 million.

Resolution

When federal regulators seized LS&L on April 14, 1989 they discovered listening devices in the room used by the FHLBB examiners. Three days later, they sent criminal referrals to the U.S. attorneys and the FBI in Phoenix and Los Angeles. In September, regulators filed a complaint charging Keating, his family, and top ACC officers with bleeding over $1 billion of federally insured deposits from LS&L.

Keating was convicted in 1991 in a California state court of 17 criminal charges. Judge Lance Ito sentenced Keating to 10 years in prison. In January 1993, while serving the sentence from his state conviction, Keating was convicted of 73 federal counts of racketeering, securities fraud, illegal loans, and similar charges. The federal judge sentenced Keating to an additional 12 years in prison.

In April 1996, an appellate court overturned Keating's 1991 California conviction, ruling that Judge Ito had given improper instructions to the jury. Keating was released from prison eight months later after a U.S. District judge overturned Keating's federal conviction, ruling that several jurors in the federal trial were biased against Keating because they were aware of his previous state conviction.

Federal prosecutors announced in January 1999 that they would seek a retrial. Keating, who was then 75 years old, reached a plea agreement wherein he admitted for the first time that he had committed fraudulent acts. In return, he was sentenced to the time he had already served in prison.

13 Bank Robbers

Because that's where the money is.

(Willie Sutton's explanation of why he robbed banks)

Between 1982 and 1989, a small group of savings and loan operators stole more money through insider loans and extravagant pay packages than gunman Willie Sutton ever dreamed of getting through holdups. Twenty-four-year-old college dropout Charles Keating III withdrew $1 million per year in salary and benefits from his father's Lincoln Savings & Loan. Other Keating family members collected similarly generous salaries, traveled extensively at company expense, and received unsecured loans at below market interest rates.

And the Keatings were not unique. Executives of Columbia Savings & Loan Association spent $100,000 of depositors' money on guns, luxury hotel rooms, and Michael Jackson tickets. Centennial Savings in Santa Rosa, California squandered more than $1 million on luxuries such as floral arrangements and pony-skin-covered stools in the thrift's private bar. The CEO's office at CenTrust Savings Bank in Miami was adorned with a gold-inlay ceiling and a $12 million original Rubens oil painting. Congressman Jim Leach (R, Iowa) complained that too many savings and loan operators acted as if their federally insured institutions were "private piggybanks."[1]

But far more money was lost through imprudent loans and bad investments than was stolen by corrupt managers. When the Garn–St. Germain Depository Institutions Act was passed in 1982, savings and loans were paying an average rate of 11.5 percent on their deposits while earning only 10.4 percent on their mortgage portfolios. Two-thirds of the nation's thrifts were losing money. After the Garn–St. Germain bill expanded the range of allowable investments, many thrifts abandoned relatively safe home loans in favor of higher-yield acquisition, development, and construction (ADC) loans. Some thrifts even made direct investments in undeveloped real estate, hoping to capitalize on rising land prices.

Unfortunately, the thrifts entered the commercial real estate market at its peak. The Texas real estate market began collapsing in 1984 following a dip in oil prices. By 1988, Texas real estate prices were 36 percent below their 1982 crest. Thousands of real estate developers defaulted on billions of dollars of loans. Property seized through foreclosure was often worth only a fraction of the outstanding loan balance.

The FHLBB liquidated or sold more than 200 insolvent savings and loans during 1988. But the enormous cost of reimbursing insured depositors left the FSLIC with a negative net worth of $75 billion. And there were still approximately 350 insolvent thrifts awaiting action. Charles Bowsher, Comptroller General of the United States, recommended that the insolvent thrifts be closed as soon as possible and estimated the cost of doing so to be $84 billion and rising.

Congressional Hearings

The House and Senate Banking Committees held hearings in early 1989 to investigate why so many savings and loans needed intervention. FHLBB chairman Danny Wall blamed falling oil prices and declining real estate values for most of the thrift failures. Frederick Wolf, director of the GAO's accounting and financial management division, claimed many failures were caused by unsound operating practices. Describing the GAO's investigation of 26 bankrupt thrifts, Wolf cited numerous examples of excessive loans to single borrowers, conflicts of interest among officers and directors, and excessive salaries and benefits paid to savings and loan executives. "Fraud or insider abuse existed at each and every one of the failed thrifts," Wolf testified.[2]

The senators and representatives demanded to know why regulators had not done more to stop abusive lending and operating practices. Former FHLBB chairman Edwin Gray recounted petitioning Reagan budget director David Stockman in 1984 for more examiners. Gray's agency had only 700 examiners with which to oversee the nation's 3,300 thrifts and some institutions waited as long as three years between examinations. But Reagan's White House staff, focused on trimming the federal budget and philosophically opposed to government regulation of business, had denied Gray's request.

Several state regulators were found to have had suspiciously cozy relationships with thrift operators. L.L. Bowman III, the chief regulator in Texas, had been in bed—literally—with the people he was supposed to be regulating. Bowman cavorted with prostitutes hired by Vernon Savings & Loan while Vernon executives squandered $6 million of depositors' money on aircraft and $5.5 million on artwork to decorate the executive offices.[3]

California's regulatory agency was little better. Larry Taggart, who served as California's savings and loan commissioner from 1983 to

1984, spent only half the funds budgeted for regulatory oversight. After 21 months as the state's top regulator, Taggart joined a San Diego investment firm affiliated with Charles Keating's Lincoln Savings & Loan. His new duties included lobbying federal and state regulators on behalf of Lincoln and other savings and loans. Taggart, an active fundraiser for the Republican Party, warned White House Chief of Staff Donald Regan in 1986 that FHLBB efforts to constrain thrift lending practices were "likely to have a very adverse impact on the ability of our party to raise needed campaign funds in the upcoming elections."[4]

During the hearings, several government regulators accused the nation's auditors of turning a blind eye to their clients' problems. A representative from the Office of Thrift Supervision testified that the deficient 1986 and 1987 audits of Lincoln Savings & Loan were "proof positive that any thrift in America could obtain a clean audit opinion despite being grossly insolvent."[5] And a GAO representative described a study of 11 savings and loan associations that failed in the Dallas Federal Home Loan Bank District between January 1, 1985 and September 30, 1987. GAO investigators concluded that "for 6 of the 11 savings and loans, CPAs did not adequately audit and/or report the [institutions'] financial or internal control problems in accordance with professional standards."[6]

The most common audit deficiency cited in the GAO report was failure to test the collectibility of high-risk loans. Examples of high-risk loans included delinquent or past due loans, loans in which terms were modified or restructured, loans insufficiently collateralized, and loans to related or inside parties. One CPA firm confessed that it had not evaluated the collectibility of ADC loans because they were new and "assumed to be collectible."[7] Another audit team relied on oral assertions from a member of the thrift's management even though the manager was also one of the borrowers on the loan. "Most of the CPAs," according to the GAO report, "did not hire ... independent appraisers to verify collateral values ... nor did they verify oral assertions by management of loan collectibility and collateral values."[8]

In addition to finding fault with the actions of specific auditors, the GAO criticized the AICPA for failing to provide adequate guidance for audits of savings and loans. The institute's *Audit and Accounting Guide for Savings and Loan Associations* had not been updated since 1979, three years before the Garn–St. Germain deregulation Act was enacted. The *Guide* contained little discussion of the risks associated with ADC loans. Nor did it instruct auditors to report material internal control weaknesses to government regulators.

AICPA president Philip Chenok defended the profession during his testimony before the congressional panels. Chenok explained that the 11 thrift audits examined by the GAO were not a representative sample and cautioned against extrapolating the results to the nation's 3,300 thrifts.

He also reminded Congress that the FASB and the AICPA had objected to the FHLBB's decision in 1981 to allow savings and loans to defer losses from sales of assets. Chenok promised that the institute would issue a revised audit and accounting guide in the very near future.

Although Chenok maintained a conciliatory tone during his testimony, other accountants were more combative. Peat Marwick's Bob Elliott complained during the hearings that CPAs were being used as "scapegoats" for bad laws, poor regulation, and incompetent management. "Congress deregulated the left side of the balance sheet by permitting thrifts to get into high risk businesses but kept regulation and deposit insurance for the right side of the balance sheet," Elliott asserted. "Now legislators are blaming accountants for creating this mess."[9]

Elliott's last sentence was an overstatement. Nobody accused auditors of causing savings and loans to lose their depositors' money—just of failing to report the losses. Representative Henry Gonzalez, chairman of the House Banking Committee, concluded at the end of the hearings that public accountants had been "derelict in their duty to sound alarms about impending disasters in the [thrift] industry."[10]

Financial Institutions Reform, Recovery, and Enforcement Act of 1989 (FIRREA)

Shortly after his inauguration in January 1989, President George H.W. Bush proposed a plan to close the nation's 350 insolvent savings and loans and reorganize the federal regulatory system.

The House and Senate passed the Financial Institutions Reform, Recovery, and Enforcement Act of 1989 (FIRREA) by margins of 412–7 and 91–8, respectively. FIRREA established the Resolution Trust Corporation (RTC) and granted the agency an initial appropriation of $50 billion with which to resolve the nation's hundreds of insolvent thrifts. Many bankrupt thrifts were seized and their assets sold at auction. Others were merged into healthy savings and loans. The RTC usually had to make direct cash payments or promise tax credits to induce healthy organizations to assume the failed thrifts' obligations. Between 1989 and 1995, the RTC disposed of 747 savings and loans. Direct payments by the RTC totaled approximately $200 billion. With the tax credits and interest on the 30-year bonds added in, the total cost to taxpayers approached $500 billion.

In an attempt to prevent future losses, FIRREA reversed many provisions of the Garn–St. Germain legislation of 1982. Thrifts were once again required to invest at least 70 percent of their assets in residential real estate loans. Commercial loans were limited to four times the institution's net worth. Investments in junk bonds were prohibited.

FIRREA also doubled the minimum net worth requirements of savings and loans. "Requiring S&Ls to put their own capital at risk ahead of taxpayers' money is the only way to prevent in the future the unsound business practices that contributed to the current crisis," said Treasury Secretary Nicholas F. Brady.[11]

Finally, FIRREA made major changes to the federal system of regulating and insuring savings and loans. FIRREA disbanded the FHLBB and made the Office of Thrift Supervision (OTS) responsible for regulating the savings and loan industry. The bankrupt FSLIC was abolished, and responsibility for insuring savings and loans was transferred to an agency of the FDIC.

Federal Deposit Insurance Corporation Improvement Act of 1991 (FDICIA)

Two years after enacting FIRREA to bail out the country's bankrupt savings and loans, Congress was forced to address a similar crisis in the nation's banking system. Only 558 banks failed between 1934, the year President Franklin D. Roosevelt established the FDIC, and 1979. But 1,085 banks failed during the 1980s, including 427 failures in 1988 and 1989 alone. An additional 169 banks failed in 1990.

A 1991 GAO report, *Failed Banks: Accounting and Auditing Reforms Urgently Needed*, blamed weak internal controls for contributing to many of the bank failures and claimed that deficiencies in GAAP enabled bank managers to hide their institutions' losses from regulators.

Of 39 failed banks investigated by the GAO, 33 were found to have had internal control problems that contributed significantly to their failure. Deficient lending practices were the most common control weakness. Many banks conducted insufficient credit analysis before granting loans and failed to maintain necessary documentation. Board of director inadequacies were found at 21 of the 39 banks. One director defied a regulatory cease and desist order and channeled $255 million of bank assets to a mortgage company he controlled. Seven of the 39 banks paid dividends in excess of net income, depleting the banks' capital reserves and enriching the directors who were major stockholders.

Government regulations required banks to submit quarterly unaudited financial statements known as "call reports." But the GAO concluded that the quarterly call reports did not accurately portray the banks' financial condition and thus provided no early warning to regulators of the banks' deteriorating financial conditions.

The most common deficiency in the failed banks' quarterly call reports was inadequate loan loss reserves. One bank recorded a loan loss reserve of $213,000 on a loan portfolio of $147 million; GAO investigators estimated actual losses of $42 million on these loans. Another bank recorded a loan loss reserve of $623,000 on a loan portfolio of $190 million; the actual losses totaled approximately $158 million.

GAAP required banks to establish a loss reserve for a specific loan when a loss on the repayment of the loan was deemed to be probable and the amount of the loss could be reasonably estimated. But the GAO observed that many bank managers appeared to interpret the word "probable" to mean "virtually certain" rather than "more likely than not." Thus, banks delayed recording losses while there was any shred of hope that a loan might one day be collected.

Accounting for investment securities was another problem area. The value of a debt instrument varies inversely with changes in interest rates. But GAAP permitted banks to carry an investment at historical cost if the bank intended, and had the ability, to hold the security until its maturity. During periods of rising interest rates, banks avoided reporting losses by feigning the intent to hold securities until maturity. The GAO observed that management's intent and ability to hold a security for up to 30 years were very subjective, but the current market values of most investment securities were objective and readily available. The GAO concluded that "the present accounting rules are so flawed that we favor market value accounting for investment securities."[12]

The GAO also expressed concern about inadequate accounting for and disclosure of related party transactions. Some holding companies controlled dozens of banks, mortgage companies, leasing companies, and insurers. Regulators sometimes lacked sufficient information to determine whether the earnings and capital of insured institutions were being diverted to nonbank entities through "sham" transactions. The GAO recommended that transactions between related parties be accounted for and reported based on their economic substance and that FASB clarify how economic substance should be determined.

President George H.W. Bush signed the Federal Deposit Insurance Corporation Improvement Act (FDICIA) on December 19, 1991. In addition to raising banks' minimum capital requirements, prescribing standards for loan documentation, and prohibiting "excessive" executive compensation, the FDICIA contained provisions to strengthen bank accounting and auditing.

The FDICIA required all banks to have their annual financial statements audited by independent public accountants. Previously, the FDIC required applicants for deposit insurance to obtain independent audits during only the first three years subsequent to obtaining deposit insurance coverage. Otherwise, unless a bank was subject to SEC regulation as a result of issuing publicly traded securities, the decision of whether to be audited had been left to the discretion of bank management and directors. To ensure the quality of bank audits, the FDICIA required all public accounting firms performing bank audits to participate in an approved peer review program. The FDICIA also authorized bank regulators to review public accountants' audit workpapers.

Two other provisions of the FDICIA—a requirement that auditors evaluate and report on the adequacy of each bank's internal accounting controls and a requirement that banks disclose the current market values of their investment portfolios—initiated substantial changes in auditing and financial reporting.

Internal Control Reporting

The Watergate investigations of the 1970s revealed dozens of instances of U.S. corporations making improper campaign contributions to domestic politicians and/or paying bribes to foreign officials. Many of these payments were disbursed through off-the-books accounts not reflected in the companies' accounting records. Top executives frequently dodged responsibility by claiming the payments were made by subordinates without the executives' knowledge or consent.

Congress sought to stop improper corporate payments by passing the Foreign Corrupt Practices Act of 1977 (FCPA). The FCPA amended the Securities Exchange Act of 1934 by requiring all public companies to establish and maintain a system of internal accounting controls sufficient to ensure that assets were disbursed only in accordance with management's authorization and transactions were recorded as necessary to permit preparation of financial statements in conformity with GAAP. Thus, public companies' internal accounting controls became a matter of law.

Less than two years later, in April 1979, the SEC proposed that (1) management include an assessment of the company's internal accounting controls in its annual report to stockholders, and (2) the company's independent auditors evaluate and report on management's statement.

The SEC proposal met fierce opposition. During the 90-day public comment period, the SEC received nearly 1,000 letters opposing mandatory internal control reporting. Many commentators objected to the higher audit fees that would surely result if public accountants were required to opine on their clients' internal accounting controls. Some letters questioned whether sufficient criteria existed with which to objectively determine whether internal controls were adequate. Other letters pointed out that it was possible for financial statements to be fairly stated in spite of internal control weaknesses. More than 500 commentators viewed the SEC's proposal as an attempt to require managers to report on their compliance with the FCPA; many argued that mandating such a statement was unconstitutional under the Bill of Rights.

Although the AICPA expressed support for *voluntary* internal control reporting, the institute strongly opposed the SEC's 1979 proposal for *mandatory* reporting, calling it "unnecessary and counterproductive."[13] The AICPA leaders, who believed adamantly that accounting and reporting standards should be set in the private sector, probably objected more strongly to the SEC's invasion of their turf than to the actual substance of the requirement. The Auditing Standards Board even issued SAS No. 30, *Reporting on Internal Accounting Control*, in 1980 describing procedures for auditors to follow when expressing an opinion on a client's internal accounting controls. The Financial Executives Institute (FEI) also supported voluntary internal control reporting while opposing mandatory reporting.

The SEC, faced with staunch opposition from the accounting profession and the business community, rescinded its proposal in June 1980, saying it would monitor voluntary internal control reporting practices and reconsider the need for mandatory reporting at a later date.

Eleven years later, the FDICIA of 1991 was the first federal regulation requiring certain businesses to publicly report on their internal accounting controls. The FDICIA required each bank's CEO and CFO to sign an annual statement acknowledging management's responsibility for maintaining an adequate internal control structure and assessing the effectiveness of the institution's internal accounting controls. Furthermore, the bank's public accountants were required to examine and report on management's statements.

In order to comply with the FDICIA's internal control reporting requirements, bank managers and auditors needed a set of criteria with which to evaluate the adequacy of a bank's internal accounting controls. Five professional accounting and finance associations (collectively nicknamed "COSO") established a committee to provide the necessary guidance.[14] The committee released its report, *Internal Control—Integrated Framework*, in September 1992. Eight months later, the ASB issued SSAE No. 2, *Reporting on an Entity's Internal Control Structure over Financial Reporting*, providing auditors with guidance for evaluating the design effectiveness of internal controls and testing their operating effectiveness.

DePaul University accounting professor Curtis Verschoor estimated the first-year costs of complying with FDICIA's internal control rules to be approximately $100 million, including $20 million of "windfall" revenues collected by public accounting firms.[15] Verschoor, who believed that the new internal control reporting and attestation requirements would soon be extended to all public companies, predicted that historians would one day refer to the FDICIA as the "Auditors' Full Employment Act of 1991."[16]

By 1993, the AICPA and the SEC had traded positions on the desirability of mandatory internal control reporting. The AICPA, perhaps motivated by the higher fees earned on bank audits, asked the SEC to compel all public companies to report whether their internal accounting controls were effective and require auditors to attest to management's assertions. ASB chairman John Sullivan claimed that if companies were required to have their internal controls audited, "some frauds would not have been perpetrated."[17]

But SEC support for internal control reporting had waned since 1979.

> I question how reporting on internal controls by independent auditors is going to deter fraudulent financial reporting resulting from cooked books when management is not deterred by the requirement for an annual audit and is able to conceal fraud during the audit

said SEC chief accountant Walter Scheutze. Scheutze expressed concern about the costs of internal control audits and said such audits would not address the basic causes of fraudulent financial reporting: "relentless, dishonest management and the application of subjective accounting principles."[18]

FEI members again voiced strong opposition to mandatory internal control reporting, and the SEC declined to require companies to have their internal controls audited. It was not until 2002, after the Enron and WorldCom scandals, that the internal control reporting requirements pioneered by the FDICIA were extended to all public companies.

Mark-to-Market Accounting

Until 1938, banks and thrifts reported their investment portfolios at current market value. But in response to the hundreds of bank failures that occurred during the early 1930s, government regulators mandated that financial institutions value investment securities at historical cost (i.e., their purchase price). Regulators believed, at the time, that historical cost accounting would encourage managers to focus on the long-run "intrinsic" values of investments and would discourage pursuit of short-term "speculative" market gains.

Unfortunately, historical cost accounting permitted financial institutions to manipulate their reported earnings through gains trading (also called "cherry-picking"). Banks and thrifts generated income at their discretion by selectively selling securities that had appreciated in value while retaining "underwater" investments and continuing to report them at historical cost. Another common abuse involved extending loans at below market interest rates to borrowers who paid large up-front application or closing fees. Lenders reported the fees immediately as income while reporting the below-market loans at their full face value.

The savings and loan crisis of the 1980s revealed the deficiencies of historical cost accounting for financial institutions. As interest rates soared during the late 1970s, the market value of thrifts' loan and investment portfolios plummeted. But the balance sheets provided to shareholders and regulators continued to report the loans and investments at their original cost. According to GAAP, the cumulative net worth of the nation's 3,300 savings and loans was approximately $33 billion at the end of 1980. If the loans and investments had been marked to market, the cumulative net *deficit* would have been $118 billion.[19]

The SEC began pushing the FASB toward mark-to-market accounting shortly after President George H.W. Bush appointed Richard C. Breeden chairman of the SEC in 1990. Breeden, who had been instrumental in drafting key provisions of FIRREA, told a Senate committee that banks and thrifts should adopt "market-based measures of valuation at the earliest possible date."[20] Breeden's chief accountant Walter Scheutze described himself as a "country boy from Texas that likes market-value accounting."[21]

In November 1991, the SEC convened a Market Value Conference at which representatives from business, government, academia, and public accounting debated the relative merits of historical cost and mark-to-market accounting. Much of the discussion focused on the banking reform legislation being debated in Congress. Referring to the thrift balance sheets of the early 1980s, an SEC representative warned, "Nothing does more to destroy the credibility of the financial reporting process, or the confidence of the investing public, than financial statements that create the impression all is well when in fact all is not well."[22] Former FHLBB member Lawrence J. White described the thrifts' cost-based financial statements as "frauds" and "cheats." White said that adopting market value accounting would be "the most important banking regulations reform for the 1990s; all else pales in comparison."[23]

Proponents of mark-to-market accounting complained that cost-based financial statements ignored economic reality. In an environment of rapidly fluctuating interest rates, the values of financial instruments could change dramatically overnight. But GAAP required companies to report how much their assets cost, not how much the assets were currently worth. Richard Breeden questioned the relevance of "once upon a time" asset values.[24] Lawrence White argued that regulators needed to know the current market values of banks' assets in order to evaluate the true solvency of insured institutions.

The banking industry vehemently opposed market value accounting. Theoreticians complained that mark-to-market accounting violated accounting's going concern assumption. It made no sense, they argued, to report the liquidation value of an asset the bank planned to keep. Pragmatists worried about the reliability of current market values. Mark-to-market accounting "is woefully bad because of the inexactness of the reported numbers," warned Bob Muth, chairman of the Independent Bankers Association of America's Bank Operations Committee. "With historical-cost accounting, you at least have solid numbers," Muth explained. Many bank assets did not trade on secondary markets and the estimated current values of such assets "would be so inexact as to be incomparable."[25]

More than anything else, bankers feared uncontrollable swings in their institutions' quarterly earnings. If banks were required to report gains (losses) equal to the net increases (decreases) in the fair market value of their financial instruments, operating earnings could be swamped by changes in the investment portfolio. Raymond V. O'Brien, chairman of the National Council of Community Bankers, called mark-to-market accounting a "serious threat" and a "movement that is worth opposing."[26]

The FDICIA, signed by President Bush in December 1991, contained a provision requiring the SEC and federal bank regulators to develop jointly a method for banks to provide supplemental disclosure of the estimated fair market value of assets and liabilities. The provision was a compromise between advocates and opponents of mark-to-market accounting. Banks could continue reporting assets and liabilities at historical cost on their balance sheets, but had to disclose current market values in the footnotes.

That same month, the FASB extended similar disclosure requirements to all American companies. SFAS No. 107, *Disclosures about Fair Value of Financial Instruments*, required companies to disclose, either parenthetically on the face of the balance sheet or in the footnotes, the fair value of their financial instruments. Receivables, payables, options, forward contracts, and equity securities were included in the statement's definition of financial instruments. FASB opted to use the term "fair" rather than "market" value because the disclosure requirement extended to assets and liabilities that might not be traded on secondary markets. For financial instruments not actively traded, companies had to estimate fair value by discounting expected future cash flows.

The Big Six public accounting firms generally supported SFAS No. 107's disclosure requirements. But most of the 204 comment letters FASB received opposed the new standard. Concerns about the costs of compliance and the subjectivity of the fair value estimates were the most common criticisms. Many worried that SFAS No. 107 was a camel's nose under the tent that would eventually lead to replacing historical cost accounting with market value accounting.

SFAS No. 107 was, indeed, the first of a series of FASB pronouncements that moved the accounting model closer to mark-to-market valuation. In May 1993, FASB issued SFAS No. 115 requiring many (but still not all) investment securities to be reported at current fair/market value on the balance sheet.[27] But to assuage companies who feared uncontrollable volatility in their reported earnings, SFAS No. 115 did not require all changes in market value to flow through the income statement. SFAS No. 119, issued in 1995, required companies to disclose more information about the values of derivative financial instruments such as interest rate swaps and futures contracts.[28]

Other Accounting Reforms

Two other accounting pronouncements can be traced directly to abuses by financial institutions in the 1980s.

In December 1986, the FASB issued new guidance on accounting for loan origination and commitment fees.[29] SFAS No. 91 required financial institutions to defer most loan origination fees and recognize them as income over the life of the loan rather than at inception. Loan commitment fees also had to be deferred if the commitment was deemed likely to result in a loan. No longer could banks and thrifts inflate their income simply by extending loans (that might never be collected).

In May 1993, the FASB issued SFAS No. 114, *Accounting by Creditors for Impairment of a Loan*. Loans had to be classified as impaired if it became probable that the lender would not collect all amounts due—interest as well as principle—under the original loan agreement. Previously, some creditors continued carrying loans at full face value in situations where they expected (hoped) to collect the principal but were willing to waive years of accrued interest. The new statement also clarified that "probable" meant "likely to occur" and that creditors should not wait until a loss was virtually certain before establishing a valuation allowance. Impaired loans had to be valued at the present value of expected future cash flows or at the fair value of the associated collateral if foreclosure was probable. An article in the *CPA Journal* predicted that SFAS No. 114 was "likely to generate higher valuation allowances for certain creditors, particularly those in the financial services industry."[30]

Aftermath

After being saddled with a half-trillion-dollar liability to bail out the nation's insolvent savings and loans, angry taxpayers and their representatives sought vengeance against crooked executives, complicit politicians, and lax auditors. The U.S. Department of Justice filed criminal charges against 1,098 former thrift executives between October 1988 and April 1992. Nearly 80 percent of the 839 convicted executives spent time in prison. Although the average prison sentence was only 22 months, a handful of the most notorious dealers, such as Don Dixon of Vernon Savings & Loan and Charles Keating of Lincoln Savings & Loan, received sentences of 10 years or more.

Investigations of failed savings and loans contributed to the resignations of Speaker of the House Jim Wright (D, Texas) and Majority Whip Tony Coelho (D, California). Both representatives had close ties to Vernon Savings & Loan. Coelho, chair of the Democratic Congressional Campaign Committee, hosted numerous fundraising events aboard Don Dixon's 112 ft. yacht, *High Spirits*. Wright asked FHLBB chairman Edwin Gray in December 1986 to restrain Dallas-based regulators who were threatening to close Vernon. When Vernon was finally shut down in 1987, 96 percent of the loans in its portfolio were in default. Vernon's bankruptcy cost U.S. taxpayers $1.3 billion.

Several public accounting firms paid dearly for their association with failed banks and thrifts. More than 300 Ernst & Young financial services clients ended up in receivership. The FHLBB initially sought $1 billion of damages from E&Y for allegedly deficient audits of 12 institutions, including Lincoln Savings & Loan, Vernon Savings Association of Dallas, the Western Savings Association of Phoenix, and the Silverado Banking, Savings & Loan Association of Denver. After the FHLBB became convinced that E&Y could not pay $1 billion and survive, the board accepted E&Y's settlement offer of $400 million. The settlement represented approximately $200,000 from each of E&Y's 2,000 U.S. partners, although much of the cost was covered by insurance.

The FHLBB filed similar claims against 10 other public accounting firms. Deloitte & Touche paid $312 million to settle 18 pending lawsuits seeking $1.4 billion. D&T also promised to improve the training and supervision of partners auditing financial institutions. Peat Marwick and Arthur Andersen paid settlements of $186 million and $82 million, respectively.

The Other Side of the Coin

Unfortunately, financial institutions were not the only organizations which published deceptive financial statements during the 1980s. In fact, many banks were themselves victimized by borrowers who submitted fraudulent statements with their loan applications. Unscrupulous fraudsters, such as Barry Minkow and "Crazy" Eddie Antar, bilked unwitting bankers out of tens of millions of dollars.

Part IV

The Expectation Gap

14 Auditors and Fraud

> No major aspect of the independent auditor's role has caused more difficulty for the auditor than questions about his responsibility for the detection of fraud.
>
> (Commission on Auditors' Responsibilities, 1978[1])

"Audit" comes from the Latin word *audire*, meaning "to listen" or "to hear." The Roman Empire required a sophisticated system of checks and controls to ensure that officials in distant lands did not skim tax receipts or misuse funds intended for public works. The Romans separated the duties of collecting revenues, authorizing payments, maintaining custody of cash, and recording financial transactions. A specially trained corps of financial officers called "quaestors" supervised scribes and oversaw financial matters in the subjugated provinces. Quaestors had to report periodically to Rome and have their records "heard" by an examiner.

Although the word "audit" comes from Latin, the practice of testing or verifying financial records predates Roman civilization by at least 3,000 years. Sumerian clay tablets dating from 3200 B.C. list payments from the king's treasury and contain small marks, dots, and circles at the side of the figures, indicating that checking had been performed. Egyptian pharaohs assigned teams of scribes to each of the royal granaries. Two scribes kept independent records of receipts and disbursements while a third scribe (the auditor) compared the two records. Darius, who ruled the Persian Empire from 521 B.C. to 486 B.C., authorized special scribes, called "the king's eyes and ears," to perform surprise audits of his provincial governors.

Public Accountants

For the first 5,000 years of recorded history, most auditors worked for the government. Few people, other than monarchs, owned more assets than they could manage personally. Only rulers of large estates or territories depended on stewards or appointed officials to maintain custody of their assets and enter into transactions on their behalf. Auditors, from ancient times through the Middle Ages, helped emperors, pharaohs and kings maintain control of their realms. Auditors ensured that those entrusted with the ruler's assets kept proper records and did not use the assets for their own benefit. Deterring and detecting theft were the auditor's primary responsibilities.

The first widespread demand for audits of private enterprises arose during the industrial revolution of the nineteenth century. British railroads, textile mills, and steamship lines required enormous amounts of capital. Such operations could be financed only through the formation of joint stock companies. Directors oversaw the huge enterprises on behalf of absentee stockholders. To protect investors from directors' incompetence and/or malfeasance, the British Companies Act of 1845 required corporations to keep detailed accounting records and undergo an annual audit by a committee of shareholders. Accounting historian C.A. Moyer described the purpose of British statutory audits as follows: "The principal function of an audit was considered to be an examination of the report of stewardship of corporation directors, and the most important duty of the auditor was to detect fraud."[2]

Although early British audits were performed by shareholders, many audit committees eventually sought advice from trained accountants. English and Scottish accountants established firms of "public accountants" to provide audit services. Within 70 years, a new profession was born. The London city directory listed 467 accountants in 1870, compared to only 11 in 1799. Familiar names from that era include S.H. Price, Edwin Waterhouse, William W. Deloitte and George A. Touche. By 1881, most English prospectuses for new securities were audited by professional accountants.

American public accountants trailed their British counterparts by approximately 50 years. Committees of stockholders began auditing American railroads as early as the 1840s, but audits by independent public accountants did not become common until the early 1900s. Charles Waldo Haskins and Elijah Watt Sells established the first native American Big Eight accounting firm in New York in 1895. Brothers Alwin C. and Theodore C. Ernst established Ernst & Ernst in Cleveland in 1903. Arthur E. Andersen completed the Big Eight when he left Schlitz Brewing Company and entered public practice in Chicago in 1913.

Disclaiming Responsibility for Fraud

Audits, from antiquity through the end of the nineteenth century, focused on detecting fraud. Auditors reviewed expenditures in exhaustive detail to learn what stewards, government officials, and corporate directors had done with the monies entrusted to them. In their objectives and methodology, British audits performed during the 1800s strongly resembled audits performed in other countries thousands of years earlier. Lawrence Dicksee, in his seminal textbook *Auditing: A Practical Manual for Auditors*, first published in 1892, described the threefold objective of a corporate audit as the detection of fraud, the detection of technical errors, and the detection of errors in principle.[3]

But the focus of audits began shifting during the early twentieth century, at least in the United States. The first truly American auditing textbook, Robert Montgomery's *Auditing Theory and Practice*, published in 1912, explained the change in audit objectives as follows:

> In what might be called the formative days of auditing, students were taught that the chief objectives of an audit were: (1) detection and prevention of fraud, and (2) detection and prevention of errors. But in recent years there has been a decided change in demand and service. Present-day purposes are: (1) to ascertain actual financial condition and earnings of an enterprise, and (2) detection of fraud and errors, but this is a minor objective.[4]

Subsequent editions of Montgomery's book placed even less emphasis on fraud detection. The fifth edition, published in 1934, described fraud detection as an "incidental, but nevertheless important" objective of the audit.[5] In 1940, the sixth edition stated, "Primary responsibility ... for the control and discovery of irregularities necessarily lies with the management."[6] Montgomery's eighth edition (1957) described fraud detection as a "responsibility not assumed."[7]

D.D. Rae Smith, in 1960, explained public accountants' deemphasis of fraud detection.

> In the distant past audits no doubt had their origin in the natural distrust felt by one man for another in matters where the handling of money or other valuables was at stake. The function of the auditor then was to obtain an account of a man's stewardship and to assure himself that no misappropriation of funds had taken place. With the passage of time, as businesses developed and grew into complex organizations, this original concept of the auditor's function became impracticable and outdated. Nevertheless, it is only in relatively recent years that it has begun to be accepted that balance sheets and profit and loss accounts are representations made by management as to a state of affairs and results of transactions; and that the function of the auditor is to express an opinion on those representations....
>
> The detection of fraud should not therefore be regarded as the main purpose, or even as one of the main purposes, of an audit.

> This does not, or course, mean that an auditor is in no way concerned with, or interested in, the discovery of frauds and defalcations. If proper application of the audit procedures necessary to enable him to express an opinion on the accounts he is examining would also discover a fraud or defalcation, then any failure by the auditor to make the discovery will be at his peril. But this should not obscure the fact that such a discovery is a by-product, and not the main purpose, of the auditor's work. The responsibility for safeguarding the assets of a business rests squarely with the management. They do not discharge this responsibility by having an independent audit.[8]

From the beginning, American auditing pronouncements emphasized the limitations of the audit process and management's responsibility for preventing fraud rather than the auditor's responsibility for detecting fraud. *Verification of Financial Statements*, written by the AIA in 1929, stated that the recommended auditing procedures would "not necessarily disclose defalcations nor every understatement of assets concealed in the records of operating transactions or by manipulation of the accounts."[9] Similarly, the AICPA's 1951 *Codification of Statements on Auditing* stated:

> The ordinary examination incident to the issuance of an opinion respecting financial statements is not designed and *cannot be relied upon to disclose defalcations and other similar irregularities*, although their discovery frequently results. In a well-organized concern reliance for the detection of such irregularities is placed principally upon the maintenance of an adequate system of accounting records and appropriate internal control. If an auditor were to attempt to discover defalcations and similar irregularities he would have to extend his work to a point where its cost would be prohibitive. It is generally recognized that good internal control and surety bonds provide protection more cheaply. On the basis of his examination by tests and checks, made in the light of his review and tests of the system of internal control, *the auditor relies upon the integrity of the client's organization* unless circumstances are such as to arouse his suspicion...[10]
>
> (Emphasis added)

Statement on Auditing Procedure (SAP) No. 30, issued in September 1960, described the auditor's responsibility for fraud in more positive terms, yet retained much qualifying language.

> In making the ordinary examination, the independent auditor is aware of the possibility that fraud may exist. Financial statements

may be misstated as the result of defalcations and similar irregularities, or deliberate misrepresentation by management, or both. The auditor recognizes that fraud, if sufficiently material, may affect his opinion on the financial statements, and his examination, made in accordance with generally accepted auditing standards, gives consideration to this possibility. However, the ordinary examination directed to the expression of an opinion on financial statements is not primarily or specifically designed, and cannot be relied upon, to disclose defalcations and similar irregularities, although their discovery may result. Similarly, *although the discovery of deliberate misrepresentation by management is usually more closely associated with the objective of the ordinary examination, such examination cannot be relied upon to assure its discovery*. The responsibility of the independent auditor for failure to detect fraud (which responsibility differs as to clients and others) arises only when such failure clearly results from noncompliance with generally accepted auditing standards.[11]

(Emphasis added)

The Great Debate

During the late 1960s and early 1970s, a series of accounting scandals, including Continental Vending, Four Seasons Nursing Home, U.S. Financial, Yale Express, Giant Department Stores, and National Student Marketing, raised questions about whether auditors were doing enough to fight financial crime.

Equity Funding, in 1973, cast new doubt on the nation's financial reporting system. "…a lot of people decided that if the auditing system didn't catch the Equity Funding fraud, then the system was a bad one," the *Wall Street Journal* reported, "…after Equity Funding, it's hard for accountants to argue that a massive swindle, with thousands of victims, is beyond the scope of a routine audit."[12] SEC chairman Ray Garrett Jr. announced at the first AICPA meeting following the discovery of the Equity Funding scandal that he wanted auditors to accept more responsibility for detecting management fraud.

Public accountants responded to the criticism by pointing to sentences in SAP No. 30 that specifically disclaimed responsibility for fraud. In addition, auditors unfurled their engagement letters in which they notified client management before beginning each audit that they would not be looking for fraud. "It is sheer ignorance," many accountants complained, "to think the purpose of the audit is to detect fraud."[13]

During the next few years, a heated debate took place regarding how much responsibility auditors should accept for detecting financial statement fraud. Auditors had many arguments for wanting to limit their responsibility for fraud. Fraud was extremely rare, they claimed, and requiring auditors to search for fraud during every engagement would increase audit costs unnecessarily for thousands of innocent clients. Plus, auditors relied on documents and information provided by management while performing their audits. It would create an adversarial relationship if auditors had to treat every management representation with suspicion. Finally, auditors were simply not trained to detect fraud. Auditors were experts in determining whether transactions were recorded in compliance with GAAP; recognizing forgeries and detecting lies were outside their expertise.

Arthur Andersen partner George R. Catlett used the following analogy to explain why it was unreasonable to expect auditors to guarantee that financial statements were free of undetected fraud.

> Those who suggest that the auditor has a joint, and presumably equal, responsibility with management for the financial statements do not in my view understand the relative roles of management and the auditor. There is no more justification for an auditor to be a guarantor than there would be for a lawyer to guarantee that he will win a lawsuit or a doctor to guarantee that an operation will be successful. A lawyer does not have a joint responsibility for a client's morals, and a doctor does not have a joint responsibility for a patient's health habits.[14]

Catlett warned auditors against accepting more responsibility for fraud, saying, "...the accounting profession must not permit itself to be destroyed by assuming responsibilities or accepting a role that cannot be successfully fulfilled."[15]

But Professor John J. Willingham, in his response to Catlett's paper, urged auditors not to resist public demands for reform. Willingham said that requests for auditors to accept more responsibility for detecting fraud should be treated as "opportunities and privileges to serve society." He answered Catlett's warning with a caveat of his own: "The accounting profession must not permit itself to be destroyed by refusing to provide requested services to society. Destruction in the latter case will be much slower but nonetheless definite."[16]

And there was plenty of evidence that investors wanted auditors to provide greater protection against fraud. A survey commissioned by Arthur Andersen in 1974 found that 66 percent of the investing public believed that "the most important function of the public accounting firm's audit of a corporation is to detect fraud."[17] A.M.C. Morison expressed the prevailing public opinion when he wrote: "The first object of an audit is to say that the accounts can be relied on, that is that they are 'all right'; it is absurd to say that they are all right subject of course to the possibility that undetected fraud may have made them all wrong."[18]

The Auditing Standards Executive Committee tried to close the debate in 1977 by issuing SAS No. 16, *The Independent Auditor's Responsibility for the Detection of Errors and Irregularities*. The new standard stated: "...the independent auditor has the responsibility, *within the inherent limitations of the auditing process* (emphasis added), to plan his examination to search for errors and irregularities that would have a material effect on the financial statements...." Inherent limitations identified in the standard included auditors examining only representative samples of recorded transactions, the possibility that management might override internal controls relied on by auditors, and the difficulty of detecting fraud concealed through forgery and collusion.

A companion standard, SAS No. 17, *Illegal Acts by Clients*, addressed the auditor's responsibility for detecting a client's violations of laws and regulations. Auditors received sharp criticism during the Watergate hearings for not detecting and reporting illegal campaign contributions made by hundreds of U.S. corporations. SAS No. 17 required auditors to consider whether a client had complied with laws and regulations, such as tax laws, that directly affected amounts presented in the financial statements. But the standard stated that audits conducted in accordance with GAAS could not be expected to provide assurance that all illegal acts would be detected. Determining the legality or illegality of many acts was beyond the auditor's professional competence.

Unfortunately, SASs Nos. 16 and 17 did not resolve the controversy over auditors' responsibility for detecting fraud and illegal acts. Only a year later, the (Cohen) Commission on Auditors' Responsibilities urged auditors to go a step beyond SAS No. 16 and agree to provide "reasonable assurance" that the financial statements were not materially misstated through fraud. "Users of financial statements should have the right to assume that audited financial information is not unreliable because of fraud..." the Commission said.[19]

John Dingell and Ron Wyden

Representatives John Dingell (D, Michigan) and Ron Wyden (D, Oregon) picked up in 1985 where Senator Lee Metcalf and Representative John Moss left off in 1978. Dingell chaired both the House Energy and Commerce Committee and its Subcommittee on Oversight and Investigations. Wyden was Dingell's top lieutenant. Angered by the costly collapses of Continental Illinois Bank and Penn Square Bank, Dingell announced plans in February 1985 to hold seven or eight hearings "to see how the accounting profession is functioning as a part of the federal regulatory system."[20] Noting that nonaudit services and competitive pressures had increased significantly during the previous seven years, Dingell expressed concern about auditors caving in to pressure from clients. Subcommittee members wanted to know why so many banks failed without receiving a modified opinion from their auditors.

The hearings did not begin well for the accountants. Dingell attacked SAS No. 16 in his opening statement: "The public expects that independent auditors will make reasonable efforts to assure that fraudulent corporate activity will not go undetected or unreported."[21] And the first witnesses recommended radical changes to the public accounting profession. Professor Abraham Briloff, a veteran of the Metcalf/Moss hearings, urged Congress to ban public accounting firms from providing management advisory services to their audit clients. Professor Robert Chatov said the SEC should take over the public function of writing accounting and auditing standards. Chatov also wanted the SEC to assign auditors to publicly held companies and rotate the auditors periodically.

House Democrats accused SEC chairman John Shad of failing to adequately monitor the nation's public accounting firms. Subcommittee members criticized the SEC for delegating too many of its responsibilities to industry-controlled private organizations such as the FASB and the AICPA's Public Oversight Board. Wyden accused the SEC of dealing harshly with small accounting firms while Ernst & Whinney—described by Dingell as a "three-time loser"—escaped punishment for alleged audit failures at Franklin National Bank, United American Bank and Continental Illinois Bank. The SEC was practically "inviting" Congress to "step in and write a whole new set of rules," Wyden warned.[22]

Shad defended the SEC's performance, claiming his agency was "coming down with hobnailed boots on audit failures."[23] He testified that the SEC filed 18 enforcement cases against accountants and auditors in 1984 compared to only 11 and three in 1983 and 1982, respectively. Shad also disputed the House Democrats' gloomy view of the country's financial reporting system. He reported that the rate of alleged audit failures among the nation's 10,000 publicly held companies was less than 1 percent. Dingell responded that he didn't know "whether we ought to have serenity of mind because there are only a few audit failures or whether we ought to be scared to death because they're so big."[24]

In May 1986, Ron Wyden introduced a Bill that would have required auditors to report *suspicions* of fraud to the SEC. Existing auditing standards required auditors to tell only company managers and directors about fraud and to resign from the engagement if the company did not respond satisfactorily. The Bill, if enacted, would have compelled auditors to inform the SEC as soon as they had "reasonable" suspicions of any illegality. Wyden claimed that provisions of his Bill would have helped prevent damage from the bankruptcies of ESM Government Securities and Drysdale Government Securities. "Who would oppose exposing fraud in light of recent scandals in brokerage firms and banking?" he asked.[25]

But many people opposed Wyden's Bill. Price Waterhouse chairman Joseph E. Connor said the proposal "would convert independent auditors into a police role."[26] Duane Kullberg of Arthur Andersen said the Bill would "make the auditor surrogate for a government investigator" and would force auditors to "reach conclusions without giving their clients a chance to defend themselves."[27] Even the SEC opposed Wyden's Bill, saying it would impose unnecessary costs on public companies.

Wyden later softened the fraud notification provisions, but his Bill never gathered enough bipartisan support to pass Congress or survive a likely veto by the pro-business, anti-regulation Reagan administration. Public outrage over accounting scandals had not yet reached the level necessary to induce government action.

Continuing Controversy

Although Reps. Dingell and Wyden failed to enact new legislation in 1986, they did not lose interest in the public accounting profession. Several notorious accounting frauds came to light during the late 1980s. And each new scandal resurrected old questions about whether auditors were doing enough to protect the public from fraudulent financial reporting.

In July 1987, a 22-year-old "wonder boy" named Barry Minkow resigned as CEO of the ZZZZ Best Carpet Cleaning Company after a reporter from the *Los Angeles Times* uncovered $72,000 of fraudulent credit card charges submitted by ZZZZ Best. Further investigation revealed that more than half of the company's revenues were completely fictitious. Although ZZZZ Best's auditors resigned the engagement in June, after uncovering some of Minkow's lies, they did not report their suspicions to the SEC until a month later—after ZZZZ Best filed for bankruptcy protection. Rep. Dingell said the ZZZZ Best scandal provided "vivid proof that the present system for independent auditors reporting fraud did not work".[28]

Less than three years later, "Crazy Eddie" Antar, one of the most recognized names in the New York metropolitan area, fled the United States after being indicted by the SEC for fraud and insider trading. Antar had inflated his electronics company's inventories by $65 million while overstating its revenues and understating its liabilities. Ron Wyden had Crazy Eddie on his mind when he reintroduced his Financial Fraud Detection and Disclosure Act in the summer of 1990.

15 ZZZZ Best

> Life is a movie. You're the actor; you're the director; you're the writer. And if you don't like the way your life is going, you'd better change the script, because it's your life and you have complete control over it.
>
> (Barry Minkow[1])

Barry Minkow published an autobiography, *Making It in America*, when he was only 19 years old. The book described how Barry founded the ZZZZ Best (pronounced "Zee Best") Carpet Cleaning Company in his parents' garage and within three years built a successful business with multiple offices and hundreds of employees. Barry encouraged other young people to stay off drugs and follow their dream.

Nine years later, Barry wrote a second book entitled *Clean Sweep*. This book described Barry's conversion to Christianity while serving time in a federal penitentiary. A note inside the front cover states that the author's proceeds from sales of the book will be used to compensate victims of the ZZZZ Best accounting fraud. But Barry will have to sell nearly as many books as Stephen King to earn the $26 million of restitution he was ordered to pay in conjunction with his 25-year prison sentence.

The Boy Wonder

Barry Minkow was smart, funny and outgoing. But like many 14-year-olds, he was insecure about his looks and dissatisfied with his finances. Barry's ample nose looked huge atop his skinny body. And he did not have as much money as most of his high school classmates. Barry's father worked at a series of low-paying jobs and his mother sold carpet cleaning services over the telephone.

To improve his appearance, Barry began lifting weights at a local gym. He cleaned the men's locker room on weekends to pay his membership dues. To supplement his small allowance, he began making sales calls for his mother's employer. Prepubescent Barry sounded just like the hundreds of housewives engaged in telemarketing.

In October 1982, at the age of 16, Barry borrowed $2,000 from a man he met at the gym and used it to buy carpet cleaning equipment. His mother made telephone calls to arrange jobs and Barry cleaned carpets after school and on weekends. The small company grew at an improbable rate. Within five years, ZZZZ Best had 1,400 employees working out of 21 offices in California, Arizona, and Nevada.

In December 1986, Barry raised more than $11 million through an initial public stock offering. His prospectus reported revenues of $575,000, $1.2 million, and $4.9 million in fiscal years 1984 through 1986, respectively. With ZZZZ Best stock trading on the Nasdaq stock exchange, Barry was the youngest CEO of a public corporation in the United States.

The price of ZZZZ Best stock peaked at $18.375 on April 6, 1987, raising the company's total market capitalization above $200 million. Later that month, the respected investment banking firm of Drexel Burnham Lambert agreed to help Barry raise $40 million so he could purchase Flagship Cleaning Services, Inc., the company that held the concession to perform carpet cleaning services through Sears Roebuck & Co.'s nationwide network of stores.

By his twenty-first birthday, most of Barry Minkow's dreams had come true. His 5.9 million shares of ZZZZ Best stock were worth approximately $100 million. He had appeared as a guest on Oprah Winfrey's top-rated television talk show and had received two commendations from Los Angeles mayor Tom Bradley—one for entrepreneurship and the second for participating in an antidrug campaign. Barry lived with his girlfriend in a $700,000 house in a gated community. His red Ferrari convertible sported the license plate ZZZZBST.

The ZZZZ Best Fraud

The sad truth is that ZZZZ Best never earned a legitimate profit during any year of its spectacular history. Competition was fierce in the carpet cleaning business and profit margins were razor-thin. Barry's army of telemarketers did not drum up nearly enough business to cover the costs of the company's fleet of carpet cleaning trucks, its 21 offices, and its corporate overhead.

Throughout most of ZZZZ Best's existence, simply meeting the payroll was a weekly challenge. Barry would do anything to raise cash. Soon after opening his first office, Barry kicked in his own door and filed an insurance claim stating that several thousand dollars of equipment had been stolen. The scam worked so well that he staged a second phony burglary six months later at another office.

Credit cards were another source of illicit cash. Almost as soon as ZZZZ Best began accepting customer credit cards, Barry started overstating the charges. He altered the amounts on the credit card receipts or submitted duplicate receipts for the same service. ZZZZ Best eventually had to refund most of the overcharges, but it often took the bank more than 90 days to process a customer complaint and adjust the company's account. In the meantime, Barry had an interest-free loan.

One factor contributing to ZZZZ Best's cash flow problems was the huge amount of cash required to service the company's debt. Banks refused to deal with Barry in the early years because he was not old enough to sign a legally binding contract. This forced Barry to seek financing from "nontraditional" sources. The friend who gave Barry the initial $2,000 to start ZZZZ Best was actually a loan shark who demanded half of ZZZZ Best's profits. Other early financing came from private investors who demanded interest of 1 percent per week.

Barry's only hope of repaying his initial loans and freeing himself from usurious interest charges was to obtain financing from a bank. To do so, he needed to convince the bankers that he was profitable. So Barry concocted the story that in addition to cleaning carpets, ZZZZ Best also repaired buildings damaged by fire or water. This story helped Barry in two ways. The fictitious revenue he claimed to be earning on the restoration contracts increased ZZZZ Best's purported net income, making it appear that the company was growing very rapidly. And the phony restoration projects provided a plausible explanation for why he wanted to borrow so much money. Barry claimed he needed short-term loans to purchase supplies and pay subcontractors. He promised to repay the loans when the projects were finished.

The ZZZZ Best fraud was simply a matter of disguising the loan proceeds and repayments. When Barry borrowed money from banks or private investors, he recorded the cash inflows as if they were revenues from customers. When he repaid loans, he recorded the cash outflows as if they were payments for wages and supplies. The large amounts of cash flowing in and out of his bank accounts created the impression that ZZZZ Best was earning large amounts of revenue and incurring the associated expenses. As long as Barry could keep borrowing larger amounts of money, he could repay his earlier loans and keep the scheme going.

Barry's Gang

The ZZZZ Best fraud was carried out by one of the strangest groups of conspirators ever assembled. Barry's gang included a former linebacker and doctoral candidate turned accountant (Mark Morze); a gun-loving white separatist (Tom Padgett); and a 300-pound amateur philosopher with a prior conviction for cocaine abuse (Mark Roddy).

Mark Morze provided the accounting knowledge that Barry lacked. Morze was a large man who played fullback and linebacker on the UCLA football team quarterbacked by future movie star Mark

Harmon. Later, Morze completed most of the course work for a doctorate in the history of science before dropping out of school to start his own bookkeeping service. By the early 1980s, Morze was grossing $100,000 per year preparing tax returns and profit and loss statements for small businesses.

Barry, who claims to have failed his eleventh grade accounting class, hired Morze in September of 1985 to help him prepare the financial statements and other documents required for ZZZZ Best's loan applications. Barry promised to pay Morze 10 percent of any loan proceeds he could raise. Morze promptly set to work producing financial statements that would impress the bankers. Over the next year and a half, Morze forged hundreds of documents and authored the journal entries that made Barry's money-losing company look like a hot investment prospect.

Tom Padgett was a 30-year-old insurance adjuster when he met Barry Minkow at the Valley Gym in 1980. Padgett wore a Nazi SS ring and belonged to the Odinist Fellowship, a white separatist organization named after the Norse god Odin. He also subscribed to *Soldier of Fortune* magazine and claimed to be a former mercenary. Young Barry admired Padgett's weightlifting ability and began hanging around during Padgett's workouts. Padgett was flattered by the attention. He offered Barry workout tips and took the boy to his apartment to show off his gun collection.

As a claims adjuster for Allstate Insurance, Padgett often recommended contractors to policyholders whose homes had suffered water or smoke damage. After Barry founded ZZZZ Best, Padgett began directing carpet cleaning business to his young friend. Barry responded by buying Padgett lunches and giving him small kickbacks. Later, while Padgett was working at Travelers Insurance, he helped convince bankers that Barry's building restoration jobs were legitimate. Padgett confirmed phony contracts to inquiring bankers over the telephone and gave Barry a package of Travelers letterheads on which Barry forged letters describing building restoration work. Eventually, Barry installed Padgett as president of Interstate Appraisal Services—a phony contractor which allegedly hired ZZZZ Best to restore damaged buildings.

Mark Roddy was a huge man with huge appetites—for food, beer, women, and cocaine. He was Padgett's primary helper at Interstate Appraisal Services and was instrumental in convincing ZZZZ Best's auditors that the phony building restoration contracts were legitimate.

Barry's Auditors

When Barry decided to offer ZZZZ Best stock to the public, he needed an auditor to bless his fraudulent financial statements. Mark Morze contacted George Greenspan in January 1986 and engaged him to audit

ZZZZ Best's April 30, 1986 financial statements. Greenspan's primary qualification, from Morze's point of view, was that he lived in New Jersey, nearly 3,000 miles from ZZZZ Best's southern California operations. Morze feared that a local auditor might eventually wonder why he had never seen reports in the newspaper about the catastrophic fires that allegedly led to ZZZZ Best's huge restoration contracts. And the geographic separation reduced the risk of Greenspan making unexpected visits to ZZZZ Best's offices.

Greenspan relied on documents and confirmations to test the building restoration contracts that comprised roughly half of ZZZZ Best's purported revenue. This was where Barry's two shell companies came into play. Barry set up a phony insurance adjustment company, Interstate Appraisal Services (IAS), in November 1985. Barry told Greenspan that IAS hired ZZZZ Best to repair damage suffered by insurance policyholders. Using IAS letterhead, Tom Padgett created phony contracts awarding multimillion dollar building restoration projects to ZZZZ Best. Padgett dutifully confirmed the terms of any contract Greenspan inquired about. On the expenditure side, ZZZZ Best made most of its payments to Marbil Marketing, ostensibly for supplies and subcontractors. Marbil was controlled by Mark Morze and the money it received was circulated back into ZZZZ Best's bank accounts. Morze forged invoices and other documents to support the amounts received from ZZZZ Best.

Soon after Greenspan issued his audit report on ZZZZ Best's April 30, 1986 financial statements, he was replaced by Ernst & Whinney. The investment banking firm underwriting Barry's stock offering insisted that he engage a nationally recognized auditing firm. Ernst & Whinney's engagement letter stated that they would review ZZZZ Best's financial statements for the quarter ended July 31, 1986, assist in preparing the registration statement to be filed with the SEC, and perform the April 30, 1987 annual audit.

ZZZZ Best's SEC registration statement claimed the company earned $5.4 million of revenue during the first quarter of fiscal 1987—more than the total revenue reported in the entire previous year. Approximately $1 million of the revenue was from ZZZZ Best's legitimate carpet cleaning operations. The other $4.4 million of purported revenue was from the completely fictitious building restoration branch of the company.

To his credit, Ernst & Whinney audit partner Larry D. Gray insisted on inspecting ZZZZ Best's largest restoration project before issuing his comfort letter to the underwriters. Barry lied and stalled, claiming that outsiders were not allowed to visit the work sites. But Gray was adamant.

In November 1986, Tom Padgett and Mark Roddy visited Sacramento to try to create something that looked like a multimillion-dollar restoration project. They told the managers of the largest building in

Sacramento, the 300 Capital Mall building, that they were interested in leasing a large amount of space. The building managers let Padgett and Roddy borrow the keys to some vacant offices so they could show the site to their "business associates" at a future date. Then Padgett and Roddy rented a small office in a neighboring building, filled it with leased furniture, and put Assured Property Management (APM) on the door. APM was supposedly in the business of supervising contractors who worked on projects for insurance claimants.

On Sunday, November 23, Mark Morze accompanied auditor Larry Gray and attorney Mark Moskowitz on an early morning flight to Sacramento. Morze drove Gray and Moskowitz to the APM office, where Mark Roddy waited, posing as the company's manager. Roddy showed them a wall map with push pins marking the locations of APM's supposed projects. After lunch, the four men went to inspect the progress on ZZZZ Best's largest contract.

Morze and Roddy told their guests that a water storage tank on the roof of the 300 Capital Mall building had ruptured, flooding the top three floors of the 18-story building and causing damage all the way down to the fifth floor. The foursome toured the pristine 17th floor, which Morze and Roddy claimed was already completely restored. They also visited several lower floors where, by happy coincidence, some actual redecorating work was in progress. Roddy had put up a couple of ZZZZ Best signs the night before to make it appear that Barry's company was doing the work. Larry Gray wrote in his memo for the audit workpapers, "ZZZZ Best's work is substantially complete and has passed final inspection. Final sign-off is expected shortly, with final payment due to ZZZZ Best in early December."[2]

After ZZZZ Best's successful stock offering in December 1986, Ernst & Whinney set to work on the audit of the fiscal year that would end April 30, 1987. Larry Gray asked to visit the site of a purported $8.2 million restoration project in San Diego.

In February, Padgett and Roddy leased a warehouse to serve as the San Diego branch of Assured Property Management and filled it with $168,000 of the cheapest carpet they could find. Then they borrowed the keys to a vacant eight-story office building, claiming they wanted to show the building to potential investors who would be in town over the weekend. Early on the morning of Saturday, February 7, Padgett and Roddy went to the building and put up ZZZZ Best signs and phony contractors' permits. Later that day, Mark Morze escorted auditor Larry Gray to APM's warehouse, where Gray observed the rolls of carpet and saw a ZZZZ Best truck parked outside. Then they visited the office building, where Gray saw lots of unfinished floor space and was told that a fire and resulting water damage had caused the evacuation of the building. To Gray, the large empty building looked like a plausible site for an $8.2 million restoration project.

Two months later, Gray called Minkow's bluff. He said he wanted to return to San Diego and see the completed project. Barry tried every excuse, but Gray refused to approve the April 30 financial statements without inspecting the site. Padgett and Roddy returned to San Diego and leased the still vacant building. With no alternative, they were forced to sign a seven-year lease on a building they had no use for.

ZZZZ Best took possession of the building on May 1. Larry Gray's visit was scheduled for May 11. What happened during the intervening ten days was one of the most audacious cover-ups ever attempted. Barry promised a large construction company $200,000 per day plus expenses if they could wire, dry-wall, paint, and carpet six floors of the building before Gray's inspection. Crews worked around the clock while Mark Roddy snapped pictures of workmen wearing ZZZZ Best t-shirts. The amount spent for the first month's rent, the security deposit, and the building renovation totaled an estimated $4 million. But the scheme worked. After touring the building on May 11, Gray wrote in his files, "Job site looks very good."[3]

ZZZZ Busted

On May 22, 1987, the *Los Angeles Times* published an article documenting at least $72,000 of fraudulent credit card charges submitted by ZZZZ Best.[4] *LA Times* reporter Daniel Akst had begun investigating the credit card overcharges after receiving numerous complaints from an outraged and persistent Burbank secretary who had been overcharged for carpet cleaning. ZZZZ Best's stock price dropped 28 percent to $11.125 on the day the article was published. Barry's explanations of the credit card problem were less than convincing and the stock continued to drop. One week after Akst's exposé, with the stock price approaching $6.00 per share, ZZZZ Best's board of directors hired an outside law firm to investigate the alleged credit card fraud.

Also in May, an accountant named Mark Rothberg called an acquaintance at Ernst & Whinney and said he had important information about ZZZZ Best. Rothberg had recently begun working at Interstate Appraisal Services and had overheard Tom Padgett and Mark Roddy discussing the fraud. Although Ernst & Whinney never discovered that the restoration projects were fictitious, they did find evidence that Minkow had lied about his relationship with Rothberg. The auditors resigned the ZZZZ Best engagement on June 2, 1987 without issuing a report on the April 30 financial statements.

On July 2, lawyers reported to ZZZZ Best's board of directors that the addresses of the purported building restoration projects could not be located and the jobs were almost certainly fictitious. ZZZZ Best CFO Bruce Andersen reported that the company had less than $100,000 in the bank despite receiving millions of dollars of loans and investments in the preceding weeks. Barry submitted his resignation that same day, citing health problems.

It took several months for the federal and state agencies to gather the necessary evidence, but on January 14, 1988, Barry Minkow, Tom Padgett, Mark Morze, Mark Roddy, and seven others were charged with a variety of criminal offenses relating to their involvement with ZZZZ Best. Padgett, Morze, and Roddy pleaded guilty and agreed to cooperate with the authorities.

Barry's trial commenced in August 1988. Ten weeks later, the prosecution rested its case after presenting voluminous evidence of Barry's involvement in the fraud. Judge Dickran Tevrizian, anxious to move on to other cases on his docket, offered Barry a maximum sentence of 12 years if he would drop his defense and plead guilty. But Barry rejected the offer. After lying so successfully for five years, he decided to give it one more try. Barry took the witness stand and claimed he had been the unwilling puppet of Padgett and Morze. The jurors were not convinced. They convicted Barry of 57 counts of stock fraud, bank fraud, mail fraud and tax evasion. Judge Tevrizian, angered by Barry's stubbornness and lack of remorse, sentenced him to 25 years in prison and ordered him to pay $26 million in restitution.

Clean Sweep

For his deficient audits of ZZZZ Best, George Greenspan was permanently barred from practicing as an accountant before the SEC.[5] When Greenspan had agreed to audit ZZZZ Best's April 30, 1986 financial statements, Mark Morze had given him a copy of ZZZZ Best's April 30, 1985 audit report signed by "Richard Evans." The SEC criticized Greenspan for relying on the audit report without contacting Evans or reviewing his audit workpapers. In fact, "Richard Evans" did not exist. Morze had written and signed the audit report himself. The SEC also concluded that Greenspan had failed to gather sufficient evidence regarding ZZZZ Best's revenues. Although insurance restoration jobs comprised nearly half of the company's alleged revenues, Greenspan had never asked to visit any of the 15 purported job sites. Finally, the SEC ruled that Greenspan was not even independent of ZZZZ Best because he represented the company as its legal counsel during two loan closings in 1985.

When a large California bank sued Ernst & Whinney, seeking to recover several million dollars it had loaned to ZZZZ Best, the appellate judge declined to hold Ernst & Whinney liable for the bank's losses because the accountants' review report clearly stated that they were not expressing an opinion on ZZZZ Best's July 31, 1986 financial statements. Later, a group of shareholders filed suit against Ernst & Whinney, ZZZZ Best's former attorneys, and ZZZZ Best's former underwriter. The suit was settled privately for a reported $35 million, but the contributions of the individual defendants are not known.

While in prison, Barry began rewriting the script of his life story. At the prompting of a Christian counselor and a devout cellmate, Barry decided to pursue a career in the ministry. He earned bachelor of arts and master of divinity degrees by watching videotaped lessons from Jerry Falwell's Liberty University. Barry impressed the parole board with his "exemplary" behavior and earned parole in 1995 after serving approximately seven years of his 25-year sentence.

Following his release, Barry served for two years as the associate pastor of the Church at Rocky Peak in Chatsworth, California before accepting a call in February 1997 to become the senior pastor of Community Bible Church in San Diego. Prison didn't diminish Barry's powers of persuasion. His congregation grew from 140 to 1,200 members during the first seven years under his leadership.

16 Crazy Eddie

> Eddie was a godlike figure to me. We all looked up to him like a leader. He worked out with weights; he carried himself like a prince or something; he was just so charismatic.
>
> (Sammy Antar[1])

Eddie Antar should have been a rich entrepreneur. When "Crazy Eddie" opened his first retail electronics store in 1968, he entered the right business at the right time. The consumer electronics market grew exponentially during the next 20 years as new products such as microwave ovens, VCRs, CD players, and personal computers became must-have items in U.S. households.

In the early 1970s, electronic appliances were sold primarily by department stores or by small retailers acting as licensed dealers for one or two brands. Eddie Antar's idea was to create an electronics "superstore" stacked to the ceiling with hundreds of products from all the major manufacturers. Eddie Antar's stores offered far greater selection than other retailers. Crazy Eddie's volume allowed him to negotiate discounts from manufacturers and underprice his competitors. After Crazy Eddie's demise, Best Buy and Circuit City built multibillion dollar national retail chains using Antar's business model. Such could have been Antar's fate if he had been a more honest merchant and a more faithful husband.

Crazy Eddie, Inc.

Eddie Antar's first store was a 12 ft. by 12 ft. cubbyhole named "Sights and Sounds" on Kings Highway in Brooklyn. After a year and a half, Eddie moved his store to a higher traffic location and renamed it "Crazy Eddie's Ultra Linear Sound Experience," using a nickname he had picked up in high school. The store stocked transistor radios, turntables, speakers, and similar items.

Eddie was a ferocious salesman. If a customer attempted to leave the store without making a purchase, Eddie slashed the price of whatever item the customer had been looking at until the customer agreed to buy it. When all else failed, Eddie was known to lock the door to prevent customers from leaving. Family members recall Eddie somehow persuading a customer to take off his shoes, then stashing the shoes behind the counter and taunting, "You want your shoes back, we're gonna make a deal."[2]

Eddie's business grew quickly. In 1973, he opened a second store on Long Island. A Manhattan store opened two years later. The key to Crazy Eddie's success was an advertising campaign built around the tag line, "Crazy Eddie—His prices are IN-SA-A-A-A-ANE!" The spokesman who screamed this line in dozens of radio and television ads was a former disk jockey named Jerry Carroll (aka "Dr. Jerry"). The company's ads became part of the popular culture. Crazy Eddie commercials scared Darryl Hannah's character during the hit movie *Splash*. Dan Akroyd parodied the ads on *Saturday Night Live*. After 15 years of relentless exposure, one survey found that Dr. Jerry was more widely recognized among New Yorkers than long-time mayor Ed Koch.

Crazy Eddie went public in 1984. The company expanded from 13 to 43 stores during the next three years, using $134 million of capital raised through several stock offerings. In 1987, its market capitalization peaked at $600 million. Crazy Eddie, Inc. generated $350 million of revenue that year through sales of televisions, audio equipment, computers, and small appliances.

The Antar Family

Eddie Antar was born in 1947 and grew up in the Bensonhurst area of Brooklyn. He dropped out of school at age 16 and was soon earning $700 per week selling appliances on commission at Crawford's department store. It was at Crawford's that some teenage girls dubbed him "Crazy Eddie" after observing his histrionics trying to sell a fryer to a reluctant customer. Although many young men might have been satisfied working regular hours and earning a steady income, Eddie dreamed of owning his own store.

Later, as CEO of his own chain of electronics stores, Eddie relished his reputation as a tough guy. He came to work wearing dark glasses and a black leather jacket, accompanied by a 100-pound German shepherd. Although not tall, Eddie was physically imposing, with a full black beard and a powerful body. He kept a weight bench in his office and often pumped iron while negotiating business deals.

Although Eddie was the founder and CEO of Crazy Eddie, Inc., the business was really a family affair. Eddie's parents, uncle, sister, two brothers, and numerous cousins worked at the company and participated in or at least benefited from the fraud.

Eddie's father Sam M. Antar ("Sam M.") was the patriarch of the Antar family. Sam M.'s parents had immigrated to the United States from Syria. Although a devout member of the Shar'aree Zion congregation, who began each day by giving prayers at shul and would not even turn on a light switch on the Sabbath, Sam M. had a peculiar sense of ethics. Regarding his role at Crazy Eddie, Sam M. said, "I skimmed millions and millions of dollars. But I never lied, I never cheated anybody. I cheated the government maybe, but not anybody."[3]

The man who orchestrated the Crazy Eddie fraud was Eddie's cousin, Sam E. Antar (called "Sammy" by members of the family). Sammy began working at Crazy Eddie in 1971 when he was 14 years old. For $10 a day, paid off the books, Sammy opened stock, swept floors, cleaned the bathroom and did anything else Eddie ordered him to do.

When Sammy finished high school, Eddie sent him to college to study accounting. It was at college that the nervous, overweight Sammy found something he was good at. He graduated *magna cum laude* from Baruch City College and, in 1980, scored in the top 1 percent on the CPA exam. After graduation, Sammy gained audit experience at the public accounting firm of Penn & Harwood—the firm that audited Crazy Eddie's financial statements. He later rejoined Crazy Eddie as the company's controller and played a major role in directing the fraud.

The Crazy Eddie Fraud

Eddie Antar and his family began breaking the law as soon as the first store opened. Initially, their schemes were aimed at avoiding taxes. Eddy M. Antar—Sam M.'s brother and Sammy's father—served as Crazy Eddie's treasurer. Each night after closing, the store managers drove to Eddy M.'s house and dropped off the day's receipts. Each store's daily receipts consisted of checks, credit card slips, and $2,000 to $3,000 of cash. The checks, credit card slips and a fraction of the cash were deposited in the bank the next morning. The remainder of the cash was kept by the family and never reported.

Some of the skimmed cash was used to pay employees off the books. Many Antar family members received small paychecks from Crazy Eddie, which they reported to the IRS, but collected large amounts of unreported cash supplements. Eddie's brother Allen, for example, claimed that his entire compensation for working as a store manager was $300 per week, yet he lived in an expensive house, drove a Jaguar and sent two of his children to an expensive private school. Another Antar family member hired "Kool and the Gang" to perform for 1,000 guests following his son's bar mitzvah.

Other cash was used to purchase inventory from independent jobbers. Because the company was underreporting its sales revenue, it also needed to hide some of its purchases to prevent its revenues and expenses from looking suspiciously out of balance.

The remaining skimmed cash was kept by the Antar family. At first, Eddy M., Sam M., and Eddie kept the cash in their houses under beds, in file cabinets, and under the floorboards. Then, in 1979, family members began making regular trips to Israel carrying hundreds of thousands of dollars of cash which they deposited in Bank Leumi. Between 1980 and 1983, the Antars deposited more than $6 million dollars in account No. 31332. It is not known how many other anonymous, numbered accounts they might have been using.

During the early 1980s, Eddie began planning an initial public offering of his company's stock. At this point, the objective of the fraud changed. Until that time, the family's skimming understated Crazy Eddie's sales revenue and made it look like the company was barely breaking even. Now Eddie needed to report profits to attract investors.

The solution was to enhance the company's actual sales growth by skimming less money each year. Eddie and his family methodically reduced their skimming from $3 million in 1980 to $2.5 million in 1981, $1.5 million in 1982, and $750,000 in 1983. Although Crazy Eddie's true earnings grew only $600,000 during those four years, the reduced skimming caused reported net income to rise from $1.7 million to $4.6 million. This impressive growth record contributed to the initial public offering being oversubscribed when shares were offered to the public in 1984.

In 1986, Sammy went one step farther in manipulating Crazy Eddie's reported revenues. One critical measure analysts use to evaluate retail businesses is "comparable store sales." Sammy had the clever idea of transferring money from the Antars' Israeli bank accounts into Crazy Eddie and counting it as sales revenue. Sammy arranged to have $1.5 million transferred from Bank Leumi Israel to the Leumi bank in Panama. Then he ordered the Panamanian bank to send bank drafts in amounts ranging from $75,000 to $150,000 to Crazy Eddie's retail stores, where they were counted as sales revenue.

Another trick Sammy devised to inflate Crazy Eddie's comparable store sales was to misclassify wholesale transactions as retail sales. Crazy Eddie's huge volume enabled the company to negotiate deep discounts from manufacturers. On occasion, Crazy Eddie acted as a wholesaler selling merchandise to other retailers at a price higher than Crazy Eddie paid but lower than the smaller company could negotiate with the manufacturer. Sammy credited these sales to his stores, overstating their true performance.

In addition to inflating revenues, Eddie and Sammy overstated the company's inventory. Like most retailers, Crazy Eddie conducted a physical count at the end of its fiscal year to determine its inventory balance. In 1985, Eddie ordered his warehouse manager to add $2 million to the amount counted. The next year, $6 million was added.

To fool the auditors, Sammy had warehouse employees stack boxes in hollow rectangles, creating the appearance of more boxes than really existed. He also persuaded two suppliers to ship several million dollars of inventory to Crazy Eddie's warehouse shortly before year end, but hold the bills for the merchandise until after year end. The "borrowed" inventory inflated Crazy Eddie's year end assets.

The final dimension of the fraud involved understating Crazy Eddie's liabilities. Under Sammy's direction, the accounts payable supervisor recorded fictitious debit memos from vendors ostensibly for returned goods and volume discounts. During the year ended March 1, 1987, $20 million of phony debit memos were subtracted from Crazy Eddie's true accounts payable.

Crazy Eddie's Auditors

During its early years, Crazy Eddie was audited by a New York accounting firm named Penn & Harwood. The firm was so small that the fees received from Crazy Eddie comprised more than one-third of the firm's total revenue. Although no evidence suggests that anybody at Penn & Harwood knew of or participated in the Crazy Eddie fraud, the small firm was certainly not in a very strong position to monitor its larger, more powerful client.

While preparing for the initial public offering, Crazy Eddie's underwriter suggested hiring a more prestigious accounting firm to increase investors' confidence in the company's financial statements. Main Hurdman, then the ninth largest U.S. accounting firm, took over Crazy Eddie's audit in 1984. KPMG Peat Marwick performed the 1987 and 1988 audits following its merger with Main Hurdman.

Since the discovery of the fraud, Sammy Antar has given numerous speeches and interviews describing the tricks he and his cousins used to fool the auditors. One key was that the auditors never visited all the Crazy Eddie stores in the same year, and they told Sammy in advance which stores they had selected for audit. Sammy moved inventory to the selected stores to cover shortages while inflating inventories as much as 300 percent at the stores not audited.

Sammy also managed to evade many of the auditors' procedures. At the completion of one physical inventory count in 1986, the auditor asked a warehouse clerk to photocopy a sheet of paper containing his test counts. The quick-witted clerk made two copies and gave the second copy to Sammy informing him of the items on which the auditor would be performing his followup tests. Later, Sammy discovered where the auditors kept the key for their workpaper trunk. From then on, Sammy spent his evenings reading the auditors' workpapers and preparing explanations for any suspicious transactions they discovered.

Discovery of the Fraud

The collapse of Eddie Antar's business began with the collapse of his marriage. Eddie married his high school sweetheart, Deborah Rosen, in 1969. While Debbie stayed at home caring for the couple's five daughters, Eddie worked 14-hour days followed by long evenings of "talking business" in uptown clubs.

Eddie's drinking and verbal abuse strained his marriage. His infidelity killed it. During 1983, Debbie learned about the attractive young Crazy Eddie employee whose rent her husband was paying. On December 31, 1983, Debbie and two of her sisters-in-law confronted Eddie as he sat in a limousine outside his girlfriend's apartment. The four-way shouting match prompted the doorman to call the police.

Many of Eddie's relatives sided with Debbie when she filed for divorce. Sam M. berated Eddie for shaming his five daughters. Eddie's sister Ellen had been with Debbie when she confronted him on December 31. Eddie threatened to fire his brother Mitchell because Mitchell's wife supported Debbie.

While Eddie was distracted with personal problems, his company floundered. The rapid growth experienced during the 1970s was impossible to sustain in the long run. Senior executives, most of whom were hired for loyalty rather than talent, proved inadequate to manage a large, public company. New competitors stole market share and reduced profit margins.

On December 22, 1986, Eddie unexpectedly resigned as president of Crazy Eddie, Inc., leaving a vacuum at the top of the organization. Mitchell, Sammy, and a third man were chosen by the board of directors to take over the "office of the president." The stock price fell to $6 per share the next spring, down from a high of $20.

The drop in stock price attracted the attention of corporate raiders who believed that Crazy Eddie was a sound company suffering from mismanagement. Elias Zinn, a Texas electronics retailer, and Victor Palmieri, a renowned turnaround specialist, bought a 17 percent stake in Crazy Eddie. Zinn and Palmieri fired the remaining Antar family members and installed their own management team in November 1987, shortly after gaining control of Crazy Eddie through a proxy contest. Bob Marmon, a veteran of the Penn Central turnaround, replaced Sammy Antar as Crazy Eddie's CFO. Marmon ordered that a company-wide physical inventory count be taken. Preliminary reports estimated a $45 million shortage of inventory compared to the amount recorded on the balance sheet. The actual shortfall was later determined to be nearly $65 million.

Fugitive Eddie

Eddie began liquidating his stock holdings almost as soon as the IPO was complete. Between 1984 and 1987, Eddie realized more than $60 million from sales of his Crazy Eddie stock. He transferred most of the money to bank accounts in Israel, Italy, Switzerland, Liberia, and Gibraltar. But in January 1990, following an SEC indictment for fraud and insider trading, a federal judge ordered Eddie to return all his funds to the United States.

Rather than surrender his assets, Eddie fled to Israel, using a black market passport he had obtained in Brazil. Eddie traveled extensively for the next two years, using at least six aliases to hide his identity. Howard Sirota, lead attorney for Crazy Eddie shareholders, was determined to find Antar and recover his clients' money. Knowing of Antar's fondness for northern Italian cuisine, Sirota sent photos of Antar to *maître d'*s of Italian restaurants throughout Europe and the Middle East, offering a $10,000 reward for information about Antar's whereabouts.

Antar ultimately blew his own cover by walking straight into a Bern, Switzerland police station. Thirty-two million dollars of Antar's money was stashed in a Swiss bank account under the name of David Jacob Levi Cohen. After U.S. authorities persuaded the bank to freeze the account, Antar hired a Swiss lawyer to help him obtain access to his money. When the lawyer failed, Antar traveled to Bern himself and asked the Swiss police to help him withdraw his money. The police tracked Antar back to Israel, where he was arrested on June 24, 1992 at a luxury apartment in a suburb of Tel Aviv.

Justice?

Considering his key role in perpetrating an $80 million fraud, Sammy Antar received an extremely lenient sentence. Sammy knew he was in trouble when Zinn and Palmieri won the proxy contest for control of Crazy Eddie. During the nine days before he received his pink slip, Sammy shredded a mountain of files. The shredding made Sammy indispensable to the government. Lacking documentary evidence, prosecutors needed Sammy's testimony to prove their case against Eddie. In return for Sammy's cooperation, the U.S. Attorney offered him six months' house arrest and 1,200 hours of community service.

In July 1993, a jury convicted Eddie Antar of 17 counts of conspiracy, fraud, and racketeering. A judge sentenced him to 12 years in prison and ordered him to pay $121 million of restitution. Antar's attorneys appealed the verdict, claiming that the trial judge, Nicholas Politan, had been biased against Eddie from the start. They cited a statement Politan made at a sentencing hearing in which he said that his objective "from day one" had been to get back the money that had been taken as a result of the defendant's fraudulent activities.[4] They also complained of the judge's unsympathetic treatment during the first week of the trial when one of Eddie's young daughters died of cancer. The Third U.S. Appeals Court found substance in the defense attorneys' arguments and overturned Eddie's conviction in April 1995.

One year later, with the U.S. Attorney's office preparing to retry him, Eddie Antar pleaded guilty to a single count of racketeering. A New Jersey District judge sentenced Eddie to six years and 10 months in a federal penitentiary.

17 Closing the Gap

> I wasn't hired to detect fraud. I was hired to do an audit.
>
> (Samuel George Greenspan[1])

Samuel George Greenspan issued a clean opinion on ZZZZ Best's 1986 financial statements without ever suspecting that nearly 50 percent of the company's reported revenues were entirely fictitious. In Greenspan's mind, he had fulfilled his professional responsibilities by confirming ZZZZ Best's building restoration contracts with Tom Padgett at Interstate Appraisal Services (IAS) and by reviewing scores of documents supporting ZZZZ Best's payments to Marbil Marketing. How was he to know that IAS and Marbil were shell companies controlled by Barry Minkow's accomplices? Greenspan saw his role as verifying that the restoration jobs were accounted for properly—not verifying that the restoration work had been performed in the first place.

ZZZZ Best and Crazy Eddie were only two of the most outrageous accounting frauds discovered during the 1980s. The ESM Government Securities fraud, discovered in March 1985, received extensive news coverage because of its effect on the Ohio thrift industry. Two years later, Wedtech founder John Mariotta, whom President Ronald Reagan had described as a "hero for the eighties," was discovered to have used bribery and fraudulent financial statements to build his $100 million company.[2] With each new scandal, investors and creditors demanded to know why the auditors had not uncovered the wrongdoing. Auditors' attempts to disclaim responsibility for fraud only enraged their critics. Pressure mounted for auditors to play a more active role in preventing fraudulent financial reporting.

The Treadway Commission

In the fall of 1985, shortly after Representative John Dingell's Commerce Committee held its first round of hearings, the AICPA and four other professional accounting associations decided to sponsor a

National Commission on Fraudulent Financial Reporting. Former SEC commissioner James C. Treadway, Jr. chaired the six-member commission, whose mission was to identify causal factors leading to fraudulent financial reporting and recommend steps to reduce its incidence.

The commission's report, released in October 1987, concluded that primary responsibility for preventing fraudulent financial reporting belonged to corporate managers.[3] The report recommended that managers establish and enforce a code of conduct for their organizations. It also recommended that corporations maintain an effective internal audit department and appoint an audit committee composed entirely of independent directors. Top executives were urged to include a written statement in the annual report acknowledging their responsibility for the accuracy of the company's financial statements.

The report stated that independent public accountants played a "secondary" but "crucial" role in detecting and deterring fraudulent financial reporting.[4] Because of the disagreement that existed among auditors, investors, and regulators, the commission recommended that auditing standards be amended to clarify the auditor's responsibility for detecting financial fraud. "The standards should restate this responsibility to require the independent public accountant to take affirmative steps to assess the potential for fraudulent financial reporting and design tests to provide reasonable assurance for detection," the report said.[5] The commission also recommended that auditors make greater use of analytical review procedures to identify suspicious account balances and review quarterly financial statements before their release.

As part of their work, the members of the Treadway Commission reviewed 119 enforcement actions brought by the SEC against public companies between 1981 and 1986. The commission concluded that fraudulent financial reporting was most likely to occur when there were both situational forces motivating fraud and institutional opportunities making fraud easier to commit or more difficult to detect. Examples of situational pressures that might increase the risk of fraud include sudden decreases in revenue, unrealistic budget pressures, and compensation plans tied to short-term accounting numbers. Weak internal controls, ineffective internal audit departments, and inattentive directors made it easier for managers to commit fraud. The commission recommended that auditors consider such factors when assessing the risk of fraudulent financial reporting.

The commission also noted that a "large majority" of the frauds investigated by the SEC had been perpetrated by the company's CEO or CFO. The report recommended that auditors not assume management integrity but apply professional skepticism in determining executives' trustworthiness.

The "Expectation Gap" Auditing Standards

In April 1988, the Auditing Standards Board (ASB) issued nine Statements on Auditing Standards (SASs) intended to narrow the "expectation gap" between what financial statement users believed auditors were responsible for and what auditors themselves believed they were responsible for. The ASB, when it announced the new standards, acknowledged that financial statement users wanted auditors to communicate more clearly, provide early warnings of possible business failures, and assume more responsibility for detecting fraud and illegal acts. AICPA vice-president of auditing Dan M. Guy and ASB chairman Jerry D. Sullivan explained the need for the new standards as follows:

> Because CPAs have long accepted responsibilities to both preparers and users of audited financial information, the profession has a duty to continually assess auditing standards in light of the expectations, concerns and criticisms of others. When such an assessment indicates a need to modify standards, it's necessary to do so. Based on such an assessment, and after due process, extensive deliberation and careful study, the ASB approved these nine new SASs. The new standards should bring the auditor's responsibility and performance closer to public expectations.[6]

SAS No. 53, *The Auditor's Responsibility to Detect and Report Errors and Irregularities*, was the most eagerly anticipated of the new standards. Whereas SAS No. 16 required auditors *to search for* material errors and irregularities, SAS No. 53 required auditors to design their audits "*to provide reasonable assurance* of detecting errors and irregularities that are material to the financial statements" (emphasis added).[7] Although the wording change was subtle, SAS No. 53 was the first standard to state the auditor's responsibility for fraud in an affirmative manner. Auditors were required not only to be on the lookout for fraud and to report it if stumbled upon, but actually to provide reasonable assurance that material fraud would be discovered if present. Of course, the new standard retained caveats warning that auditors should not be presumed negligent if a material fraud escaped detection because of forgery or collusion.

Most auditors believed that SAS No. 16 allowed them to assume that management was honest unless they found evidence suggesting otherwise. But SAS No. 53 required auditors to treat management representations with professional skepticism—assuming neither honesty nor dishonesty. The new standard required auditors to look for client characteristics frequently associated with fraud. Examples of "red flag" client characteristics included domination of operating and financing decisions by a single person, a decentralized and inadequately monitored organizational structure, and contentious or difficult accounting issues. When client characteristics suggested that the risk of material misstatement might be higher than normal, auditors were advised to assign more experienced personnel, gather more persuasive audit evidence, and exercise a heightened degree of professional skepticism in critical audit areas.

SAS No. 53 required auditors to report material irregularities to senior management and the board of directors or its audit committee. In most situations, however, auditors were not required to report fraud to outside parties except by means of a modified audit report.

SAS No. 54, *Illegal Acts by Clients*, superseded SAS No. 17. Because U.S. businesses were subject to a host of laws and regulations—such as those governing occupational safety, environmental protection, equal employment, and patent rights—the ASB maintained that it was not feasible to ask auditors to provide reasonable assurance of detecting all illegal acts that could have a material effect on the financial statements. Consequently, SAS No. 54 held auditors responsible only for illegal acts having both a direct and a material effect on line item amounts in the financial statements. For example, auditors were required to provide reasonable assurance of detecting income tax evasion because testing tax compliance was a necessary step in evaluating the client's tax expense and tax liability accounts. But auditors had no responsibility to evaluate a client's waste disposal policies because such laws were outside the auditor's area of expertise and because contingent liabilities arising from violations had only an indirect effect on the financial statements. Although auditors were not required to search for many kinds of illegal acts, SAS No. 54 did obligate auditors to notify senior management and the board if evidence of an illegal act was discovered.

At the same time the ASB clarified auditors' responsibility for errors, irregularities and illegal acts, the board issued three new standards intended to improve audit effectiveness. SAS No. 55, *Consideration of the Internal Control Structure in a Financial Statement Audit*, required auditors to understand and document in all audits the client's control environment, accounting system, and control procedures. The auditor's understanding of the client's internal controls had to be sufficient to identify types of potential misstatements and design appropriate substantive tests. SAS No. 56, *Analytical Procedures*, replaced SAS No. 23 and required auditors to use analytical procedures during the planning and final review stages of all audits. The ASB believed that auditors might have more luck detecting material misstatements if they used ratio analysis, industry comparisons, and trend analysis to evaluate the overall reasonableness of clients' financial statements. SAS No. 57, *Auditing Accounting Estimates*, instructed auditors to evaluate significant accounting estimates by reviewing the process used by management to develop the estimate, developing an independent expectation of the estimate, or by reviewing subsequent events occurring prior to completion of fieldwork.

SAS No. 58, *Reports on Audited Financial Statements*, was the first substantial revision of the standard auditor's report since 1948. SAS No. 58 expanded the introductory paragraph by adding two sentences that differentiated management's responsibility to prepare the financial statements from the auditor's responsibility to express an opinion on the financial statements. The revised auditor's report included a scope paragraph that explained briefly what an audit entailed and specified that an audit provided only *reasonable assurance* that the financial statements were free of *material* misstatement. The ASB hoped that the new report, with its explicit references to reasonable assurance and materiality, would help readers understand the inherent limitations of the audit process.

SAS No. 59, *The Auditor's Consideration of an Entity's Ability to Continue as a Going Concern*, addressed another important dimension of the expectation gap. Financial statement users wanted auditors to provide an early warning if a client might be forced to discontinue operations. SAS No. 59 required auditors to issue a modified audit report if there was "substantial doubt" about the client's ability to meet its obligations as they came due for a reasonable period of time, not to exceed one year from the balance sheet date. Many auditors objected to this standard on the basis that it required them to predict the future. But Congress and the investment community were adamant about auditors accepting more responsibility for warning investors and creditors of a client's impending collapse.

Two final SASs sought to improve communication between auditors and clients. SAS No. 60, *Communication of Internal Control Structure Related Matters Noted in an Audit*, required auditors to notify senior management and the audit committee of any material internal control weaknesses discovered during an audit. And SAS No. 61, *Communication with Audit Committees*, required auditors to inform the client's audit committee of any significant audit adjustments, disagreements with management, or serious difficulties encountered during the audit engagement.

Together, the nine "expectation gap" auditing standards affected almost every phase of the audit process from initial planning through to the final audit report. SAS Nos. 53–54 and 59 clarified auditors' responsibilities for detecting errors, irregularities, and illegal acts, and for evaluating the client's ability to continue as a going concern. SAS Nos. 55–57 sought to enhance audit quality by improving auditors' procedures for evaluating internal controls, performing analytical procedures, and evaluating accounting estimates. SAS Nos. 58 and 60–61 were aimed at improving auditors' communications with clients and financial statement readers. The ASB hoped the new standards would satisfy critics for years to come.

Fraudulent Financial Reporting: 1987–1997

Ten years after the Treadway report was issued, the same five sponsoring organizations commissioned three researchers to analyze cases of alleged fraudulent financial reporting described in Accounting and Auditing Enforcement Releases (AAERs) issued by the SEC during the period 1987 through 1997. The researchers examined a random sample of 200 of the nearly 300 instances of fraudulent financial reporting alleged in AAERs during those years.

Their report, *Fraudulent Financial Reporting, 1987–1997: An Analysis of U.S. Companies*, summarized key company and management characteristics of the companies involved in instances of alleged financial statement fraud. The researchers observed that in 83 percent of the cases, either the CEO or the CFO or both were named as participants in the fraud. And few of the companies appeared to have a properly functioning audit committee. Approximately half the frauds involved recording revenues prematurely or fictitiously. Overvaluing assets was another common means of committing fraud. Overall, the report highlighted the importance of an effective and independent audit committee and emphasized the importance of the organization's control environment.

The researchers also examined a subset of 45 cases in which the SEC alleged deficiencies in the auditors' performance. Misapplying GAAP, over relying on management representations, not obtaining sufficient evidence to evaluate significant estimates, failing to recognize related party transactions, and placing too much reliance on weak internal controls were some of the most common criticisms leveled by the SEC against the auditors.

Subsequent Auditing Standards

SAS No. 53 was certainly not the last word on auditors' responsibility for financial statement fraud. SAS No. 82, *Consideration of Fraud in a Financial Statement Audit*, superseded SAS No. 53 in 1997. The new standard explained auditors' responsibilities as follows:

> The auditor has a responsibility to plan and perform the audit to obtain *reasonable assurance* about whether the financial statements are free of *material* misstatement, *whether caused by error or fraud*. Because of the nature of audit evidence and the characteristics of fraud, the auditor is able to obtain reasonable, but not absolute, assurance that material misstatements are detected. The auditor has no responsibility to plan and perform the audit to obtain reasonable assurance that misstatements, whether caused by errors or fraud, that are not material to the financial statements are detected.[8]
>
> (Emphasis added)

AICPA representatives insisted that SAS No. 82 clarified, but did not expand, auditors' responsibilities for fraud. Auditors' responsibilities were still limited by the bounds of reasonable assurance and materiality.

SAS No. 82's primary contribution was that it provided more detailed guidance to help auditors assess the risk of fraud. Paragraphs 16 and 17 identified more than 30 risk factors commonly associated with fraudulent financial reporting. Auditors were instructed to look for "red flags" such as high turnover among senior management, disputes with former auditors, domineering management behavior, declining industry conditions, and highly complex transactions. Paragraph 18 identified risk factors related to misappropriation of assets. Clients lacking proper internal controls and possessing material amounts of high-value, easily convertible assets such as jewels or computer chips posed the highest risk. SAS No. 82 required auditors to document their risk assessments in their workpapers and adjust their audit procedures to provide reasonable assurance of detecting material fraud should it exist. SAS No. 82's requirements for reporting fraud, if discovered, remained similar to those of SAS No. 53.

Only five years later, in the wake of the Enron and WorldCom scandals, the ASB replaced SAS No. 82 with SAS No. 99. This most recent attempt to improve auditors' fraud detection capabilities is described in Chapter 29.

Conclusion

Much of the impetus for SAS Nos. 53, 82 and 99 came from court decisions. Although auditors tried disclaiming responsibility for frauds concealed through forgery and collusion, judges and juries kept ordering auditors to pay damages to the victims of financial statement fraud. Successful lawsuits against auditors led to changes in auditing standards, new federal statutes, and the reorganization of public accounting firms. During the early and mid-1990s, repelling class-action lawsuits and seeking litigation reform became the public accounting profession's top priorities.

Part V

The Litigation Crisis

18 Auditors' Legal Liability

> Be careful what you wish for lest it come true.
>
> (Author unknown)

Auditors in the early 1900s were subject to scant discipline. State agencies set requirements for obtaining CPA licenses, but few states spent much effort monitoring auditors' behavior. The American Association of Public Accountants (AAPA) rarely disciplined its members and had no authority over accountants who did not belong.

An editorial in the *Journal of Accountancy* in 1912 advocated holding auditors legally liable for investors' losses as a means of promoting higher-quality audits and disciplining negligent or dishonest auditors.

> If an auditor's certificate is to command the respect of the banking and investing community the opinions expressed in his certificate must be based upon sound judgment and careful investigation. It would therefore seem to follow, if an auditor has failed to exercise reasonable care ... that he should be held in some measure at least, responsible for losses sustained by investors.
>
> One of the strongest inducements to this exercise of conservatism ... would be the possibility of fixing upon the auditor legal liability for statements made. The great majority of American accountants today regard the moral liability for their work as equally imperative with any legal liability, but it must be admitted that there are members of the profession—happily their numbers are small—who require to have some sort of legal obligation in order to stimulate their sense of honor and their respect for integrity....
>
> ...in order to protect the public against inefficiency ... and in order to protect the profession against the inclusion of undesirable members, we strongly advocate the theory that if the laws today do not fix legal liability upon the auditor they should be so amended as to bring about that condition of affairs.[1]

It wasn't long before public accountants came to rue the *Journal's* wish. In subsequent decades, accounting firms paid hundreds of millions of dollars to reimburse investors for losses attributed to auditors' negligence or fraud. By the 1990s, accountants were begging Congress for relief from legal liability.

Auditors' Legal Liability

Auditors can be held liable to their clients and to third parties, such as creditors and investors, who suffer losses after relying on audited financial statements. Accountants' liability may derive from common law (i.e., laws established by court decisions) or from statutory law (i.e., laws enacted by federal or state legislatures).

Clients may recover damages from accountants for breach of contract, negligence, or fraud. Examples of breach of contract include failing to deliver an audit report on time or withdrawing from an audit engagement without justification. An example of negligence would be failing to discover an employee embezzlement that normal auditing procedures should have revealed. Instances of fraud by auditors are rare, but an example would be an auditor conspiring with client management to publish materially misleading financial statements.

Third parties who rely on audited financial statements may seek judgments against accountants under common law. An example would be a banker who issues a loan after reviewing a loan applicant's audited financial statements. If the borrower defaults and the financial statements are discovered to contain material misstatements, the bank may seek damages from the auditor.

The Securities Act of 1933 and the Securities Exchange Act of 1934 are the primary federal statutes governing auditors' liability to third parties. Both statutes hold auditors liable to investors who suffer loss caused by relying on materially misstated financial statements.

Auditors' Liability to Clients

One of the earliest court decisions establishing auditors' liability to their clients was *Craig* v. *Anyon* (1925). James T. Anyon was the managing partner of the accounting firm Barrow Wade Guthrie & Co. (BWG&C). Anyon's firm audited the financial statements of Bache & Co. from 1913 to 1917. In May 1917, a Bache employee confessed to having embezzled more than $1 million during the preceding five years. Bache & Co. filed suit against BWG&C, alleging that, had the audits been performed with reasonable care, the embezzlement would have been discovered sooner and the losses would have been substantially less. In May 1922, a jury found in favor of the plaintiff. Although the jury recommended that BWC&G reimburse Bache & Co. for its entire loss, the judge believed there had been contributory negligence on the part of the plaintiff and held BWC&G liable for only the aggregate fees it had collected for its audits. An appellate court affirmed the judgment three years later.

Since the 1920s, hundreds of clients have filed lawsuits charging their auditors with negligence. One example is a 2003 suit filed by Micrel, Inc. against Deloitte & Touche. Micrel claimed that, for three years, Deloitte approved its accounting for stock options granted to employees. But after a new supervising partner was assigned to Micrel's audit, Deloitte required Micrel to change its accounting and restate its prior earnings. Micrel claimed to have incurred more than $50 million in expenses because of Deloitte's flipflop. Deloitte denied the charges, arguing that Micrel's managers and directors were responsible for the company's misstated financial statements.

Auditors' Liability to Third Parties in Common Law

Auditors' liability to third parties under common law hinges on a legal concept called "privity of contract." The doctrine of privity provides that a contract does not confer rights or impose obligations on any person except the contracting parties. Early U.S. court decisions held auditors responsible only to the client who hired them to perform the audit. Parties who were not specifically named in the engagement contract could not recover damages from the auditor. More recent court decisions have permitted third party "beneficiaries" of the audit to recover damages from auditors.

In *Landell* v. *Lybrand* (1919), a plaintiff sued the accounting firm of Lybrand Ross Bros. & Montgomery after his $2,000 investment in the Employers' Indemnity Company (EIC) became worthless. The plaintiff asserted that EIC's financial statements were false and that the auditors had been negligent in certifying them. The trial judge dismissed the case on the basis that the auditor was responsible only to the client who hired him. The Pennsylvania Supreme Court upheld the decision, stating:

> There were no contractual relations between the plaintiff and defendants, and, if there is any liability from them to him, it must arise out of some breach of duty.... The averment in the statement of claim is that the defendants were careless and negligent in making their report; but the plaintiff was a stranger to them and to it, and, as no duty rested upon them to him, they cannot be guilty of any negligence of which he can complain.[2]

Twelve years later, the New York Court of Appeals issued a similar opinion in *Ultramares Corp.* v. *Touche* (1931). Fred Stern & Co., a rubber importer, hired Touche Niven & Co. (TN&C) to audit its December 31, 1923 balance sheet. The auditors failed to detect that Stern's assets included $950,000 of fictitious accounts receivable and its reported liabilities omitted more than $300,000 of accounts payable. TN&C supplied Stern with 32 copies of the certified balance sheet, knowing the reports would be distributed to banks and other creditors. Ultramares Corporation loaned $165,000 to Stern based on the company's purported solvency. When Stern defaulted on the loans, Ultramares filed suit against the auditors. Although the jury concluded that the auditors had conducted the audit negligently, the Appeals Court refused to hold the auditors liable to third-party creditors, stating:

> If liability for negligence exists, a thoughtless slip or blunder, the failure to detect a theft or forgery beneath the cover of deceptive entries, may expose accountants to a liability in an indeterminate amount for an indeterminate time to an indeterminate class....[3]

The *Ultramares* decision set a precedent that shielded auditors from liability to third parties for more than 30 years. But that protection began to erode in 1965 when the *Restatement of Torts* advised that third parties who are members of a known or intended class of financial statement users can be considered secondary beneficiaries of the audit engagement and are thus eligible to recover damages for negligence. For example, if an auditor knew that a client intended to submit audited financial statements to obtain debt financing, the auditor would be liable to any lender who suffered damages caused by the client's materially misstated financial statements. A Rhode Island court followed the *Restatement of Torts* approach in holding an auditor liable for a lender's losses in *Rusch Factors* v. *Levin* (1968).

Auditors' potential liability expanded further in 1983 when courts in Wisconsin (*Citizens State Bank* v. *Timm Schmidt & Co.*) and New Jersey (*Rosenblum, Inc.* v. *Adler*) ruled that all parties whom the auditor should reasonably foresee as recipients of audited financial statements have the same rights as those with privity of contract. Under this broad interpretation, auditors can be held liable for losses sustained by virtually any investor or creditor who relies on misstated financial statements.

Auditors' Liability under Statutory Law

The Securities Act of 1933 (the "1933 Act") was designed to protect investors from false and misleading statements. Because Congress was in a punitive mood following Ivar Kreuger's colossal fraud, the 1933 Act placed an unusually harsh burden on auditors. Investors must prove only that they suffered damages and that the audited financial statements contain a material misstatement or omission. Plaintiffs need not prove that they relied on the financial statements or that the auditors were negligent. To avoid liability, auditors have the burden of proving that they conducted a proper audit in accordance with GAAS, that the financial statements are fairly stated, or that the investor's loss was caused by factors other than the misleading financial statements. Essentially, the defendant auditor is presumed guilty under the 1933 Act unless proven innocent.

Price Waterhouse partner George O. May complained bitterly of the 1933 Act's liability provisions.

> I cannot believe that a law is just or can long be maintained in effect which deliberately contemplates the possibility that a purchaser may recover from a person whom he has not bought, in respect of a statement which at the time of his purchase he had not read, contained in a document which he did not then know to exist, a sum which is not to be measured by injury resulting from falsity in such statement. The Securities Act not only abandons the old rule that the burden of proof is on the plaintiff, but the doctrine of contributory negligence and the seemingly sound theory that there should be some relation between the injury caused and the sum recovered.[4]

By the time the Securities Exchange Act of 1934 (the "1934 Act) was enacted, Congressional ire over Kreuger's fraud had cooled. Auditors can be held liable under Rule 10b-5 of the 1934 Act if they certify materially false financial statements. But, to recover damages, plaintiff-investors have the burden of demonstrating that: (1) the auditor made a false statement; (2) upon which the plaintiff relied; that (3) caused the plaintiff to suffer damages. Thus, the plaintiff's burden of proof is substantially higher than under the 1933 Act.

A question that remained unresolved for 40 years was whether the 1934 Act required plaintiffs to prove that the auditor *intended* to deceive the investors. Rule 10b-5 contains the phrase "employment of manipulative and deceptive devices" in its title. Accountants contended that the phrase demonstrated that the rule was intended to apply only to *intentional* misstatements, not misstatements caused by errors. But the SEC argued that Congress intended, when it wrote the statute, to hold auditors liable for both fraudulent and negligent conduct. In *Hochfelder* v. *Ernst & Ernst* (1976), the U.S. Supreme Court sided with the accountants and ruled that auditors could not be held liable to third parties for ordinary negligence under the 1934 Act. Justice Lewis F. Powell, Jr. wrote that plaintiffs could not recover damages unless the auditor acted with "intent to deceive, manipulate or defraud."[5]

Justice Powell issued his opinion while Senator Metcalf's staff was in the midst of its investigation of Equity Funding and other accounting failures. Metcalf's report, *The Accounting Establishment*, recommended that Congress amend the 1934 Act to hold auditors liable for losses attributable to their negligence. Representative John Moss and Senator Thomas Eagleton introduced such a Bill in 1978, but it was never enacted.

Six years after the *Hochfelder* ruling, the Second Circuit Court of Appeals decided in *Howard Sirota* v. *Solitron Devices, Inc.* (1982) that proof of recklessness could satisfy the requirement of intent and was sufficient to hold an auditor liable under Rule 10b-5. Subsequent lawsuits filed under the 1934 Act have tended to charge auditors with recklessness or gross negligence (i.e., failure to use minimal care) because it is easier to prove the auditor made a series of serious mistakes than that the auditor knew of a client's fraud and intentionally helped cover it up.

The third federal statute that has had a significant impact on the accounting profession is the Racketeer Influenced and Corrupt Organization (RICO) section of the Organized Crime Control Act of 1970. When RICO was originally drafted, the list of prohibited offenses included kidnapping, bribery, extortion, and drug trafficking. But because the SEC was concerned that organized crime organizations were beginning to sell stolen and counterfeit securities, the Senate added mail fraud and wire fraud to the list of RICO offenses. RICO allowed victims of organized crime to file private lawsuits in federal court and recover treble damages plus legal costs if successful.

Although even the worst public accounting firms bear little resemblance to the Cosa Nostra, imaginative plaintiffs began filing RICO lawsuits against accounting firms claiming that auditors who recklessly certified a client's false financial statements engaged in organized crime. A statute originally intended to battle silk-shirted mafia dons began to be used against pinstriped accountants. Auditors found guilty under RICO had to reimburse plaintiffs for three times their actual damages.

Other Influential Court Decisions

1136 Tenants' Corporation (1967). Between 1963 and 1965, Jerome Riker embezzled $130,000 from the tenants who owned the cooperative apartment building at 1136 Fifth Avenue on Manhattan. The tenants sued Max Rothenberg & Co., the firm that prepared the cooperative's annual financial statements and tax returns, claiming the accountants were negligent in not discovering Riker's embezzlement. Rothenberg's attorneys argued their client had been hired to perform only bookkeeping and write-up services, not to conduct an audit. Unfortunately for Rothenberg, the firm had no engagement letter specifying its responsibilities. And there was some evidence supporting the tenants' claim that Rothenberg had been hired to perform an audit. The cooperative's income statement, prepared by Rothenberg, listed the fees paid to the firm as "Audit expense." Rothenberg's report accompanying the financial statements did not express an opinion as to their fairness but neither did the report expressly disclaim such an opinion. A New York appellate court upheld the trial court's decision requiring Rothenberg to pay $230,000 in damages to the tenants.

The *1136 Tenants'* case influenced accounting practice in two ways. Accounting firms began insisting that all clients sign and return an engagement letter confirming the services to be performed. And shortly after the *1136 Tenants'* case was decided, the AICPA established the Accounting and Review Services Committee to set standards for accountants to follow when performing nonaudit services.

Yale Express (1967). In May 1964, the treasurer of Yale Express notified the company's board of directors that the previous year's financial statements should have reported a loss instead of a profit. Peat Marwick & Co., the company's auditors, investigated the allegations and discovered that the Yale Express's 1963 expense accruals had been understated by approximately $1 million. Auditing standards of the time did not specifically address what auditors should do when errors were discovered in previously issued financial statements. Consequently, the 1963 misstatements were not reported to the public until the 1964 financial statements were distributed.

The disclosure of the errors prompted investors to file suit against Yale Express and Peat Marwick asserting that the inaccuracies in the 1963 financial statements should have been disclosed as soon as they were discovered. The trial judge sided with the plaintiffs, stating, "The common law has long required that a person who has made a representation must correct that representation if it becomes false and if he knows people are relying on it."[6] The judge's decision led the AICPA to issue SAP No. 41, *Subsequent Discovery of Facts Existing at the Date of the Auditor's Report*. The standard requires the client (and the auditor if necessary) to notify financial statement users and the SEC if material errors are discovered in a previously issued set of financial statements.

BarChris Construction Corporation (1968). In May 1961, BarChris Construction Corporation sold $1.7 million of bonds to the general public. Before the S-1 registration statement was filed with the SEC, Peat Marwick & Co. dispatched a senior auditor to review the company's latest interim financial statements, read the minutes of all 1961 board of directors meetings, inquire about any changes in material contracts, and inquire about any newly discovered liabilities. The purpose of the procedures was to determine whether any events had occurred during 1961 which suggested the December 31, 1960 financial statements might be misstated.

After BarChris declared bankruptcy in 1962, the bondholders filed suit against BarChris and Peat Marwick. The trial judge concluded that BarChris had incorrectly accounted for several construction projects and that Peat Marwick had failed to exercise due diligence in reviewing the S-1 registration statement. The auditor who performed the review was not a CPA, had only recently been promoted to senior, and was unfamiliar with the construction industry. And according to the judge, "Most important of all, he was too easily satisfied with glib answers to his inquiries."[7]

Shortly thereafter, the AICPA amended SAS No. 1 (AU 560) to provide additional guidance on procedures auditors should perform when reviewing events subsequent to the balance sheet date. The BarChris case also led accounting firms to place greater emphasis on making sure auditors understand the client's business and industry.

U.S. Financial (1975). U.S. Financial materially overstated its 1970 and 1971 net income by recognizing improper gains on bogus "sales" of real estate to affiliated companies. Touche Ross & Co. issued clean audit opinions for each year after failing to recognize that U.S. Financial's owners facilitated the alleged sales by arranging financing, signing repurchase agreements, or guaranteeing the purchasers against loss. The SEC censured Touche Ross for its deficient audits and barred the firm's San Diego office from accepting new publicly traded audit clients for 12 months. The SEC also required Touche Ross to adopt procedures ensuring "that in all audit engagements specific review shall be made which is designed to determine the management's direct or indirect involvement in material transactions which are included in the financial statements."[8]

In 1975, the AICPA issued SAS No. 6, *Related Parties*, requiring auditors to perform procedures designed to identify non-arm's length transactions between clients and affiliated entities. The FASB subsequently issued SFAS No. 57, *Related Party Disclosures*, providing guidance for how related party transactions should be disclosed in the financial statements.

Increasing Liability

Although auditors' liability under common law was established as early as 1905 and the U.S. Congress imposed statutory liability during the early 1930s, lawsuits against accounting firms were relatively rare until the 1970s. Few individual investors or creditors had the resources to battle a well funded accounting firm. The potential damages that might be recovered rarely justified the certain legal costs of filing a lawsuit.

But contingency fees and class action lawsuits, two legal innovations that gained popularity during the 1970s, changed the risk/return calculus of suing accounting firms. In a class action the legal claims of many investors are consolidated into one joint claim. In a contingency fee arrangement, attorneys agree to represent plaintiffs in return for a percentage of the damages recovered. Under these circumstances, investors and creditors have little to lose from suing auditors. The plaintiffs incur no legal fees if they lose and stand to receive damages if they win. Attorneys gladly accept such engagements because of the potential to earn as much as one-third of the damages awarded to thousands of plaintiffs.

The frequency of lawsuits against accounting firms accelerated during the 1980s and the size of the settlements began to seriously hurt the firms' profits. Arthur Andersen was ordered to pay $81 million in 1981 for its deficient audit of Fund of Funds. The amount was more than double what any accounting firm had ever been required to pay. Andersen's executives refused to disclose the amount of insurance the firm carried, but lawyers from other Big Eight firms said the norm was between $50 million and $60 million. Andersen's partners, who were personally liable for the debts of the partnership, probably paid at least some of damages out of their own pockets.

In 1992, a Texas jury ordered Coopers & Lybrand to reimburse MiniScribe Corp. bondholders for $20 million of actual losses. Then, to punish the auditors for their negligence, the jurors ordered Coopers & Lybrand to pay an additional $200 million of punitive damages. The MiniScribe decision, and others like it, motivated accountants to launch an aggressive lobbying campaign aimed at convincing Congress to reform the nation's tort liability system.

19 Fund of Funds

> We're in the business of totally converting the proletariat to the leisured class painlessly. It's revolutionary and it's God-damn exciting
>
> (Bernie Cornfeld[1])

"Do you sincerely want to be rich?" That was the first question Bernie Cornfeld asked each potential sales agent who wanted to join Investors Overseas Services (IOS). Cornfeld's IOS started out selling mutual funds to American military personnel stationed in Europe. The company, headquartered in Geneva, eventually expanded to dozens of countries throughout the world.

Although few IOS agents or investors ever became rich, Cornfeld made a fortune. Ten years after its founding, IOS had 16,000 sales agents, one million investors, and more than $2 billion of total assets. Cornfeld's share of IOS was worth approximately $200 million. The 5 ft. 5 in. Cornfeld was a giant in the world of international finance.

But Cornfeld met his match in John McCandish King. Like Cornfeld, King was a self-made millionaire. King invested $1,500, one-half of his net worth, in an Oklahoma oil drilling venture in 1952. During the next 15 years, King showed an amazing knack for finding oil under previously undrilled property. By the mid-1960s, King Resources was one of the country's largest independent oil companies and its founder was worth an estimated $300 million. King dressed like Hollywood's vision of a Texas oil man, wearing expensive cowboy boots and 10-gallon hats, and owning 3,000 pairs of cufflinks.

In 1968, an IOS subsidiary began buying oil and gas rights from King Resources. During the next two years, King swindled Cornfeld out of tens of millions of dollars by overcharging for speculative properties. By 1973, Cornfeld had been ousted from IOS, King Resources was bankrupt, and King had been indicted for fraud.

Bernie Cornfeld and IOS

Bernie Cornfeld was born in Istanbul, Turkey in 1927. His parents immigrated to the United States three years later. Young Bernie's first job was guessing contestants' ages and weights at a Brooklyn fairground sideshow. He spent the early 1950s driving a taxi in New York and campaigning for political candidates endorsed by the revolutionary Socialist Youth League.

In 1956, Cornfeld abandoned his socialist leanings and embraced free market capitalism. He moved to Paris and established a family of mutual funds geared toward the needs of U.S. soldiers stationed abroad. Cornfeld's salesmen canvassed door-to-door persuading soldiers and their families to invest $25 or $50 per month in one of IOS's mutual funds. Later, the salesmen solicited funds from Europeans anxious to invest in the booming American economy. IOS's importance to the New York Stock Exchange grew as millions of new investment dollars flowed into the company. By 1965, IOS transactions sometimes comprised 5 percent of the NYSE's daily trading volume.

Cornfeld loved mingling with celebrities. Princess Ira von Fürstenberg and fashion designer Oleg Cassini attended lavish parties at Cornfeld's twelfth-century chateau in France. Tony Curtis, Cary Grant, and Audrey Hepburn were frequent guests at his 22-bedroom Hollywood mansion.

And Cornfeld surrounded himself with enough beautiful women to make Hugh Hefner jealous. Two voluptuous, leather-clad female chauffeurs piloted Cornfeld's limousine. Several young women at a time shared Cornfeld's residences. He complained that one-to-one relationships were "too complicated."[2] Actress Victoria Principal was a member of Cornfeld's harem before attaining fame in the television series *Dallas*. Heidi Fleiss had a three-year relationship with Cornfeld before embarking on her career as "Hollywood's Madam."

Fund of Funds, Ltd.

The Fund of Funds, Ltd., with assets of nearly $500 million, was IOS's largest mutual fund. As its name implied, Fund of Funds invested in other funds. Thus, an investment in Fund of Funds was really an investment in many mutual funds which, in turn, invested in corporate stocks and bonds. The extensive diversification offered by Fund of Funds made it attractive to small investors.

When the stock market stagnated in the late 1960s, Cornfeld decided to change Fund of Funds' investment strategy. Fund of Funds established a natural resources proprietary account (NRPA) in 1968 for the purpose of investing in oil and gas properties. At a Fund of Funds board of directors meeting in Acapulco, Mexico, John McCandish King proposed supplying properties to the NRPA. The minutes described the proposed relationship between King Resources and Fund of Funds as follows:

> The role of King Resources with respect to the contemplated [NRPA] would be that of a vendor of properties to the proprietary account, with such properties to be sold *on an arm's length basis at prices no less favorable* to the proprietary account than the prices charged by King to its 200-odd industrial and other purchasers.[3]
>
> (Emphasis added)

Between 1968 and 1970, the NRPA purchased 400 properties from King Resources and its affiliates for a total of approximately $120 million. Fund of Funds' investments in natural resource interests were made as follows: (1) King identified properties and determined their worth, (2) King telephoned a Fund of Funds representative in Geneva to recommend the properties and tell Fund of Funds their price, (3) the Fund of Funds representative approved the investment, and (4) King Resources sent Fund of Funds a bill. Although the Fund of Funds representative in Geneva had the authority to reject investments, not one of King's hundreds of recommendations was ever turned down. For all practical purposes, King had *carte blanche* authority to make investments for the NRPA.

King's Fraud

Unfortunately, King abused Cornfeld's trust. The agreement between Fund of Funds and King Resources stated that King would sell properties to Fund of Funds at prices no less favorable than the prices King charged his other customers. But King took advantage of Fund of Funds by purchasing inexpensive oil and gas properties one day and selling them to the NRPA days later for prices 10 or 20 times higher than King had paid. Although not all the properties sold to the NRPA were so outrageously overpriced, King consistently charged higher prices to the NRPA than he charged his other customers. An analysis performed by Arthur Andersen during its audits of King Resources revealed that selling prices to the NRPA were roughly twice as high as the prices charged to other customers.

The second aspect of the fraud involved inflating the estimated market value of the NRPA's real estate holdings. Because Fund of Funds was an open-ended mutual fund, it was required to calculate a net asset value (NAV) every day. A mutual fund's NAV is computed by dividing the number of outstanding mutual fund shares into the total market value of the fund's net assets. The NAV determines the proceeds distributed to mutual fund shareholders who redeem their shares on a given day.

Fund of Funds' investments in oil and gas properties made it difficult to calculate the fund's NAV; there was no readily available market value of its real estate holdings. To try to determine the current value of Fund of Funds' assets, King arranged periodically for investors to purchase a fraction of the NRPA's properties. Fund of Funds used the prices paid by the investors as a basis for valuing its remaining land.

Unknown to Fund of Funds, King used side agreements to induce people to pay inflated prices for the NRPA's property. For example, King once provided an investor with the down payment to purchase a piece of NRPA land and promised to repurchase the land two years later if the investor wanted to sell. The inflated prices received from the "engineered" land sales led Fund of Funds to believe that its oil and gas holdings were increasing in value. Thus, Fund of Funds continued purchasing more property from King Resources.

Investors who exited Fund of Funds during 1969 and 1970 benefited from King's manipulations because they received payouts based on inflated NAVs. Investors who held their Fund of Fund shares ultimately bore the cost of the fraud. The residual investors were left with a fund holding oil and gas properties that were worth far less than their purchase price.

Arthur Andersen's Role

By the early 1960s, each of the Big Eight accounting firms maintained dozens of offices worldwide enabling them to audit multinational companies. Arthur Andersen's Geneva office was in charge of IOS's annual audit. Andersen's New York office was responsible for auditing Fund of Funds. The Denver office performed most of the audit work related to Fund of Funds' NRPA.

Andersen's Denver office also audited King Resources. In fact, Andersen partner Phil Carr supervised the audits of both King Resources and the NRPA. Because all of the NRPA's property was purchased from King Resources, the NRPA audit was performed using documents obtained from King. Andersen auditors sometimes worked on the King Resources and NRPA audits contemporaneously.

In connection with Fund of Funds' 1968 audit, Andersen's Denver auditors prepared a schedule showing the prices charged by King Resources to Fund of Funds and other customers. The schedule showed clearly that King Resources' profit margins were higher on sales to the NRPA than to others. Although the auditors knew the terms of the agreement between King and Fund of Funds, they chose not to report the unusually high markups to Fund of Funds.

In late 1968, John King arranged for Robert Raff to purchase 10 percent of a certain natural resource interest owned by the NRPA. Raff made a down payment of $88,000 toward the $440,000 purchase.

Based on the price paid by Raff, Fund of Funds recorded $820,000 of unrealized appreciation on its remaining 90 percent interest.

Phil Carr learned in January 1969, before the completion of Fund of Funds' 1968 audit, that King had advanced the down payment to Raff in the form of a non-interest bearing loan. Carr notified John Robinson, the New York partner in charge of the Fund of Funds audit, that the sale the NRPA was using to estimate the market value of its remaining property was not an arm's-length transaction. Discussions within Arthur Andersen reached the highest levels of the partnership. In the end, the auditors decided that the unrealized appreciation, while probably unwarranted, was not material relative to Fund of Funds' total assets. The partners never told representatives of Fund of Funds or IOS that the sale was not *bona fide*.

One year later, a similar transaction took place on a much larger scale. King tried in late 1969 to find a buyer for a portion of the mineral rights owned by the NRPA in the Canadian Arctic. After Standard Oil of Indiana and an independent group of investors declined to buy the property, King arranged for his friend John Mecom to purchase 9.375 percent of the NRPA's interest. Mecom paid a $266,000 down payment and promised to make subsequent payments of $10 million. Based on the per acre price agreed to by Mecom, Fund of Funds recorded a $119 million upward revaluation of its remaining Arctic interest.

The auditors did not know at the time that King had provided Mecom with the down payment. Nor did they know that King rewarded Mecom's cooperation by purchasing certain Alaskan property from Mecom for $15 per acre only four months after refusing to buy the same property for $3 per acre.

But the auditors should have known, because they also audited Mecom's company, that Mecom was experiencing severe cash flow problems as of December 1969. Andersen chairman Leonard Spacek had even met with Mecom in 1968 to discuss refinancing Mecom's debts. The auditors also knew that King and Mecom were friends and frequent business associates.

There was considerable discussion within Arthur Andersen about possibly qualifying Fund of Funds' audit report because of the size of the revaluation. One partner argued that the transaction resulted in "a great deal of maneuvering of values based on very little cash received at the time."[4] But Alan Broad of Andersen's Geneva office warned that Fund of Funds' response to a qualification would be "an explosion."[5] In the end, the auditors issued a "subject to" qualified audit report wherein they disclaimed an opinion on whether the NRPA's oil and gas assets were fairly valued.

Fund of Funds v. *Arthur Andersen*

Fund of Funds' bankruptcy trustee filed suit against Arthur Andersen in February 1975, alleging fraud and breach of contract. Fund of Funds contended that its contract with Andersen required the auditors to report any known irregularities. The following excerpt from Arthur Andersen's engagement letter for the 1968 Fund of Funds audit described the auditors' responsibility for fraud.

> While certain types of defalcations and similar irregularities may be disclosed by this kind of an examination, it is not designed for that purpose and will not involve the audit of a sufficiently large portion of the total transactions to afford assurance that any defalcations and irregularities will be uncovered. Generally, primary reliance for such disclosure is placed on a company's system of internal control and effective supervision of its accounts and procedures. *Of course, any irregularities coming to our attention would be reported to you immediately.*[6]
>
> (Emphasis added in the judge's opinion)

Fund of Funds' lawyers argued that the auditors neglected their responsibilities by failing to report King Resources' higher than normal markups and the suspicious land sale to Robert Raff.

Fraud is defined as an intentional misrepresentation or concealment of a material fact that causes damage to another person. The requirement of a "misrepresentation" may be satisfied by a defendant failing to disclose facts necessary to keep other statements the defendant made from being misleading. Fund of Funds contended that Andersen committed fraud by issuing clean audit opinions stating that the Fund's assets were fairly stated while withholding information about dubious transactions that might have caused the assets to be overvalued.

Fund of Funds claimed that Arthur Andersen's actions caused damage to the Fund's shareholders in two ways. First, the auditors' failure to notify Fund of Funds about King Resources' higher than normal markups in 1968, when the auditors first learned of them, caused Fund of Funds to continue paying excessive prices in subsequent years. Second, the unwarranted upward revaluation of Fund of Funds' Canadian Arctic mineral rights in December 1969 resulted in excessive payments to redeeming shareholders, to the detriment of continuing shareholders.

Arthur Andersen contended that Fund of Funds' board of directors was solely responsible for the Fund's investment decisions, and that auditors are not obligated to evaluate whether prices paid by their clients are fair. Further, Andersen claimed that state laws and professional standards regarding client confidentiality prevented the auditors from revealing to Fund of Funds information gained from King Resources. As to the revaluation of the Arctic property, Andersen claimed that its auditors satisfied generally accepted auditing standards by confirming the purchase with Mecom and the firm had no way of knowing about the side agreements between Mecom and King.

The trial commenced on July 13, 1981 with Judge Charles E. Stewart, Jr. presiding. After 55 days of testimony and two weeks of deliberation, the jury found in favor of the plaintiffs and ordered Arthur Andersen to pay $81 million of damages.

The jury rejected Andersen's confidentiality defense largely because of the unusual circumstances wherein King Resources routinely provided evidence used during Fund of Funds' audit. The jury also felt that if Andersen had truly perceived an irreconcilable conflict between its duty to Fund of Funds and its duty to King Resources, the auditors should have resigned one of the two engagements.

And the jury was not satisfied that Andersen had done everything necessary to audit the sale of the Arctic property rights. The auditors had information casting doubt on Mecom's ability to satisfy the contract, but did not make specific inquiries to King or Mecom regarding the existence of side agreements.

In assessing damages related to King Resources' overcharges, the jury tried to estimate the difference between the prices Fund of Funds paid and what they "should have paid" according to the agreement. Based on the average markup charged by King Resources to other customers, the jury estimated that Fund of Funds had been overcharged $48 million. As to the revaluation claim, the jury determined that Fund of Funds would not have entered into the transaction that resulted in the revaluation if Andersen had shared its concerns about Mecom. Thus, the jury held Andersen liable for $33 million of related damages.

Postscript

Robert Vesco wrested control of IOS from Bernie Cornfeld in 1970. Vesco fled to Cuba three years later to escape criminal charges of embezzling $224 million from various IOS mutual funds. Vesco lived in Havana under Fidel Castro's protection until 1996, when a Cuban court convicted him of defrauding investors in a cancer treatment venture. A Cuban judge sentenced Vesco to 13 years in prison.

John King was convicted in 1976 of conspiracy and fraud related to the sale of the Canadian Arctic prospecting rights. He spent most of the next two years in prison.

Bernie Cornfeld may not have been the innocent victim he claimed to be. Cornfeld spent 11 months in a Swiss prison in 1973 awaiting trial on charges of defrauding IOS investors. When Cornfeld was finally tried, however, a Geneva court acquitted him of all charges. Cornfeld returned immediately to Hollywood and resumed his Playboy lifestyle. Cher, the Jacksons, and other icons of the 1970s were his frequent guests. His mansion served as a filming location for Joan Collins' *Dynasty* television show and Madonna's *Who's That Girl?* music video.

Cornfeld fled the United States in the 1980s to avoid the IRS. He spent most of his remaining years in England, France, and Israel. Lavish living and bad investments eventually eroded Cornfeld's IOS fortune. After Cornfeld died of pneumonia in a London hospital in February 1995, friends had to raise £80,000 to pay his outstanding medical bills.

20 MiniScribe

> You can fool all the people some of the time, and some of the people all the time, but you can't fool all the people all of the time.
>
> (Abraham Lincoln)

Joe Jamail and James Paul Linn were legal heavyweights.

Jamail was a "bare knuckles" personal injury lawyer renowned for his ability to wring huge judgments from Texas juries. In 1986, Jamail helped Pennzoil win a $10.3 billion judgment against rival Texaco. The judgment was the largest ever upheld on appeal and netted Jamail $345 million in fees. Five years later, Jamail represented a group of Texans who had lost $20 million on MiniScribe Corp. debentures. The bondholders sought damages from MiniScribe's officers, the auditors, and the bond underwriters.

Linn was the polished attorney chosen by MiniScribe's auditors to defend their reputation and assets. Linn's international clientele included former Philippines first lady Imelda Marcos, British rock star David Bowie, and Saudi arms dealer Adnan Khashoggi. "It's going to be a good fight," Linn said shortly before his bout with Jamail. "I expect to prove that the auditors were the victims."[1]

The two lawyers traded blows in front of a jury in Galveston, Texas for three months in late 1991 and early 1992. The one fact on which they agreed was that a huge fraud had taken place at MiniScribe. Jamail accused the auditors of conspiring with MiniScribe's managers and knowingly certifying the company's false financial statements. Linn argued that Coopers & Lybrand had performed a proper audit, but had been deceived by lies, forged documents, and packages of bricks labeled as inventory.

Jamail appeared to score a knockout when the jury awarded his clients $550 million—$20 million of actual losses plus $530 million of punitive damages. MiniScribe's chairman Q.T. Wiles was assessed $250 million in punitive damages; the firm's underwriters, $80 million; Linn's client Coopers & Lybrand, $200 million. "Mr. Linn got his Oklahoma

... kicked," Jamail crowed after the trial. "It was bloody when it came back across the Red River."[2]

Linn rebounded two weeks later when Judge Roy Engelke overturned the jury's verdict, saying it was "contrary to the great weight and preponderance of the evidence."[3] One of the jurors bolstered Linn's bargaining position by signing an affidavit stating that the bailiff had pressured the jury into awarding high damages. Allegedly, Jamail had promised to donate a portion of the settlement to Galveston charities. The juror also claimed she had been offered free legal services to side with the plaintiffs. The juror's accusations led to a year-long grand jury investigation, although no charges were ever filed.

In the end, Coopers & Lybrand agreed to pay $45 million without admitting guilt. The settlement allowed both attorneys to claim victory. "The question Joe has to answer, and he can't, is why would he take a $550 million judgment and settle it for a fraction," taunted Linn. "There was so much error in the case that Jamail ... knew there was no way it could stand on appeal."[4] Jamail dismissed Linn's question, saying his clients had decided to accept Coopers & Lybrand's settlement offer rather than bankrupt the firm. "It became a business decision rather than a legal one," Jamail said. "It became a question of how much money they could pay."[5]

MiniScribe Corporation

MiniScribe Corporation was founded in 1980 in Longmont, Colorado. Initially, the company produced $5\frac{1}{4}$ in. disk drives for personal computers. MiniScribe grew quickly thanks to its relationship with IBM, which purchased nearly 60 percent of MiniScribe's early output. Although MiniScribe earned more than $75 million of revenue by its fourth year, research and retooling costs consumed most of the company's profits as $5\frac{1}{4}$ in. floppy disks gave way to $3\frac{1}{2}$ in. disks and hard drives.

MiniScribe faced a crisis in 1985 when personal computer sales slowed and IBM decided to produce its own disk drives. A MiniScribe director placed a desperate phone call to William Hambrecht, president of the venture capital firm Hambrecht & Quist (H&Q). The director told Hambrecht that MiniScribe needed an immediate capital infusion of at least $10 million to avoid bankruptcy.

H&Q specialized in acquiring and turning around small manufacturers of computer parts and accessories. After evaluating MiniScribe's technology and concluding the company was worth saving, H&Q invested $20 million for a 12 percent stake in the disk-drive maker. H&Q then installed its in-house turnaround specialist, Q.T. Wiles, as MiniScribe's chairman and CEO.

Quentin Thomas Wiles was known as "Dr. Fix-it" for his ability to revive troubled companies. Wiles honed his management skills during the 1960s cleaning up small electronics companies acquired by conglomerate TRW. Since joining H&Q in 1972, Wiles had been dispatched to a dozen ailing high-tech companies, generating $250 million of equity profits from $50 million in original investments. Wiles, who lived and worked in Sherman Oaks, California, sometimes acted as the CEO of as many as seven H&Q-controlled companies, using color-coded folders to keep them straight.

Wiles laid off 20 percent of MiniScribe's workforce and organized the remaining employees into 15 autonomous units, each responsible for a specific product, customer, or research project. Each business unit had its own budget and financial targets that became the sole basis on which employees were evaluated.

MiniScribe executives traveled from Colorado to Sherman Oaks four times a year to report their accomplishments and set goals for the next quarter. Although Wiles often presided over the meetings wearing a baseball cap and golf shirt, the atmosphere was far from relaxed. Wiles threw, shredded, or kicked reports that displeased him. Managers who failed to meet quarterly financial objectives could be fired on the spot.

"Dr." Wiles's medicine appeared to work miracles at MiniScribe. The company reported modest profits during the second half of 1985 after losing $19.6 million during the first six months. During the next three years, MiniScribe reported 13 consecutive quarters of rising sales and earnings. Its stock price increased from $3 at the time Wiles arrived in May 1985 to $13 in July 1988.

Wiles, who was 66 years old in 1985, decided he wanted to be remembered as the man who made MiniScribe a billion-dollar company. Wiles set increasingly ambitious quarterly sales goals for MiniScribe, paying generous bonuses to employees who hit the targets and accepting no excuses from those who failed. MiniScribe's sales soared from $114 million in 1985 to $185 million in 1986 and $362 million in 1987. Wiles boldly promised analysts that MiniScribe's revenues would surpass $660 million in 1988.

MiniScribe's reported sales and profits were suspiciously good during the first three quarters of 1988. Although personal computer sales slipped during the summer and fall and other disk-drive makers laid off hundreds of employees, MiniScribe continued to astound Wall Street. MiniScribe announced September 30 year-to-date revenues of $486 million. Reported nine-month earnings of $40.4 million exceeded those of the prior year by 83 percent.

Packaging Bricks

Unfortunately, MiniScribe's true performance was not nearly as impressive as its financial statements suggested. The company's 1986, 1987, and 1988 profits were inflated through overstated sales revenue, understated reserves, and fictitious inventory.

MiniScribe's harried managers devised a number of schemes to meet their quarterly sales quotas. One former sales manager confessed to shipping twice as many disk drives as a computer manufacturer had ordered. The extras were returned, but not before MiniScribe had reported an extra $9 million of sales revenue.

MiniScribe produced many of its disk drives in Singapore. It took up to two weeks for the inventory to cross the Pacific by ship. Normal sales terms specified that customers did not take title to the drives until they were delivered in the United States. But at the end of at least one quarter in 1986, MiniScribe executives altered purchase orders to make it appear that customers took title to the inventory when it was shipped from Singapore. This sleight-of-pen allowed MiniScribe to recognize revenue for goods still asea.

A third scheme involved recognizing revenue when goods were shipped from MiniScribe's factory to one of its own warehouses. MiniScribe maintained several warehouses around the country so it could provide just-in-time delivery to important customers. MiniScribe shipped drives to the warehouses at its own discretion and didn't issue sales invoices until customers took possession. In 1987, MiniScribe began shipping excess quantities of inventory to the warehouses and recording the shipments as sales. One former employee estimated that between $80 million and $100 million of unordered disk drives were shipped to a distribution warehouse in Los Angeles.

MiniScribe also inflated net income by understating reserves. In 1985, MiniScribe reported a bad debt allowance of $752,000 for $15.6 million of accounts receivable. A year later, the allowance was only $736,000 even though receivables had more than doubled to $40 million. MiniScribe's reserve for obsolete inventory decreased $2 million during 1986 while inventory increased $22 million. In 1988, MiniScribe reported a bad debt allowance equal to less than 1 percent of its $177 million of accounts receivable; other disk-drive manufacturers reported reserves ranging from 4 percent to 10 percent of gross receivables.

MiniScribe's most outrageous accounting tricks involved fictitious inventory. The $45.1 million inventory balance reported on MiniScribe's December 31, 1986 balance sheet was overstated by $4.5 million. To prevent the auditors from discovering the misstatement, MiniScribe's controller and another employee broke into the auditors' locked trunk and copied the list of items the auditors had test-counted during their observation of MiniScribe's physical inventory. The controller then inflated the quantities of high-value inventory items the auditors had not sampled.

A year later, MiniScribe's top officers colluded to overstate the company's inventory by $15 million. Executive vice-president Owen

Taranta and several other MiniScribe employees met in a company warehouse on December 18, 1987, and packed bricks into crates labeled as disk-drive inventory. Taranta even brought his wife and children to help with the packing. The crates were shipped to two MiniScribe distributors shortly before year-end. The distributors held the crates for two weeks before sending them back to MiniScribe as "returned goods." MiniScribe reported the bricks as inventory-in-transit on its December 31, 1987 balance sheet.

The inventory fraud continued into 1988 as employees repackaged scrap materials and defective disk drives and counted them as good inventory. Other employees prepared false inventory tickets to inflate inventory quantities.

Disk Failure

The first sign of trouble at MiniScribe was a December 9, 1988 press release announcing a production cutback due to slowing sales. The bad news slashed 20 percent from MiniScribe's stock price.

On February 9, 1989, MiniScribe revealed it had lost $14.6 million during the fourth quarter of 1988. The year-end balance sheet hinted of further problems. MiniScribe's ratio of inventory to sales was 43 percent, dangerously high for a company whose inventory was susceptible to obsolescence and far above the industry average of 24 percent. The accounts receivable balance represented 122 days of sales, compared to an industry average of 70 days.

Q.T. Wiles resigned from MiniScribe on February 22, stating that "his family position did not allow him to spend the time and energy required to act as chief executive."[6] The managers who replaced Wiles soon discovered problems with the company's inventory and receivables. MiniScribe recalled its 1986–1988 financial statements on May 18, 1989, stating that they were inaccurate and could not be relied upon.

MiniScribe's outside directors conducted a six-month investigation before issuing a report in September 1989 concluding that senior management had "perpetrated a massive fraud on the company, its directors, its outside auditors and the investing public."[7] The 1,500-page report described in detail how MiniScribe employees had accelerated sales, understated reserves, and even written a computer program called "Cook Book" to generate fictitious inventory numbers.

MiniScribe, whose stock price fell below $2 following the revelation of the fraud, filed for Chapter 11 bankruptcy protection on January 1, 1990. Its assets were acquired several months later by rival disk-drive maker Maxtor.

MiniScribe's Auditors

Coopers & Lybrand's Denver office issued clean audit opinions on MiniScribe's fraudulent 1986–1988 financial statements. The MiniScribe directors' investigative report did not accuse the auditors of participating in the fraud, but did state that Coopers & Lybrand had "failed the company at a time when their services were most needed."[8] The directors criticized the auditors for errors in judgment and "allowing themselves to be pushed too hard and too far."[9]

Raymond MacFee, the partner in charge of MiniScribe's 1986 audit, was not an easy man to push around. Described by colleagues as "strong-willed and principled," MacFee withstood a lot of abuse from Wiles. During one telephone conversation regarding a disputed sales transaction, Wiles shouted so loudly that MacFee had to hold the phone away from his ear.

MiniScribe's preliminary 1986 income statement showed $22.7 million of profits. But MacFee was not comfortable with the numbers. Among other things, MiniScribe had recorded $16 million of sales on the last day of its fiscal year—more than the $14 million earned during the previous 28 days. Internal Coopers & Lybrand memos expressed concern about MiniScribe's revenue recognition, heavy shipments at month end, and accounts receivable aging.

MacFee asked Wiles to record adjusting journal entries reducing MiniScribe's earnings by $1.5 million. Wiles, who planned to include the 1986 financial statements in an April 1987 bond prospectus, balked at recording the adjustments. When MacFee persisted, Wiles requested a private meeting with Jack Grace, head of Coopers & Lybrand's Denver office. Wiles proposed his own post-closing adjustments to *increase* profits by $900,000.

Grace notified MacFee of the hastily arranged Saturday meeting with Wiles, but when MacFee was struck ill, Grace finished the negotiations and signed the audit report himself. When MacFee returned to work three days later, he learned that Grace had issued a clean audit opinion certifying that MiniScribe had earned $22.7 million. Grace had not only allowed Wiles to net his $900,000 of last-minute entries against MacFee's $1.5 million of income-reducing adjustments, but he had also waived the remaining $600,000 difference as immaterial.

Aftermath

Jamail's lawsuit on behalf of MiniScribe's bondholders was only one of more than a dozen legal actions taken against Wiles, Coopers & Lybrand, and Hambrecht & Quist. Coopers & Lybrand agreed in June 1992 to pay $95 million to settle civil suits brought by MiniScribe creditors and investors. The $140 million in MiniScribe-related claims caused Coopers & Lybrand to reduce 1992 profit distributions to partners.

The SEC charged Wiles and 14 former employees with conspiring to inflate MiniScribe's net income from 1986 through 1988.[10] During the three years Wiles was in charge of MiniScribe, senior managers collected undeserved bonuses totaling $290,000 and sold more than 300,000 shares of MiniScribe stock at artificially high prices. Without admitting or denying guilt, most of the former MiniScribe officers agreed to refund their bonuses and trading gains plus interest thereon.

On June 17, 1994, a federal jury convicted MiniScribe CFO Patrick Schleibaum of fraud and insider trading. Several MiniScribe executives who had been granted immunity from prosecution testified about Schleibaum's role in the fraud. The jury's deliberations were made easier by Schleibaum's admission that he had participated in packing bricks in disk-drive containers.

Three weeks later, Q.T. Wiles stood trial in the same Denver courtroom where Schleibaum had been convicted. Federal prosecutors charged Wiles with concealing a $15 million inventory shortage and submitting false financial statements to Standard Chartered Bank to obtain a $90 million loan. They also claimed that Wiles profited by selling $1.7 million of MiniScribe stock before the inventory shortfall became public knowledge. "Wiles wanted his management team to make the numbers," said Assistant U.S. Attorney Gerald J. Rafferty in his opening statement. "And when his management team could not make the numbers, he told them to cheat, and they did."[11]

Wiles' attorney H. Alan Dill acknowledged that fraud had been committed at MiniScribe, but said his client was not involved in the scheme. Dill described Wiles as a "hands-off" manager who oversaw seven companies simultaneously from his California headquarters and entrusted operating decisions to MiniScribe's managers in Colorado. He presented evidence that Wiles had visited MiniScribe's headquarters only twice during the three years he served as CEO. Dill pinned the blame on MiniScribe's financial officers, claiming they misstated the accounting records without Wiles' knowledge or consent.

The same MiniScribe employees who helped convict Schleibaum returned to testify against Wiles. Owen Taranta provided the most damning testimony by describing a meeting on October 14, 1987 in which he, Wiles and other Miniscribe officers discussed MiniScribe's $15 million inventory shortage. Taranta testified that Wiles suggested the problem could "go away" with a little "creative bookkeeping."[12] Taranta said he interpreted Wiles' comments as an order to make up fictitious inventory to cover the shortage.

Prosecutors also introduced memos and faxes allegedly linking Wiles to the fraud. One memo from a MiniScribe executive read "No cooking without Q.T.'s approval." Another note stated, "Q.T. does not want to lie to the world again," implying that Wiles was aware of earlier accounting abuses.[13] Dill complained that the sentences were taken out of context; he suggested more innocent interpretations of their true meaning.

The jurors deliberated for nine hours before convicting Wiles of fraud and insider trading. Although there was little hard evidence tying Wiles directly to the fraud, the jurors accepted the prosecutors' portrayal of Wiles as a tyrannical boss who intimidated his subordinates into breaking the law. In the end, they held Wiles responsible for the massive fraud committed at MiniScribe while he was in charge. "There wasn't a single piece of paper that convicted him," said one juror, "but after a while it just started adding up."[14]

Wiles, who was 75 years old at the time of his conviction, was sentenced to three years in prison and ordered to reimburse the government $125,000 for the cost of his incarceration. His lawyers appealed the sentence, arguing that, at Wiles' advanced age, three years was a de facto life sentence. Prosecutors were determined, however, to send a strong message that they would not tolerate financial fraud. After more than two years of appeals, Wiles reported to a minimum security facility on March 31, 1997. At 78, Wiles was one of the oldest prisoners in the federal prison system's population. He returned home in 1999, still in good health, after serving two and a half years in prison.

21 Litigation Reform

> It's the single worst thing that has ever happened to the accounting profession.
>
> (Peat Marwick general counsel Victor M. Earle III, describing the $81 million judgment against Arthur Andersen[1])

The jury's $81 million judgment against Arthur Andersen in the Fund of Funds case stunned the entire public accounting profession. The amount was more than double what any accounting firm had ever been required to pay for losses sustained by a client's shareholders. Representatives of all the major accounting firms expressed concern that the Fund of Funds verdict would stimulate more frequent claims against auditors. And auditors feared that future plaintiffs would use the Fund of Funds case as a precedent to seek higher amounts of damages. Coopers & Lybrand's general counsel warned, "When people think there's a pot of gold at the end of the rainbow, they persevere in their claims."[2]

Accountants' fears were confirmed in 1992 when a Galveston jury ordered Coopers & Lybrand to pay $220 million for its deficient audits of MiniScribe. The judgment included $200 million of punitive damages on top of $20 million of actual damages. The MiniScribe verdict prompted a flurry of articles in professional accounting journals protesting the unfairness of holding auditors liable for amounts far in excess of the actual harm they might have caused.[3] Although Coopers & Lybrand eventually settled the MiniScribe bondholders' suit for "only" $45 million, the prospect that a single audit failure could expose an accounting firm to virtually unlimited liability focused accountants' minds on the need for litigation reform.

A Litigation Crisis

In April 1992, *Time* magazine reported that U.S. accounting firms faced 6,000 liability suits seeking more than $15 billion in damages.[4] Several months later, the chief executives of the Big Six accounting firms composed a white paper entitled *The Liability Crisis in the United States: Impact on the Accounting Profession*. The document opened with the statement, "The tort liability system in the United States is out of control" and went on to warn that "the consequences could prove fatal to accounting firms of all sizes."[5]

The six executives revealed that their firms, collectively, had paid $477 million—9 percent of their domestic accounting and auditing revenue—defending and settling lawsuits in 1991. But, to generate support for litigation reform, the executives emphasized the potential harm to the public. The "epidemic of litigation" was impairing accounting firms' abilities to hire and retain talented employees. Unless the "brain drain" stopped, audit quality would eventually suffer, exposing investors to greater risk. The accounting firms claimed to be reducing their liability exposure by avoiding high-risk clients such as technology firms and private companies making initial public offerings. The executives warned that the country's economy would stagnate if small companies could not obtain the professional services necessary to raise capital. Finally, the accounting executives complained that a "tort tax" was being levied on the entire country as accountants and other professionals raised their fees to recoup higher legal costs.

The white paper alleged that the firms' high litigation costs were caused, not by the accountants' own negligence, but by "flaws" in the nation's tort liability system. Topping the list of complaints was the doctrine of joint and several liability. Each defendant found guilty of contributing to a plaintiff's losses could be held liable for 100 percent of the judgment, regardless of the degree of fault. The philosophy behind joint and several liability was that in situations where one defendant was unable to pay, it was better for the other guilty parties to pay the entire damages than for the innocent victim to not be compensated fully for his loss. But accounting firms were often the only solvent defendant following a client's bankruptcy. Auditors sometimes had to pay 100 percent of the damages in situations where they were guilty, at worst, of failing to detect a fraud planned, executed, and concealed by corrupt corporate managers.

A second purported "flaw" in the tort liability system was that victorious defendants could not recover their legal costs, even if the plaintiff's case was without merit. Plaintiffs needed only to demonstrate damages to invoke the discovery system, during which they could compel the auditors to turn over thousands of pages of documents. Securities lawyers used the threat of a lengthy and disruptive discovery process to "extort" settlements from innocent auditors. Accountants claimed they frequently agreed to pay damages simply to avoid the costs of defending themselves.

Finally, the accounting executives complained about the unfairness of punitive damages. Punitive damages were allowed in civil tort cases to deter and punish misconduct. But some states placed few, if any, restrictions on the amount of punitive damages juries could award. In cases such as MiniScribe, punitive damages far exceeded the plaintiff's actual losses. Defendant accountants had little idea at the beginning of a trial how high their potential liability might be. Fear that a jury might award the plaintiff excessive punitive damages led auditors to settle claims privately rather than argue them in court.

The auditors' white paper concluded that "substantive reform of both federal and state liability laws" was needed "to restore equity and sanity to the liability system."[6] The accountants asked that joint and several liability be replaced with a proportionate liability standard that assessed damages based on each defendant's degree of fault. The accountants wanted plaintiffs to reimburse the defendant's legal fees if the court determined that a suit was without merit. And the accounting executives asked for "reasonable limitations on punitive damages."

Tort Reform

The AICPA established a political action committee (PAC) in 1976 to fend off reforms proposed by Senator Lee Metcalf and Representative John Moss. The AICPA also established a "key persons" program to lobby federal legislators. More than 1,500 CPAs maintained personal contacts with representatives from their states and advocated the AICPA's position on Bills affecting the accounting profession. An AICPA branch office in Washington, DC supported the institute's political activities.

Accountants' lobbying efforts intensified during the early 1990s. In 1991, the Big Six accounting firms helped organize the Coalition to Eliminate Abusive Securities Suits (CEASS). Other CEASS members included investment banks, high-tech companies, corporate directors and other frequent targets of securities-related litigation. Each of the Big Six pledged $2 million in 1992 toward promoting litigation reform legislation.

The Securities Subcommittee of the Senate Banking Committee held hearings during the summer of 1993 to investigate the need for securities litigation reform. Senator Christopher Dodd (D, Connecticut), who received more than $500,000 in donations from accounting-related PACs between 1990 and 2005, listened sympathetically as representatives from the Big Six testified that they faced legal claims totaling 20 times their aggregate net assets. Although several investor and consumer advocates testified that auditors must be held responsible for their misdeeds, the accountants were delighted when the final subcommittee report concluded that "some modification of joint and several liability appears to be justified."[7]

Senators Dodd and Pete Domenici (R, New Mexico) sponsored a bipartisan reform Bill in March 1994 calling for the adoption of proportionate liability in place of joint and several liability. They also recommended adoption of the so-called "English Rule" requiring losing parties to reimburse the winner's legal costs. But President Bill Clinton, who received generous support from trial lawyers during his two presidential campaigns, showed little interest in securities litigation reform. House Commerce Committee members John Dingell (D, Michigan) and Edward Markey (D, Massachusetts) succeeded in blocking the proposed legislation.

The litigation reform movement gained momentum later in 1994 when 300 Republican congressional candidates endorsed Newt Gingrich's "Contract with America." One provision of the "Contract" stated that within 100 days of taking office, House Republicans would introduce legislation capping punitive damages at three times actual damages and requiring losers of civil lawsuits to reimburse the winner's legal expenses. Accountants donated $3.6 million to congressional candidates during the 1994 election cycle, up 50 percent from the $2.4 million donated in 1992. Although accounting PACs had traditionally given nearly 60 percent of their contributions to Democrats, the split was nearly even in 1994 as last-minute contributions went to Republicans endorsing tort reform.

In late 1995, both Houses of Congress passed the Private Securities Litigation Reform Act (PSLRA). Senator Dodd sponsored the Bill in the Senate and Representative Billy Tauzin (D, Louisiana) sponsored the companion Bill in the House. The Bill established proportionate liability for defendants who did not knowingly engage in securities fraud. Juries would be required to allocate responsibility for the plaintiffs' losses among the defendants. And, subject to some exceptions to protect small investors from catastrophic loss, each defendant would be responsible only for his or her "fair share" of the loss.

The PSLRA also required plaintiffs to state with particularity specific facts suggesting that the defendants acted with fraudulent intent. No longer could plaintiffs file suits based on vague claims of fraud and then "fish" through thousands of pages of subpoenaed documents searching for every judgment that might be second-guessed. Finally, the Act, as originally drafted, included a provision requiring unsuccessful plaintiffs to reimburse the defendants' legal costs.

President Clinton, who had earlier expressed tepid support for the Bill, vetoed the PSLRA, saying the heightened pleading requirement would make it too difficult for victims of securities fraud to recover their losses. Senator Dodd then defied his own party's leader by urging congressional Democrats to override the President's veto. After the "loser pays" provision was dropped to garner additional support, the House and Senate adopted the amended Bill by votes of 319 to 100 and

68 to 30, respectively. It was the first veto override of the Clinton presidency.

Because the PSLRA applied only to securities lawsuits filed in federal court, plaintiffs' lawyers began filing more securities claims in state courts instead of in federal district courts. And because corporations had shareholders living in nearly every state, attorneys could select the state with the most "advantageous" laws. Congress closed this loophole in 1998 when it passed the Securities Litigation Uniform Standards Act requiring class action suits about accounting issues to be filed in federal court.

Limited Liability Partnerships

Laventhol & Horwath (L&H) was once the seventh largest accounting firm in the United States, with 425 partners and nearly 3,500 employees in 51 offices. L&H increased its revenues from $70 million in 1980 to $275 million in 1986 by acquiring smaller CPA firms and aggressively marketing consulting services to audit clients.

During the late 1980s, L&H lost a series of court cases charging the firm with negligence and fraud. L&H executives blamed the losses on bad luck and the unfair tort liability system. Outsiders wondered whether the firm had elevated revenue growth over audit quality. Former L&H employees complained that pursuit of profits made partners too willing to accept clients of dubious character and too reluctant to reject questionable accounting practices.

Jim Bakker's PTL ("Praise the Lord") Ministry was one of the clients L&H acquired during its 1980s growth spurt. PTL was the largest client of L&H's Charlotte, North Carolina office. Bakker resigned in disgrace in March 1987 after it was discovered that PTL funds had been disbursed to a young woman with whom the famous televangelist had been breaking the seventh commandment.[8]

Investors sued L&H, alleging the auditors had helped Bakker and PTL convert a $19 million loss into a $26 million profit in 1986. Even more damning was an allegation that the L&H partner in charge of the audit had maintained a secret PTL bank account that was unknown even to PTL's chief financial officer. The account had been used to funnel thousands of dollars to Bakker's friends and to firms that provided no legitimate services. The plaintiffs sought to recover damages of $184 million—roughly half of L&H's 1989 firm-wide revenue.

Another of L&H's most lucrative clients was Grabill Corporation, which paid nearly $1 million per year for its audit. After Grabill declared bankruptcy in 1989, the court-appointed trustee could locate only $2 million of the $69 million of real estate listed on Grabill's books. An episode of the CBS newsmagazine *60 Minutes* in early 1990 questioned what L&H had been doing to earn its annual $1 million fee.

By late 1990, L&H had only $146 million of assets compared to $153 of firm liabilities. And the recorded liabilities were almost certainly understated because the firm was named as a defendant in 100 outstanding lawsuits seeking $2 billion in damages. After failing to negotiate a merger with a Big Six accounting firm, the L&H partners voted in November to disband their 75-year-old firm.

But the partners couldn't simply walk away from the accounting firm's liabilities. Because L&H was a general partnership, each partner was jointly and severally liable for all the firm's debts. After L&H's liquidation, individual partners had to contribute $47 million of personal assets to satisfy the firm's remaining obligations. At least ten L&H partners declared personal bankruptcy to shelter their homes and savings from L&H creditors.

Until January 1992, Rule 505 of the AICPA *Code of Professional Conduct* allowed accounting firms to practice only as proprietorships, partnerships, or professional corporations. After the AICPA amended Rule 505 to allow accountants to practice in any form permitted under their state's laws, accountants embarked on a nearly three-year-long campaign to convince state legislatures and boards of accountancy to allow accounting firms to reorganize as limited liability partnerships (LLPs).

Accountants claimed it was unfair that a partner in Boston might have his personal assets seized because of an error made by a partner in Dallas. Representative Ron Wyden (D, Oregon) disagreed. "It's outrageous that partners so well paid for their firms' opinions are asking for liability protection," Wyden said. "They want it both ways: Get rich from their professional credentials but avoid being culpable for the acts of their partners. They're saying, 'To heck with people who depend on our work and opinions.' "[9] Auditors countered that the entire assets of the accounting firm were still at risk. LLPs merely provided partners a "doomsday defense" in the event of the firm's failure.

Only 20 states amended their regulations to permit accounting firms to practice as LLPs. But in August 1994, Hawaii became the fiftieth state to allow out-of-state LLPs to practice accounting within its jurisdiction. Most states required LLPs to carry a specified minimum amount of professional liability insurance coverage and maintain a minimum net worth. Accountants gladly accepted such requirements in return for sheltering their personal assets. By the end of September, all of the Big Six accounting firms had reorganized as LLPs.

The Courts Provide Relief

Between 1992 and 1994, several state and federal court decisions granted accountants relief from legal liability.

Bily v. *Arthur Young & Co.* (1992). Osborne Computer produced the world's first portable personal computer in 1981. Sales peaked at

$10 million per month in early 1983, but plummeted soon after when consumers rejected machines that were not "IBM compatible." A group of venture capitalists, including a member of Osborne's board of directors, sued Arthur Young, claiming Osborne's 1982 earnings were overstated by $3 million. A jury awarded the plaintiffs $4.3 million of damages after the trial judge instructed the jurors that auditors were liable to all "third parties who reasonably and foreseeably rely on an audited financial statement prepared by the accountant."[10]

In 1992, the California Supreme Court, by a 5–2 vote, overturned the trial court's verdict. The majority opinion stated that the auditor "owes no general duty of care regarding the conduct of an audit to persons other than the client."[11] The court noted that financial statement users tend to be sophisticated business enterprises capable of performing their own due diligence reviews. It stated that investors should be encouraged to hire their own auditors to verify information the investors consider important. Although the *Bily* decision was binding only in California, accountants hoped the strongly worded opinion would influence judges in other states.

Reves v. *Ernst & Young* (1993). Jack White, the general manager of the Farmers' Cooperative in Van Buren, Arkansas, funneled $4.1 million of the co-op's funds into his personal gasohol business. After several years of operating losses, White unloaded his money-losing enterprise by transferring its ownership to the co-op. The co-op's 1980 and 1981 balance sheets listed the gasohol business as an unconsolidated subsidiary valued at $4.5 million even though the plant's market value was no more than $1.5 million.

After the co-op declared bankruptcy in February 1984, investors accused Arthur Young of helping conceal White's misuse of co-op funds. A federal jury found the auditors guilty of securities fraud and awarded $6.1 million in damages. But the trial judge denied the plaintiffs' request for triple damages under RICO. The judge ruled that RICO was not intended to be used against outside professionals who provided services to a corrupt organization. A federal appeals court in St. Louis affirmed the trial judge's ruling, saying: "It is clear that Arthur Young committed a number of reprehensible acts, but these acts in no way rise to the level of participation in the management or operation of the co-op."[12]

When the plaintiffs appealed to the U.S. Supreme Court, arguing that Congress intended RICO to apply to all wrongdoers, the Supreme Court justices voted 7–2 to uphold the appeals court ruling. Justice Blackmun wrote in the majority opinion, "it is clear that Congress did not intend to extend RICO liability … beyond those who participate in the operation or management of an enterprise."[13] Accountants hoped the *Reves* decision would help protect them from claims for triple damages.

Central Bank of Denver v. *First Interstate Bank of Denver* (1994). Section 10(b) of the Securities Exchange Act of 1934 permits victims of securities fraud to recover damages through private litigation from parties who perpetrate fraud. And for approximately 30 years, beginning in the 1960s, federal courts held secondary parties, such as accountants and lawyers, liable for aiding and abetting. An "aider and abettor" is one who has knowledge of a crime and assists in its commission through advice or financial support.

The Colorado Springs–Stetson Hills Public Building Authority (the "Building Authority") issued $26 million of bonds in 1986 and 1988 to finance improvements in a planned real estate development. After the Building Authority defaulted on the bonds, a group of investors, led by First Interstate Bank of Denver, filed suit accusing the Building Authority and the bond underwriters of fraudulently failing to disclose the fact that the appraised value of the land securing the bonds had fallen below the minimum value stipulated in the bond covenants. Central Bank of Denver, which had acted as the indenture trustee for the bond issues, was named as a defendant for allegedly aiding and abetting the fraud.

In April 1994, the U.S. Supreme Court dismissed the claims against Central Bank of Denver. The Court ruled that because Section 10(b) of the 1934 Act does not specifically mention aiding and abetting, private litigants may not recover damages from parties who are only peripherally involved in the fraud. Investors may sue the corporate managers who perpetrate fraud, but not the professionals who advise the primary wrongdoers, the court concluded. Leaders of the AICPA and the major public accounting firms hoped the decision would reduce the number of lawsuits against auditors.

Ernst & Young wasted no time before trying to take advantage of the *Central Bank* decision. The firm's lawyers cited *Central Bank* in asking a federal judge for summary adjudication of claims filed by ZZZZ Best investors. The petition stated that because Ernst & Young had simply performed professional services for ZZZZ Best, the firm was guilty, at worst, of aiding and abetting Barry Minkow's fraud and should not be held liable for the investors' losses. Although the judge dismissed the plaintiffs' claims against Ernst & Young for aiding and abetting, the judge ruled that because the auditors had been so intricately involved with false statements made by ZZZZ Best, the plaintiffs could continue pursuing their claims, naming the auditors as primary wrongdoers. Because of the *Central Bank* decision, lawsuits against auditors under the 1934 Act must demonstrate that the actions of the auditors rise to the level of primary wrongdoing.

Conclusion

In spite of the favorable court decisions of the early 1990s and the Private Securities Litigation Reform Act of 1995, public accounting firms continue to pay multimillion-dollar settlements to shareholders and creditors of bankrupt clients. Ernst & Young paid $335 million in 1999 to Cendant Corporation shareholders for failing to detect accounting fraud at one of Cendant's merger partners. KPMG paid $125 million in 2003 to settle a class action suit filed by shareholders of drugstore chain Rite Aid. Deloitte & Touche paid an estimated $250 million in 2005 to reimburse three Japanese insurance companies for losses suffered from the collapse of D&T client Fortress Re. PricewaterhouseCoopers was ordered in 2005 to pay $182 million to shareholders of Ambassador Insurance Company.

And investors continue seeking damages in amounts that threaten the accounting firms' survival. In 2003, Amerco, Inc., the parent of truck rental company U-Haul International, sued PricewaterhouseCoopers for $2.5 billion, claiming the auditors had given the company incorrect advice about how to account for its special purpose entities. Parmalat, SpA filed a $10 billion suit against Deloitte & Touche and Grant Thornton in 2004 for allegedly deficient audits of the Italian dairy company. The Parmalat suit led the two U.S. accounting firms to file legal briefs disavowing responsibility for the actions of their foreign affiliates.

Litigation played a major role in the collapse of Arthur Andersen. Audit failures at Sunbeam and Waste Management during the late 1990s cost the firm $110 million and $75 million, respectively. Lawsuits for failed audits at Enron, WorldCom, and the Baptist Foundation of Arizona might well have bankrupted Arthur Andersen even if the firm had survived its 2002 criminal indictment. Lawyers representing Global Crossing and Qwest shareholders filed additional legal claims against Andersen even after the firm's demise. The only good news for the Andersen partners was that, unlike their unfortunate counterparts at Laventhol & Horwath, they have been shielded from personal liability by Andersen's status as a limited liability partnership.

Part VI

Beginning of the End

22 Auditor Independence

> Public faith in the reliability of a corporation's financial statements depends upon the public perception of the outside auditor as an independent professional. If investors were to view the auditor as an advocate for the corporate client, the value of the audit function itself might well be lost.
>
> (Warren Burger,[1] U.S. Supreme Court Justice)

Independence is the cornerstone of auditing. Investors and creditors demand that an objective third party examine corporate financial statements because they fear (rightly) that the management-prepared reports might be biased. Independent auditors add credibility to the information provided by self-interested corporate managers. Auditors who rubber-stamp managers' assertions are as useless as lifeguards who cannot swim.

Auditor Independence

Independence is a state of mind. The AICPA's second general standard of auditing requires that "In all matters relating to the assignment, an independence in mental attitude is to be maintained by the auditor or auditors."[2] Auditors' judgments must be objective, impartial, unbiased, and unaffected by self-interest.

But because it is impossible to measure, let alone regulate, an auditor's mental attitude, AICPA and SEC rules focus on prohibiting situations in which the auditor would have an obvious incentive to render an undeserved favorable audit report. SEC chairman Arthur Levitt summarized the Commission's requirements very simply, "Independence means the auditor should not be in bed with the corporate managers whose numbers they audit."[3]

One of the SEC's first enforcement actions, *In the Matter of Cornucopia Gold Mines* (1936), illustrates how closely entwined early auditors sometimes were with their clients. Cornucopia leased space in the accounting firm's office and paid an audit fee based, in part, on its annual gold sales. In addition, the auditor in charge of Cornucopia's audit owned shares of Cornucopia's common stock and served simultaneously as the company's controller.

During the next 70 years, the AICPA and SEC adopted progressively stricter rules governing auditors' relationships with their clients. Rule 101 of the AICPA *Code of Professional Conduct* currently prohibits auditors from having a direct or material indirect financial interest in an audit client; serving as an officer or director of a client company; lending money to or accepting loans from an audit client; or auditing a company where a close relative is responsible for preparing the financial statements.[4] More than 100 detailed rulings by the AICPA Professional Ethics Executive Committee address issues such as whether an auditor may accept a gift from an audit client, whether an auditor may maintain a checking account at a client financial institution, and even whether an auditor may share a vacation home with an audit client.

The AICPA *Code of Professional Conduct* requires auditors to be independent *in appearance* as well as in fact.[5] That is, auditors must avoid situations that would cause reasonable people to doubt their independence. Because the auditor's primary role is to enhance investors' and creditors' faith in audited financial statements, AICPA secretary John L. Carey wrote in 1946, "The accounting profession must be like Caesar's wife. To be suspected is almost as bad as to be convicted."[6]

But in spite of the many SEC and AICPA rules enacted to protect auditors' perceived independence, doubts about auditors' independence persisted throughout the second half of the twentieth century. Significant numbers of investors questioned the propriety of: (1) clients selecting and paying their own auditors, (2) auditors accepting jobs with their former audit clients, (3) accounting firms performing management advisory services for their audit clients, and (4) public accountants entering into joint ventures with their audit clients.

Auditors Hired and Paid by Clients

One of the great ironies of the public accounting profession is that although auditors are expected to render impartial opinions, they are hired and paid by the organizations whose financial statements they audit. Skeptics liken this arrangement to allowing the home baseball team to hire the umpires or permitting authors to choose their own book reviewers. The (Cohen) Commission on Auditors' Responsibilities acknowledged the conflict of interest when it stated, "The independent auditor is selected and paid by someone affected by his work. Consequently, total independence is a practical impossibility."[7]

Corporations paying multimillion-dollar fees have significant economic power over their auditors. Partners at large accounting firms claim they would never accede to a client's improper demands because no single client represents more than a tiny fraction of the firm's total revenue. But this argument ignores the importance a single client might have to a particular office or an individual partner. Lincoln Savings & Loan accounted for 20 percent of Arthur Young's Phoenix office revenue. Equity Funding provided 60 percent of Wolfson Weiner Ratoff & Lapin's Los Angeles office revenue. Penn & Harwood depended on Crazy Eddie for one-third of its New York office revenue. The partners and auditors in the aforementioned offices had strong incentives to maintain friendly relations with their lucrative clients.

The Public Oversight Board's Advisory Panel on Auditor Independence (1994) recommended strengthening corporate audit committees to shield auditors from management's influence. Other safeguards, such as partner rotation and second partner review, help ensure that the engagement partner does not become too close to management or succumb to management pressure.

Mandatory audit firm rotation has often been suggested as a means of reducing clients' economic power over their auditors. Consumer advocate Ralph Nader recommended in 1976 requiring corporations to engage their auditors for five-year noncancellable, nonrenewable terms. Auditors' judgments would no longer be influenced by fear of being fired or by hope of extending the engagement. And knowledge that auditors from a rival accounting firm would soon review the client's accounting records would be a strong inducement toward audit quality.

In 1991, the U.S. Comptroller General considered requiring the nation's 50 largest banks to rotate audit firms every five to seven years. The proposal was similar to the auditor rotation policy then practiced by Canadian banks. Big Six leaders estimated the proposal would increase annual audit costs by at least 10 percent. Moreover, they warned that the risk of audit failure is highest in the early years of the auditor/client relationship when auditors are not as familiar with the client's operations. The Comptroller General rejected the proposal after concluding that the costs of mandatory audit firm rotation outweighed the potential benefits. But rotation was discussed periodically throughout the 1990s whenever Congress or the SEC grew worried about corporate managers' influence over auditors.

The Revolving Door

Only a small minority of young auditors remain in public accounting longer than five years. Audit clients routinely raid their accounting firms' staffs, seeking experienced accountants who already understand the clients' operations. And accounting firms often encourage departing auditors to join a client, believing the relationship between the accounting firm and the client will be strengthened.

The "revolving door" between accounting firms and their clients poses a number of threats to auditor independence. Job-seeking auditors may spend more time trying to impress potential employers than critically examining the fairness of the financial statements. At best, the auditor might find it difficult to objectively evaluate the integrity of client personnel. At worst, a client might use a lucrative job offer to reward an auditor for a favorable report.

Potential problems continue after an auditor joins a client. The former auditor's knowledge of the audit firm's testing techniques might enable the client to manipulate the financial statements in ways that are least likely to be detected. And continuing auditors might relax their skepticism when questioning a friend and former colleague.

Jack D. Atchison, the Arthur Young partner who supervised Lincoln Savings & Loan's audits, became the poster boy for the revolving door. Atchison earned $225,000 per year at Arthur Young before accepting a $930,000 position with Lincoln's parent company. Congressman Richard H. Lehman (D, California) questioned Arthur Young chairman William Gladstone about Atchison's role reversal.[8]

CONGRESSMAN LEHMAN: Did anyone at Arthur Young have any contact with Mr. Atchison after he left and went to work for Lincoln?

MR. GLADSTONE: Yes, sir.

LEHMAN: In the course of the audit?

GLADSTONE: Yes.

LEHMAN: So he went from one side of the table to the other for $700,000 more?

GLADSTONE: That is what happened.

LEHMAN: Did the job he had there have anything to do with interfacing with the auditors?

GLADSTONE: To some extent, yes.

LEHMAN: What does "to some extent" mean?

GLADSTONE: On major accounting issues that were discussed in the Form 8-K, we did have conversations with Jack Atchison.

LEHMAN: So he was the person Mr. Keating had to interface with you in major [accounting] decisions?

GLADSTONE: Him, and other officers of American Continental.

Unfortunately, Atchison is not the only auditor whose defection raised doubts about independence. The *New York Times* reported in October 1992 that the California State Board of Accountancy was investigating six companies accused of committing accounting fraud after luring former auditors to fill key financial positions.[9] In one such case, Deloitte & Touche paid $65 million to investors and creditors of bankrupt Bonneville Pacific Corporation to settle a suit alleging that

D&T's independence was impaired by the fact that Bonneville's chairman, controller, and four other financial employees were recent D&T alumni.

The AICPA asked the SEC in June 1993 to prohibit public companies from hiring their audit partner for one year following the completion of the audit. Such a rule would have been similar to federal laws restricting former government employees from lobbying their previous agencies. But the SEC rejected the AICPA proposal, arguing that such a rule would be too difficult to enforce. The SEC suggested that the AICPA amend its *Code of Professional Conduct* to require the one-year cooling-off period. The AICPA then abandoned the proposal, not wanting to be responsible for restricting its members' career opportunities.

Nonaudit Services

Throughout much of the twentieth century, auditors and regulators debated the propriety of public accounting firms providing management advisory services to their audit clients. *Journal of Accountancy* editor A.P. Richardson observed in 1925:

> Accountancy is developing two schools of thought ... eccentric and concentric. The eccentric school is more aggressive and ready to spread out into fields new and untried and in short to do all things which may seem to be required by the client whether those things are of accountancy or otherwise. The concentric school has taken as its motto: "Sutor ne supre crepidam judicaret" ... or "Let the cobbler stick to his last."[10]

Price Waterhouse chief George O. May belonged to the more conservative, "concentric" school. He published a letter in the September 1925 *Journal of Accountancy* warning that unrestrained expansion of services was "fraught with danger."[11] Arthur E. Andersen, founder of the firm that bore his name, advocated the more expansive, "eccentric" view. Andersen delivered a speech in Chicago in November 1925 urging accountants to seek "newer and broader fields of service to business management."[12]

Andersen's aggressive "eccentric" viewpoint dominated the public accounting profession during and after World War II. But accountants' expansion into management advisory services sparked concerns about potential conflicts of interest. The SEC's 1957 annual report alleged that some accountants were failing to maintain a clear distinction between giving advice to management and making business decisions for them. Robert Mautz and Hussein Sharaf warned in *The Philosophy of Auditing* (1961) that auditors' performance of management advisory services could erode their perceived independence.[13] Several public opinion surveys in the 1960s, 1970s, and 1980s revealed that significant numbers of financial statement users believed that consulting services could impair auditors' independence.

Critics of accountants' expansion into management consulting argued that lucrative consulting engagements increased the client's financial power over the accounting firm. The more services an accounting firm provided to a client, the more pressure the audit partner felt to submit to the client's wishes rather than risk losing the engagement.

And performing certain services, such as information system design, could potentially put the auditor in the position of evaluating his own firm's work. An auditor would need extraordinary courage to report control weaknesses in an information system designed by the accounting firm's consulting arm.

Finally, consulting and auditing require different mindsets. A consultant is an ally and advocate of management, whereas an auditor is responsible to the public and must maintain professional skepticism. CUNY–Baruch accounting professor Abraham Briloff expounded:

> It should be patently self-evident ... that a firm undertaking the management consulting responsibility has, in effect, allied itself with management and has become an integral part of such management. To presume such a firm could then don the robes of an independent auditor for that enterprise would be to perpetrate a hoax.[14]

Leaders of the major accounting firms denied vehemently that there was anything improper about accountants performing consulting services for their audit clients. Big Eight representatives claimed that consulting services actually improved audit quality by giving accountants a deeper understanding of their clients' operations.

The AICPA strongly supported its members' expansion of services. The Institute's Ad Hoc Committee on Independence (1969) reported that none of the 44 state boards of accountancy which responded to their inquiry had ever disciplined an accountant for alleged lack of independence involving consulting services. A 1969 AICPA Council resolution stated, "It is an objective of the Institute, recognizing that management services are a proper function of CPAs, to *encourage* all CPAs to perform the entire range of management services consistent with their professional competence, ethical standards and responsibility" (emphasis added). [15]

The first serious attempt to rein in accountants' nonaudit services came during the mid-1970s. Senator Lee Metcalf's 1976 staff report, *The Accounting Establishment*, recommended prohibiting accounting firms from performing management advisory services for their audit clients.

Instead of banning consulting services, the SEC issued Accounting Series Release No. 250 in 1978 requiring corporations to disclose in their proxy statements information about the fees paid to their accounting firms for nonaudit services. The first round of proxy statements revealed that the consulting fees paid by public corporations to their accountants averaged only 8 percent of total audit fees. Fewer than 12 percent of public companies paid consulting fees greater than 50 percent of audit fees. This information helped convince the SEC that nonaudit fees did not pose a serious threat to auditor independence at that time. The agency repealed the disclosure requirement in 1982.[16]

Joint Ventures with Clients

Co-contracting is a common business practice through which two or more firms pool their expertise to provide services superior to those any single company can provide. For example, a consulting firm hired to improve a client's management information system often finds it advantageous to co-contract with a computer hardware manufacturer and a software designer.

Although the AICPA allows accountants to co-contract with their audit clients as long as the revenues are not material to the auditor, Section 602.02g of the SEC's *Codification of Financial Reporting Policies* forbids direct business relationships between public accounting firms and their publicly traded audit clients. This SEC rule prevents the auditors of companies such as IBM and Microsoft from entering into joint consulting engagements with these desirable potential partners.

Three of the Big Eight accounting firms petitioned the SEC in 1988 to relax its prohibition against co-contracting between accountants and their audit clients. The firms claimed the SEC's rule was a restraint of trade and hurt the public by preventing services from being provided in the most economically efficient manner. But the SEC rejected the petition, arguing that direct business relationships between accountants and audit clients would impair the accountants' perceived independence.

A year later, the accounting firms proposed four safeguards they would be willing to accept if allowed to co-contract with audit clients. The proposed safeguards were: (1) the accounting firm and the audit client must not have a continuing co-contracting relationship (i.e., they may collaborate on *individual* projects, but may not pool their capital to form a continuing joint venture), (2) accounting firm personnel involved in the consulting engagement may not participate in the audit, (3) there must be no litigation between the accounting firm and its client concerning the co-contracting engagement, and (4) peer review teams would periodically examine the accounting firm's co-contracting relationships. But the SEC once again refused to amend Section 602.02g after concluding that the proposed safeguards were insufficient to preserve the appearance of independence. The SEC's decision infuriated the accounting firms' consulting partners, who continued to believe that the SEC's independence requirements put them at a competitive disadvantage vis-à-vis stand-alone consulting firms.

The Independence Standards Board (ISB)

A number of events during the early 1990s raised doubts about auditors' independence. Several Ernst & Young partners who participated in the audit of RepublicBank were discovered to have accepted millions of dollars of loans from their client. KPMG Peat Marwick was forced by the SEC to resign from two audit clients because of conflicts arising from the clients' dealings with a KPMG-affiliated investment bank. SEC chief accountant Walter Scheutze accused public accountants of acting as "cheerleaders for their clients" when expressing opinions about FASB exposure drafts.[17]

And public accounting firms' consulting practices continued to grow. By the mid-1990s, the Big Six accounting firms were earning more than 40 percent of their revenue, and an even larger share of their profits, from management advisory services. The major accounting firms offered services ranging from tax planning and feasibility studies to market analysis and interior design. While consulting revenues soared, audit fees stagnated due to aggressive price cutting as firms competed for clients. SEC chairman Arthur Levitt warned accountants against using audits as "loss leaders retained as a foot in the door for higher-fee consulting services."[18]

In 1997, Levitt pressured the AICPA leadership into forming a new Independence Standards Board (ISB) to establish requirements for accountants auditing publicly traded companies. William Allen of the Delaware Court of Chancery agreed to chair the ISB, which was composed of four practicing accountants and four public representatives.

Although SEC chief accountant Michael Sutton cited the growing diversity of nonaudit services performed for audit clients as one of the primary factors leading to the ISB's formation, reform would not come easily. The four accounting profession representatives—Price Waterhouse chairman James J. Schiro, KPMG Peat Marwick chairman Stephen G. Butler, Ernst & Young chairman Philip A. Laskawy, and AICPA president Barry Melancon—were fiercely committed to defending and expanding their firms' consulting practices.

The ISB's first three standards sidestepped the controversial topic of nonaudit services. The first standard required auditors to disclose to the client's audit committee all relationships between the auditor and the client. The second standard relaxed restrictions on auditors investing in firm-audited mutual funds. The third standard established guidelines for auditors accepting jobs with audit clients.

The ISB spent much of its first three years trying to develop a conceptual framework for auditor independence. The Board issued a discussion memorandum in February 2000 seeking advice on topics such as how to define independence, whether standards should be based on perceptions of independence, and how to measure the costs and benefits of auditor independence.

Conclusion

Arthur Levitt hoped the ISB would restore confidence in auditors' independence. But during the first year of the ISB's existence, two audacious accounting frauds further eroded investors' faith in auditors' ability to enforce proper accounting. Waste Management, the nation's largest waste disposal company, announced in February 1998 that it had overstated its 1992 through 1997 earnings by $1.4 billion. Eight months later, Sunbeam Corporation recalled its 1996 and 1997 financial statements, saying they were materially misstated.

The most troubling aspect of both cases was that the auditors had uncovered, but failed to report, many of the accounting violations. Waste Management's auditors waived $128 million of proposed adjustments at the end of the 1993 audit based on company executives' promise to correct the misstatements in the future. The partner in charge of Sunbeam's audit ignored known misstatements totaling 16 percent of the company's reported 1997 income. The SEC eventually disciplined five auditors for their deficient audits of the two companies.

Were the Sunbeam and Waste Management audit failures caused by lack of independence? No one will ever know because independence is an unobservable state of mind. But the auditors' approval of flawed financial statements raised serious doubts about their ability or willingness to stand up to client management.

23 Waste Management

One man's trash is another man's treasure.

(French proverb)

When Dean Buntrock took over his in-laws' small trash collection business in 1956, the company operated 15 trucks and earned $750,000 of annual revenues. Forty years later, WMX Technologies (WMX or Waste Management) was the largest waste disposal organization in the world, with operations in 21 countries and revenues approaching $10 billion.

Buntrock made far more money hauling trash than he was ever likely to have earned in his previous job selling insurance. His $12.3 million of total compensation in 1990 ranked fourth highest among American CEOs, according to *Business Week* magazine.[1] Buntrock's salary and $150 million of stock holdings allowed him to pursue interests ranging from art collecting to big game hunting. He served as a director of Chicago's prestigious Terra Museum of American Art. An Alaskan brown bear and a Canadian grizzly, trophies from two of Buntrock's many hunting expeditions, guarded the hallway to WMX's executive offices.

Buntrock won praise as a philanthropist in February 1997 by donating $26 million to St. Olaf College for construction of Buntrock Commons, a state-of-the-art facility housing a bookstore, theater, game rooms, dining facilities, and three ballrooms.

Twelve months later, Buntrock earned notoriety of a different sort when WMX announced a pretax charge of $3.5 billion and recalled its 1992 through 1996 financial statements. At the time, it was the largest earnings restatement in U.S. history.

Waste Management

The Huizenga family had been in the garbage collection business since 1894. Buntrock's wife, Elizabeth Huizenga, inherited Ace Scavenger

Service upon her father's death in 1956. Elizabeth's cousin, Wayne Huizenga, operated a similar small trash hauling company in Florida. The garbage collection industry at that time consisted of hundreds of family-owned companies, each servicing three or four municipalities with a handful of aging trucks. The situation was ripe for somebody to consolidate the industry and reduce the cutthroat competitive bidding that kept profits low.

Buntrock, Wayne Huizenga, and Lawrence Beck, owner of Acme Disposal Company, merged their three companies in 1968, naming the new company Waste Management. Waste Management used the proceeds from its 1971 initial public offering to begin buying other trash haulers. Buntrock and his partners acquired 1,500 garbage companies between 1956 and 1993, swallowing 168 firms in 1988 alone.

Wayne Huizenga left Waste Management in 1984 to apply the same acquisition-oriented growth strategy to the video rental industry. During the next 10 years, Huizenga built Blockbuster Entertainment from 19 stores to more than $1 billion in annual revenues. He eventually became one of the wealthiest men in south Florida after diversifying into hotels, cable television, professional sports franchises, and used car sales.

Waste Management's growth accelerated after Huizenga's departure. Revenues increased from $1.3 billion in 1984 to nearly $10 billion in 1993. The company's split-adjusted stock price increased from $3.41 in 1984 to a peak of $46.63 in 1992.

Buntrock renamed the giant company WMX Technologies in 1993. WMX was actually a holding company with majority interests in four public subsidiaries. Waste Management International, PLC accounted for half of WMX's operating revenues through its traditional solid waste collection and disposal operations. Chemical Waste Management (Chem-Waste) specialized in transporting and incinerating hazardous materials such as cancer-causing PCBs. Wheelebrator Technologies built scrubbers and electrostatic precipitators to reduce air pollutants. Rust International was an environmental engineering and consulting firm capable of evaluating a customer's waste problem, designing and constructing a solution, or handling the necessary cleanup.

Waste Management's growth during the 1970s was marred by allegations of price fixing and illegal trade practices. The company paid fines and settled lawsuits for colluding with other trash carriers to allocate territories, refrain from soliciting each other's customers, and submit rigged bids for municipal contracts. A general manager in Illinois was convicted of bribing a mayor and trustee to obtain a small town's trash collection contract. SEC investigators discovered that Waste Management spent $36,000 of corporate funds on illegal campaign contributions.

The 1980s brought fines and other sanctions for environmental violations. A large waste disposal site in Ohio was closed temporarily after four employees charged that the company had disposed of hazardous chemicals illegally. Alabama's attorney-general fined the company $600,000 for illegally storing PCBs at one of its landfills. Managers in Chicago confessed that pollution monitoring equipment had been shut off four times in 1986 and 1987 while toxic wastes were fed into an incinerator at unacceptably high rates.

Buntrock and other top executives dodged blame for the company's transgressions by claiming the misdeeds were committed by operating personnel without upper management's knowledge or consent. Waste Management's decentralized organization may have fostered aggressive risk taking. The company's hundreds of business units operated as independent profit centers. Employees sometimes complained that headquarters staff showed far more interest in the amount of profits produced than in the means used to generate the profits.

But Waste Management's growth slowed during the early 1990s. After acquiring more than 1,500 waste disposal companies in the last 30 years, there were few available for continued expansion. It had overpaid for recent overseas acquisitions and was struggling to earn an adequate return. Recycling and chemical waste disposal profits slumped due to higher than expected operating costs. The stock price fell from $46 in 1992 to $23 in late 1993. Pressure to produce higher profits grew more intense than ever.

Revolving CEOs

Nell Minow was an odd mixture of corporate raider, turnaround specialist, shareholder advocate, and corporate governance reformer. Her investment company, LENS, Inc., sought the worst-run companies in America. After acquiring a stake in a troubled company, Minow and her partner Bob Monks used negative reports in the press to shame the company's board into replacing top management. Nine of the first 10 companies LENS targeted, including American Express, Kodak, and Westinghouse, replaced their CEOs. In 1995, Minow took aim at Waste Management.

Waste Management was a classic example of entrenched management. By hand-picking Waste Management's board of directors, Buntrock had been able to maintain near absolute control over the company as it evolved from a small, family-owned enterprise to a huge, publicly traded corporation. Minow wanted Buntrock replaced. She gained a powerful ally in 1996 when financier George Soros purchased 6 percent of WMX's outstanding stock for $1 billion.

Buntrock retired as CEO in June 1996, temporarily retaining his position as chairman of the board. Phillip Rooney, WMX's long-time chief operating officer, succeeded Buntrock. Rooney spent the next six months working on a restructuring plan to improve Waste Management's profits. Although the plan called for 3,000 job cuts, Minow dismissed it as "cosmetic and disappointing."[2] She wanted WMX to restructure its board and sell more of its money-losing operations. Rooney resigned in February 1997 under pressure from Minow and Soros.

Buntrock came out of retirement to serve as interim CEO following Rooney's resignation. In March, Minow and Soros recruited Robert S. "Steve" Miller to serve on WMX's board of directors. Miller was a former vice-chairman of Chrysler Corporation and a veteran of corporate turnarounds at Federal Mogul and Morrison Knudsen. He led the effort to restructure WMX's board and find a permanent successor to Buntrock.

Ronald T. LeMay left his job as president of Sprint Corporation to become WMX's new CEO in July 1997. Some observers questioned the wisdom of hiring a CEO with no experience in the waste disposal business, but Miller specifically wanted an outsider over whom Buntrock would have little influence.

LeMay shocked Miller, Minow, and Soros by resigning on October 30 after only three months on the job. His terse press release stated merely that Waste Management's needs presented different challenges than he had expected when he took the job. The simultaneous resignations of John D. Sanford and James E. Koenig, WMX's current and former chief financial officers, fueled speculation that LeMay had discovered accounting problems he did not want to deal with.

After LeMay's abrupt departure, Miller became WMX's fourth CEO of 1997. Miller made it clear that he was serving only on an interim basis and that his top priority would be recruiting a permanent CEO. One of the candidates Miller spoke to about the WMX position was Sunbeam's Al Dunlap. Dunlap showed little interest in the job, however, calling Miller an "arrogant professional director playing at being an executive."[3]

Miller never succeeded in recruiting a new CEO. One of the outside directors Miller brought to WMX's board was former SEC chairman Roderick (Rod) Hills. Hills and other members of WMX's audit committee, aided by auditors from Ernst & Young, undertook a thorough investigation of the company's accounting practices. On February 25, 1998, Waste Management announced $3.54 billion of special charges and restated earnings all the way back to 1992. After the stunning announcement, Miller, Minow, and Soros decided it made more sense to sell Waste Management than to try to fix all its problems. They announced an agreement on March 11 to sell Waste Management to rival USA Waste Services.

Waste Management's Accounting

Waste Management's aggressive accounting practices were a poorly kept secret. Abraham Briloff wrote an article for *Barron's* in 1990 challenging the company's purchase accounting.[4] Waste Management allocated $566 million of the $732 million spent on acquisitions during the previous three years to goodwill. Briloff questioned the propriety of amortizing goodwill over 40 years in an industry characterized by rapid technological and regulatory change. Briloff also exposed Waste Management's use of a $70 million one-time gain in 1989 to offset operating expenses. *Business Week* published an article two years later describing how Waste Management boosted its 1991 earnings more than $50 million through one-time gains on securities transactions by three subsidiaries.[5]

Unfortunately, these articles only scratched the surface of Waste Management's accounting problems. From 1993 to 1996, Waste Management fraudulently overstated its pretax earnings by $1.4 billion. The fraud consisted primarily of delaying recognition of current operating expenses until future periods. Specifically, Waste Management understated its depreciation expenses, improperly capitalized interest, delayed recognizing asset impairments, and manipulated environmental cleanup reserves.

Waste disposal is a capital-intensive industry. Garbage trucks cost about $150,000 apiece. Standard industry practice was to depreciate trucks over eight to 10 years with no salvage value. During the early 1990s, Waste Management began depreciating its trucks over 12 years and claiming a $25,000 salvage value. With nearly 20,000 vehicles in its fleet, the reduction in depreciation expense was significant. Waste Management cut expenses further by depreciating its 1.5 million steel dumpsters over 15 to 20 years compared to the industry standard of 12 years.

Waste Management's 137 landfills contained nearly as many GAAP violations as discarded tires. The company exaggerated the capacity of many landfills so it could stretch out the amortization period of upfront costs such as construction, legal fees, inspections, and permits. It continued capitalizing interest on certain development projects past the time when the landfills were ready for use. Rarely did Waste Management record impairment charges for nonproductive assets such as hazardous waste sites and idle recycling facilities.

Waste Management also inflated earnings through its accounting for acquisitions. Waste Management made very generous estimates of acquired companies' future environmental cleanup costs. Under the purchase method of accounting, higher remediation reserves in the liability section of the balance sheet were offset by higher amounts of purchased goodwill in the asset section. The goodwill was amortized over 40 years, while current operating costs were recorded not as expenses, but as reductions of the inflated liabilities.

Waste Management's record-breaking $1.4 billion earnings restatement included corrections to depreciation expense of $509 million; capitalized interest, $192 million; environmental liabilities, $173 million; remediation reserves, $128 million; asset impairment losses, $214 million; and other mistakes, $216 million.[6]

Partners in Crime

Very few of Waste Management's accounting manipulations were unknown to the company's auditors. The Arthur Andersen audit team recognized as early as 1988 that Waste Management routinely made fourth-quarter adjustments to reduce vehicle and container depreciation cumulatively from the beginning of the year. The auditors also discovered and documented Waste Management's non-GAAP method of capitalizing interest on landfill development, its inflation of acquired environmental remediation liabilities, and its practice of improperly charging current operating expenses to the environmental reserves.

The planning documents for the 1993 audit identified Waste Management as a "high risk client" due to its practice of "actively managing reported results," its "history of making significant fourth quarter adjustments," and the fact that it operated in an industry requiring "highly judgmental accounting estimates or measurements."[7]

The auditors subsequently identified $128 million of current and prior period misstatements in Waste Management's 1993 financial statements. But Buntrock and his financial officers refused to record the proposed adjustments, which would have reduced Waste Management's net income before special items by 12 percent. Engagement partner Robert E. Allgyer consulted Andersen's Chicago office Practice Director and the Audit Division Head before issuing the audit report. The Andersen partners concluded that because many of the misstatements originated in prior years, the impact on Waste Management's 1993 income statement was not material.

Allgyer informed Waste Management in early February 1994 that he would issue a clean audit report if Waste Management would agree to change its non-GAAP accounting policies in the future and begin reducing the amount of its cumulative misstatements. Allgyer drafted a list of "Action Steps" to eventually bring Waste Management's financial statements into compliance with GAAP. The list required Waste Management to change its accounting for depreciation, capitalized interest, and environmental cleanup reserves. The document also required Waste Management to write down its overstated assets over the next five to seven years. Buntrock agreed to the Action Steps, as did Waste Management's chief financial officer and chief accounting officer, who signed the document signifying their promise to comply.

But when the auditors returned the next year, they learned that Waste Management had complied with few, if any, of the Action Steps. The auditors identified current and prior period misstatements in Waste Management's 1994 financial statements totaling $163 million—11.7 percent of pretax income. Allgyer met again with Andersen's Chicago office Practice Director and Audit Division Head to discuss his findings. Although the partners expressed disappointment that Waste Management had not yet corrected its cumulative errors, they authorized Allgyer to issue another clean audit opinion.

During 1995, Waste Management recognized a $160 million gain when it exchanged its interest in a privately held subsidiary of ServiceMaster for stock in ServiceMaster itself. Waste Management took this opportunity to write down some of its impaired assets and accrue necessary liabilities. On its income statement, Waste Management netted $160 million of unrelated operating expenses and prior period adjustments against the one-time gain under the caption "Sundry Income." No disclosure was made regarding the amount of the ServiceMaster gain or the items offset against it.

Because of the $160 million of adjustments recorded during 1995, the auditors identified only $67 million of cumulative misstatements remaining in the 1995 financial statements. Allgyer deemed these misstatements immaterial. He issued another unqualified opinion, although he later wrote a private memorandum criticizing Waste Management for using "other gains to bury charges for balance sheet clean ups."[8]

During 1996, auditors discovered and documented what became known as the "Second Quarter Sweep." After Waste Management's field offices had closed their books, senior management directed the field controllers to reexamine their accrued liabilities and asset valuation reserves to identify amounts that could be reversed into income. Waste Management ultimately increased its second-quarter earnings from $.41 to $.45 per share, enabling it to meet analysts' expectations.

The auditors by this time had given up monitoring Waste Management's (non)compliance with the previously agreed upon Action Steps. Allgyer's team identified cumulative misstatements in 1996 totaling $105 million—7.2 percent of Waste Management's pretax income. In addition, Waste Management offset 1996 operating expenses and prior period adjustments against a portion of the gains realized from the sale of two discontinued operations. In spite of these ongoing problems, Allgyer issued an unqualified opinion on Waste Management's 1996 financial statements.

Taking out the Garbage

Waste Management's $3.5 billion adjustment in February 1998 prompted an SEC investigation of the company's accounting and

Arthur Andersen's audits. Because at least six partners, including supervising partners from Andersen's headquarters, approved the audit reports, the SEC took the rare step of charging the entire firm with fraud.[9] This marked the first time since 1985 that the SEC had charged a major public accounting firm with fraud. The SEC censured Arthur Andersen and fined the firm $7 million for countenancing Waste Management's repeated accounting violations. In addition, four Andersen partners were fined and/or barred from auditing public companies.

The SEC pointed out that the auditors had documented in their workpapers most of the errors in Waste Management's accounting procedures. The SEC criticized the auditors for failing to estimate the extent of the misstatements caused by Waste Management's improper accounting methods and for abusing the concept of "materiality" to allow known misstatements to pass. The Commission also condemned the auditors' decision to tolerate current-period accounting misstatements in return for promises from Waste Management to correct the misstatements in the future. The SEC staff described the Action Steps drafted by Allgyer after the 1993 audit as "an agreement between [Waste Management] and its auditor to cover up past frauds by committing additional frauds in the future."[10] In a severe warning to auditors not to repeat Andersen's behavior, the SEC said:

> Unless the auditor stands up to management as soon as it knows that management is unwilling to correct material misstatements, the auditor ultimately will find itself in an untenable position: it either must continue issuing unqualified audit reports on materially misstated financial statements and hope that its conduct will not be discovered or it must force a restatement or qualify its report and thereby subject itself to the liability that likely will result from the exposure of its role in the prior issuance of the materially misstated financial statements.[11]

Andersen did indeed face liability for blessing Waste Management's false financial statements. Nell Minow told a reporter from *Business Week*, "Andersen owes the shareholders some money. They are there to prevent exactly this kind of surprise...."[12] The accounting firm eventually paid $75 million to compensate investors who purchased WMX stock between November 1994 and February 1998. Waste Management contributed an additional $145 million to the investors' compensation fund.

The SEC filed civil charges against Dean Buntrock, Phillip Rooney, and four other Waste Management officers, seeking monetary damages and to bar them from serving as officers or directors of public companies. The complaint described Buntrock as "the driving force" behind the fraud, claiming he set earnings targets and directed his financial staff to use "top-level adjustments" to conform the reported results to the predetermined goals.[13] Buntrock and the other defendants received performance-based bonuses tied to Waste Management's earnings. Buntrock, who owned more than 3 million shares of WMX stock, was also motivated to avoid declines in the company's share price.

Buntrock filed a countersuit against the SEC, claiming that certain top officials were biased because they had been paid by Waste Management's audit committee. SEC chief accountant Robert Herdman, a former Ernst & Young partner, had headed his firm's investigation of Waste Management before joining the SEC. Similarly, SEC chief enforcement accountant Charles Niemeier had performed services for Waste Management's audit committee while in private practice. Buntrock also alleged that the $3.5 billion writeoff authorized by interim CEO Miller was unnecessary and was part of a scheme to enrich Miller and his associates. According to Buntrock, Miller announced the "big bath" to drive down the stock price, issued options to himself and others at the new lower price, and three weeks later announced the merger with USA Waste Services.

Former vice-president of finance Bruce Tobecksen settled the SEC's charges on September 30, 2004. Without admitting or denying the allegations regarding his role in the alleged fraud, Tobecksen refunded $400,000 of performance-based compensation plus nearly $300,000 of prejudgment interest thereon and paid a $120,000 fine. The SEC's charges against the other defendants and Buntrock's countersuit are still outstanding.

24 Sunbeam

> I'm a superstar in my field, much like Michael Jordan in basketball and Bruce Springsteen in rock 'n' roll.
>
> ("Chainsaw Al" Dunlap[1])

Al Dunlap was certainly paid like a superstar. He came away with $100 million after 20 months of work at Scott Paper Company. Critics accused Dunlap of enriching himself at the expense of thousands of laid-off employees. But Dunlap proudly pointed out that he had increased Scott's shareholder value from $2.5 billion to $9 billion. "My $100 million was less than 2 percent of the wealth I created for all Scott shareholders," Dunlap wrote. "Did I earn that? Damn right I did."[2]

Dunlap specialized in turning around troubled companies. Before restructuring Scott Paper, he helped turn around at least six other companies, including Sterling Pulp & Paper, American Can, Lily-Tulip, Crown-Zellerbach, and Consolidated Press Holdings. Dunlap earned the nickname "Chainsaw Al" by slashing costs at each of these companies. He laid off tens of thousands of employees during his 30-year career, including 11,200 at Scott Paper alone. Dunlap never apologized for the layoffs, claiming he worked in situations where it was necessary to cut 35 percent of the jobs in order to save the other 65 percent. He blamed the layoffs on previous managers who created the problems he was called in to fix.

Sunbeam Corporation's board hired Dunlap in July 1996, hoping he could revive the struggling home appliance maker. Their decision was rewarded immediately as Sunbeam's stock jumped from $12.50 to $18.63 on the day Dunlap's hiring was announced. The stock eventually reached a high of $53 in March 1998. But three months later, in June 1998, Sunbeam's board fired their superstar CEO for withholding important information about the company's deteriorating condition. Dunlap learned firsthand what it felt like to be laid off.

Chainsaw Al

Lieutenant Albert J. Dunlap graduated from the U.S. Military Academy at West Point in 1960. He was the first member of his family to attend college and the first resident of Hasbrouck Heights, New Jersey admitted into the prestigious Academy. At West Point, Dunlap displayed more tenacity than brilliance. He graduated 537th in a class of 550, but boasted of surviving a rigorous program that four of every 10 entering cadets failed to complete. Dunlap called West Point the best business school in the world because it taught him how to lead, think, and handle adversity.

Dunlap made a career out of doing the dirty work most CEOs dreaded. Thirty years of closing factories and cutting payroll made him one of the most hated business executives in the country. It was probably prudent that he lived in a highly secure gated community, owned a bullet-proof vest, and was accompanied at all times by an armed bodyguard.

Newspapers and business magazines regularly criticized Dunlap's heavyhanded management style. Government officials ranging from small-town mayors to Labor Secretary Robert Reich complained about his layoffs. Dunlap accepted criticism as the price of success. He wrote in his autobiography: "You're not in business to be liked. Neither am I. We're here to succeed. If you want a friend, get a dog. I'm not taking any chances; I've got two dogs."[3]

Dunlap was devoted to his two German shepherds. When he relocated to Philadelphia to oversee Scott Paper's restructuring, Dunlap rented a separate suite for the dogs at the posh Four Seasons hotel. His will designated $2 million for their care. But although Dunlap loved dogs, he identified even more closely with fiercer predators. His home and office were decorated with pictures and sculptures of lions, eagles, alligators and sharks.

Although Dunlap was best known as "Chainsaw Al," he had several other nicknames. His enemies called him "the Shredder" for the way he dismantled Scott Paper Company. One of his best friends, Sir James Goldsmith, dubbed him "Rambo in Pinstripes." Dunlap embraced his various monikers. He even posed for a publicity photograph with a black bandanna tied around his head, two ammunition bandoleers draped across his shoulders, and an Uzzi-style machine pistol clutched in each hand.

While Dunlap's corporate restructurings generated billions of dollars of returns for investors, he apparently didn't trust other CEOs to do the same for him. Dunlap kept most of his $200+ million fortune invested in government Treasury bonds, calling the stock market a "fool's game."[4]

Sunbeam

Sunbeam was one of the most widely recognized brand names in America during the second half of the twentieth century. Few households lacked a Sunbeam toaster, iron or mixer. Oster Company, acquired by Sunbeam in 1960, produced blenders, barber's clippers and electric blankets.

Unfortunately for Sunbeam, it got caught up in the merger wave of the early 1980s and was acquired in 1981 by conglomerate Allegheny International. For the next seven years, Allegheny sucked nearly all the profits out of Sunbeam, leaving little for product development or factory renovation.

Investment fund managers Michael F. Price and Michael H. Steinhardt gained control of Sunbeam after Allegheny filed for bankruptcy protection following the stock market collapse of October 1987. Price and Steinhardt sold 24 percent of Sunbeam's shares through an initial public offering in 1992, keeping the remaining shares for themselves and maintaining control over the company's board of directors.

Paul Kazarian was the first CEO hired by Price and Steinhardt to run Sunbeam. Under Kazarian's leadership, Sunbeam reported $120 million of profits during 1992. Kazarian was fired early the next year, however, when Sunbeam's senior managers rebelled against his "eccentric" management style. Roger Schipke replaced Kazarian in 1993, but couldn't maintain the company's forward progress. Sunbeam's blenders, mixers, toasters, gas grills, and outdoor furniture all lost market share from 1993 to 1995.

Price and Steinhardt hired Al Dunlap in July 1996. Dunlap's compensation package—$1 million annual salary, $2.5 million of stock options, and $12.2 million of restricted stock—reflected both Dunlap's reputation as a turnaround artist and the magnitude of what he was expected to accomplish at Sunbeam. Amazingly, Price and Steinhardt recovered their investment in only one day. Although Chainsaw Al was feared by employees and despised by managers, he was revered on Wall Street. The 49 percent increase in Sunbeam's stock price on the day Dunlap's hiring was announced was the largest one-day increase in the NYSE's history.

Four months later, on November 12, Dunlap outlined to Sunbeam's board his plans to restructure the company. Dunlap proposed closing 18 of 26 factories and shedding 6,000 of Sunbeam's 12,000 employees. The downsizing, he said, would reduce company costs by $225 million per year. At the same time, he announced plans to double the company's sales revenue within three years by introducing new products and expanding exports.

Dunlap's plan appeared to work. First and second-quarter sales during 1997 were 13 percent above the prior year. Dunlap attributed the company's improved operating margins to his cost-cutting initiatives. Third-quarter sales of $289 million were 25 percent higher than 1996. Sunbeam's stock increased steadily as the company met or exceeded analysts' earnings forecasts each quarter. The share price reached $47 following the announcement of the blockbuster third quarter.

Sunbeam's Collapse

By late 1997, Dunlap was ready to sell Sunbeam. He had promised his management team that Sunbeam was a 12- to 18-month project—discontinue the unprofitable products, close the inefficient factories, cut the unnecessary costs, and then sell the company to somebody who would run it for the long term. Sunbeam's investment bankers approached numerous companies, including Gillette, Black & Decker, Rubbermaid, Maytag, and Whirlpool. If Sunbeam's stock price had merely risen from $12.50 into the low $30s, Dunlap probably could have sold the company and walked away with $100 million from his stock options. But with the stock trading near $50 per share, no other company was interested in acquiring Sunbeam. Dunlap was stuck operating a company he had intended only to restructure.

When Sunbeam's investment bankers failed to find a buyer, they suggested that Dunlap instead use his company's inflated stock to acquire other companies. Sunbeam announced on March 2, 1998 that it had reached agreements to acquire three companies: Coleman Company, maker of camping and recreation equipment; First Alert, maker of smoke alarms; and Signature Brands USA, maker of "Mr. Coffee" brand coffee machines. The three companies' combined annual revenues of $1.5 billion more than doubled Sunbeam's size. Sunbeam's stock reached an all-time high of $53 per share two days after the acquisitions were announced.

Dunlap planned to issue $700 million of zero-coupon bonds to help pay for the acquisitions. While the underwriters were performing their due diligence work for the bond offering, they discovered that Sunbeam's first-quarter 1998 sales were coming in significantly below forecasted amounts. The underwriters insisted that Sunbeam disclose its lower-than-expected sales before issuing the bonds.

On March 19, against Dunlap's strong objections, Sunbeam issued a press release announcing that its first-quarter sales would probably fall short of Wall Street analysts' projections of $285 million to $295 million. The press release went on to say that sales were still expected to exceed 1997 sales of $253 million. Sunbeam's stock dropped 9 percent to $45 following the announcement.

But the March 19 press release did not come close to revealing the actual extent of Sunbeam's problems. In fact, Sunbeam's first-quarter sales were only $169 million as of March 17. There was no reasonable basis for expecting that Sunbeam's first-quarter revenues would match those of the previous year. On April 3, two days after its loan was funded and one day after the First Alert and Signature Brands acquisitions were completed, Sunbeam issued a new press release announcing that it would report a loss for the first quarter. The stock price plummeted 24 percent to $34 following the announcement.

Sunbeam released its first-quarter financial statements on May 11. The statements showed a net loss of $44.6 million on sales of $244 million. At a press conference attended by stock analysts and news reporters, Dunlap tried to divert attention from the first-quarter loss by emphasizing the "good" news that he planned to close eight recently acquired factories and lay off 6,400 Coleman, First Alert, and Signature Brands employees. In spite of this rather unique public relations ploy, Sunbeam's stock slid to $26 per share.

The fatal blow to Dunlap's reputation and Sunbeam's stock price was delivered by *Barron's* magazine on June 8.[5] Jonathan P. Laing's article "Dangerous Games: Did 'Chainsaw Al' Dunlap Manufacture Sunbeam's Earnings Last Year?" accused Sunbeam of overstating its 1997 revenues and understating its expenses. Sunbeam's stock price dropped below $21 the day after the article appeared.

Sunbeam's board held an emergency meeting on Tuesday, June 10 to discuss the *Barron's* article. Dunlap and his two top accounting officers denied Laing's allegations. Phillip Harlow, the Arthur Andersen partner in charge of Sunbeam's audit, reiterated his belief that Sunbeam's 1997 financial statements were fairly presented.

Near the end of the meeting, one of the directors asked, almost as an aside, how Sunbeam's second quarter was progressing. Without answering the question, Dunlap exploded into one of his trademark tirades. He berated the board members for their skepticism and threatened to quit unless they gave him their unconditional support. Afraid of losing their superstar CEO, the directors did what they could to placate Dunlap and adjourned the meeting.

Early the next morning, Sunbeam's general counsel David Fannin called one of the board members and revealed what Dunlap had withheld the previous afternoon. Sunbeam was facing a $100 million revenue shortfall for the second quarter and was in danger of violating important loan covenants. The directors spent most of the next two days on the telephone with Sunbeam employees, learning what they could about the company's sad condition. By the end of the week, Chainsaw had been axed.

Sunbeam's Accounting

The answer to Jonathan Laing's question in *Barron's* was a resounding "Yes." Sunbeam had indeed used a variety of accounting tricks to inflate its 1997 revenues and profits. When Sunbeam eventually revised its financial statements, it restated 1997 net income to $38.3 million from the $109.4 million originally reported.

Al Dunlap's first official act as CEO of Sunbeam had been to hire Donald Kersh as the company's chief financial officer. Kersh possessed two characteristics that made him invaluable to Dunlap. First, he was loyal. Kersh had followed Dunlap to four companies since 1983. He was one of the few people on earth who could stand working with Dunlap for more than a few months. Second, he was a creative accountant. As each quarter ended, Dunlap instructed Kersh to use the contents of his "ditty bag" to make sure Sunbeam met the analysts' forecasts.[6] Kersh, himself, joked of being Sunbeam's "biggest profit center."[7]

Kersh began filling his "ditty bag" during the fourth quarter of 1996 when Sunbeam recorded $338 million of restructuring charges to cover the costs of Dunlap's reorganization plan. The SEC later determined that Sunbeam padded the charges with at least $35 million of prematurely recognized expenses, excessive writedowns, and improper reserves. Sunbeam expensed in 1996 more than $18 million of advertising, consulting, and product redesign costs that should have been recognized during 1997. Kersh also wrote off $2.1 million of good inventory along with the obsolete and discontinued products. Sales of these items at normal prices during 1997 artificially boosted Sunbeam's profit margins. Finally, Kersh set up a $12 million reserve for a lawsuit regarding a hazardous waste site. Sunbeam recorded $9 million of income during the fourth quarter of 1997 after settling the lawsuit for $3 million.

As early as the first quarter of 1997, Sunbeam began engaging in "channel stuffing." That is, the company offered customers discounts and other incentives to place orders earlier than they would otherwise have done so. Sales soared during early 1997, creating the impression of a quick turnaround. Yet Sunbeam's early "success" made it that much more difficult for the company to meet subsequent sales targets. As 1997 progressed, Sunbeam had to offer increasingly generous terms to get customers to place more orders.

Sunbeam soon began recording revenue for bill-and-hold transactions. Sunbeam persuaded customers to place orders early for goods they would not need until several months in the future. For example, Sunbeam reported revenue in November 1997 for summer products such as barbecue grills and outdoor furniture that customers would not need until the following spring. Sunbeam continued to hold the goods so customers' warehouses would not be burdened with out-of-season merchandise. The customers often retained the right, through explicit agreement or winks and nods, to cancel their orders prior to delivery. In spite of these unusual terms, Sunbeam recognized revenue when the orders were received.

As the end of the year approached, Sunbeam resorted to even more aggressive sales tactics. The company established a "distributor program" in December that offered discounts, extended payment terms, and return rights to customers willing to accept delivery before year-end. Sunbeam recorded $24.7 million of revenue during the fourth quarter for items customers had the right to return in the future. In fact, significant amounts of the inventory "sold" during the fourth quarter were returned to Sunbeam during 1998.

By the first quarter of 1998, it had become almost impossible for Sunbeam to sell anything. Wal-Mart's warehouses were loaded with a 20-week supply of mixers and a 31-week supply of bread makers. K-Mart was holding more mixers, bread makers, and rotisseries than it normally sold in an entire year. In one last effort to meet its sales targets, Sunbeam changed its quarter-end from March 29 to March 31. The Coleman acquisition was completed on March 30. The change in reporting period allowed Sunbeam to record an additional $5 million in net sales of Sunbeam products and almost $15 million of net sales from Coleman, a suspiciously high amount for the last two days of a quarter.

Sunbeam's Auditors

Phillip E. Harlow was the engagement partner in charge of Sunbeam's audits from 1994 through 1998. In May 2001, the SEC filed a civil injunction alleging that Harlow's unqualified audit opinions on Sunbeam's 1996 and 1997 financial statements were false and misleading.[8] Contrary to the audit reports signed by Harlow, Sunbeam's financial statements were not fairly stated and Arthur Andersen's audits had not been performed in accordance with professional auditing standards.

The SEC accused Harlow of failing to exercise appropriate skepticism while conducting Sunbeam's audits. Specifically, the SEC staff criticized Harlow for not challenging Sunbeam's $12 million environmental litigation reserve during the fourth quarter of 1996. Harlow did not independently verify the amount, but relied almost exclusively on Sunbeam's general counsel's opinion that the reserve was appropriate. Harlow also failed to critically examine the purpose of Sunbeam's 1997 bill-and-hold transactions. An impartial observer would have concluded that the deals were driven by Sunbeam's desire to meet analysts' quarterly sales and earnings forecasts rather than by any legitimate business purpose.

Even more damning, the SEC found evidence that Harlow had knowingly permitted Sunbeam to misreport several transactions. The auditors had correctly identified $18 million of costs that should not have been included among Sunbeam's December 1996 restructuring charges. Harlow proposed several journal entries to bring Sunbeam's books into compliance with GAAP. But when Dunlap and Kersh refused to record the adjustments, Harlow went ahead and issued a clean audit opinion on the 1996 statements after concluding that the $18 million of uncorrected errors were immaterial in relation to Sunbeam's overall financial condition.

Harlow discovered, but permitted, more accounting shenanigans in 1997. In probably the most bizarre transaction Sunbeam attempted, Kersh recorded $11 million of revenue and $8 million of profit on the "sale" of spare parts to the contractor Sunbeam used to handle its warranty claims. Except the contractor never actually agreed to purchase the parts and certainly not for $11 million. The contractor had merely signed an "agreement to agree" to buy the parts at a price to be determined. When Harlow concluded that no gain should be reported on this apparently sham transaction, Kersh reduced the profit by $3 million. Rather than insisting that the entire transaction be erased from Sunbeam's books, Harlow concluded that the remaining profit was immaterial and allowed it to remain. Harlow also proposed, but ultimately passed, a $2.9 million entry to correct overvalued Mexican inventory and $563,000 of other miscellaneous adjustments. Approximately 16 percent of Sunbeam's reported 1997 income came from items Harlow had proposed as adjustments in 1996 or 1997, but which had not been corrected.

Harlow and his firm paid dearly for allowing Sunbeam to have its way with its accounting. Arthur Andersen paid $110 million to settle a lawsuit filed by Sunbeam's investors. Harlow was suspended from appearing or practicing before the SEC as an accountant.

Burnt Toast

Throughout the SEC's investigation of Sunbeam and the company's restatement of its 1996, 1997, and 1998 earnings, Dunlap insisted that he was not responsible for the company's accounting problems. Dunlap defended the propriety of the bill-and-hold transactions, claiming they were done to smooth out sales of seasonal products. According to Dunlap, "There was a clear transfer of title, risk of loss, etc., to the customer, the inventory was properly segregated, and all revenue recognition criteria under GAAP were met."[9] As to the other accounting issues, Dunlap said he relied on advice from his accounting staff, the three outside directors on his audit committee, and Arthur Andersen. Dunlap denies ever directing his employees to do anything improper.

While no Sunbeam employees have publicly accused Dunlap of ordering or even approving improper accounting, several have described a hostile work environment in which employees were under intense pressure to "make the numbers."[10] Quarterly sales and earnings goals were nonnegotiable. Failure was not tolerated. Sunbeam's director of international sales recalled a meeting at which top executives were given earnings targets and told, "Your life depends on hitting that number!"[11]

Employee stock options created another powerful incentive for Sunbeam's aggressive accounting. Dunlap's crew of roving turnaround specialists had little affection for Sunbeam. They had even less fondness for Dunlap, due to his abusive personality and habit of humiliating employees. Sunbeam's top managers worked at the company and tolerated Dunlap's abuse only because they thought they could make a lot of money quickly. All the senior managers knew that if Sunbeam failed to meet the analysts' forecasts, their work and suffering would be for naught.

The SEC charged Dunlap, Kersh, and four other Sunbeam executives with conspiring to fraudulently misrepresent the company's operations.[12] No criminal charges were filed, however, and Dunlap and Kersh were permitted to settle the civil charges without admitting or denying guilt. Each was permanently barred from serving as an officer or director of a public company. Dunlap paid a $500,000 fine, while Kersh paid $200,000. Dunlap's only real punishment, other than the damage to his reputation, came through private litigation. He paid $15 million in January 2002 to settle a class action suit filed by Sunbeam shareholders.

25 End of the Millennium

> One last word on auditor independence. During our rulemaking, many argued the problem was only in our minds, as we couldn't cite examples of audit failures where the auditors had also provided significant consulting or other non-audit services. We put this notion to rest last week when we sued Arthur Andersen for having issued false and misleading audit reports in the Waste Management debacle.
>
> (SEC Commissioner Laura S. Unger,[1] June 25, 2001)

Arthur Andersen's home office in Chicago was less than 10 miles from Waste Management's Oak Brook, Illinois headquarters. And the two firms shared more than a telephone area code. Fourteen former Andersen auditors worked at Waste Management during the 1990s, often in key financial and accounting positions. Every Waste Management chief financial officer and chief accounting officer from 1971 to 1997 was an Andersen alumnus.

Andersen partner Robert E. Allgyer took over the Waste Management audit in 1991. Shortly after Allgyer's appointment, Waste Management froze Andersen's audit fees at their 1990 level while allowing Andersen to earn additional revenues for "special work." During the next six years, Andersen collected $7.5 million in audit fees and $11.8 million for other services. Allgyer, who also served as the marketing director of Andersen's Chicago office, was compensated, in part, based on his firm's total billings to Waste Management.

Andersen auditors identified hundreds of millions of dollars of misstatements in Waste Management's 1993 through 1996 financial statements without insisting that the misstatements be corrected. SEC commissioner Laura Unger inferred that Andersen's willingness to condone Waste Management's flawed accounting might have been related to Waste Management's payment of high nonaudit fees and employment of Andersen alumni. She cited Andersen's flawed audits of Waste Management as justification for stricter auditor independence requirements.

8,064 Violations

The Sunbeam and Waste Management audits demonstrated to the SEC how tolerant auditors had become of their clients' aggressive accounting. But it was an even more blatant scandal that triggered the most extensive revision of SEC independence requirements in 70 years.

In the winter of 1997, an anonymous letter to the SEC prompted an investigation that uncovered 8,064 independence violations by PricewaterhouseCoopers partners and employees. More than half of the firm's 2,700 U.S. partners—including six of the 11 partners responsible for the firm's independence policies—owned investments in the firm's audit clients. Even chairman James Schiro, a member of the Independence Standards Board, was guilty of a minor violation involving $1,600 of an audit client's stock.

PwC spokesmen protested that many of the 8,000 violations were technical in nature, such as one partner who was cited because each of his children owned a single share of Walt Disney Company stock framed and hanging in their bedrooms. But nearly 40 percent of the violations were direct employee investments in clients. Investigators identified 140 instances of partners and managers owning stock issued by companies they helped audit.

The PwC scandal, which was revealed to the public in January 2000, created a dilemma for the AICPA. The Institute had always claimed responsibility for disciplining its members. But what should the AICPA Professional Ethics Executive Committee do with more than 1,500 PwC auditors accused of violating professional standards?

AICPA president Barry Melancon opted to absolve the guilty parties by attacking the rules. The day after PwC disclosed its violations, Melancon issued a press release urging the SEC to soften its independence requirements. When *Business Week* (February 7, 2000) published an editorial citing PwC's noncompliance as evidence that auditors had abandoned their commitment to the public trust, Melancon responded with a letter to the editor saying that the proper conclusion to draw from PwC's 8,064 violations that the existing rules were unreasonable:

> CPAs play a critical role in protecting the public interest and in promoting the smooth functioning of our capital markets. Objectivity and independence are professional obligations we take seriously. However, the profession has the right to expect the rules to remain current and relevant. Many of the independence rules for auditors were created decades ago, before working spouses and ubiquitous 401(k) plans, for example. No one disagrees that auditors must remain independent from the companies they audit, but forcing partners' spouses to divest themselves of their pension plan because it includes investments in an audit client supervised by a partner

> they don't know 3,000 miles away defies common sense. It's time to write independence rules that make sense in today's world.[2]

PwC's pervasive noncompliance with SEC rules naturally sparked questions about whether similar problems existed at other accounting firms. SEC chief accountant Lynn Turner asked the AICPA's Public Oversight Board (POB) to oversee investigations at the other Big Five accounting firms. But in a move than enraged SEC chairman Arthur Levitt, the AICPA sent a letter to POB chairman Charles Bowsher stating that it would "not approve nor authorize payment for invoices submitted by the POB or its representatives that contain charges for the special reviews. . . ."[3] The AICPA, which funded the POB, flatly refused to investigate whether auditors at other accounting firms were investing in their clients' securities.

Chairman Levitt had harbored doubts about auditors' independence ever since his appointment by President Bill Clinton in 1993. Levitt frequently criticized accountants' performance of management advisory services for audit clients. After more than six years in office, and with the likely end of his term in sight, Levitt finally had the case he needed to build public support for substantive reform. PwC's complaints that its employees had been confused by the SEC's Byzantine independence rules earned more scorn than sympathy. And the AICPA's blatant refusal to enforce its own *Code of Conduct* cost it the moral high ground. Levitt decided to devote his last months in office to reforming the SEC's auditor independence requirements. With George W. Bush leading Al Gore in public opinion polls, it was now or never.

The SEC's Proposal to Modernize the Rules Governing Auditors' Independence

In June 2000, Levitt proposed the first major overhaul of SEC auditor independence requirements since 1983. The new rules were based on four principles for evaluating an auditor's independence. The SEC stated that an auditor is not independent when the auditor (1) has a mutual or conflicting interest with the audit client, (2) audits his or her own work, (3) functions as management or employee of the audit client, or (4) acts as an advocate for the audit client.[4]

The SEC conceded in its proposal that some of the rules that had tripped up PwC's employees were unnecessarily restrictive. The old SEC rules prohibited all partners, and their family members, from investing in any entity audited by the firm. When Price Waterhouse merged with Coopers & Lybrand in 1998, thousands of employees had been forced to divest themselves of stock in the other firm's audit clients. Few auditors worked directly on more than a handful of the combined firm's 3,000 public clients, yet many employees had incurred large tax liabilities from selling significant portions of their investment portfolios. Proposed rule 2-01(c)(1) prohibited direct investments in the firm's audit clients only by those participating in the client's audit and their immediate family members.

The proposal also loosened restrictions on accountants auditing organizations where their family members were employed. The old SEC rules, adopted before dual-career families were common, limited where auditors' spouses and other family members could work. Several spouses of Price Waterhouse and Coopers & Lybrand partners had been forced to quit their jobs in 1998 even though the spouses' jobs had nothing to do with accounting and the partners did not participate in the employers' audits. Proposed rule 2-01(c)(2) stated that an auditor's independence would be considered impaired only if a close relative was employed in an accounting or financial reporting oversight role.

Other proposed rule changes were not received so warmly by the AICPA and the Big Five accounting firms. The proposal identified ten nonaudit services that, if provided to an audit client, would impair an auditor's independence. Most of the identified services, such as bookkeeping and executive recruiting, were already precluded by SEC and AICPA rules. Many accountants objected strongly, however, to the proposed addition of internal audit outsourcing and information systems design and implementation to the list of prohibited services. These were two of the most profitable and fastest-growing services in the public accounting profession.

When Arthur Levitt met with the chairmen of Arthur Andersen, KPMG, and Deloitte & Touche to explain his proposal, they listened impassively, showing no willingness to negotiate. Levitt asked for a counterproposal, but they refused to even discuss limiting their consulting services to audit clients. Andersen chairman Bob Grafton warned Levitt at the end of the meeting, "Arthur, if you go ahead with this, it will be war."[5]

The AICPA unleashed its 14 paid lobbyists on Capital Hill and mailed thousands of sample letters for AICPA members to copy on to their own letterhead and send to their congressional representatives. Arthur Andersen, KPMG, and Deloitte & Touche employed their own lobbyists and conducted their own letter-writing campaigns. Total lobbying expenditures by the AICPA and the Big Five exceeded $12 million during 2000. But this was a small price to pay to protect their $10 billion consulting practices.

The lobbying efforts produced results. Forty-six members of Congress wrote to Levitt urging him to withdraw, amend, or delay the independence proposal. And Levitt learned that Senator Richard Shelby (R, Alabama) was preparing an "appropriations rider" that would bar the SEC from spending any of its funds to implement or enforce the proposed rules. Levitt implored Senate majority leader Trent Lott

(R, Mississippi) not to let Congress cut the SEC's funding. He informed Lott that numerous publications, including the *New York Times*, *Washington Post*, *Los Angeles Times*, and *Business Week*, had endorsed the proposal. "Well, Arthur," Lott replied, "I'm not familiar with what you're proposing to do, but if those liberal publications are in favor of it, then I'm against it."[6]

But Levitt was not without allies. Four former SEC chairmen endorsed the revised independence requirements. Several expert witnesses, including influential money manager John H. Biggs, Comptroller of the Currency John D. Hawke, Jr., and former Federal Reserve chairman Paul A. Volcker testified in favor of the proposal at the SEC's public hearings.

And there was dissension among the normally unified leaders of the Big Five. Although KPMG partner Robert Elliott vowed not to let the SEC "bomb the profession back into the Stone Age," Ernst & Young chairman Philip Laskawy endorsed the proposed ban on information systems design work and internal audit outsourcing.[7] Ernst & Young was in the process of selling its consulting division to Cap Gemini and had little to lose from the new restrictions. PricewaterhouseCoopers did not endorse Levitt's proposal, but with 8,064 recent independence violations on its record, the firm was in no position to publicly oppose regulatory reform.

The five SEC commissioners were scheduled to vote on the independence proposal at their November 15, 2000 meeting. The AICPA and several influential congressional committee chairmen urged delay, complaining that the SEC had not allowed sufficient time for public comment. In reality, Levitt's foes wanted the vote delayed until after the new President took office and appointed a new SEC chairman.

During the final 48 hours preceding the SEC's scheduled vote, Levitt reached a compromise with AICPA president Barry Melancon and the leaders of the major accounting firms. Levitt, wanting to avoid litigation and fearing retaliatory budget cuts, offered to allow accounting firms to continue performing information systems design work for their audit clients on the condition that companies disclose in their annual proxy statements the amounts paid to their accountants for consulting services, with information systems fees broken out separately. Levitt also proposed allowing accounting firms to perform up to 40 percent of their clients' internal auditing work.

Melancon and the Big Five chairmen were drawn to the negotiating table by the GOP's disappointing performance on November 7. Fearing that their congressional allies would not be able to block Levitt's original proposal and not knowing who would eventually win the presidency, the accounting industry leaders dropped their opposition to the diluted proposal. The SEC commissioners adopted the new auditor independence requirements on November 15.

Impact of the SEC's New Rules

When the first proxy statements containing the mandated fee disclosures appeared in 2001, even the SEC was shocked by the amounts some companies were paying their accountants for tax and consulting work. In 2000, the companies comprising the S&P 500 paid a total of $1.2 billion for audit work and $3.7 billion for nonaudit services. KPMG, for example, earned only $4 million performing Motorola, Inc.'s audit but collected $62 million for computer consulting and other services. General Motors paid Deloitte & Touche $17 million to perform its audit and $79 million for other services. Sprint Corporation paid Ernst & Young $2.5 million for auditing and another $64 million for consulting and other services. The size of some of the consulting contracts led Arthur Levitt to comment:

> I'm not suggesting that each of these audit firms has compromised its independence. But I have to wonder if any individual auditor, working on a $2.5 million audit contract, would have the guts to stand up to a CFO and question a dubious number in the books, thus possibly jeopardizing $64 million in business for the firm's consultants. The chances of that happening seem even smaller when you consider that many auditors are compensated partly on the basis of how much nonaudit business they sell.[8]

Several investor groups reacted to the fee disclosures by sponsoring shareholder resolutions demanding that corporations stop purchasing management advisory services from accountants. One such resolution at Walt Disney Company in 2002 received support from 42 percent of the company's shareholders. Although the Disney resolution failed to win a majority of votes cast, the shareholders' "higher than expected" support for the proposal prompted Disney's board to stop purchasing management advisory services from auditor PricewaterhouseCoopers. Ann Yerger, director of research at the Council of Institutional Investors, warned corporate executives that "Shareholders are sending a powerful and strong message that they believe the [auditing and nonauditing] functions should be separated."[9]

As shareholders and corporate governance watchdogs became increasingly outspoken about potential conflicts of interest between auditing and consulting, corporate directors began discouraging companies from hiring accountants to perform management advisory services. Board members were frequently named as defendants in lawsuits alleging accounting fraud. Many directors feared that lucrative consulting engagements awarded to accountants would be cited as evidence of lax oversight if the company's financial statements were ever called into question. The safest strategy, from the directors' standpoint, was to look elsewhere for consulting advice. Apple Computer, Sara Lee, Johnson & Johnson and several other prominent companies decided in 2002 to stop purchasing internal audit and information technology consulting services from their auditors.

The two-year period surrounding the SEC's revision of its independence requirements saw the breakup of most of the Big Five accounting firms. Ernst & Young sold its information technology division to French consulting firm Cap Gemini in May 2000 for $11.1 billion. KPMG's consulting division spun off into an independent, publicly traded company named Bearing Point. PricewaterhouseCoopers negotiated with Hewlett-Packard and considered an initial public offering before finally selling its technology services unit to IBM. Only Deloitte & Touche kept its consulting division and that wasn't entirely by choice. D&T planned to sell its consulting practice through an initial public offering in early 2002, but cancelled its plans due to insufficient interest in the stock offering.

Thus, Arthur Levitt succeeded in significantly reducing the consulting services performed by accounting firms for their audit clients. Many corporate boards adopted policies restricting the services purchased from accountants, and three of the four largest public accounting firms disposed of large portions of their consulting branches.

Materiality Guidance

Auditing standards require auditors to provide reasonable assurance that their clients' financial statements contain no "material" misstatements. The FASB, in Financial Accounting Concepts Statement No. 2, *Qualitative Characteristics of Accounting Information*, defined materiality as:

> the magnitude of an omission or misstatement of accounting information that, in light of surrounding circumstances, makes it probable that the judgment of a reasonable person relying on the information would have been changed or influenced by the omission or misstatement.

The primary problem with the FASB's definition of materiality was that it was difficult to apply in practice. Who could predict how a "reasonable person" might react to a particular accounting error? So auditors developed various rules-of thumb to help them evaluate whether misstatements were material enough to require adjustment. Some auditors deemed an error material if it exceeded 10 percent of earnings before taxes. Other auditors used 1 percent of the client's total revenue or total assets as their yardstick for determining materiality.

Some clients abused the concept of materiality by refusing to correct misstatements that fell short of the auditors' materiality threshold.

Negotiating audit adjustments became a routine part of the audit process. After the auditors presented their list of findings, the CEO and CFO bargained with the audit partner to determine the minimum adjustment needed before the partner would issue a clean opinion.

Auditors frequently approved financial statements containing millions of dollars of known, but "immaterial," errors. Andersen partner Phillip Harlow ignored $18 million of known misstatements in Sunbeam's 1996 financial statements. Robert Allgyer overlooked $128 million of errors in Waste Management's 1993 financial statements in return for Dean Buntrock's promise to correct the errors in the future. And Arthur Andersen was not the only accounting firm allowing its clients to issue "immaterially" false financial statements. W.R. Grace & Co. manipulated its 1991 through 1994 earnings by recording arbitrary liabilities in good years and reversing the accruals in lean years. Price Waterhouse auditors documented the manipulations in their audit workpapers, but issued clean audit reports after concluding that the effects on Grace's annual earnings were not material.[10]

Arthur Levitt addressed the issue of materiality in a September 1998 speech at New York University's Center of Law and Business.

> But some companies misuse the concept of materiality. They intentionally record errors within a defined percentage ceiling. Then they try to excuse the fib by arguing that the effect on the bottom line is too small to matter. If that's the case, why do they work so hard to create the errors? Maybe because the effect can matter, especially if it picks up that last penny of the consensus estimate.[11]

Eleven months later, the SEC issued Staff Accounting Bulletin (SAB) No. 99, *Materiality*. SAB No. 99 rejected a bright-line materiality cutoff based on some arbitrary percentage of a financial statement component. Instead, the SAB required auditors to consider both quantitative *and qualitative* characteristics of known misstatements. Quantitatively small misstatements might be considered material if they changed a loss into income, concealed an unlawful transaction, affected a company's compliance with loan covenants, converted an earnings decrease into an earnings increase, or enabled a company to just meet analysts' expectations. SAB No. 99 also forbid companies from knowingly recording misstatements of any size for the purpose of managing or smoothing reported earnings.

Conclusion

Surprisingly, the Sunbeam and Waste Management earnings restatements, announced within eight months of each other in 1998, had little effect on Arthur Andersen's reputation. The two scandals were almost lost among revelations of similar accounting failures at Phar-Mor (Coopers & Lybrand), Cendant (Ernst & Young), Rite-Aid (KPMG), W.R. Grace (Price Waterhouse), and Livent (Deloitte & Touche).

Nor did the two bungled audits lead to significant improvements in Andersen's auditing procedures. To the extent that Andersen leaders even acknowledged that errors had occurred during the Sunbeam and Waste Management audits, they dismissed the mistakes as aberrations, not indicative of pervasive flaws in the firm's culture or audit methodology.

But the failed Waste Management audit ultimately played a significant role in Andersen's downfall. Andersen promised in its consent decree to permanently refrain from future securities law violations. In effect, the SEC placed Andersen on probation with a warning that future audit failures would result in severe punishment. A year later, the Justice Department cited Andersen's fear of violating its probation as the firm's motive for shredding hundreds of pounds of Enron-related documents.

Part VII

From Profession to Regulated Industry

26 Professionalism

> The certified public accountant acknowledges a moral responsibility … to be as mindful of the interests of strangers who may rely on his opinion as of the interests of the client who pays his fee. This is at the same time a heavy burden and a proud distinction. It marks the certified public accountant as an individual of the highest integrity … a highly useful servant to society as a whole.
>
> (John L. Carey, 1946[1])

Sociologists define a profession as an occupation whose practitioners must master a specialized body of knowledge, satisfy formalized admission requirements, adhere to a code of ethics, and serve the public.

Public service distinguishes a profession from a business. Society grants professionals the exclusive right to perform certain services. Only licensed physicians may prescribe medication. Registered attorneys, alone, may practice law. Certified public accountants possess an exclusive franchise to sign audit reports. In return, society expects professionals to promote the public good. Physicians must heal the sick. Attorneys should promote justice. CPAs are expected to protect the public from erroneous or fraudulent financial information.

The founders of the American public accounting profession readily acknowledged their obligation to serve the public. Price Waterhouse chief George O. May explained the auditor's public responsibility as follows:

> The high-minded accountant who undertakes to practice in this field assumes high ethical obligations, and it is the assumption of such obligations that makes what might otherwise be a business, a profession. Of all the groups of professions which are closely allied with business, there is none in which the practitioner is under a greater ethical obligation to persons who are not his immediate clients.[2]

Accountants' responsibility to the public is recognized formally in Article II of the AICPA *Code of Professional Conduct*, which requires members to "accept the obligation to act in a way that will serve the public interest, honor the public trust, and demonstrate commitment to professionalism."

Serving Two Masters

Jesus of Nazareth warned his disciples: "No man can serve two masters. Either he will hate the one and love the other, or he will be devoted to the one and despise the other."[3] While professing an obligation to society, American public accountants have struggled for more than 100 years to balance their responsibility to serve the public with their need to please the corporate managers who pay their fees. Public opinion polls reveal that investors expect auditors to be corporate policemen—enforcing strict accounting standards and blowing the whistle on corporate wrongdoing. But the "watchdog" role places auditors in an adversarial relationship with the CEOs and CFOs who have traditionally had significant influence over the selection, retention, and compensation of corporate auditors. Corporate managers often prefer auditors who are "cooperative" and who provide the most valuable business advice.

For the first 70 years of the twentieth century, most auditors managed to earn a comfortable living while fulfilling their obligations to the public. The growth in the economy and the increase in the number of publicly traded companies ensured a steady increase in public accounting firms' revenues. AICPA prohibitions against advertising, direct solicitation and competitive bidding stifled competition between accounting firms, making it difficult for clients to switch auditors. Accounting firm partners, who were in most cases assured of tenure until they retired, could enforce proper accounting knowing that the client was unlikely to retaliate by firing the auditor and that the partner's position in his firm was reasonably secure even if he did lose the client.

But auditors' economic security began to erode during the 1970s. Under pressure from the Federal Trade Commission, the AICPA rescinded its restrictions on competitive bidding, advertising, and direct solicitation. Competitive bidding reduced audit fees and cut accounting firm profits. Audit partners faced increased pressure to retain clients and sell additional value-added services such as tax planning and management advisory services.

Some clients exploited the increased competition among accounting firms by engaging in "opinion shopping." That is, they asked prospective auditors during the selection interviews how they would require the client to account for certain transactions. Auditors who interpreted accounting standards strictly risked losing the engagement to auditors who permitted the client more leeway. When Arthur Young partner Larry Gray questioned ZZZZ Best's accounting practices, Barry

Minkow chided, "You know, Larry, I just know Coopers & Lybrand would love this account."[4]

Advertising

Early public accountants announced their services by distributing handbills and purchasing advertisements in city directories. But in 1922, the American Institute of Accountants banned most forms of self-promotion by public accounting firms. AICPA secretary John Carey commented on the ban in 1966:

> The general prohibition against advertising is accepted today without much question. To be sure, there is nothing illegal or immoral about advertising as such, but it is almost universally regarded as unprofessional.[5]

Other professional associations, such as those representing doctors, lawyers and optometrists, also banned advertising by their members. Although the restrictions had been in place for decades, the Federal Trade Commission (FTC) alleged during the 1970s that the rules against advertising were an illegal restraint of trade. With the aid of the Antitrust Division of the U.S. Department of Justice, the FTC pressured all the major professional associations to drop their bans on advertising. In 1978, AICPA members reluctantly amended Rule 502 of the *Code of Professional Conduct* to permit advertising that was not "false, misleading, or deceptive."

Few CPA firms were quick to launch major advertising campaigns. Accountants' complex services were difficult to explain in a one-page ad or a 30-second commercial. And it didn't seem efficient to try to reach accountants' very narrow target audience—corporate CEOs and CFOs—through the mass media.

But by the mid-1990s, the Big Five accounting firms were spending millions of dollars on advertising. PricewaterhouseCoopers launched a $60 million advertising campaign in March 1999 built around the tag line, "Join us. Together we can change the world." Several months later, Ernst & Young launched a $50 million advertising campaign touting the firm's ability to solve clients' problems. Such advertisements, aimed squarely at high-level corporate managers, heightened concerns about whether public accountants were placing client service above public service. After seeing a newspaper advertisement that read, "Think of us as partners, Deloitte Haskins & Sells & You," Congressman John Dingell (D, Michigan) observed, "That doesn't sound too independent to me."[6]

Certain advertisements, designed to promote an individual firm's interests, had the unfortunate side effect of degrading the overall profession. In early 1998, Deloitte & Touche taunted its largest rival with full-page ads in *USA Today*, the *Wall Street Journal*, and the *Financial Times* that proclaimed:

> Andersen Consulting: Distracted by infighting
> Deloitte Consulting: Focused on our clients

Although a Coopers & Lybrand spokesman described the ads as "unseemly," Deloitte's managing partner James E. Copeland, Jr. expressed impish pride in his firm's mudslinging. "I would be severely disappointed if our competitors were not critical of our marketing efforts," Copeland responded.[7]

Direct Solicitation

Until the late 1970s, Rule 502 of the AICPA *Code* prohibited not only advertising but also "direct solicitation," defined as uninvited in-person visits, conversations or telephone calls to a potential client. Although the AICPA rescinded its rule against direct solicitation in 1979, approximately a dozen states maintained statutes or board of accountancy rules prohibiting direct solicitation.

When Scott Fane moved from New Jersey to a Miami suburb in 1985, his efforts to establish a public accounting practice were hampered by Florida's regulations banning direct solicitation. After growing frustrated that he was not even permitted to offer his services to potential clients over the telephone, Fane filed suit against the Florida State Board of Accountancy (FSBoA) alleging that the board's restrictions violated his First Amendment right to free speech.

Attorneys representing the FSBoA argued that the ban was necessary to protect consumers from "overreaching" CPAs. A former state board chairman testified that CPAs who solicit clients are "obviously in need of business and may be willing to bend the rules."[8] The judge, however, concluded that the Florida board had not provided sufficient evidence to demonstrate a causal relationship between in-person solicitation and accountant misconduct.

After a U.S. district court and a federal appeals court ruled in Fane's favor, the FSBoA appealed to the U.S. Supreme Court. By a vote of 8–1, the Court struck down Florida's restrictions on direct solicitation. Justice Anthony Kennedy observed that the ban on direct solicitation was as likely to harm consumers as help them.

> In denying CPAs and their clients the considerable advantages of solicitation in the commercial context, Florida's law threatens societal interests in broad access to complete and accurate commercial information that the First Amendment is designed to safeguard.[9]

But Justice Sandra Day O'Connor, in her dissent, worried that accountants would soon sink to the level of lawyers: "Commercialization has an incremental, indirect, yet profound effect on professional culture, as lawyers know all too well."[10]

Competitive Bidding

In 1934, the AIA council adopted a resolution condemning competitive bidding.

> RESOLVED, That the council of the American Institute of Accountants regards competitive bidding for professional accounting engagements as contrary to the best interests of members' clients and of the public generally and urges members of the Institute to endeavor by all means at their disposal to eliminate the practice of competitive bidding.[11]

For the next 40 years, a variety of professional rules and state statutes limited price competition among public accountants.

After the AICPA rescinded its ban on competitive bidding in 1972, many large corporations adopted the practice of soliciting bids from several accounting firms before appointing an auditor. Hewlett-Packard, for example, received proposals from 10 accounting firms desiring to perform its 1978 audit.

And auditors didn't necessarily wait for an invitation before pitching their services. "Five years ago if a client of another firm came to me and complained about the service, I'd immediately warn the other firm's chief executive," said Deloitte chairman J. Michael Cook in 1985. "Today I try to take away his client."[12]

Competition led to price wars. Accounting firms underbid each other in pursuit of new engagements and incumbent auditors had to freeze or even reduce their fees to retain existing clients. Audit partner Eugene Bertorelli of Oppenheim Appel & Dixon complained in 1985 that many of his clients were "treating the audit like a commodity, like shopping for cheaper gasoline."[13]

As audit fees dropped, accounting firms had to cut costs in order to maintain profits. The primary determinant of an audit's cost is the amount of testing performed. Lower audit fees led to tighter time budgets and smaller sample sizes. The (Treadway) Commission on Fraudulent Financial Reporting warned in 1987 that "intense competition among accounting firms contributes to significant pressure on audit fees, often with corresponding pressure to reduce staff, time budgets and partner involvement in audit engagements."[14] A senior partner at Spicer & Oppenheim in New York described the situation more bluntly:

> The guys in charge of Big Eight audits today are very bottom-line oriented. That's how they got their jobs. They'll do whatever is necessary to make a profit on the engagements. But they're caught in a crossfire. Because management has quoted low-ball fees, making money on the job is impossible—impossible, that is, unless the firm cuts corners on the audit, limiting the scope of its review below prudent levels and crossing its fingers that everything will turn out all right. With people on the job more concerned with profits than with quality, the chance for serious errors and oversights is always great.[15]

Unfortunately, evidence began to mount that fee reductions were indeed affecting audit quality. The (Cohen) Commission on Auditors' Responsibilities cited a survey of auditors in which 58 percent of the respondents admitted having signed off a required audit program step without completing the work.[16] Time budget pressure was the most frequently reported reason for not performing the required work. Professors Tim Kelley and Loren Margheim discovered in a subsequent survey of staff auditors that more than half of the respondents had committed one or more "audit quality reduction acts" such as prematurely signing off an audit program step, making a superficial review of client documents, or accepting a weak client explanation.[17]

Assurance Services

Because of corporate mergers and competitive bidding for audit engagements, the inflation-adjusted accounting and auditing revenues of the 60 largest accounting firms remained flat from 1987 through 1992. The Big Six employed fewer auditors in 1993 than they did in 1988.

The AICPA, growing alarmed about the stagnant market for its members' accounting and auditing services, commissioned a Special Committee on Assurance Services in 1994 to explore the expansion of "audit-like" services into new areas.

After months of study, special committee chairman Robert K. Elliott reported that the profession's signature product—the financial statement audit—faced a dim future. Because all audits had to comply with professional standards and government regulations, it was difficult for auditors to introduce innovative improvements. Clients, perceiving all audits to be alike, shopped for the lowest price. And advances in technology might soon enable investors and creditors to monitor companies themselves, reducing the demand for auditors' services.

> Over the last few years, the concept of electronic data interchange (EDI) between suppliers and customers has become a reality. Capital suppliers (banks and investors) are just another class of

> supplier. They, too, can be linked by EDI. Once capital suppliers have real-time access to an enterprise's databases, they will have little interest in annual financial statements—and, by extension, auditors' opinions on them—issued well after the entity's fiscal year-end. What they might be far more interested in is real-time assurance from the auditor that either the information in the enterprise's databases is reliable or the system itself is highly likely to produce reliable data.[18]

The special committee recommended that CPAs expand from the accounting business into the information business. The profession's most valuable asset (at least at that time) was its members' reputation for honesty and integrity. Committee member Don Pallais, after noting that "people trust CPAs," urged public accountants to "leverage their reputation and skills into new areas."[19]

The special committee identified more than 200 potential service opportunities for public accountants and prepared business plans for the six services deemed most promising. One proposed assurance service, named WebTrust, involved reviewing the security controls of commercial Web sites to enhance customers' confidence. Another proposed service, SysTrust, would provide assurance on whether an information technology system was designed and operating properly. ElderCare would involve managing elderly clients' financial affairs and providing assurance that health workers and other care providers were performing their services effectively. Other proposed assurance services involved helping clients measure performance and assess risks.

Because these services were purportedly based on consumer demand, rather than regulatory requirements, the special committee estimated that the new services had the potential to double or triple public accounting firms' revenues. The AICPA devoted considerable resources during the late 1990s and early 2000s to promoting these new services and training AICPA members to perform them.

A Herd of Wild Cognitors

As public accountants contemplated a future farther removed from traditional audit and tax services, some grew dissatisfied with their previously cherished title of Certified Public Accountant. Consultants hired by the AICPA reported that the CPA brand was "no longer helpful," in part, because CPAs were stereotyped as narrowly focused historians, not forward thinkers.[20] Another consultant claimed, "If I walked into a room and introduced myself as a certified public accountant, people would ask me about accountancy or tax. These are not product lines that will make money for accountants."[21]

So in April 2000, the AICPA began efforts to introduce an entirely new professional certification. Holders of the new designation would be qualified to help "people or organizations achieve their objectives through the strategic use of knowledge or knowledge management systems."[22]

The new credential was intended to be interdisciplinary. The certification exam would cover subjects such as economics, law, marketing, organizational behavior, business strategy, and information systems design. While a CPA certificate demonstrated expertise in financial matters, the new credential would signify broad knowledge in multiple business disciplines. And unlike the CPA designation, which was valid only in the United States, the new designation would be international. The AICPA enlisted the cooperation of accounting societies in six other countries in an effort to create a business credential that would be recognized around the globe. Finally, the new designation would be free of government regulation. State legislatures determined the requirements for obtaining a CPA license, but the AICPA and its international partners would establish the requirements for holders of the new credential. AICPA leaders claimed the new designation would attract more young people to the profession and would reflect more accurately the broad range of abilities possessed by most AICPA members.

The proposal lost momentum in October 2000 when the English, Irish, and Scottish Institutes of Chartered Accountants withdrew their support, citing fear that the new designation would diminish the "Chartered Accountant" brand. And the proposal faced significant opposition from several state CPA societies, including those of New York and Illinois. Atop their list of objections was a belief that the proposal for the new professional credential implied that the existing CPA credential was somehow deficient. Many CPAs opposed the AICPA's plans to allow non-CPAs to obtain the new credential.

But the factor that probably doomed the new designation was its proposed name—"Cognitor," derived from the Latin word for "knowledge." A prominent accounting journalist said the proposed name reminded him of a "pterodactyl-type dinosaur swooping over the mountaintops."[23] One puzzled accounting firm partner commented, "Cognitor—it sounds like you need a helmet to be one."[24] Another CPA complained that "Cognitor" sounded like Latin for "know-it-all."[25]

Acknowledging that the proposed name was a public relations fiasco, the AICPA withdrew the name "Cognitor" and began referring to the new credential as "XYZ," meaning that its actual name would be determined later. No new name was ever adopted, however. AICPA members, in a referendum in late 2001, rejected the "Cognitor/XYZ" proposal by a margin of 63 percent to 37 percent.

The Growth of Nonaudit Services

Public accountants in the United States have always done more than just perform audits. During the earliest years of the twentieth century, accounting firms offered a variety of services including installations of factory cost systems, studies of organizational efficiency, and investigations of potential acquisition targets. Commencement of the federal income tax in 1913 created a market for tax compliance and planning services. The advent of computerized data processing during the 1950s created new opportunities for information systems consulting.

In 1980, management advisory services (MAS) accounted for about 13 percent of the Big Eight accounting firms' total revenues. But tax and MAS fees grew considerably more rapidly than audit fees during the 1980s and 1990s. By 1998, MAS provided more than half of the major accounting firm's total revenue while accounting and auditing brought in only 30 percent. The Big Five even stopped referring to themselves as "accounting firms." "Calling us an accounting firm is like calling Disney a cartoon maker or G.E. an appliance manufacturer," explained an Arthur Andersen spokesman in 1998. "While we were founded on accounting, as Disney was on cartoons and G.E. on appliances, we have outgrown that." Arthur Andersen, he said, was a "multidisciplinary professional services firm."[26]

Continuing price competition in the audit market forced audit partners to assume a new role—salesman. In spite of aggressive efforts to control costs, many audits generated only marginal profits. After obtaining an engagement through a low-ball audit fee, the only way to earn a satisfactory profit was to persuade the client to purchase higher-margin tax and consulting services. Many public accounting firms adjusted their partner compensation schemes to reward auditors for cross-selling tax and consulting services. Partners who failed to meet their annual sales quotas faced dismissal from the partnership.

Increased pressure on audit partners to sell nonaudit services posed at least two risks to audit quality. Auditors' attention turned from carefully examining their clients' financial statements toward identifying potential service opportunities. And auditors found it increasingly difficult to confront corporate executives about questionable accounting practices. CFOs who were forced to record significant audit adjustments were rarely receptive to their auditors' sales pitches.

Arthur Andersen

The history of Arthur Andersen & Co. closely parallels the history of the American public accounting profession.

Arthur E. Andersen was born to Norwegian immigrant parents in 1885. After being orphaned at age 16, Andersen worked as a mail clerk during the day while finishing high school and attending college at night. The 23-year-old Andersen became the youngest CPA in Illinois in 1908. He worked for three years in the Chicago office of Price Waterhouse, served briefly as the controller of the Schlitz Brewing Company in Milwaukee, and was appointed chairman of the accounting department in Northwestern University's new School of Commerce before opening his own public accounting practice in 1913.

According to most accounts, Arthur Andersen possessed high ethical standards and great courage. During Andersen's second year in practice, the president of a large client demanded that Andersen approve an unusual accounting treatment that would have inflated the client's reported profits. Andersen reportedly told the man there was "not enough money in the city of Chicago" to make him approve the improper accounting.[27] Andersen lost the client, but enjoyed the last laugh when the former client declared bankruptcy a year later.

During Andersen's lifetime, Arthur Andersen & Co. grew into a prominent national firm with more than a dozen offices arrayed from Boston to Los Angeles. The firm specialized in auditing public utilities and was instrumental in averting the bankruptcy of Samuel Insull's two mammoth investment trusts, each controlling hundreds of power companies.

After Andersen's death in December 1947, the 25 surviving partners voted to disband the firm. But a young partner named Leonard Spacek convinced his fellow partners to change their minds. Spacek led Arthur Andersen & Co. for the next 26 years.

One of Spacek's most important contributions was his decision to support Joseph Glickauf's experiments in electronic data processing. After Glickauf successfully designed and installed the world's first automated payroll system at a General Electric factory in 1953, Spacek formed a new Administrative Services Division to tackle similar projects. Skeptical audit partners dubbed the new division "Spacek's Folly" and complained when the division's early revenues were insufficient to cover its costs. But because of Glickauf's vision and Spacek's early financial support, Andersen became the industry leader in information technology (IT) consulting.

By 1988, Andersen's consulting division was generating 40 percent of the firm's total revenues. The partnership agreement at that time called for all partners—whether engaged in auditing, tax work, or consulting—to share a single firm-wide profit pool. But the consultants, who averaged annual revenues of $2.3 million per partner, resented sharing their loot with the accountants and auditors who generated only $1.4 million of revenues per partner. And the consultants wanted greater representation on firm-wide committees, which continued to be dominated by auditors.

In 1989, the consultants formed an independent business unit named "Andersen Consulting" while the auditors and tax accountants continued to practice under the name "Arthur Andersen & Co." The two entities were linked through an international umbrella organization, Andersen Worldwide. The partners in each group drew from separate profit pools subject to an agreement that the group earning the higher profit would share up to 15 percent of its earnings with the other group.

By the late 1990s, the transfer payments from Andersen Consulting to Arthur Andersen & Co. approached $200 million per year. Each of Andersen Consulting's 1,100 partners was forfeiting more than $150,000 per year to provide a $100,000 per partner subsidy to the 1,700 audit and tax partners.

The Andersen Consulting partners, wanting to keep more of their own profits, voted unanimously on December 17, 1997 to withdraw from Andersen Worldwide. But the auditors, recalling the support they had provided to the consulting division during its early years and citing a provision in the partnership agreement that required the partners of a departing business unit to pay 1.5 times the unit's annual revenues, demanded $14 billion of compensation.

The Andersen Consulting partners refused to pay. Instead, they filed for binding arbitration with the International Chamber of Commerce, claiming that Arthur Andersen & Co. had violated the 1989 separation agreement by maintaining its own IT consulting division that had competed illegally for Andersen Consulting's clients.

Guillermo Gamba, a Harvard-educated Colombian lawyer, was selected to decide the dispute. After nearly two years of fact finding and deliberation, Gamba concluded in August 2000 that Andersen Worldwide had violated its obligation to Andersen Consulting. The consultants were permitted to walk away from their former partners for only $1 billion and a requirement to stop using the Andersen name. The consultants were only too happy to adopt a new name—Accenture—and erase the Andersen name from their identity.

Gamba's decision devastated Arthur Andersen & Co. Many of the audit partners had spent the previous two years daydreaming about yachts, vacation homes, and early retirement. A $14 billion settlement would have yielded each Arthur Andersen partner almost $8 million. Now they would receive only a tiny fraction of that amount. And Arthur Andersen would no longer collect the $100,000 per partner annual subsidy formerly received from Andersen Consulting. Andersen Consulting's departure dropped Arthur Andersen & Co. to fifth place among the Big Five public accounting firms in terms of total revenue. With profits and partner compensation lagging their larger rivals, Andersen audit partners faced even greater pressure to retain existing clients, cut audit costs, and sell additional services.

Conclusion

Accountants and accounting scholars began warning in the 1980s that creeping commercialism threatened audit quality. NASBA president Robert Block complained in 1983 about the "present pell-mell campaign to grab the other fellow's client" and warned that an "atmosphere of commercialism" would destroy accountants' professionalism.[28] The AICPA's Special Committee on Standards of Professional Conduct for CPAs reported in 1986 that "the competitive environment has placed pressure on the traditional commitment to professionalism in the practice of public accounting."[29] Art Wyatt, when he resigned from the FASB in 1988, criticized the Big Eight for being more commercially than professionally oriented.[30]

But worst was yet to come. Competitive pressures increased substantially during the 1990s. Arthur Andersen dismissed 10 percent of its audit partners in 1992. Older partners, those with the most experience and the deepest commitment to protecting the public, were let go while the "rainmakers" were retained. Similar purges occurred at KPMG and Grant Thornton as accounting firms trimmed partners who failed to meet their sales quotas.

During the late 1990s, the dam finally burst. U.S. public companies announced 919 earnings restatements during the five and a half years between January 1997 and June 2002. Approximately 10 percent of all listed companies announced at least one restatement during that time period. In comparison, there were only 292 restatements during 13 years from 1977 through 1989. Many believed the rise of commercialism within the public accounting profession and the increased number of financial reporting problems were related.

Two of the most notorious earnings restatements were made by Enron and WorldCom. On November 8, 2001, Enron restated its 1997 through 2001 earnings by $586 million. One month later, the nation's seventh largest company was bankrupt. WorldCom made an even more shocking announcement on June 25, 2002 when it slashed its previously reported earnings by $3.8 billion. WorldCom's final restatement, issued months later, totaled $11 billion. The Enron and WorldCom restatements caused the collapse of Arthur Andersen & Co. and led to the most extensive revision of federal securities laws since the Securities Acts of 1933 and 1934.

27 Enron

We're on the side of angels. We're taking on the entrenched monopolies. In every business we've been in, we're the good guys.

(Enron president Jeffrey K. Skilling[1])

Fortune magazine named Enron America's "most innovative" company six years in a row.[2] Industry observers marveled at Enron's transformation from traditional natural gas distributor to high-flying commodities broker. CEO Ken Lay boasted in an August 1996 interview that 40 percent of Enron's 1995 earnings came from businesses that did not exist in 1985. And Lay expected the trend to continue. "We expect that five years from now, over 40 percent of our earnings will come from businesses that did not exist five years ago. It's a matter of recreating the company and the businesses we're in," Lay explained.[3]

Enron's innovation led to phenomenal growth. Revenues increased from $13.3 billion in 1996 to $100.8 billion four years later. Enron's fiscal 2000 revenues ranked seventh among U.S. companies. When the stock price peaked at $90 in August 2000, Enron's market capitalization approached $80 billion.

But on December 2, 2001, less than ten months after being voted one of the 25 most admired companies in the world, Enron filed for Chapter 11 bankruptcy protection. The company had been accounting for its energy contracts and special purpose entities (SPEs) in ways that were certainly innovative but not at all admirable. The bankruptcy trustee blamed Enron's board of directors for failing to exercise proper oversight over the company's finances. More than two dozen Enron executives were indicted on charges of conspiracy, fraud, and insider trading.

Ken Lay and Enron's Founding

Kenneth ("Ken") Lay was born and raised in rural Missouri. His father, a Baptist minister and failed shopkeeper, sold farm equipment and worked in a feed store to support the family. Lay spent many hours of his youth sitting on a tractor, dreaming of becoming the next John D. Rockefeller.

Lay earned a master's degree in economics from the University of Missouri in 1965. After working briefly as a speechwriter for the president of Humble Oil, Lay enlisted in the Navy, where he was assigned to study the economic impact of a U.S. withdrawal from Vietnam. His research led to a doctorate in economics from the University of Houston.

Lay entered the natural gas business shortly after his discharge from the Navy. He began at Florida Gas and spent several years at Transco Energy before Houston Natural Gas (HNG) recruited him in 1981 to serve as chairman and CEO.

HNG was acquired by rival InterNorth in 1985. Although InterNorth was the larger company and the dominant partner in the merger, Lay emerged as chairman and CEO of the combined company. Shortly after the merger, Lay announced with great fanfare that HNG/InterNorth would change its name to "Enteron." Several days later, a chagrined Lay shortened the new name to "Enron" after learning that "enteron" is a medical term for the digestive tract from the intestines to the anus, making it an especially bad name for a company in the natural gas business.

The InterNorth–HNG merger created the most extensive natural gas pipeline system in North America. Enron's 40,000 miles of pipe stretched from Canada to Mexico and from the Atlantic to the Pacific. Enron, with the ability to buy gas wherever prices were lowest and sell gas wherever prices were highest, was uniquely positioned to take advantage of deregulation in the natural gas market.

Jeffrey Skilling and Enron's Transformation

Jeffrey Skilling was born in Pittsburgh in 1953. When he was only 13 years old, Skilling served briefly as the production manager of a community cable-access television station after the previous manager quit unexpectedly and Skilling was the only other person who knew how to operate the equipment. He earned a business degree from Southern Methodist University in Dallas before entering Harvard University's MBA program, where he graduated in the top 5 percent of his class. "I've never not been successful in business or work—ever," Skilling told a reporter from *Business Week*.[4]

Skilling's first job out of Harvard was with the energy and chemical consulting practice of McKinsey & Co. While working on a consulting engagement with Enron, Skilling sold Ken Lay on the idea of creating a Gas Bank—a place where consumers and producers of natural gas could enter into long-term contracts to purchase or sell fixed quantities of gas at stable prices. Companies that consumed large quantities of natural gas jumped at the opportunity to hedge against the risk of future price increases. Gas producers eventually recognized the wisdom of guarding against future price declines.

Skilling joined Enron as a full-time employee in 1990. Ten years later, Enron was an entirely different company. Only 3 percent of the company's revenues came from delivering natural gas to customers via Enron's pipeline network. More than 90 percent of the revenues were generated by Enron's Wholesale division, which bought and sold energy-related derivative contracts.

Enron was truly innovative in introducing new types of contracts. The company even wrote contracts tied to changes in the weather. It turns out that many companies are interested in protecting themselves from the effects of unfavorable weather conditions. A clothing cataloger who sells a lot of winter outerwear, for example, suffers reduced sales if temperatures are mild. Enron created a derivative contract wherein Enron agreed to pay the cataloger a certain dollar amount for every degree above normal temperature during a given time period; the retailer promised to pay Enron for every degree below normal. Enron then hedged its exposure to high temperatures by entering into a complementary contract with a soft drink manufacturer who feared unusually cold weather. By the end of the decade, Enron earned most of its revenues selling "risk positions" rather than selling tangible products such as gas or electricity.

Enron was also an innovator in electronic commerce. In October 1999, Enron launched Enron Online (EOL), an Internet-based marketplace through which traders could buy and sell commodities such as paper, plastics, and metals. Within a year, EOL was the largest e-commerce Web site in the world, offering 1,150 products related to 35 commodities in 13 currencies.

Andy Fastow and Enron's Accounting

Andy Fastow joined Continental Illinois Bank shortly after earning his MBA from Northwestern University's Kellogg School of Business. He worked on leveraged buyouts and asset securitizations until Jeffrey Skilling recruited him in 1990 to join Enron. The two became close friends. Fastow was named Enron's CFO in 1998 when he was only 36 years old.

During the late 1990s, Enron expanded into new industries and new geographic markets. The Houston-based natural gas company purchased Portland [Oregon] General Electric in 1997 for $3.2 billion. A year later, Enron spent $2.4 billion to acquire a water treatment company in England and paid $1.3 billion to buy an electricity distributor in São Paolo, Brazil. In 1999, Enron began constructing a $1.2 billion nationwide fiber optic network. The plan was to sell high-speed

Internet access to companies during the day and on-demand movies to households in the evening.

Enron's enormous capital budget created a financial dilemma. "We couldn't just issue equity and dilute shareholders in the near term," Fastow explained to a reporter from *CFO* magazine. "On the other hand, we couldn't jeopardize our [debt] rating by issuing debt, which would raise the cost of capital and hinder our trading operations."[5]

Fastow's solution was to raise capital through hundreds of special-purpose entities. SPEs were a popular tool for raising capital and isolating risk. If Enron wanted, for example, to build a new power plant, it would sponsor an SPE dedicated to that purpose. The SPE would build the power plant, using money borrowed from insurance companies, pension funds, investment banks, and wealthy individuals. The SPE would then lease the power plan to Enron, which would operate it.

Enron used more than 3,000 SPEs for off-balance sheet financing. Accounting rules permitted Enron to exclude an SPE's assets and liabilities from its consolidated financial statements as long as at least 3 percent of the SPE's equity was owned by an outside investor. In the above example, Enron would not list the power plant among its assets but neither would it report as a liability the money borrowed to build the plant. If Enron had borrowed the funds and built the power plant itself, without the SPE, Enron's debt-to-asset ratio would have increased.

But Enron abused the accounting rules for SPEs. Many of Enron's SPEs were not independent entities because they were controlled by related parties and because Enron promised to reimburse losses suffered by the SPEs. Thus Enron, not the SPE's nominal owners, bore most of the risk. And Enron's financial statements did not adequately disclose the extent of Enron's commitments or the amounts for which Enron was contingently liable.

The second significant accounting issue at Enron was the company's practice of marking its energy contracts to "market value" at the end of each quarter. Enron petitioned the SEC in 1991 for permission to use mark-to-market accounting. Ironically, Enron's request came at the same time the nation's banks were fiercely resisting SEC efforts to get them to mark their financial instruments to market. The SEC, chaired by fair-value advocate Richard Breeden, approved Enron's request.

Mark-to-market accounting enabled Enron to book future anticipated profits in the current year. For example, a typical energy contract obligated Enron to supply a fixed quantity of natural gas to a customer at a price of, say, \$3.00 per thousand cubic feet for the next ten years. Ordinarily, a gas supplier would record revenue each year as the gas was delivered to the customer. But with mark-to-market accounting, Enron could simply "assume" that it would be able to supply the gas at an average cost of \$2.80 per thousand cubic feet and immediately recognize revenue equal to the present value of the $0.20 per thousand cubic feet expected future profit. If gas prices fell in a subsequent year, Enron recorded additional revenue on the basis that the contract had increased in value.

Mark-to-market accounting works well in situations where market prices are readily observable. But there was no established market for many of the contracts Enron entered into. Valuing Enron's contracts each quarter required estimates and assumptions about future commodity prices, transportation costs, and discount rates. And FASB provided no detailed guidance on how the values should be calculated. "There are just too many models and too many different types of instruments for us to have a one-size-fits-all type of model," said the FASB's director of research.[6] Consequently, Enron had wide discretion over how to value its contracts and when to recognize holding gains.

Enron's use of mark-to-market accounting was not a secret. It was disclosed with the rest of Enron's accounting policies in the company's annual reports. *Wall Street Journal* reporter Jonathan Weil warned readers in September 2000 that much of Enron's reported profits were unrealized.[7] In fact, unrealized gains on derivative contracts comprised one-third of Enron's 1999 net income and approximately one-half of the company's 2000 profits. Enron would have reported a loss in the second quarter of 2000 absent the estimated holding gains.

Enron's Collapse

Enron's troubles began in 2000. British regulators cut the rates Enron's water utility was permitted to charge, slashing the entity's profits. And the largest customer of Enron's $3 billion power plant in Dabhol, India stopped paying for service. Indian politicians, who had complained for years that Enron's rates were too high, sided with the customer in the dispute. Many of Enron's recent South American acquisitions proved unprofitable.

Enron's stock price, which reached $90 in the summer of 2000, declined with each piece of bad news. The price dipped below $60 in March 2001 when Blockbuster backed out of its agreement to distribute on-demand movies via Enron's fiber optic network.

California's 2000/2001 energy crisis was a mixed blessing for Enron. The company reaped huge profits supplying electricity at wholesale prices as much as 900 percent higher than the previous year. But Enron also made some powerful enemies. "Every trading company in the country has been feasting on California, and Enron is the shrewdest of them all. They are like sharks in a feeding frenzy," complained the executive director of the Utility Consumers' Action Network in San Diego.[8] The City of San Francisco joined other plaintiffs in a civil lawsuit alleging that Enron engaged in unlawful market manipulation. Governor

Gray Davis instructed his attorney-general to investigate allegations of illegal price fixing.

Skilling, who had served as Enron's president and chief operating officer since 1997, succeeded Lay as CEO in February 2001. Although even Skilling's harshest critics acknowledge his intelligence and creativity, Skilling lacked the diplomacy and tact necessary to lead a highly visible company in troubled times. During an April 2001 conference call with Wall Street analysts, Skilling called fund manager Richard Grubman an "asshole" after Grubman asked why Enron was slow releasing a balance sheet and cash flow statement for the first quarter. It was a juvenile and dangerous comment coming from the CEO of a public corporation whose stock price depended on the goodwill of analysts and institutional investors.

Two months later, Skilling asked an audience at a technology conference in Las Vegas if they knew the difference between the state of California and the *Titanic*. "At least when the Titanic went down the lights were on," Skilling joked.[9] Millions of Californians were not amused. California's attorney-general responded that he would love to escort Ken Lay to an 8 ft. by 10 ft. prison cell and introduce him to a tattooed inmate named Spike.[10]

Skilling shocked Wall Street by resigning from Enron on August 14, 2001. His meager explanation—that he wanted to travel, learn a foreign language, and master dirt-bike riding—raised more questions than it answered. Enron's stock price dropped 14 percent from \$43 to \$37 within the week amid speculation that undisclosed internal problems had driven Skilling from his post.

Shortly after Ken Lay resumed his old job as Enron's CEO, he received a disturbing letter from Sherron Watkins, the company's vice-president of corporate development. "I am incredibly nervous that we will implode in a wave of accounting scandals," Watkins wrote. "Skilling's abrupt departure will raise suspicions of accounting improprieties and valuation issues. Enron has been very aggressive in its accounting...." Watkins went on to complain that Enron had booked undeserved profits on inadequately disclosed transactions with related parties.[11]

Lay asked Arthur Andersen and Enron's lawyers Vinson & Elkins to investigate Watkins's allegations. Their investigation revealed that two of Enron's SPEs did not qualify as independent entities because they were not adequately capitalized. The accountants also concluded that Enron had improperly accounted for \$1.2 billion of notes receivable issued by an SPE in exchange for Enron stock. Enron had included the notes among its assets when they should have been reported as a reduction of stockholders' equity.

On October 16, 2001 Enron announced a \$638 million loss for the quarter ended September 30. The loss resulted from \$1.01 billion of non-recurring expenses, including $180 million of severance costs and restructuring charges in Enron's broadband division; $287 million of asset impairments at its water treatment facilities in England; and $544 million of investment losses resulting from the consolidation of the two inadequately capitalized SPEs. Lay downplayed the losses, pointing out that, excluding the special charges, Enron's third-quarter profits were 35 percent higher than the previous year. "As these numbers show, Enron's core energy business fundamentals are excellent," Lay told analysts.[12]

As analysts and journalists scrutinized Enron's surprising earnings announcement, their attention soon focused on two partnerships established by CFO Andy Fastow in 1999. The partnerships, LJM1 and LJM2, were capitalized with a few million dollars of Fastow's money and more than $400 million raised from banks and investments banks that did business with Enron. From 1999 to 2001, the LJM partnerships bought tens of millions of dollars of assets from Enron. The transactions created an obvious conflict of interest for Fastow. As Enron's CFO, he had a fiduciary duty to the corporation's shareholders to negotiate a high selling price. But as an investor in the LJM partnerships, he clearly wanted to purchase the assets at the lowest possible price.

Fears of financial chicanery heightened when the *Wall Street Journal* reported on October 19 that Fastow had personally earned more than $7 million in management fees plus $4 million in capital gains on an investment of only $3 million.[13] Fastow resigned from Enron on October 24, two days after the SEC asked Enron for information about its dealings with the Fastow-run partnerships. Subsequent investigation revealed that Fastow earned more than $30 million from the partnerships during their two-year existence.

Enron's stock traded at $34 shortly after the third-quarter loss was announced on October 16. Ten days later it was trading at $16. The price dropped below $9 on November 8 when Enron restated its 1997 through 2001 earnings, cutting previously reported profits by $586 million or 20 percent. The restatement corrected improper accounting for transactions with partnerships headed by Andy Fastow and Michael Kopper, a former member of Fastow's staff. The adjustments also increased Enron's liabilities by $628 million at the end of 2000.

Ken Lay spent much of November trying desperately to negotiate a merger with cross-town rival Dynegy. When Dynegy backed away from the troubled company, Enron was forced to declare bankruptcy.

Enron and Arthur Andersen

Enron was Arthur Andersen's second largest client at the turn of the twenty-first century. Andersen's Houston office billed Enron $52 million in 2000—$25 million for auditing Enron's financial statements plus $27 million for nonaudit services. Andersen employees, many of whom were assigned to the Enron engagement year-round, occupied nearly an entire floor of Enron's 50-story headquarters. So many Andersen employees accepted jobs with Enron that members of Enron's accounting department jokingly referred to Arthur Andersen as "Enron Prep."

Chief accounting officer Richard Causey was one of the nearly 90 Andersen alumni employed at Enron. While he was at Andersen, one of Causey's closest friends was a fellow auditor named David Duncan. Causey and Duncan maintained their friendship after Causey left to become Enron's CAO and Duncan took over as the engagement partner in charge of Enron's audit. Each spring, the duo led a group of Andersen and Enron "coworkers" on a tour of elite golf courses around the country.

Arthur Andersen's independence was called into question shortly after Enron disclosed that a large portion of the 1997 earnings restatement consisted of adjustments the auditors had proposed at the end of the 1997 audit but had allowed to go uncorrected. Congressional investigators wanted to know why Andersen tolerated $51 million of known misstatements during a year when Enron reported only $105 million of net income. Andersen chief executive Joseph F. Berardino explained that Enron's 1997 earnings were artificially low due to several hundred million dollars of non-recurring expenses and write-offs. The proposed adjustments were not material, Berardino testified, because they represented less than 8 percent of "normalized" earnings. Other accounting experts disputed Berardino's claim that the $51 million of misstatements were immaterial. Berardino's testimony served primarily to remind people of previous situations, such as Sunbeam and Waste Management, in which Andersen auditors discovered tens of millions of dollars of accounting errors but backed down after management declined to record the proposed adjustments.

Internal Andersen memorandums revealed that members of the firm's Professional Standards Group (PSG) questioned Enron's accounting as early as 1999. The PSG was an elite group of accounting experts who advised Andersen auditors on their clients' most complex accounting issues. PSG member Carl Bass wrote a memo in December 1999 objecting to Enron's accounting for the Blockbuster deal. Two months later, Bass questioned the legitimacy of one of Enron's partnerships. "This whole deal looks like there is no substance," Bass wrote in an email to PSG members at Andersen's Chicago headquarters.[14]

Bass continued resisting Enron's aggressive accounting practices until March 2001, when Enron management persuaded Andersen executives to remove Bass from the audit team. David Duncan, who didn't follow Bass's advice very often anyway, relayed Enron's complaints about Bass to Bass's superiors in Chicago. Duncan didn't want his office's most lucrative client relationship soured by an auditor Enron managers described as "caustic and cynical."

Lay and Skilling Charged

Federal prosecutors charged Ken Lay with six criminal counts of wire fraud and conspiracy to commit securities fraud. Most of the charges stemmed from allegations that Lay lied to employees, credit rating agencies, and analysts by claiming Enron was healthy when he knew otherwise. Jeffrey Skilling was indicted on 28 counts of conspiracy, securities fraud, insider trading, and making false statements to auditors. Prosecutors alleged that Skilling filed false quarterly and annual reports with the SEC in 2000 and 2001 and sold $62 million of Enron stock at a time when he knew the price was inflated by false information.

Lay's and Skilling's trial commenced on January 30, 2006 in the U.S. District Court in Houston with Judge Simeon Lake presiding. Judge Lake demonstrated his no-nonsense approach to the showcase trial by seating the jury in only one day. Although Lay and Skilling were represented by the best legal talent $60 million could buy, Lake was determined not to let the high-powered defense team complicate the proceedings unnecessarily.

The government's star witness was Andy Fastow. The former CFO described in detail how Enron used related party transactions with the LJM partnerships to manipulate its reported earnings. In one illustrative transaction, Skilling approached Fastow near the end of a quarter in 1999 and offered to sell LJM an interest in an Enron power plant project in Brazil. "That plant is a piece of sh—," Fastow responded. "No one would buy it."[15]

But Fastow changed his mind after Skilling promised to protect LJM from any losses on the transaction. Enron recognized a gain on the sale of the power plant in 1999, enabling the company to meet its quarterly earnings target. A little more than a year later, Enron repurchased the power plant interest from LJM at a higher price even though the plant continued to lose money.

The Brazilian power plant transaction was not an isolated event. Between 1999 and 2001, Enron reported millions of dollars of improper gains from selling assets to SPEs at inflated prices. Enron also avoided reporting millions of dollars of losses by parking money-losing assets in off-balance-sheet entities.

The defense attorneys tried to deflect Fastow's testimony by claiming that he was making up lies to earn a more lenient sentence for himself after pleading guilty to two counts of conspiracy to commit fraud. Skilling's lawyer said Fastow and other former Enron employees "had been robbed of their free will" and were saying "false things about Jeff and Ken" to satisfy prosecutors. "These witnesses were not unvarnished," Lay's attorney complained. "They were shellacked."[16]

Sherron Watkins' testimony was more difficult to refute. The former Enron vice-president, who had earned international acclaim for blowing the whistle on Enron's accounting practices, testified that Lay had not done enough to investigate her allegations. She also said that some of Lay's public comments during fall 2001 were misleading.

Lay and Skilling each testified in their own defense. Lay described himself as an extreme optimist who believed right up until the end that Enron was "one of the strongest companies" in America.[17] Skilling insisted that he thought Enron was a healthy company when he resigned in August 2001 and when he sold $15 million of Enron stock the following month. Both men blamed the company's collapse on the bear market that followed the September 11 terrorist attacks in New York and Washington, "manipulative" trading practices by short-sellers, and panic caused by "irresponsible" news articles in the *Wall Street Journal*.[18]

In their closing arguments, the defense attorneys denied that any crimes had occurred at Enron, other than those committed by Andy Fastow. SPEs were as "common as grass," the attorneys claimed. And every transaction had been approved by Enron's independent auditors and attorneys. "There was no evil," Skilling's lawyer said, adding that if what his client did was illegal "we might as well put every CEO in jail."[19]

But prosecutors said it was "absurd" to claim that no crimes had taken place at Enron. Lay and Skilling conspired to cover up Enron's deteriorating financial condition while dumping millions of their own shares, the government claimed. Lead prosecutor Kathryn Ruemmler urged the jury to "Hold [Lay and Skilling] accountable for the choices they made and the lies they told."[20]

On the sixth day of deliberations, the jurors did exactly as Ms. Ruemmler asked. They convicted Ken Lay on all six counts of conspiracy and fraud. Jeffrey Skilling was acquitted on nine counts of insider trading, but convicted on 19 other felony charges. The jury didn't believe Skilling's claim that he was unaware of Enron's problems at the time he resigned. There were "red flags everywhere," one juror said. Nor did the jurors believe that Lay and Skilling were innocent victims of Fastow's deceit. They were "very controlling people" another juror said describing Enron's two top executives. At a news conference after the verdicts were announced, one juror said she hoped other corporate CEOs would realize that "those in charge have responsibility. There's too much hurt here. If something good can come out, companies can be aware that they must be conscientious."[21]

After listening to Enron investors and employees tearfully describe the harm Enron's collapse had caused them, Judge Lake sentenced Jeffrey Skilling to 24 years and four months in prison. Skilling had doomed many investors and employees to "a life sentence of poverty," Lake said in explaining the harsh verdict.[22] Skilling will have to serve at least 85 percent of his sentence before becoming eligible for parole. His remaining assets, estimated at $45 million, went to a fund to compensate Enron victims.

Andy Fastow, who was originally charged with 98 felonies, was sentenced to only six years in prison followed by two years of community service. The government dropped the 98-count indictment in 2004 after Fastow pleaded guilty to two counts of conspiracy and agreed to testify against Lay and Skilling. Prosecutors praised Fastow's cooperation and called his testimony "critical" to winning the convictions of Enron's two top executives.

Ken Lay was never sentenced. Lay died of heart failure six weeks after the conclusion of his trial. His conviction was later vacated on the basis that a defendant who dies while his appeal is in process isn't considered convicted. Although Lay's criminal record was wiped clean, his legacy is marred forever. Enron's "Crooked E" will always be remembered as a symbol of corporate greed and corruption.

28 WorldCom

There was only one right path to take, and I would take it again.
(Cynthia Cooper[1])

Betty Vinson and Cynthia Cooper had much in common. Both grew up in Mississippi and studied accounting at state universities. Both eventually moved to Clinton, Mississippi and joined telecommunications giant WorldCom, where they reported to CFO Scott Sullivan. Vinson worked in the general accounting department as the director of management reporting. Cooper was WorldCom's director of internal audit. Both possessed strong religious faith. Vinson taught her daughter's Sunday school class. Cooper recited the 23rd Psalm during times of stress.

But in 2002, their lives turned in opposite directions. Vinson confessed to FBI agents on June 24 that she had helped prepare more than $3.7 billion of improper journal entries. She later pled guilty to two criminal counts of conspiracy and securities fraud. Cooper led the internal investigation that discovered Vinson's bogus entries. *Time* named Cooper one of the magazine's 2002 "Persons of the Year" for her role in uncovering the largest accounting fraud (to date) in U.S. history.[2]

WorldCom

Bernard ("Bernie") Ebbers was born in Alberta, Canada in 1941. The Ebbers family moved to California and then to New Mexico, where Bernie attended a boarding school and worked in the maintenance department of a Navajo reservation. After flunking out of two colleges, Ebbers worked for several years as a milkman and bouncer until a former high school basketball coach helped him obtain a scholarship from Mississippi College. Ebbers's first job following graduation was teaching middle school science and coaching basketball. Later, he managed a warehouse for a garment factory.

Ebbers turned to managing hotels in 1974 because he thought it matched his abilities. "It didn't require any technical skills," Ebbers said, "It was mostly about getting along with people. I thought I could do that."[3] By the early 1980s, Ebbers owned eight motels, including some in the Hampton Inn and Courtyard by Marriott chains.

Ebbers and three other entrepreneurs met in a coffee shop in 1983 and hatched a plan to start their own telephone company. The company, originally named Long Distance Discount Service (LDDS), sold long distance telephone services to retail customers in Mississippi and surrounding states. Founding a long distance phone company did not require a huge initial investment in cables or transmission equipment. LDDS simply purchased excess capacity from major long distance carriers and resold the capacity to retail customers. Ebbers was named LDDS's CEO in 1985.

In 1991, LDDS embarked on a string of mergers that transformed the company from a little-known, regional long distance carrier into a major player in the telecommunications industry. By the end of 1993, LDDS had revenues of approximately $1.5 billion per year and was the fourth largest long distance telephone company in the United States behind only AT&T, MCI, and Sprint. The company changed its name to WorldCom in 1995 to reflect its global aspirations.

Additional acquisitions boosted WorldCom's revenues to $7.4 billion by 1997. Most of the acquisitions were stock-for-stock trades. Wall Street rewarded the company's rapid growth with a steadily increasing stock price. Ebbers used the highly valued stock as currency to buy more companies, perpetuating WorldCom's growth.

Ebbers opened merger negotiations with MCI in 1998. Although MCI, with annual revenues of $20 billion, was almost three times the size of WorldCom, Ebbers was able to acquire his larger rival for $7 billion of cash and 1.1 billion shares of stock valued at $32 billion. The $39 billion deal was the largest corporate merger to date.

The MCI deal vaulted WorldCom over Sprint into second place in the telecommunications industry. The company's 60,000 employees offered local, long distance, and wireless telephone services to more than 20 million customers. WorldCom was also the largest Internet carrier in the world, providing services in more than 100 countries on six continents. Consolidated revenues exceeded $30 billion per year.

Ebbers profited greatly from WorldCom's growth. He collected compensation of $36 million and $31 million in 1999 and 2000, respectively. And the value of his stock holdings exceeded $1.1 billion in late 1999. Ebbers pledged his WorldCom stock as collateral to take out almost $1 billion in personal and business loans. He used the proceeds to buy an assortment of businesses, including a rice farm, a lumber mill, a country club, a trucking company, a minor league hockey team, and a marina. His personal assets included a luxury yacht christened *Aquasition*.

I'm Sorry, your Call Cannot be Completed…

After completing more than 60 acquisitions between 1985 and 1999, Ebbers set his sights on Sprint. WorldCom announced plans in October 1999 to merge with the rival phone company. But the merger plans were terminated in July 2000 when the U.S. Department of Justice blocked the union of the country's second and third largest telecommunications companies.

The collapse of the Sprint deal marked the beginning of trouble for Ebbers and WorldCom. For 15 years, WorldCom had used mergers and acquisitions to fuel its growth. With fewer small telecommunications companies available for purchase and the Justice Department growing concerned about industry consolidation, rapid growth through mergers was no longer possible. In addition, industry-wide overcapacity was leading to significant price cuts in telephone and Internet service.

When WorldCom's profits began stagnating in early 2000, Ebbers grew fanatical about cutting the company's costs. He shut off the supply of free coffee to employees at WorldCom's headquarters and ordered a nightwatchman to refill bottled water dispensers with tap water.

But such costs were negligible at the $30 billion company. WorldCom's largest expense was "line costs." Line costs are the amounts paid to other phone companies to carry some portion of a WorldCom customer's call. For example, a call from a WorldCom customer in Boston to a friend in Paris might originate on a local Boston company's phone line, be transferred to a WorldCom transatlantic cable, and end up on a French phone company's network. WorldCom would have to pay the Boston phone company and the French company for relaying the WorldCom customer's call. During the 1990s, WorldCom spent between 40 percent and 50 percent of its annual revenues on line costs.

Wrong Numbers

Scott Sullivan was the controller of Advanced Telecommunications Corporation (ATC) when it was acquired by WorldCom in 1992. Sullivan, the son of a former railroad accountant, had worked as an auditor at a major public accounting firm before joining ATC. Sullivan advanced quickly within WorldCom and was promoted to chief financial officer in 1994.

Sullivan and Ebbers worked closely for the next eight years. Ebbers, who had never taken an accounting course, relied heavily on Sullivan to structure WorldCom's acquisitions and finance the company's growth. *CFO* magazine referred to Sullivan as a "whiz kid" and awarded him a CFO Excellence Award in 1998.[4] Although Sullivan lived modestly in a rented townhouse for most of the years he worked at WorldCom, he sold $18 million of WorldCom stock in August 2000 and began building a 28,000 sq. ft. home in Boca Raton, Florida.

Ebbers was fixated on WorldCom's revenue growth. He trumpeted WorldCom's growth during quarterly conference calls with stock analysts and personally approved (some would say dictated) the company's revenue forecasts. Sullivan urged Ebbers to scale back his aggressive revenue targets after the collapse of the Sprint deal. But Ebbers continued promising Wall Street impressive growth, fearing WorldCom's stock price would fall if the company failed to maintain the impressive growth rate it established during the 1990s.

Ebbers applied tremendous pressure on his subordinates, especially Sullivan, to meet his aggressive revenue goals. He ordered the accounting department to prepare a special monthly report so he could monitor revenues. Top executive bonuses were tied to achieving double-digit revenue growth each quarter. A former executive reported that the focus on revenue was "in every brick in every building" and was a constant topic of conversation within management.[5]

During the first quarter of 1999, Sullivan began using a variety of tricks to close the gap between WorldCom's actual revenues and Ebbers's forecasts. During the next three years, WorldCom accountants regularly recorded adjusting journal entries to bring each quarter's reported revenues into line with the previously released forecasts. The revenue adjustments, which were usually recorded in round dollar amounts weeks after the quarter closed, totaled $958 million between the first quarter of 1999 and the first quarter of 2002. Although relatively small in relation to the $110 billion of revenues WorldCom reported during those three years, the adjustments enabled WorldCom to report 11 consecutive quarters of double-digit revenue growth. Without the adjustments, revenue growth would have dipped into single-digits in five of the 11 quarters.

The second number, besides revenue growth, that Ebbers worried about was the ratio of line cost expense to revenue, called the "line cost E/R ratio." An increase in a phone company's E/R ratio alerts analysts that the company has either leased more capacity than its volume of calls warrants or is overpaying for its leased capacity.

Each month, WorldCom had to estimate the amounts it would eventually have to pay local and regional phone companies for calls placed through the other companies' networks. The accrued liabilities were quite large because some companies did not bill WorldCom until several months after calls were made. And the amounts, especially for international service, could be very difficult to estimate. WorldCom sometimes had to accrue liabilities for line costs before the foreign company (or the relevant government agency) had even informed WorldCom of the per-minute rate for use of its lines.

WorldCom accountants, at the direction of Scott Sullivan, began manipulating the company's line cost accruals in 1999. They understated WorldCom's line costs by $3.3 billion between the second quarter of 1999 and the fourth quarter of 2000 by reducing the amounts accrued for likely future payments. The reductions to WorldCom's line cost accruals were recorded after the close of each quarter and were not supported by contemporaneous analysis or documentation. Sullivan used the line cost adjustments to smooth WorldCom's quarterly earnings amounts.

By the end of 2000, WorldCom's accrued liabilities for line costs were significantly understated. Sullivan and the accounting staff could no longer get away with simply underestimating the line cost accruals each quarter. This forced Sullivan to come up with a new scheme for reducing WorldCom's reported line cost E/R ratio.

Beginning in the first quarter of 2001, WorldCom accountants began capitalizing line costs as additions to WorldCom's property and equipment instead of reporting the costs as operating expenses. The accounting treatment violated GAAP because the line costs were ongoing operating expenses that should have been recognized as expenses when incurred. But the treatment aided Sullivan's goal of inflating WorldCom's declining profits. WorldCom's accountants improperly capitalized $3.8 billion of line costs between the first quarter of 2001 and the first quarter of 2002.

Reluctant Participants

Betty Vinson was one of many WorldCom employees who reluctantly participated in the fraud. David Myers worked directly under Scott Sullivan as WorldCom's controller. Myers's friend Buford ("Buddy") Yates served as WorldCom's director of general accounting. Vinson reported to Yates, as did Troy Normand, who oversaw the accounting for WorldCom's property and equipment.

In October 2000, Yates told Vinson and Normand that Myers and Sullivan wanted the accounting staff to slash the company's accrued line costs by $828 million. When Vinson and Normand objected to the post-closing adjustment, Yates relayed Myers's promise that he would never ask them to do anything like that again.

Vinson suffered pangs of guilt after recording the adjustment. She told Yates on October 26 that she planned to resign from WorldCom. Normand expressed similar misgivings. Several days later, Scott Sullivan met with Vinson and Normand and promised to assume full responsibility for WorldCom's accounting. Vinson, who earned a higher salary than her husband and didn't want to leave town to find a comparable job, was persuaded to stay at WorldCom. Normand stayed as well.

Vinson's situation grew worse during the first quarter of 2001 when Yates instructed her to capitalize $771 million of line costs. Myers, who rejected an earlier proposal to capitalize line costs as unsupportable under GAAP, authorized the new accounting treatment under pressure from Sullivan. Yates argued against capitalizing the costs, but eventually passed the order on to Vinson. Vinson felt trapped. With Normand's help, she prepared and posted journal entries transferring the line costs out of WorldCom's operating expenses into five fixed asset accounts. The entries were made in April but backdated to February by changing the dates in the computer. During the next four quarters, Vinson prepared similar journal entries totaling approximately $3 billion.

The adjusting journal entries made by Vinson and Normand at WorldCom's headquarters created a dilemma for the property accounting group in Tulsa, Oklahoma who kept the detailed records of WorldCom's fixed assets. Because of the capitalized line costs, the amount reported for fixed assets on WorldCom's balance sheet exceeded the sum of the individual items listed in the property ledger. Several members of the property accounting group refused to adjust the property ledger to match the corporate records when they learned the nature of the costs being capitalized. Some threatened to resign. None, however, reported their objections to WorldCom's auditors or directors.

Night Detectives

Cynthia Cooper joined LDDS in 1994. Ebbers placed the 30-year-old accountant in charge of the company's internal audit department. The petite former prom princess didn't frighten many people, but that wasn't her job. WorldCom's internal auditors acted more as internal consultants than corporate policemen. They concentrated on operational audits, looking for ways to cut unnecessary costs and improve efficiency. Cooper was proud of the fact that her 24-member department paid for itself several times over through its cost-saving recommendations.

WorldCom's internal auditors rarely investigated the company's financial accounting practices. But in early 2002, the head of WorldCom's wireless division complained to Cooper that the corporate accounting staff had reduced his division's bad debt reserves by $400 million. The accounting adjustment appeared unwarranted to Cooper. Although Sullivan defended the adjustment, he backed down after Cooper raised the topic at the next meeting of WorldCom's audit committee.

The next day, Sullivan called Cooper's cell phone while she was at the hair salon and warned her angrily not to interfere with his plans again. Sullivan had charmed or bullied WorldCom's entire corporate accounting department into obeying his instructions, but his anger only piqued Cooper's interest. "When someone is hostile," Cooper said, "my instinct is to find out why."[6]

On March 7, 2002, WorldCom received a "Request for Information" from the SEC. The regulators were puzzled by WorldCom's uncanny ability to earn record profits at the same time most other telecommunications companies, such as AT&T, were reporting losses. Specifically, the SEC asked for information about WorldCom's revenue recognition policies, bad debt reserves, goodwill valuation, and loans to officers.

At about that same time, it became apparent that WorldCom would have to replace its long-time auditor, Arthur Andersen. Andersen had audited WorldCom's financial statements since 1990, but the firm was drowning in Enron's wake. Cooper grew worried that if any accounting problems existed, they might be overlooked during the transition to a new auditor. She decided, without the permission of her superiors, to begin probing WorldCom's accounting records.

Several weeks later, Mark Abide, an accountant who helped keep track of WorldCom's property and equipment, forwarded to the internal audit department an article from the *Fort Worth Weekly* describing a former WorldCom accountant who claimed to have been wrongfully discharged after raising questions about WorldCom's accounting for capital expenditures. "This is worth looking into from an audit perspective," Abide said.[7]

Cooper directed her two top managers, Gene Morse and Glyn Smith, to investigate WorldCom's fixed asset accounts. They soon discovered that the amount of expenditures capitalized during 2001 far exceeded the capital spending authorized by WorldCom's board of directors.

Morse, the internal audit department's resident computer expert, persuaded a senior IT manager to grant him access to WorldCom's electronic ledger. Working at night to avoid detection, Morse wrote programs that scanned millions of recorded transactions. By early June, he had identified $2 billion of questionable accounting entries.

When Cooper realized the significance of Morse's findings, she became worried that the guilty parties might try to destroy the evidence. Morse began copying the evidence on to CDs, using equipment he purchased with his own money.

In spite of Cooper's efforts to maintain secrecy, Sullivan learned from subordinates that the internal auditors were asking questions about WorldCom's capital expenditure accounts. He summoned Cooper and Smith to his office on June 11 and asked what they were working on. Smith described the audit without revealing the improprieties they had already discovered. Sullivan coolly urged them to delay their audit for several months, saying there were some problems he intended to take care of in the third quarter.

Worried that Sullivan might sabotage their investigation, Cooper called Max Bobbit, the head of WorldCom's audit committee. Bobbitt met with Cooper and Smith on June 14. After hearing their concerns, he instructed them to brief the new auditors from KPMG. But Bobbit did not report their suspicions at the next day's board of directors meeting.

On June 17, Cooper decided to force the issue. She and Smith went to Betty Vinson and asked for documentation to support the suspicious adjusting journal entries. Vinson admitted recording the entries, but said she had no documents to explain them. Buford Yates referred the auditors to David Myers. Myers, when confronted, admitted that the accounting treatment was wrong.

Apprised of Myers's confession, Max Bobbitt scheduled a special audit committee meeting for June 20. Cooper explained her findings and Farrell Malone, the KPMG partner assigned to WorldCom, expressed his opinion that the line costs should not have been capitalized. Sullivan requested four days to prepare a defense of his accounting treatment.

When the audit committee reconvened on June 24, Sullivan tried to defend the accounting using a concept known as the "matching principle." Sullivan argued that WorldCom had entered into long-term lease agreements to obtain sufficient capacity for anticipated future needs. Thus, WorldCom was justified in capitalizing the line costs as "prepaid capacity" and deferring the expense until future periods when the capacity would be used to generate revenue.

It was a tenuous argument, at best. But even if accounting rules could be stretched to allow capitalization of the line charges, Sullivan could not show how the capitalized amounts were calculated, explain why they were allocated to accounts such as furniture and fixtures that had no correlation with underutilized network capacity, or justify how the capitalized amounts were being depreciated.

The audit committee accepted KPMG's judgment that the accounting treatment was wrong. Myers complied with the committee's request that he resign; Sullivan refused and was fired the next day. Following a meeting of the full board on June 25, WorldCom announced that it would restate its 2001 and 2002 profits by $3.8 billion. After a thorough investigation lasting several months, the total restatement reached $11 billion.

The stress of the investigation took a severe toll on Cooper. Friends estimate she lost 30 pounds during and immediately after the ordeal. Her mother noticed a strange lack of cadence in her speech and thought she appeared unusually tired. "There have been times that I could not stop crying," Cooper later confessed.[8]

WorldCom's Outside Auditors

Melvin Dick, Arthur Andersen's managing partner for technology, media, and communications, assumed responsibility for WorldCom's audit in 2001. Dick had more than 25 years of auditing experience and had previously supervised the audits of U.S. West and Level 3 Communications.

WorldCom was one of Arthur Andersen's 20 most lucrative clients. Between 1999 and 2001, WorldCom paid Andersen approximately $64 million. But about $50 million of the fees were for consulting, litigation support, and tax services. Andersen representatives told WorldCom's audit committee in 2000 that Andersen's cost of performing the WorldCom audit exceeded the amount billed, and that Andersen considered the unbilled costs a "continuing investment" in WorldCom.[9] Thus, Andersen was in a dangerous position. The firm wanted desperately to retain the WorldCom audit so it could continue providing profitable nonaudit services, but at the same time needed to cut audit costs to recover past losses.

Dick's audit team relied on analytical procedures and tests of internal controls to reduce the amount of detailed tests performed on WorldCom's accounting records. That is, the auditors compared each quarter's account balances with those of previous quarters and concentrated their tests on the accounts showing the largest fluctuations. The auditors also documented WorldCom's procedures for recording transactions, and performed only minimal testing on accounts where the accounting procedures were deemed adequate to prevent material errors.

The auditors' heavy reliance on analytical procedures and internal controls proved ineffective in detecting the WorldCom fraud. The auditors interpreted WorldCom's consistent quarterly line cost E/R ratio as evidence that the reported line costs were reasonable. But Sullivan's staff deliberately manipulated recorded line costs to keep the line cost E/R ratio at about 42 percent. The auditors failed to consider that management might manipulate the financial statements to *eliminate* quarter-to-quarter variations. In fact, WorldCom's 2000 through 2002 quarterly financial statements showed surprising stability given the highly volatile business environment.

Regarding WorldCom's capital expenditures, the auditors concluded, after reviewing a small sample of equipment purchases, that WorldCom's internal controls were adequate. Unfortunately, the journal entries reclassifying line costs as fixed assets were recorded outside the normal process for recording capital additions. Sullivan's staff at headquarters had the ability, through "top-side" journal entries, to significantly alter the numbers generated by WorldCom's normal accounting system.

WorldCom's accounting staff took several steps to conceal the fraud from the auditors. The monthly revenue reports given to the auditors, while purported to be the same reports used by Ebbers and Sullivan to monitor the company's sales, were altered to make it more difficult to identify the post-closing revenue adjustments. And Sullivan and Myers refused numerous requests from Andersen for access to WorldCom's computerized general ledger. Without access to the ledger, the auditors had to accept management's word that there were no significant adjustments to the accounting records. Melvin Dick testified before a congressional committee that the auditors planned their audit "in general reliance on the honesty and integrity of the management of the company."[10] In hindsight, this reliance could not have been more misplaced.

Aftermath

After the proposed Sprint acquisition fell through in the spring of 2000, WorldCom's stock price began a long descent, falling from $61 in June 1999 to $15 in December 2001. WorldCom's declining stock price created a financial crisis for Ebbers. Most of his stock holdings were pledged as collateral for almost $1 billion of personal and business loans. As the value of the shares fell, nervous lenders demanded that Ebbers repay the loans or provide additional security.

Ebbers asked WorldCom's compensation committee in September 2000 to lend him $50 million of corporate funds so he could satisfy his outside lenders without having to sell his WorldCom stock. The compensation committee advanced the funds to Ebbers without stipulating an interest rate or repayment date. During the next 18 months, WorldCom extended additional direct loans and issued loan guaranties that, by April 2002, totaled more than $400 million.

WorldCom's board eventually became distressed over Ebbers' reluctance to collateralize the loans and by the discovery that Ebbers was using the loan proceeds to subsidize several money-losing businesses. WorldCom's outside directors met on April 26 to discuss replacing Ebbers. Several directors were unhappy with Ebbers' failure to establish a sustainable growth strategy since the collapse of the Sprint merger. Others feared that Wall Street had lost confidence in him. Ebbers submitted his resignation three days later in exchange for a severance package promising him $1.5 million per year for life.

After WorldCom's board learned of the massive fraud in June 2002, it commissioned a special committee chaired by former FASB chairman Dennis Beresford to investigate the fraud. The committee found no evidence tying Ebbers directly to the improper line cost accounting. But their report blamed Ebbers for creating a corporate culture that discouraged dissent and emphasized "making the numbers" above all else. The committee faulted WorldCom's corporate culture for cultivating the largest accounting fraud ever discovered.

> This culture began at the top. Ebbers created the pressure that led to the fraud. He demanded the results he had promised, and he appeared to scorn the procedures (and people) that should have been a check on misreporting. When efforts were made to establish

> a corporate Code of Conduct, Ebbers reportedly described it as a "colossal waste of time." He showed little respect for the role lawyers played with respect to corporate governance matters within the Company. While we have heard numerous accounts of Ebbers' demand for results—on occasion emotional, insulting, and with express reference to the personal financial harm he faced if the stock price declined—we have heard none in which he demanded or rewarded ethical business practices.[11]

Federal prosecutors worked for almost two years to build a criminal case against Ebbers. Their efforts were hampered by a shortage of documentary evidence. Ebbers never used e-mail and rarely issued instructions in writing. Finally, in March 2004, Scott Sullivan agreed to testify against his former boss. Ebbers was indicted the next day on nine counts of conspiracy, securities fraud, and filing false statements with the SEC.

When the trial began in January 2005, Sullivan testified that he had warned Ebbers numerous times that WorldCom's accounting practices were improper. "I told him that the adjustments we made were not right and they were made to hit the earnings per share. I told him we didn't even have a name to call these adjustments," Sullivan testified. "We have to hit our numbers," Ebbers allegedly replied.[12]

Ebbers's defense team, led by Reid Weingarten, tried to sow doubt about Sullivan's credibility by bringing up Sullivan's acknowledged adultery and cocaine use. Weingarten argued that Sullivan's testimony should be discounted because it was being given in an effort to win a reduced sentence for his own role in the fraud.

In a controversial and risky move, Ebbers took the witness stand and adamantly denied knowing anything about the fraud. "I wasn't advised by Scott Sullivan of anything being wrong," Ebbers claimed. "He's never told me he made an entry that wasn't right. If he had, we wouldn't be here today."[13] Ebbers claimed that Sullivan and the accounting department falsified WorldCom's reports without his knowledge or consent.

The jury deliberated eight days before convicting Ebbers of all charges. The jurors doubted the truthfulness of Sullivan's testimony, but ultimately rejected Ebbers' claim that he was simply unaware of how $7.1 billion of line costs were accounted for. "He was the man in charge," said one juror. "It's kind of hard to sit here and think he didn't know what was going on."[14]

U.S. District Judge Barbara S. Jones sentenced Ebbers to 25 years in federal prison. "I recognize this sentence is likely to be a life sentence," the judge told the 63-year-old Ebbers. "But I find a sentence of anything else would not reflect the seriousness of the crime."[15]

Scott Sullivan was rewarded richly for his testimony against Ebbers. Although he pled guilty to three criminal charges carrying a potential sentence of 27 years, Judge Jones sentenced Sullivan to only five years in prison, saying that "he provided information … without which Mr. Ebbers could not have been convicted."[16] Ebbers' attorney Reid Weingarten griped about Sullivan's good fortune, saying that lenient sentences for informants "create overwhelming incentives for snitches to fabricate evidence against superiors, which is exactly what happened in this case."[17]

David Myers and Buddy Yates were each sentenced to one year and one day in prison, while Troy Normand escaped with three years of probation. Betty Vinson's path led to five months in prison followed by five months of house arrest.

29 The Perfect Storm

> The day Arthur Andersen loses the public's trust is the day we are out of business.
>
> (Steve Samek, 1999[1])

Steve Samek, managing partner of Arthur Andersen's U.S. audit practice, never spoke a truer sentence in his life. An auditor's only real product is his or her credibility. When an auditor's written opinion is no longer deemed trustworthy, no client will pay a nickel for the auditor's signature.

Samek epitomized the "new" Andersen. Unlike Leonard Spacek's derby-clad technicians, Samek was an aggressive salesman and an extroverted showman. Samek rose to prominence within Andersen through his work on the Boston Chicken account. In one of his annual performance reviews, Samek was praised for turning Boston Chicken's $50,000 audit into a $3 million full-service engagement.

After being named head of Andersen's U.S. operations in 1998, Samek spent much of the next four years touring the country urging audit partners to sell more services. A violinist sometimes accompanied Samek as he exhorted audit partners to think of themselves as maestros directing a diverse "orchestra" of auditors, tax specialists, and consultants. Client service was stressed more than ever before. Samek even penned an 80-page manual that included advice on how to empathize with clients.

Samek implemented a "2×" performance appraisal system that encouraged audit partners to generate at least twice as much nonaudit revenue as audit revenue. A partner whose clients paid $3 million in annual audit fees, for example, was evaluated based on how close his clients came to purchasing $6 million of tax and consulting services. Young partners knew the only route to advancement within the firm was through selling more services. Even veteran partners had to generate new revenues or risk being forced into early retirement.

The Fall of Arthur Andersen

Enron's bankruptcy threatened Andersen's profits, but wasn't expected to threaten Andersen's existence. Since 1997, Andersen partners had shelled out more than $500 million to settle lawsuits arising from alleged audit failures at Sunbeam, Waste Management, McKesson HBOC, Colonial Realty, DeLorean Motors, and Baptist Foundation of Arizona. Andersen's attorneys began the unpleasant, but familiar, task of negotiating a monetary settlement with Enron's creditors and shareholders.

When Andersen's internal lawyers arrived in Houston in January 2002, they were dismayed to find that hundreds of Enron-related e-mail messages had been deleted from auditors' computers. Further investigation revealed that 20 boxes of Enron-related documents had been shredded on the orders of Andersen partner David Duncan.

Andersen CEO Joseph Berardino informed the SEC on January 10 that company personnel had destroyed a "significant but undetermined number of Enron-related documents."[2] Four days later, Berardino fired Duncan, saying he "wanted to send a message … that this was not a culture that would stand that kind of behavior."[3]

Berardino spent the next month trying to calm anxious clients and convince government regulators that Andersen was serious about adopting meaningful reforms. Berardino hired John C. Danforth, an Episcopal minister and retired U.S. senator, to represent the firm. After Arthur Levitt declined an invitation to join a special advisory board, Berardino persuaded former Federal Reserve chairman Paul A. Volcker to assume a leadership role. Volcker joined Andersen on the condition that he be allowed to separate the firm's auditing and consulting practices.

On March 2, Andersen's general counsel informed Berardino that the Justice Department was considering filing criminal charges against the entire firm. Only two weeks earlier, lawyers from Davis Polk & Wardwell had advised Andersen's board that an indictment was unlikely. Because Andersen had voluntarily notified the SEC that documents had been destroyed and had aided government investigators in recovering as much information as possible, the attorneys expected the government to treat the firm leniently.

Andersen's lawyers begged the Justice Department not to indict the firm. A letter to Assistant Attorney General Michael Chertoff outlined the negative impact an indictment would have on the firm's 28,000 U.S. employees, hundreds of retired partners, and thousands of clients. But after a federal grand jury concluded there had been "widespread criminal conduct" by Andersen involving "wholesale destruction of tons of paperwork," Chertoff charged the firm with obstruction of justice.[4] The decision was influenced by Andersen's recent failures at Sunbeam and

Waste Management, which convinced Chertoff that Andersen was a recidivist offender.

Andersen partners complained that the indictment was politically motivated. Congressional Democrats were demanding justice for the thousands of shareholders and employees hurt by the Enron fraud. And the Bush administration, which had close ties to several Enron executives and board members, was anxious to appear tough on corporate wrongdoing. Thousands of Andersen employees staged street demonstrations protesting that government prosecutors were destroying an 88-year-old firm merely to satisfy public blood lust. "I didn't shred; my kid needs to be fed," read one placard. "It takes a real Jack-Ashcroft to put 28,000 people in the streets," said another.[5]

News of the indictment led dozens of Andersen's most lucrative clients to sever their ties with the disgraced firm. Andersen attempted to merge with Deloitte & Touche and Ernst & Young, but negotiations collapsed when lawyers were unable to assure the other firms that they would not inherit Andersen's legal woes along with its clients and employees. Andersen's global network began unraveling on March 12 when its Spanish affiliate defected to Deloitte & Touche.

While awaiting trial, the once proud accounting firm became a national laughingstock. Talk show hosts David Letterman and Jay Leno made numerous jokes about the accountants who couldn't count. "I hope this doesn't turn kids off to an exciting career in accounting," Leno quipped.[6] Even President George W. Bush couldn't resist joining the fun. "I have good news and bad news from Saddam Hussein," the President told a group of dinner guests. "The good news is he is willing to let us inspect his biological and chemical warfare installations. The bad news is he insists Arthur Andersen do the inspection."[7]

When the trial began on May 6 in Houston, Andersen put its fate in the hands of defense attorney Rusty Hardin. Hardin, a Houston native who favored cowboy boots and mustard yellow suits, was known for his ability to sway Texan juries. During the trial, Hardin earned a rebuke from Judge Melinda Harmon for making fun of the two lead prosecutors' Boston and Brooklyn origins.

David Duncan was the government's star witness. "I obstructed justice," Duncan told the jury. "I instructed people on the engagement team to follow the document retention policy, which I knew would result in the destruction of documents."[8] A representative from the SEC described the consent decree Andersen signed after the agency's investigation of Waste Management stipulating that Andersen could be held in contempt of court if it engaged in future wrongdoing. Prosecutors claimed that fear of violating the consent decree motivated Duncan to hide incriminating information from the SEC. E-mail messages between David Duncan and personnel in Andersen's Chicago headquarters were introduced as evidence that Duncan had not acted alone in destroying documents.

After four weeks of testimony and ten days of deliberation, the jury convicted Arthur Andersen of one count of obstruction of justice. Surprisingly, the verdict was not based on the hundreds of pounds of shredded documents. Several jurors accepted Hardin's explanation that the auditors had simply complied with Andersen's routine document retention policy. Nor were the jurors persuaded by Duncan's testimony. Several jurors believed prosecutors had coerced Duncan into making a false confession by threatening him with a lengthy jail sentence if he resisted and promising him leniency if he cooperated. One juror reported that if Duncan had been on trial, he would have been acquitted.

Instead, the jurors concluded that Andersen in-house attorney Nancy Temple committed a crime when she advised Duncan in an e-mail message to revise an internal memorandum discussing Enron's October 15 earnings announcement. The original memo documented how Duncan had warned Enron CAO Richard Causey that certain language in the earnings announcement might be misleading. The final draft of the memo mentioned no such reservations. "Arthur Andersen did not approve that [earnings release] and Enron went along anyway and [issued] it," said jury foreman Oscar Criner. "Then Arthur Andersen set about to alter documents to keep that away from the SEC."[9] Prosecutor Andrew Weissman called the altered memo "a perfect example of Arthur Andersen sanitizing the record so the SEC would have less information."[10]

Judge Harmon fined Arthur Andersen $500,000 and sentenced the firm to five years' probation. But the indictment itself had already been a death penalty. Arthur Andersen relinquished its licenses to practice and ceased performing audits as of August 31, 2002. By the end of 2002, only a couple hundred employees remained at Arthur Andersen, most of whom were occupied settling the firm's legal affairs.

Three years later, the U.S. Supreme Court unanimously overturned Andersen's conviction on the basis that Judge Harmon had issued improper instructions to the jury. Rusty Hardin called the government's decision not to retry the case "vindication for those thousands and thousands of employees whose organization was destroyed and who went on with the rest of their lives adamantly believing that the company they had given their career to did not commit a crime."[11] Most of the displaced Andersen employees considered the Supreme Court's decision a hollow victory. "You feel better for a second, then you realize what was lost as a result of the government's action," said a former Andersen tax partner. "There's really not much else you can say."[12]

Sarbanes–Oxley

Eleven congressional committees held hearings in early 2002 investigating various dimensions of Enron's collapse. Ken Lay and Andy Fastow invoked the Fifth Amendment, but Jeffrey Skilling testified at length, blaming any accounting violations on faulty advice from Arthur Andersen. Numerous expert witnesses, including pension fund TIAA-CREF chairman John Biggs and former SEC chairman Arthur Levitt, urged the senators and representatives to adopt harsher penalties for accounting fraud and impose more stringent oversight over public accountants. The AICPA responded with a $2 million public relations campaign promoting accountants as "passionate about getting it right."

More than 30 Bills were drafted during the months following the congressional hearings. The Bill that eventually passed the House was written by Representative Michael Oxley, a Republican from Ohio. Oxley's Bill required the SEC to establish a new independent disciplinary board to regulate auditors and directed the agency to restrict the consulting services accountants could perform for their audit clients. But the Bill was short on details, leaving the SEC to set limits on auditors' services and decide the specific duties of the new disciplinary board. The House approved Oxley's Bill by a vote of 334 to 90 on April 24, 2002, with the only opposition coming from Democrats who wanted to impose tighter restrictions on public accounting firms.

The Senate moved more slowly. Senator Paul Sarbanes, a Democrat from Maryland, was determined to enact a stricter law than the one approved by the House. But with Democrats holding only a 51 to 49 seat majority in the Senate, Sarbanes needed bipartisan support to avoid having his Bill stalled by a Republican filibuster. After weeks of negotiation, Sarbanes persuaded Wyoming Senator Mike Enzi, a Republican and the only accountant in the Senate, to support his proposals. In addition to restricting consulting work performed by auditors and establishing an independent oversight board to regulate public accounting firms, the Sarbanes Bill provided stronger protections for corporate whistleblowers and extended the statute of limitations on accounting fraud cases. The Bill adopted new disclosure requirements for insider trading and corporate loans to officers and directors. Accounting firms would have to rotate supervising partners every five years and there would be a one-year cooling-off period before an auditor would be permitted to join a client as a CEO, CFO, or controller.

By the time the Senate Banking Committee approved the Sarbanes Bill on June 19, the Senate's summer calendar was already full. When Senate majority leader Tom Daschle (D, South Dakota) scheduled the floor debate for September, after the summer recess, it began to look like no accounting reform legislation would be enacted in 2002. Public interest in accounting was waning and as the November elections drew closer, the senators' thoughts were turning toward more politically rewarding issues. Senator Phil Gramm (R, Texas) vowed to defeat the Sarbanes Bill when it was introduced to the full Senate. And even if the Bill passed, it did not appear likely that House Republicans on the conference committee would approve a Bill imposing strict governmental oversight over public accounting firms. A representative from the Consumer Federal of America lamented to a colleague on June 25: "The only thing that's going to get this ball moving again is another major accounting scandal."[13]

That very afternoon, WorldCom announced that its 2000 through 2002 earnings were misstated by at least $3.8 billion. Tom Daschle decided the next morning to schedule the Senate vote for July. Although the AICPA proposed seven amendments to the Sarbanes Bill, the institute's lobbyists could not find a sponsor for any of them. Even Senator Christopher Dodd (D, Connecticut), who had received more than $500,000 from the accounting industry since 1990, abandoned his former friends and supported the proposed reforms. The Senate adopted the Sarbanes Bill on July 15 by a vote of 97 to 0.

Michael Oxley still wanted to water down the reforms in the House–Senate conference committee, but found little support among his fellow Republicans. Representatives Mark Foley (R, Florida) and Mike Rogers (R, Michigan) circulated a petition asking GOP leaders to abandon Oxley's Bill and accept the Senate version. Billy Tauzin (R, Louisiana), who had championed the accounting profession's cause during the litigation reform debate of 1995, said it was time for Congress to "pass tough new laws which will prevent future abuses and restore investor confidence."[14]

Although the final legislation is known as the Sarbanes–Oxley Act of 2002, the law is much closer to the Sarbanes Bill than to Oxley's version, especially in its provisions to enhance auditor independence. The Act stopped short of banning management advisory services to audit clients, but did prohibit nine specific services deemed incompatible with auditing. The outlawed services include bookkeeping, financial information systems design and implementation, actuarial services, internal audit outsourcing, investment banking services, legal advice, appraisal services, and executive recruiting. The Act required auditing firms to rotate the lead engagement partner every five years. And the Act prohibited accounting firms from auditing a company if the CEO, CFO, CAO, or controller was previously employed at the accounting firm and participated in the audit of that company within the previous year.

Audit committee members were subject to new restrictions and charged with new responsibilities. Each audit committee member was required to be independent, meaning that s/he could not be employed by the company or any subsidiary and could not accept any fees other than compensation for serving on the board. The Act made corporate audit committees expressly responsible for appointing, compensating, and overseeing the company's independent auditors. Audit committees were also required to establish a mechanism, such as an anonymous "hot line," for receiving and investigating complaints about accounting and auditing matters.

Corporate executives were required by the Act to certify in writing that the financial statements comply with the Securities Acts and present fairly, in all material respects, the financial condition of the company. Executives who knowingly certify false financial statements became subject to criminal penalties. Other miscellaneous provisions of the Act prohibit corporate loans to officers and directors, require more disclosures of off-balance sheet financing, and increase the maximum prison sentences for securities, mail, and wire fraud.

Auditing the Auditors

The Sarbanes–Oxley Act established a five-member committee, the Public Company Accounting Oversight Board (PCAOB or "Peek-a-boo"), to regulate auditors of publicly traded companies. The board's responsibilities include registering public accounting firms and conducting periodic inspections to ensure that auditors comply with applicable accounting and auditing standards. The board was also authorized to investigate alleged audit failures and impose sanctions. And Sarbanes–Oxley dealt a blow to public accountants' professional autonomy by giving the PCAOB authority to establish auditing, ethics, and quality control standards. Formerly, these standards had been written by committees of the AICPA.

SEC chairman Harvey Pitt, who never really liked the idea of the PCAOB, was charged with nominating the first Board members. The *New York Times* reported on October 1, 2002 that Pitt had asked John H. Biggs to serve as the PCAOB's first chairman.[15] Biggs was the CEO of TIAA-CREF, one of the nation's largest pension funds. As the custodian of $265 billion of debt and equity securities, Biggs had a strong interest in financial reporting. He was well known in the financial community as a strong advocate of accounting reform. News of Biggs's nomination was applauded enthusiastically by Paul Volcker, Arthur Levitt, Paul Sarbanes, and many others.

But Pitt issued a press release that afternoon contradicting the *New York Times* article and saying the SEC had "made no decision on the composition of the PCAOB or offered the position of chairman to any person."[16] The AICPA, the large accounting firms, and their few remaining friends in Congress opposed Biggs's nomination. TIAA-CREF rotated audit firms every five to seven years and never purchased consulting services from their auditors. Many accountants feared Biggs would try to impose similar policies on all public companies. A spokeswoman for Representative Michael Oxley said the congressman had "strong objections" to Biggs and preferred a candidate with "moderate views."[17]

Three weeks later, the five SEC commissioners elected William H. Webster chairman of the PCAOB by a partisan vote of 3 to 2. Webster was a 78-year-old retired judge who had directed the FBI and CIA under Ronald Reagan. The SEC's two Democrats criticized Webster's lack of accounting experience, and accused Pitt at a public hearing of caving in to pressure from the accounting profession. Paul Sarbanes said Pitt had "missed the opportunity to put in place an oversight board with widespread credibility."[18] Lynn Turner, the chief accountant at the SEC when Arthur Levitt was chairman, blasted the selection of Webster over Biggs, saying, "It appears that the accounting firms, the Republicans and now Chairman Pitt are trying to circumvent the Sarbanes legislation by making certain that the board does not include any reform-minded persons."[19]

Webster's selection became even more controversial only days later when it was discovered that he had served on the audit committee of a company that was being sued for accounting fraud. Furthermore, the company had fired its auditors without disclosing to the SEC that the auditors had discovered material weaknesses in the company's internal controls. Webster, who denied wrongdoing and was not named as a defendant in the civil litigation, told Pitt and SEC chief accountant Robert Herdman about the fraud accusations during the selection interviews. But Pitt and Herdman did not share the information with Congress, the White House, or the other four SEC commissioners.

Pitt already had many enemies on Capitol Hill. Before being named SEC chairman by President George W. Bush in August 2001, Pitt represented the AICPA and the Big Five accounting firms in civil litigation. Many Democrats had long doubted Pitt's willingness to police his former clients. Pitt's trouble selecting a qualified PCAOB chairman only confirmed their belief that he was not fit for his job. "Just when you think Mr. Pitt's judgment can't get any worse, he surprises us," said Representative Edward Markey (D, Massachusetts).[20] The Webster controversy caused even Pitt's few friends to abandon him. White House chief of staff Andrew Card, who had personally lobbied for Webster's selection, was furious that Pitt had withheld potentially embarrassing information.

Pitt submitted his resignation on November 6 and Webster resigned from the PCAOB shortly thereafter. In April 2003, Pitt's successor William H. Donaldson selected William J. McDonough to lead the PCAOB. McDonough was the president of the New York Federal Reserve Bank and a former CFO of First Chicago Corporation. McDonough's experience as a bank regulator and his reputation as a tough negotiator made him an attractive candidate. "The task before us is to restore the confidence of the American people and others around the world that the accounting statements issued by public companies ... present a complete, true and timely report that can be relied upon," McDonough said when his nomination was announced.[21] Later, he added, "I adore accounting theory. I think it is one of the most interesting things that one can get involved in."[22]

The PCAOB established its headquarters in Washington, DC—in office space recently vacated by Arthur Andersen—and began hiring auditors to inspect the nation's public accounting firms. The first inspections, performed in late 2003, uncovered "significant audit and accounting issues" at each of the Final Four public accounting firms.[23] All four firms were criticized for instances of failing to keep adequate documents to support their judgments. McDonough emphasized, however, that "none of our findings has shaken our belief that these firms are capable of the highest quality auditing."[24] The PCAOB continues to perform annual inspections of firms auditing 100 or more public companies and triennial inspections of smaller accounting firms.

Section 404

The most onerous provision in Sarbanes–Oxley, from the business community's viewpoint, was Section 404. This section requires corporate executives to assess their companies' internal accounting controls every year and attest that their companies have adequate internal control over financial reporting. Any material internal control weaknesses must be disclosed in the company's annual report to shareholders. And auditors are required to assess and report on the adequacy of their clients' internal accounting controls. To guide auditors' work, the PCAOB issued Auditing Standard No. 2, *An Audit of Internal Control over Financial Reporting in Conjunction with an Audit of Financial Statements.*

When the SEC set the requirements for Section 404, commission staff members estimated the aggregate annual compliance costs to be approximately $1.24 billion, an average of $91,000 per company. SEC commissioner Harvey Goldschmid justified the cost saying, "Strong internal controls will significantly deter management from committing fraud."[25] But two years later, an editorial in the *Wall Street Journal* cited a study that estimated the total first-year compliance costs to be $35 billion—28 times the SEC's prediction.[26] The millions of dollars companies were paying their auditors to report on internal controls were dwarfed by the tens of millions of dollars companies spent on consultants and software to document their controls in the first place. Deloitte & Touche reported that some of its large multinational clients were spending 70,000 man-hours—the equivalent of 35 full-time employees—complying with Section 404. And an even larger, but not easily quantified, cost was the amount of energy corporate executives were forced to spend on improving internal controls rather than running their companies. "The real cost isn't the incremental dollars," said General Motors CAO Peter Bible. "It is having people that should be focused on the business focused instead on complying with the details of the rules."[27] Sun Microsystems CEO Scott McNealy described the effects of Section 404 as throwing "buckets of sand into the gears of the market economy."[28]

Because Section 404 added significantly to the cost of selling securities in the United States, foreign-based companies began looking elsewhere to list their securities. Between 1996 and 2001, an average of 50 non-U.S. companies per year joined the New York Stock Exchange. But only 16 and eight foreign companies joined the exchange in 2003 and 2004, respectively. New public companies in China, India and Eastern Europe flocked to the London Stock Exchange, which raised $16 billion in 2005 from non-U.S. initial public offerings while the NYSE raised only $3.4 billion. A 2004 survey conducted by law firm Foley and Lardner found that 20 percent of U.S. public companies were considering going private to avoid the costs of complying with Sarbanes–Oxley.

Statement on Auditing Standards No. 99

The Enron and WorldCom scandals prompted the Auditing Standards Board to issue yet another new standard addressing financial statement fraud. SAS No. 99, *Consideration of Fraud in a Financial Statement Audit*, superseded SAS No. 82 for periods beginning on or after December 15, 2002. The new standard requires more procedures specifically designed to detect fraud than did its 1997 predecessor.

SAS No. 99 requires audit teams to hold a "brainstorming" session during which auditors discuss where fraud is most likely to occur. Auditors should try to imagine ways in which a bookkeeper might embezzle funds without being caught or senior management might try to overstate the company's earnings. The dual objectives of the brainstorming session are to identify areas of risk and instill in the audit team a proper degree of professional skepticism.

SAS No. 99 also requires audit team members to interview senior management, audit committee members, internal auditors, operating personnel, and in-house legal counsel regarding suspicious transactions and client procedures to prevent, deter, and detect fraud. Auditors should pose the same questions to multiple people and compare answers to identify inconsistencies in the responses.

The new standard requires auditors to pay particular attention to revenue, inventory, and account balances requiring significant estimates. Because approximately half of all known frauds involve misstatement of revenue, SAS No. 99 instructs auditors to "presume that there is a risk of material misstatement due to fraud relating to revenue recognition." In situations where there is risk of inventory fraud, auditors are advised to perform surprise inventory counts and examine more carefully the contents of boxed items and the manner in which goods are stacked. Auditors are required to perform a retrospective review of prior-year accounting estimates to identify biases in management's assumptions.

Two other provisions of SAS No. 99 seek to uncover fraud committed by top management. Auditors must presume a risk that management can override internal controls and address that risk by examining significant journal entries, especially entries made near the end of a reporting period. And auditors must vary their auditing procedures from year to year to make it more difficult for clients to anticipate and evade the auditors' tests.

Conclusion

The Dow Jones Industrial Average reached an all-time high of 11,723 on January 14, 2000. But 316 earnings restatements in 2000 and 2001 revealed that many high-flying technology firms of the late 1990s were not nearly as profitable as had been claimed. Enron's bankruptcy in December 2001 shattered investors' confidence. The DJIA dropped more than 2,000 points during the first half of 2002 amid fears that other "Enrons" remained undiscovered. "This is the biggest crisis investors have had since 1929," said accounting analyst Howard M. Schilit. "Investors don't know who they can trust."[29] Clearly, investors didn't trust accountants. CPAs, once held in high esteem by the American public, fell below politicians and journalists in public opinion polls.

WorldCom was the proverbial straw that broke the camel's back. *New York Times* columnist Floyd Norris attributed Sarbanes–Oxley to WorldCom CEO Bernie Ebbers. "His name is not on the law, but maybe it should be," Norris wrote. "Perhaps more than either Senator Paul S. Sarbanes or Representative Michael G. Oxley, Bernard J. Ebbers is responsible for the most far-reaching change in American securities laws since the Depression."[30]

The long-term effects of Sarbanes–Oxley are not yet known. The first-year costs of complying with Section 404 were astronomical. But average total compliance costs fell approximately 30 percent during the second year. Costs declined because companies understood the requirements better and relied less on outside consultants to document and evaluate their controls. Unfortunately, nobody has yet documented a discernible improvement in earnings quality post-Sarbanes–Oxley.

Sarbanes–Oxley's effects on the public accounting profession have been mixed. Audit revenues soared in 2003, 2004 and 2005. The number of billable hours increased as audit committees asked more questions and instructed auditors to look more closely at high-risk transactions. Audit fees paid by firms comprising the DJIA rose 40 percent between 2003 and 2004, due primarily to the requirement that firms have their internal controls audited. The Final Four accounting firms were so overwhelmed helping their largest clients comply with Section 404 that they began resigning many small and mid-sized public company engagements. Second-tier public accounting firms, such as Grant Thornton and BDO Seidman, picked up more than 400 former Final Four clients in 2003 and 2004. Grant Thornton's total revenue grew 30 percent in 2004.

On the negative side, many accounting firms have been hurt by Sarbanes–Oxley's restrictions on nonaudit services. Fees paid by DJIA members unrelated to tax or audit work declined 85 percent in 2003. Tax accountants and management consultants employed at public accounting firms complain that Sarbanes–Oxley's independence requirements make it difficult for them to compete with stand-alone consulting firms. And Sarbanes–Oxley caused many small CPA firms to stop auditing public companies. Only about 600 of the 850 public accounting firms who audited public companies in 2002 opted to register with the PCAOB. The other 250 firms resigned their public company engagements rather than bear the costs of complying with the PCAOB's membership requirements. Finally, Sarbanes–Oxley's requirement that accounting firms rotate the lead engagement partner every five years has disrupted the personal lives of many audit partners. Accounting firms are finding it necessary to transfer partners from office to office on a regular basis to comply with the partner rotation requirement.

30 Conclusion

> We ought not to look back unless it is to derive useful lessons from past errors.
>
> (George Washington)

Throughout the twentieth and into the early twenty-first century, clever fraudsters exposed flaws in the nation's financial reporting system. Some scandals led accountants to write new accounting standards closing perceived loopholes. Other frauds prompted auditors to adopt more rigorous testing procedures. When Congress or the SEC concluded that accountants were not responding adequately to protect the public interest, new safeguards were mandated. Dozens of accounting scandals, including the 14 highlighted in this book, significantly influenced the volume and content of required financial disclosure, the development of GAAP, auditors' testing procedures, the organizational structure of public accounting firms, and government regulation of the American public accounting profession.

Mandatory Financial Reporting and Compulsory Audits

More than two years passed after the stock market crash of 1929 without substantive action from Congress. But the discovery of Ivar Kreuger's massive accounting fraud brought new demands for reform. Representative Fiorello LaGuardia accused the New York Stock Exchange of abetting Kreuger's fraud. The New York *Daily Mirror* asserted that if corporations underwent regular audits, "gigantic swindles like the Kreuger & Toll Concern could not be organized."[1]

Within a year of Kreuger's suicide, Congress passed the Securities Act of 1933 requiring U.S. corporations to publish audited financial statements before selling securities to the public. Representative Sam Rayburn described the Act as a response to "the reticence of financiers."[2] Nobody was more reticent than Kreuger, a tight-lipped stoic who once attributed his success to "silence, more silence, and even more silence."[3]

The volume of information corporations must disclose has increased exponentially since 1933. When annual financial statements proved insufficient for investors' needs, the SEC mandated quarterly reporting. Although quarterly statements are still not audited, the Sarbanes–Oxley Act of 2002 requires auditors to review the quarterly statements before their release. Worries about opinion shopping led to a requirement that companies notify the SEC within five business days of an auditor's dismissal or resignation. Public companies must disclose, in a public filing, whether there have been any disagreements between management and the auditors within the previous three years. Kenneth Lay's sale of hundreds of thousands of shares of Enron stock during the months preceding his company's bankruptcy led to rules requiring more complete disclosure of insider trading.

Development of GAAP

The Securities Exchange Act of 1934 granted the SEC authority to establish GAAP. But rather than set standards directly, the SEC has allowed a series of private sector committees to write the detailed accounting rules. GAAP developed slowly during the twentieth century as the CAP, APB, and FASB dealt with reporting problems on a largely *ad hoc* basis. Many accounting standards can be traced directly to weaknesses exposed by accounting scandals.

Accounting for mergers and acquisitions was a problem area for decades. Cort Randell's National Student Marketing Corporation concealed its operating losses by acquiring 23 other companies through stock trades. But when the APB attempted to outlaw pooling-of-interests accounting in 1969, the backlash from accounting firms and the business community was so strong that it contributed to the dissolution of the APB. Twenty years later, Waste Management acquired more than 1,500 companies en route to becoming the largest waste disposal company in the world. WorldCom used stock-based acquisitions to become the world's second largest telecommunications company. Finally, in 2001, the FASB abolished pooling-of-interests accounting and established new rules requiring companies to periodically review purchased goodwill for impairment.

The savings and loan crisis of the 1980s revealed several weaknesses in financial institutions' accounting practices. Until 1987, banks and thrifts could inflate their short-term earnings by charging high application fees for low interest rate loans. And many troubled banks and thrifts concealed their true financial condition from regulators by understating their loan loss reserves. SFAS No. 91 required financial institutions to defer most loan origination fees and recognize them as income over the life of the loan rather than at inception. SFAS No. 114, issued in 1993, set stricter guidelines for when a loan had to be classified as impaired.

One of the most contentious accounting issues during the last 100 years has been whether assets should be reported at historical cost or at current market value. The SEC, believing that some companies had reported arbitrary market values during the 1920s, decided early on to require corporations to report their assets at historical cost. But rapidly fluctuating interest rates during the 1970s and 1980s revealed the inadequacies of historical cost accounting. Balance sheets didn't reveal the extent to which financial institutions' security and loan portfolios had declined in value. And companies manipulated their reported income by cherry-picking securities from their portfolios.

The SEC reversed course in the early 1990s and began advocating fair value accounting for financial instruments. Ironically, Enron was one of the few companies that shared SEC chairman Richard Breeden's enthusiasm for mark-to-market accounting. During 1999 and 2000, Enron reported hundreds of millions of dollars of unrealized holding gains on its energy contracts. In spite of Enron's opportunistic behavior, the FASB and SEC continue moving toward expanded use of fair value accounting.

Enron had more influence on other aspects of accounting. The FASB adopted tighter guidelines for special-purpose entity accounting in 2003. And the Enron fiasco prompted widespread discussion of whether the United States should abandon its rules-based approach to standard setting in favor of a European-style principles-based approach.

Auditing Procedures

Many accounting frauds led to significant changes in testing procedures as auditors tried to close loopholes exploited by clever fraudsters. Today's auditors examine more outside evidence, perform more analytical procedures, review management estimates more thoroughly, and pay more attention to related party transactions than did their counterparts of 100 years ago.

Early American audits involved examining the client's accounting records in exhaustive detail. Auditors traced journal entries to the general ledger and recomputed the account balances. Hundreds of hours were spent verifying that individual transactions were recorded and summarized correctly. But auditors spent relatively little time reviewing third-party documents. Nor did auditors routinely examine assets to test the year-end balances.

In 1939, while the SEC was investigating the McKesson & Robbins fraud, an AIA committee chaired by Patrick Glover recommended that auditors observe clients' physical inventory counts and confirm receivables via direct communication with debtors. If the Price Waterhouse auditors had performed either procedure at McKesson & Robbins, F. Donald Coster would have found it far more difficult to conceal his bootlegging activities and fictitious transactions. Auditors, since 1940, have been required to verify the existence of their clients' primary assets through physical examination or third-party confirmation.

The advent of electronic data processing in the 1950s improved accountants' lives immensely. Computers removed the drudgery from bookkeeping and significantly reduced the occurrence of posting and summarization errors. But swindlers soon learned how to use computers to commit and conceal fraud. Employees at Equity Funding programmed the company's computer to generate account numbers and phony data for 64,000 fictitious life insurance policies. Shortly after the Equity Funding fraud was discovered, the Auditing Standards Executive Committee issued SAS No. 3 identifying risks posed by computerized accounting systems. Since the mid-1970s, auditors have developed sophisticated software programs to sort and evaluate clients' electronic data.

Accounting frauds, such as the one at ZZZZ Best, led to greater use of analytical procedures. SAS No. 56, adopted within a year of the ZZZZ Best scandal, requires auditors to perform analytical procedures during the planning and final review stages of all audits. If Barry Minkow's auditors had performed simple year-to-year ratio comparisons, they might have noticed that ZZZZ Best's operating expenses and fixed assets lagged far behind the company's purported revenues. Unfortunately, new standards, alone, cannot ensure effective audits. Arthur Andersen's overreliance on badly performed analytical procedures contributed to their failure to detect WorldCom's accounting fraud. The auditors apparently never considered that WorldCom managers might manipulate the accounts to *eliminate* quarter-to-quarter fluctuations. Instead, the auditors naively interpreted WorldCom's stable line cost E/R ratio as evidence that the reported line cost expense was reasonable.

Many accounting frauds involve the manipulation of estimated account balances. Charles Keating deliberately understated Lincoln Savings & Loan's loan loss reserves. Waste Management improperly extended the estimated useful lives of its landfills. Scott Sullivan directed his accounting staff to decrease WorldCom's accruals for future line charges. Estimated account balances are especially difficult to audit because, by definition, the proper account balance will not be known until some time in the future. In 1988, the ASB issued SAS No. 57 providing auditors more guidance on how to test significant accounting estimates. SAS No. 99, issued in 2002, requires auditors to perform a retrospective review of prior-year accounting estimates to identify biases in management's assumptions or methodology.

Related-party transactions are another tool many fraudsters use to hide losses or inflate profits. Alan Novick concealed $300 million of losses by shifting them from ESM Government Securities to an affiliated—but unconsolidated and unaudited—company. Enron avoided recording losses by transferring money-losing assets to SPEs controlled by CFO Andy Fastow. In 1975, shortly after the U.S. Financial fraud was uncovered, the Auditing Standards Board issued SAS No. 6 requiring auditors to perform procedures designed to identify non-"arm' length" transactions between clients and affiliated entities. A revised SAS issued in 1983 and a Practice Alert published in 1995 provided updated guidance for auditing related-party transactions. In December 2001, weeks after Enron's bankruptcy, the AICPA distributed to its members a Related Party Toolkit emphasizing the importance of understanding the client's transactions and relationships.

Auditors' Responsibility for Fraud

British author Lawrence Dicksee commented in 1892: "The auditor who is able to detect fraud is—other things being equal—a better man than the auditor who cannot."[4] But for much of the twentieth century, American auditors tried to evade responsibility for detecting frauds committed by their clients. The first authoritative compilation of auditing procedures, published by the AIA in 1929, warned that audits would not necessarily disclose defalcations concealed through manipulation of the accounts. From 1912 through 1957 successive editions of Robert Montgomery's *Auditing Theory and Practice* placed progressively less emphasis on fraud detection.

The 1940 edition of Montgomery's auditing text disclaimed responsibility for fraud, saying that searching for irregularities would "require an examination of such detail that its cost ... would be prohibitive."[5] But that same year, the SEC said in its report on McKesson & Robbins: "We believe that ... accountants can be expected to detect gross overstatements of assets and profits whether resulting from collusive fraud or otherwise."[6] For the remainder of the century, public accountants faced an "expectation gap" between their self-defined responsibilities and public/regulatory expectations.

Public outrage over the Equity Funding scandal prompted the AICPA in 1977 to issue SAS No. 16 clarifying auditors' responsibility for fraud. The new standard required auditors to plan their examinations "to search for errors and irregularities that would have a material effect on the financial statements." Similarly, the Watergate hearings of the mid-1970s led to SAS No. 17, clarifying the auditor's responsibility for detecting and reporting illegal acts committed by clients.

Only ten years later, the savings and loan crisis and other well publicized accounting scandals of the 1980s forced the AICPA to try again. SAS No. 16 warned of "inherent limitations" in the auditing process. But American taxpayers, who would soon pay several hundred billion dollars to bail out failed financial institutions, were in no mood for excuses. The public wanted greater protection from swindlers such as

Charles Keating and Don Dixon. And the ZZZZ Best fraud, which received nationwide media coverage during the summer of 1987, left people wondering how a major public accounting firm could permit a 22-year-old carpet cleaner to claim tens of millions of dollars of fictitious revenues.

SAS No. 53, issued in 1988, required auditors to design their audits "to provide reasonable assurance of detecting errors and irregularities that are material to the financial statements." The new standard required auditors to treat management representations with professional skepticism. No longer could auditors simply assume that management was honest barring evidence to the contrary.

In 1997, shortly after the discovery of costly accounting frauds at Phar-Mor and Leslie Fay, the Auditing Standards Board provided more detailed guidance to help auditors assess the risk of fraud. SAS No. 82 identified more than thirty risk factors commonly associated with fraudulent financial reporting. The new standard required auditors to document their risk assessments in their workpapers and adjust their audit procedures to provide reasonable assurance of detecting material fraud should it exist.

The Enron and WorldCom scandals led the Auditing Standards Board to issue SAS No. 99. This latest fraud standard requires auditors to perform more procedures specifically designed to detect fraud. Audit teams must hold brainstorming sessions during which they try to imagine how a client might try to commit fraud. Auditors must conduct extensive interviews to learn about the client's procedures for preventing, deterring, and detecting fraud. Auditors are advised to pay special attention to the client's inventory and revenue accounts and are required to vary their auditing procedures from year to year to make it more difficult for clients to anticipate and evade the auditors' tests.

Public Accounting Firms

Six of the Big Eight accounting firms were established during the 1800s. The other two, Ernst & Ernst and Arthur Andersen, were established in 1903 and 1913, respectively. Of the original Big Eight, only Arthur Andersen no longer exists. Mergers consolidated the other seven firms down to four. Although they still bear their founders' names, the Final Four are vastly different than William W. Deloitte, S.H. Price, and A.C. Ernst probably ever imagined. Partners have far less autonomy. And after evolving from public accounting firms into multidisciplinary professional services organizations, the firms have largely returned to their accounting and auditing roots.

Public accounting firms in the United States have always been organized as partnerships. A common characteristic of many partnerships is weak central authority. Small partnerships operate largely on friendship and trust. Each partner trusts the others to conduct proper audits and sign the firm's name to the audit report. When firms grow, partners are reluctant to surrender their autonomy and submit their professional judgments to review by other partners. But modern firms, with upward of 1,500 partners, will inevitably contain a few bad apples. Jose Gomez certified ESM Government Securities' fraudulent financial statements while accepting thousands of dollars of "loans" from ESM's managers. David Duncan ignored advice from Arthur Andersen's Professional Standards Group and ordered Enron-related documents and e-mail messages destroyed.

Because accounting firms invariably try to dodge responsibility for audit failures by blaming rogue auditors or claiming the failures were caused by isolated errors in judgment, both Congress and the SEC have forced public accounting firms to adopt stronger internal controls. When the AICPA established a division for CPA firms in 1977, members of the SEC practice section had to assign a concurring partner to each publicly traded audit client. The Sarbanes–Oxley Act of 2002 requires that the lead engagement partner be rotated every five years.

Another characteristic of general partnerships is that the partners are jointly and severally liable for the partnership's debts. This fact exposed public accounting partners to significant risk during the litigation crisis of the 1980s and early 1990s. After Laventhol & Horwath collapsed in 1990, accountants launched a nationwide lobbying campaign seeking permission to reorganize their firms as limited liability partnerships. By the end of 1994, all the major public accounting firms were LLPs.

From their inception, public accounting firms provided a wide range of management advisory services to their clients. Until the 1970s, however, accounting and tax services provided at least 80 percent of most firms' revenues. And all public accounting firm partners had to be CPAs, even those engaged exclusively in consulting.

Consulting revenues grew faster than audit fees during the 1970s and 1980s until, by 1995, more than 50 percent of the Big Six firms' revenues, and a larger share of their profits, came from management advisory services. CPAs, jealous of their consulting colleagues' success, even toyed with the idea of becoming Cognitors.

The growth of nonaudit services led to decades of debate. Public opinion polls revealed that significant numbers of financial statement users believed that consulting services impaired auditors' independence. Witnesses at the Metcalf/Moss hearings of the 1970s and the Dingell/Wyden hearings of the 1980s recommended banning accounting firms from providing management advisory services to their audit clients.

Public accounting firms' consulting revenues continued growing until scandals at Sunbeam and Waste Management raised new concerns about auditors' close ties to their clients. Even then, SEC chairman Arthur Levitt's 2000 proposal to prohibit internal audit outsourcing and information systems design work met fierce opposition from public accountants and their friends in Congress. It was not until two years later, after Enron and WorldCom, that the Sarbanes–Oxley Act prohibited nine specific services deemed incompatible with auditing.

Government Regulation

During the 1933 Senate hearings, Haskins & Sells partner Arthur Carter urged Congress to entrust public accountants with the task of auditing corporate financial statements. "Who will audit you?" a skeptical Senator asked. "Our conscience," Carter boldly replied.[7]

And for much of the twentieth century, public accountants operated with few external restraints. States issued licenses to practice public accounting but rarely disciplined auditors for malpractice. The SEC issued only 114 Accounting Series Releases between 1937 and 1969 and fewer than 25 of them related to disciplinary action against public accountants. It was not until the 1970s that the federal government began regularly punishing auditors for deficient audits. Two Seidman & Seidman auditors were prosecuted in 1973 for performing incomplete audits of Equity Funding. And the Justice Department indicted two Peat Marwick auditors in 1974 for making false statements regarding National Student Marketing's proxy statement. The SEC banned both Seidman & Seidman and Peat Marwick from accepting new publicly traded audit clients for six months.

But even in the aftermath of National Student Marketing and Equity Funding, Senator Lee Metcalf and Representative John Moss failed to enact new legislation strengthening government oversight over public accountants. Senator Metcalf, after issuing a report highly critical of the public accounting profession, decided to give accountants one more chance to reform themselves. Representative Moss introduced a Bill in 1978 calling for the creation of a new federal agency to inspect public accounting firms and investigate allegations of substandard auditing, but the Bill stalled in committee and never reached the House floor.

Eight years later, Representatives John Dingell and Ron Wyden held another series of hearings investigating the public accounting profession. Although several witnesses urged Congress to enact substantial reforms, Dingell and Wyden didn't attempt to implement Professor Abraham Briloff's recommendation to separate auditing and consulting or Professor Robert Chatov's plan to have the SEC assign auditors to publicly held companies. Wyden's repeated attempts to require auditors to report suspicions of fraud directly to the SEC were unsuccessful. Finally, a provision of the Private Securities Litigation Reform Act of 1995 required auditors to report fraud to the SEC if the client's management failed to do so.

Only in 2002, after the Enron and WorldCom debacles, did Congress adopt tight controls over the public accounting profession. The Sarbanes–Oxley Act created the Public Company Accounting Oversight Board (PCAOB) to audit the auditors. The PCAOB's duties include registering public accounting firms and conducting periodic inspections to ensure that auditors comply with applicable accounting and auditing standards. Auditing, ethics, and quality control standards for audits of publicly traded companies are now written by the PCAOB rather than by accountants themselves.

Conclusion

American financiers boast of having the most efficient capital markets in the world. If their claim is true, much of the credit belongs to the nation's accountants for creating a relatively transparent system of financial reporting. The *Wall Street Journal* commented in 2001:

> When the intellectual achievements of the 20th century are tallied, GAAP should be on everyone's Top 10 list. The idea of GAAP—so simple yet so radical—is that there should be a standard way of accounting for profit and loss in public businesses, allowing investors to see how a public company manages its money. This transparency is what allows investors to compare businesses as different as McDonald's, IBM, and Tupperware, and it makes U.S. markets the envy of the world.[8]

Although American standard setters have tried for decades to establish a uniform set of accounting principles, alternative methods of accounting for similar transactions still complicate the process of comparing companies' earnings. And 1,818 earnings restatements in 2004 and 2005 demonstrate that accounting errors occur far more frequently than one might hope. The FASB still has much work to do to improve accounting standards for leases, pensions, and derivative securities.

American auditors like to remind their critics that fewer than 1 percent of public company audits are ever challenged by the SEC or through civil litigation. But PCAOB inspections in 2003 and 2004 discovered deficiencies at each of the Final Four public accounting firms. The PCAOB found instances of auditors using inadequate sample sizes, failing to align audit tests with risk assessments, and not maintaining control over audit confirmations. Similar problems were found at many second-tier and smaller public accounting firms. Auditors still need to improve their own internal controls and develop more effective procedures for detecting corporate fraud.

American auditing and financial reporting improved dramatically during the twentieth century, largely in response to accounting scandals.

Unfortunately, many of the most recent accounting and auditing reforms have imposed high costs on the American economy. One academic study of stock market reactions to the Sarbanes–Oxley Act concluded that the legislation cost U.S. companies billions of dollars in lost market value.[9] Since 2003, hundreds of Indian and Chinese companies have chosen to issue their securities in London rather than New York.

George O. May warned Congress in 1933: "All these things are a question of balancing risks against the cost. If you erect machinery of protection that is too expensive you will kill industry."[10] Accountants struggled throughout the twentieth century to provide relevant and reliable financial information at a reasonable cost. Many times they succeeded. Too often they failed. Future accountants must find cost-effective ways to correct today's financial reporting weaknesses and address tomorrow's inevitable accounting scandals.

Appendix A
Discussion Questions

1 Scandal and Reform

1. How did President Franklin Delano Roosevelt respond to Ivar Kreuger's investment scam?
2. What accounting reforms did Senator Lee Metcalf and Representative John Moss contemplate during the late 1970s?
3. How did the Federal Deposit Insurance Corporation Improvement Act of 1991 influence auditing and financial reporting?
4. Have American auditors always accepted responsibility for detecting and reporting their clients' financial statement fraud?
5. Why did the general counsel of a Big Eight accounting firm describe a jury's $81 million judgment against Arthur Andersen as "the single worst thing that has ever happened to the accounting profession"?
6. What did SEC chairman Arthur Levitt conclude from Arthur Andersen's audit failures at Sunbeam and Waste Management? How did Chairman Levitt respond?
7. What effect did the Sarbanes–Oxley Act of 2002 have on American auditing and financial reporting?

2 Out of Darkness

1. What reasons did American corporate executives give for not publishing audited financial statements in the early 1900s?
2. How did trendsetters such as U.S. Steel, John B. Stetson Company, and Equitable Life create pressure on other companies to publish audited financial statements?
3. According to William Z. Ripley, what economic and social problems were caused by inadequate financial reporting?
4. How did the Federal Reserve Board (indirectly) encourage American corporations to prepare audited financial statements?

3 Ivar Kreuger

1. Why did Swedish Match Company need to raise large sums of money?
2. How was Swedish Match Company able to pay interest and dividends far in excess of the company's actual profits?
3. Describe at least one fraudulent act Ivar Kreuger used to overstate Swedish Match Company's reported assets.
4. How did Kreuger conceal Swedish Match Company's true financial condition from the company's directors and underwriters?
5. What role did auditors play in the discovery of Kreuger's fraud?

4 McKesson & Robbins

1. How did the four Musica brothers "skim" profits from McKesson & Robbins?
2. What audit procedures would have detected McKesson & Robbins' fictitious sales and inflated inventories?
3. How was the McKesson & Robbins fraud discovered?

5 Into the Spotlight

1. How did the Securities Act of 1933 attempt to prevent financial frauds?
2. What proposal did Congress consider in 1933 that seriously threatened the nation's public accounting firms?
3. How did the Securities Exchange Act of 1934 attempt to prevent financial frauds?
4. What changes in auditing practice did the SEC recommend after investigating the McKesson & Robbins fraud?

6 Generally Accepted Accounting Principles

1. Accounting existed for centuries without generally accepted accounting principles. What economic changes in the late nineteenth and early twentieth centuries created a need for GAAP?
2. Why was the CAP unable to eliminate alternative accounting treatments for items such as inventory, depreciation, pensions, and income taxes?
3. What factors led to the CAP's dissolution?
4. Why did the APB reject the accounting principles proposed in ARS No. 3?
5. The SEC claims to want to reduce the number of alternative accounting treatments. Have the SEC's actions always matched its words? What role does politics play in setting accounting standards?

6. Why did growth-oriented companies prefer to account for their acquisitions as poolings-of-interests?

7 National Student Marketing

1. How was NSMC able to increase its annual revenues from $723,000 to $68 million in only two years?
2. What factors led to Cort Randell's ouster from NSMC?
3. What questions should PMM have asked Arthur Andersen before accepting the NSMC audit engagement?
4. What audit procedures should PMM have performed to test NSMC's fixed-fee marketing contracts?
5. What should PMM have done upon learning that $1.4 million of the $1.7 million of revenue accrued by NSMC at the end of fiscal year 1968 was written off during the first three quarters of 1969?
6. What should PMM have done in October 1969 when NSMC refused to issue a revised proxy statement to its shareholders?

8 Equity Funding

1. How did EFCA use phony life insurance policies to generate cash? What long-term problem did these phony policies create for EFCA?
2. How did EFCA convince the auditors that the phony life insurance policies were real? What audit procedures would have detected the fictitious policies?
3. According to the SEC, what "flagrant violations" of SEC rules and professional accounting standards did WWR&L commit?
4. Did Seidman & Seidman audit partner Bob Spencer err in giving copies of Ray Dirks's notes to Stanley Goldblum? Why or why not?

9 Déjà Vu

1. What factors led to the dissolution of the APB?
2. How is the FASB different from the CAP and the APB?
3. How did Watergate and the Arab oil embargo create pressure for accounting reform?
4. What recommendations did Senator Lee Metcalf and Representative John Moss make for reforming the accounting profession?
5. What recommendations did the (Cohen) Commission on Auditors' Responsibilities make for reforming the public accounting profession?
6. What reforms did the AICPA adopt in response to the Moss/Metcalf congressional hearings?
7. According to SAS No. 3, what risks are posed by computerized accounting systems?

10 It's a Wonderful Life?

1. Explain the phrase "borrowing short and investing long." Why were savings and loans vulnerable to interest rate risk?
2. What caused banks and thrifts to lose so much money during the late 1970s and early 1980s?
3. Why didn't financial institutions' financial statements communicate the full extent of their losses?
4. How did Regulatory Accounting Principles (RAP) help savings and loans hide their insolvency?
5. Define the term "moral hazard." Explain how reducing the net worth requirement from 5 percent to 3 percent of insured deposits encouraged S&L owners to invest in risky assets.

11 ESM Government Securities

1. How did Alan Novick conceal ESM's losses on the financial statements?
2. What is a "repo"? How did ESM use repos to maintain a positive cash flow while suffering enormous trading losses?
3. How did accountant Laurie Holtz discover that ESM's financial statements were misstated by approximately $300 million?
4. How did ESM's bankruptcy affect the citizens and taxpayers of Ohio?
5. Why did Jose Gomez not report the ESM fraud as soon as he learned about it?
6. Why did the SEC charge the entire Alexander Grant accounting firm with fraud?

12 Lincoln Savings & Loan

1. What "red flags" might have warned Arthur Young that LS&L was a high risk client?
2. What motive did Charles Keating have to understate LS&L's loan portfolio when he purchased the thrift?
3. LS&L reported $153 million of gains on real estate sales in 1986 and 1987. What facts might have caused the auditors to question whether such gains were feasible?
4. Why wasn't LS&L closed in spring 1987 as investigators from the San Francisco office of the FHLBB recommended?
5. Auditors must maintain independence in fact and appearance. What events might raise doubts about whether Jack Atchison and the Phoenix office of Arthur Young were independent of Charles Keating and LS&L?

13 Bank Robbers

1. What was the most common audit deficiency cited by the GAO in its 1989 report about S&L failures?
2. What contributing factor did the GAO find in nearly all the bankrupt banks it examined in 1991?
3. Why did the GAO recommend in 1991 that banks adopt market value accounting for investment securities?
4. What reasons did people give for opposing mandatory internal control reporting in 1979?
5. Did the AICPA support or oppose mandatory internal control reporting in 1979? In 1993?
6. Explain the term "gains trading." How did the use of historical cost accounting permit financial institutions to manipulate their reported earnings?
7. What reasons did bank executives give for opposing mark-to-market accounting?
8. Describe two pronouncements the FASB issued to improve financial institutions' accounting.

14 Auditors and Fraud

1. What was the primary purpose of auditing from antiquity through the late nineteenth century?
2. How did the auditor's responsibility for detecting financial statement fraud evolve during the twentieth century?
3. What reasons did auditors give for wanting to limit their responsibility for detecting and reporting financial statement fraud?
4. According to a survey commissioned by Arthur Andersen in 1974, what did 66 percent of investors say was the most important function of auditors?
5. What reasons did auditors and the SEC give for opposing Representative Ron Wyden's 1986 Bill that would have required auditors to report suspicions of fraud to the SEC?

15 ZZZZ Best

1. How did Barry Minkow record loan proceeds and repayments to make ZZZZ Best appear more profitable than it really was?
2. What role did Interstate Appraisal Services and Marbil Marketing play in the ZZZZ Best fraud?
3. Describe the procedures Arthur Young partner Larry Gray performed to verify the existence of ZZZZ Best's restoration projects. Were these audit procedures sufficient?
4. What events led to ZZZZ Best's collapse?

5. According to the SEC, what errors did auditor George Greenspan make in auditing ZZZZ Best's April 30, 1986 financial statements?

16 Crazy Eddie

1. Why did the Antar family initially understate their company's sales revenue?
2. What methods did Eddie and Sammy Antar use from 1980 forward to overstate Crazy Eddie's sales revenue?
3. How did Eddie and Sammy Antar conceal the fact that Crazy Eddie's inventory balance was overstated by $65 million?
4. What led to the discovery of the Crazy Eddie fraud?
5. Why was Sammy Antar, the architect of the Crazy Eddie fraud, never sentenced to prison?

17 Closing the Gap

1. What did the National Commission on Fraudulent Financial Reporting recommend to combat financial statement fraud?
2. How did SAS No. 53 differ from SAS No. 16?
3. Describe the requirements of SAS Nos. 55–57, which were adopted in 1988 to make audits more effective.
4. In what ways did SAS No. 58 change the standard auditor's report?
5. According to the SEC, what were the most common audit deficiencies from 1987 to 1997?
6. What did SAS No. 82 add to SAS No. 53?

18 Auditors' Legal Liability

1. Why did the Journal of Accountancy advocate holding auditors legally liable for clients' losses in 1912?
2. How did auditors' common law liability to third parties evolve during the twentieth century?
3. According to George O. May, how was the 1933 Securities Act unfair to accountants?
4. What must plaintiffs prove in order to recover damages from auditors under the Securities Exchange Act of 1934?
5. Describe the auditing reforms that followed each of the following legal cases: (a) 1136 Tenants' Corp., (b) Yale Express, (c) BarChris Corporation, (d) U.S. Financial.
6. Why did the number of civil lawsuits filed against public accounting firms increase during the 1970s?

19 Fund of Funds

1. How did King Resources cheat Fund of Funds?
2. How did King Resources convince Funds of Funds that its oil and gas properties were increasing in value?
3. Why did Arthur Andersen not modify Fund of Fund's 1968 audit report after learning that the land purchased by Robert Raff was not an arms-length transaction?
4. What reasons did Arthur Andersen give for not telling Fund of Funds about King Resources' higher than normal price markups?
5. Why did the jury reject Arthur Andersen's "confidentiality" defense?
6. How did the jury estimate the damages suffered by Fund of Funds?

20 MiniScribe

1. What might have motivated MiniScribe employees to overstate their company's earnings?
2. What methods did MiniScribe employees use to overstate the company's sales revenues?
3. How did MiniScribe employees prevent the auditors from discovering the overstated inventory?
4. What common financial statement ratios should have alerted the auditors to MiniScribe's overstated inventory and accounts receivable balances in 1988?
5. What did Q.T. Wiles do when audit partner Raymond McFee asked him to record adjusting entries reducing MiniScribe's 1986 earnings by $1.5 million?

21 Litigation Reform

1. What "flaws" did the chief executives of the Big Six accounting firms identify in the U.S. tort liability system?
2. Describe major provisions of the Private Securities Litigation Reform Act of 1995 that reduced auditors' legal liability.
3. Why did public accounting firms wish to reorganize as limited liability partnerships?
4. Describe how each of the following court decisions reduced auditors' legal liability: (a) Bily *v.* Arthur Young & Co., (b) Reves *v.* Ernst & Young, (c) Central Bank of Denver *v.* First Interstate Bank of Denver.

22 Auditor Independence

1. Why is it important that auditors maintain independence in appearance as well as in fact?
2. In what ways might mandatory audit firm rotation increase auditor independence and improve audit quality? What reasons did the leaders of the Big Six accounting firms give for opposing mandatory audit firm rotation?
3. How is auditor independence threatened when auditors accept jobs with former audit clients?
4. How might auditors' performance of management advisory services erode their perceived independence? How might management advisory services improve audit quality and efficiency?
5. Why does Section 602.02g of the SEC's Codification of Financial Reporting Policies forbid direct business relationships between public accounting firms and their publicly traded audit clients?
6. What events led to the establishment of the Independence Standards Board?

23 Waste Management

1. What events of the 1970s and 1980s suggest that Waste Management might have had inadequate internal controls and/or a corrupt corporate culture?
2. What motive did Waste Management have to overstate estimated liabilities for environmental cleanup costs when acquiring other companies?
3. What methods did Waste Management use to delay recognition of current operating expenses until future periods?
4. Why did Arthur Andersen classify Waste Management as a "high risk" client?
5. What actions did Arthur Andersen partner Robert E. Allgyer take after discovering $128 million of misstatements in Waste Management's 1993 financial statements? According to the SEC, how did Allgyer's actions place Arthur Andersen in an "untenable position"?
6. Why did the SEC charge the entire Arthur Andersen accounting firm with fraud?

24 Sunbeam

1. Why was Al Dunlap unable to sell Sunbeam in 1997?
2. What events led to Dunlap's ouster and the discovery of the Sunbeam fraud?
3. What motive did Al Dunlap and Donald Kersh have to record $35 million of excessive writedowns and unnecessary reserves in 1996?

4. What methods did Sunbeam use to accelerate sales in 1997? How did these tactics affect Sunbeam's 1998 sales?
5. According to the SEC, what errors did Phillip E. Harlow make during his audits of Sunbeam's 1996 and 1997 financial statements?
6. How might Al Dunlap's management style have created a culture wherein fraud could occur without being reported?

25 End of the Millennium

1. What was the nature of PricewaterhouseCoopers' 8,064 independence violations? What actions did Barry Melancon and the AICPA take in response to PwC's violations?
2. In what ways did SEC chairman Arthur Levitt propose relaxing auditor independence requirements in 2000? In what ways did Levitt propose tightening auditor independence requirements?
3. How did the AICPA and the leaders of the Big Five accounting firms respond to Chairman Levitt's independence proposal? What events motivated Levitt and the auditors to compromise?
4. How did Levitt succeed in significantly reducing the consulting services performed by public accounting firms for their audit clients?
5. According to SAB No. 99, under what circumstances might quantitatively small misstatements be considered material?

26 Professionalism

1. What distinguishes a profession from a business?
2. Why did the AICPA amend its Code of Professional Conduct in 1978 to permit public accountants to advertise?
3. Why did the U.S. Supreme Court overturn Florida's restriction on direct solicitation?
4. How might competitive bidding for audit engagements hurt audit quality?
5. According to the AICPA Special Committee on Assurance Services, why did auditing face a dim future in the early 1990s? What did the committee recommend?
6. What were the anticipated benefits of the proposed Cognitor designation?
7. How might compensating audit partners for cross-selling tax and consulting services hurt audit quality?
8. How might the breakup of Arthur Andersen and Andersen Consulting have hurt Andersen's audit quality?

27 Enron

1. In what ways did Enron violate accounting rules for special purpose entities?
2. How did Enron's use of mark-to-market accounting give executives the ability to manipulate quarterly earnings?
3. What events led to Enron's collapse?
4. What was Arthur Andersen's rationale for concluding that $51 million of known misstatements in Enron's 1997 financial statements were immaterial?
5. According to Andrew Fastow's testimony, how did Enron manipulate its reported earnings through trades with the LJM partnerships?

28 WorldCom

1. How was WorldCom able to report 11 consecutive quarters of double-digit revenue growth between the first quarter of 1999 and the first quarter of 2002?
2. How did WorldCom understate its line cost expense by $3.3 billion between the second quarter of 1999 and the fourth quarter of 2000?
3. How did WorldCom understate its line cost expense by $3.8 billion between the first quarter of 2001 and the first quarter of 2002?
4. What motivated Cynthia Cooper to begin examining WorldCom's capital expenditures and fixed asset accounts?
5. What rationale did Scott Sullivan use to try to justify capitalizing WorldCom's line cost expenses?
6. What audit procedures did Arthur Andersen perform to test WorldCom's line costs and capital expenditures? Why were these procedures ineffective?
7. What criticism did the special investigative committee chaired by Denny Beresford level against Bernie Ebbers?

29 The Perfect Storm

1. Why did Assistant Attorney General Michael Chertoff decide to charge Arthur Andersen with obstruction of justice? According to prosecutors, what was Andersen's motive for obstructing justice?
2. Describe the provisions of the Sarbanes–Oxley Act of 2002 intended to enhance auditor independence.
3. Describe the responsibilities of the PCAOB.
4. What does Section 404 of the Sarbanes–Oxley Act of 2002 require auditors and company executives to do?
5. Describe the major requirements of SAS No. 99.

6. What effect did the Sarbanes–Oxley Act of 2002 have on public accounting firms' audit and nonaudit revenues?

30 Conclusion

1. Cite examples of financial disclosures that were uncommon during the 1920s but are mandatory today.
2. Cite examples of accounting rules that were adopted in response to financial scandals.
3. How do modern auditing procedures differ from those employed 80 years ago?
4. How did auditors' responsibility for financial statement fraud evolve between 1892 and 2002?
5. How have public accounting firms changed during the last 50 years?
6. How did the Sarbanes–Oxley Act of 2002 reduce certified public accountants' professional autonomy?

Appendix B

Suggestions for Integrating *Called to Account* with Popular Auditing Texts

Each four-chapter part within *Called to Account* is a self-contained unit. The parts can be read in almost any order without significant loss of continuity. This flexible structure allows *Called to Account* to be used in a wide variety of auditing and forensic accounting courses. Table 2 provides suggestions for integrating the seven parts of *Called to Account* with the chapters of several popular auditing texts.

Table 2

Called to Account	Alvin Arens *et al.*, *Auditing and Assurance Services: An Integrated Approach*, 12th ed., Prentice-Hall, 2008.	William Messier, Jr., *et al.*, *Auditing & Assurance Services: A Systematic Approach*, 6th ed., McGraw-Hill/Irwin, 2008.	Timothy Louwers, *et al.*, *Auditing & Assurance Services*, 3rd ed., McGraw-Hill/Irwin, 2008.	Whittington and Pany, *Principles of Auditing and Other Assurance Services*, 16th ed., McGraw-Hill/Irwin, 2008.	Rittenberg, *et al.*, *Auditing: A Business Risk Approach*, 6th ed., South-Western, 2008.
Part I: Birth of a Profession	1. The Demand for Audit and Other Assurance Services	1. An Introduction to Assurance and Financial Statement Auditing	1. Auditing and Assurance Services	1. The Role of the Public Accountant in the American Economy	1. Auditing: Integral to the Economy.
Part II: The Profession's Principle Problem	2. The CPA Profession	2. The Financial Statement Auditing Environment	2. Professional Standards	2. Professional Standards	2. Corporate Governance, Audit Standards
Part III: The Savings & Loan Crisis	16. Completing the Tests in the Sales and Collection Cycle: Accounts Receivable	10. Auditing the Revenue Process	7. Revenue and Collection Cycle	11. Accounts Receivable, Notes Receivable, and Revenue	11. Auditing Revenue and Related Accounts
Part IV: The Expectation Gap	6. Audit Responsibilities and Objectives	2. The Financial Statement Auditing Environment	3. Management Fraud and Audit Risk	6. Planning the Audit	9. Auditing for Fraud
	11. Fraud Auditing				
Part V: The Litigation Crisis	5. Legal Liability	20. Legal Liability	C. Legal Liability	4. Legal Liability of CPAs	18. Professional Liability
Part VI: Beginning of the End	4. Professional Ethics	19. Professional Conduct, Independence, and Quality Control	B. Professional Ethics	3. Professional Ethics	3. Ethics: Meeting and Understanding Ethical Expectations
Part VII: From Profession to Regulated Industry	4. Professional Ethics	19. Professional Conduct, Independence, and Quality Control	B. Professional Ethics	3. Professional Ethics	3. Ethics: Meeting and Understanding Ethical Expectations

Notes

Acknowledgments

1. *Wilhelm Meister's Lehrjahre* (1796).

1 Scandal and Reform

1. Dale Flesher and Tonya Flesher, "Ivar Kreuger's Contribution to U.S. Financial Reporting," *Accounting Review* 61 (July 1986): 426.
2. Ron Wyden, "The First Line of Defense," *New Accountant* (December 1990): 15.
3. Mary B. Malloy and Walter M. Primoff, "The S&L Crisis: Putting Things in Perspective," *CPA Journal* 59 (December 1989): 12.
4. American Institute of Accountants, *Verification of Financial Statements* reprinted in *Journal of Accountancy* 47 (May 1929): 324.
5. Robert H. Montgomery, *Auditing Theory and Practice*, 8th ed. (New York: Ronald Press, 1957) quoted in Commission on Auditors' Responsibilities, *Report, Conclusions, and Recommendations* (1978), 34.
6. Paul Gigot, "Big Fraud Verdict Against Andersen Shakes Up Accounting Profession," *Wall Street Journal*, February 3, 1982.
7. *United States* v. *Arthur Young & Co.*, 465 U.S. 805 (1984).

2 Out of Darkness

1. Richard Brief, "Corporate Financial Reporting at the Turn of the Century," *Journal of Accountancy* 163 (May 1987): 144.
2. Ibid., 148.
3. William Z. Ripley, *Main Street and Wall Street* (Lawrence, KS: Scholars Book Company, 1972), 164.
4. J.E. Sterrett, "The Present Position and Probable Development of Accountancy as a Profession," *Journal of Accountancy* 7 (February 1909): 267.
5. John Carey, *The Rise of the Accounting Profession, 1896–1936* (New York: American Institute of Certified Public Accountants, 1969): 46.
6. "Certified Public Accountants," *Fortune*, June 1932, 63.
7. "Annual Audit for the Equitable," *Journal of Accountancy* 1 (January 1906): 233–234.
8. "The Reports of American Corporations," *Journal of Accountancy* 2 (October 1906): 458–459.
9. "Safeguarding Investment," *Journal of Accountancy* 27 (January 1919): 61–66.
10. William Z. Ripley, "Stop, Look, Listen!" *Atlantic Monthly*, September 1926, 380–399.

11. Ripley, *Main Street and Wall Street*, 110.
12. Ibid., 109.
13. Ibid., 29.
14. Ibid., 28.
15. Ibid., 37–38.

3 Ivar Kreuger

1. Dale Flesher and Tonya Flesher, "Ivar Kreuger's Contribution to U.S. Financial Reporting," *Accounting Review* 61 (July 1986): 425–426.
2. Joseph T. Wells, *Frankensteins of Fraud* (Austin, TX: Obsidian Publishing Company, 2000), 369.
3. "Kreuger Books Are 'Grossly Wrong,' Some Assets False," *New York Times*, April 6, 1932.
4. "Kreuger's Defalcations Shown to Be $115,800,000," *Barron's*, January 16, 1933, 22.

4 McKesson & Robbins

1. *Marmion*, Canto vi, Stanza 17 (1808).
2. Charles Keats, *Magnificent Masquerade: The Strange Case of Dr. Coster and Mr. Musica*, (New York: Funk & Wagnalls, 1964): 3.
3. Ibid., 98.

5 Into the Spotlight

1. K.L. Austin, "Ivar Kreuger's Story in Light of Five Years," *New York Times*, March 7, 1937.
2. See, for example, Max Winkler, "Playing With Matches," *The Nation*, May 25, 1932.
3. Dale Flesher and Tonya Flesher, "Ivar Kreuger's Contribution to U.S. Financial Reporting," *Accounting Review* 61 (July 1986): 426.
4. Ibid.
5. James M. Landis, "The Legislative History of the Securities Act of 1933," *George Washington Law Review* 28 (October 1959): 30.
6. "Man who Trapped Kreuger Describes Deals to Senators," *New York Times*, January 12, 1933.
7. "Ivar Kreuger III," *Fortune*, July 1933, 72.
8. Ibid.
9. John L. Carey, *The Rise of the Accounting Profession, 1937–1969* (New York: American Institute of Certified Public Accountants, 1970), 186–188.
10. "Musica Case Presages New Steps to Safeguard U.S. Investors," *Newsweek*, December 26, 1938, 9; "Ledgers and Legends," *Newsweek*, January 2, 1939, 12.
11. "After Coster, Accounting Reform," *Business Week*, January 7, 1939, 15.
12. "The McKesson & Robbins Case," *Journal of Accountancy* 67 (February 1939): 65.
13. Securities and Exchange Commission, Accounting Series Release No. 19, *In the Matter of McKesson & Robbins*, December 5, 1940.
14. Ibid.
15. Ibid.
16. "The McKesson & Robbins Case," 68–69.

6 Generally Accepted Accounting Principles

1. Henry Rand Hatfield, "What Is the Matter With Accounting?" *Journal of Accountancy* 44 (October 1927): 271–272.
2. Stephen A. Zeff, "Some Junctions in the Evolution of the Process of Establishing Accounting Principles in the U.S.A., 1917–1972," *Accounting Review* 59 (July 1984): 451.
3. Carman Blough, "The Need for Accounting Principles," *Accounting Review* 12 (March 1937): 30–31.
4. Hatfield, "What Is the Matter With Accounting?" 273.
5. Stephen A. Zeff, "The Evolution of U.S. GAAP, 1930–1973," *CPA Journal* 75 (January 2005): 23.
6. Accounting Principles Board, Opinion No. 3, *The Statement of Source and Application of Funds.*
7. Securities and Exchange Commission, Accounting Series Release No. 4, *Administrative Policy on Financial Statements.*
8. Accounting Principles Board, Opinion No. 2, *Accounting for the "Investment Credit."*
9. Securities and Exchange Commission, Accounting Series Release No. 96, *Accounting for the Investment Credit.*
10. Accounting Principles Board, Opinion No. 4, *Accounting for the "Investment Credit."*
11. "The Biggest, Wildest Merger Year Ever," *Fortune*, June 15, 1968, 43–44.
12. "Asset Pooling Debate Heats Up," *Business Week*, October 26, 1968, 160.
13. J.A. Seidman, "Pooling Must Go," *Barron's*, July 1, 1968; Abraham J. Briloff, "Dirty Pooling," *Barron's*, July 15, 1968.
14. Briloff, "Dirty Pooling," 1.

7 National Student Marketing

1. Sharon Warren Walsh, "Cortes Randell Sets Up Shop All Over Again," *Washington Post*, October 12, 1987.
2. "President's Use of Forged Document Was Fraud on Court, Says Judge," *Delaware Corporate Litigation Reporter*, August 19, 2002.
3. Andrew Tobias, *The Funny Money Game* (London: Michael Joseph, 1972), 63–64.
4. Alan Abelson, "Up and Down Wall Street," *Barron's*, December 22, 1969.
5. "National Student Marketing Says It Erred Over Deficit," *Wall Street Journal*, February 26, 1970.
6. Securities and Exchange Commission, Accounting Series Release No. 173, *In the Matter of Peat, Marwick, Mitchell & Co.*, July 2, 1975.
7. Ibid.
8. Frederick Andrews, "Fraud Trial of Peat Marwick Attracts Anxious Attention of Other Accountants," *Wall Street Journal*, October 29, 1974.
9. Wyatt Olson, "Hustling for Models," *New Times Broward–Palm Beach*, September 6, 2001.
10. Ibid.

8 Equity Funding

1. Joseph T. Wells, *Frankensteins of Fraud* (Austin, TX: Obsidian Publishing Company, 2000), 166.
2. "The Fifty Largest Diversified Financial Companies," *Fortune*, May 1972, 215.

3. Securities and Exchange Commission, Accounting Series Release No. 196, *In the Matter of Seidman & Seidman*, September 1, 1976.
4. Ibid.
5. Dialogue between Ray Dirks and Bob Spencer taken from Raymond Dirks and Leonard Gross, *The Great Wall Street Scandal* (New York: McGraw-Hill, 1974), 270.

9 Déjà Vu

1. John L. Carey, *The Rise of the Accounting Profession, 1937–1969* (New York: American Institute of Certified Public Accountants, 1970), 136.
2. All quotations in paragraph from Stephen A. Zeff, "Some Junctures in the Evolution of Establishing Accounting Principles in the U.S.A., 1917–1972," *Accounting Review* 59 (July 1984): 464.
3. "Wheat Committee: Establishing Financial Accounting Standards," *Journal of Accountancy* 163 (May 1987): 134.
4. Lee Berton, "Frustrated CPAs: Accounting Body Fails in Attempts to Change Some Firms' Reporting," *Wall Street Journal*, January 8, 1969.
5. John H. Allan, "Accountants Get Report on Rules," *New York Times*, March 30, 1972.
6. American Institute of Certified Public Accountants, *Code of Professional Conduct*, Rule No. 203, *Accounting Principles.*
7. Securities and Exchange Commission, Accounting Series Release No. 150, *Statement of Policy on the Establishment and Improvement of Accounting Principles and Standards*, December 20, 1973.
8. Financial Accounting Standards Board, SFAS No. 19, *Financial Accounting and Reporting by Oil and Gas Producing Companies.*
9. Securities and Exchange Commission, Accounting Series Release No. 253, *Adoption of Requirements for Financial Accounting and Reporting Practices for Oil and Gas Producing Activities*, August 31, 1978.
10. Wallace E. Olson, *The Accounting Profession: Years of Trial, 1969–1980* (New York: American Institute of Certified Public Accountants, 1982), 39.
11. Senate Committee on Government Operations, Subcommittee on Reports, Accounting and Management, *The Accounting Establishment: A Staff Study* (Washington, D.C.: Government Printing Office, 1976), 2.
12. Ibid., 8.
13. Ibid., 17.
14. H.G. Rickover, "The Accounting Establishment: Comments on the Metcalf Report," *Government Accountants Journal* 26 (fall 1977): 5.
15. The Commission on Auditors' Responsibilities, *Report, Conclusions, and Recommendations* (New York: American Institute of Certified Public Accountants, 1978), xii.
16. Ibid., 31.
17. Ibid., 96.
18. Ibid., 71.
19. See, for example, Felix Pomerantz, "Securing the Computer," *CPA Journal* 44 (June 1974): 23–26.

10 It's a Wonderful Life?

1. By the 1950s, most building and loan associations had changed their names to "savings and loans." Building and loans or savings and loans are also commonly referred to as "thrift organizations" or simply "thrifts."

2. David L. Mason, *From Building and Loans to Bail-outs* (Cambridge and New York: Cambridge University Press, 2004), 44.
3. "Building and Loan Program Aims to Get More Homeowners," *Business Week*, July 30, 1930, 22.
4. Negotiable order of withdrawal ("NOW") accounts were essentially interest-bearing checking accounts.
5. Robert H. Mills, "Accounting Alchemy: It Turns S&L Red Ink Into Black," *Barron's*, May 31, 1982, 30.

11 ESM Government Securities

1. Brian Dickerson, "The Lonely Death of Stephen Arky," *Miami Herald*, December 7, 1986.
2. Kathy Sawyer, "ESM Scandal Extinguished a Rising Star," *Washington Post*, July 28, 1985.
3. Donald Maggin, *Bankers, Builders, Knaves, and Thieves* (Chicago: Contemporary Books, 1989), 82.
4. "Cincinnati Savings & Loan Facing Loss," *Cincinnati Enquirer*, March 6, 1985.
5. Martha Brannigan, "Auditor's Downfall Shows a Man Caught in Trap of His Own Making," *Wall Street Journal*, October 17, 1986.
6. Maggin, *Bankers, Builders, Knaves, and Thieves*, 215.
7. Brannigan, "Auditor's Downfall Shows a Man Caught in Trap of His Own Making."

12 Lincoln Savings & Loan

1. Michael Binstein and Charles Bowden, *Trust Me: Charles Keating and the Missing Billions* (New York: Random House, 1993), 122–123.
2. Joe Morganstern, "Profit Without Honor," *Playboy*, April 1992, 68.
3. Michael C. Knapp, *Contemporary Auditing*. 4th ed. (Cincinnati: South-Western College Publishing, 2001), 60.
4. David J. Jefferson, "Keating of American Continental Corp. Comes Out Fighting," *Wall Street Journal*, April 18, 1989, B2.
5. David B. Hilder and John E. Yang, "Bank Board Appointee Has Close Ties to Thrift With Controversial Investment," *Wall Street Journal*, December 18, 1986.
6. Paulette Thomas and Brooks Jackson, "Regulators Cite Delays and Phone Bugs in Examination, Seizure of Lincoln Savings and Loan," *Wall Street Journal*, October 27, 1989.
7. Merle Erickson, Brian Mayhew, and William Felix, Jr., "Why Do Audits Fail? Evidence from Lincoln Savings and Loan," *Journal of Accounting Research* 38 (spring 2000): 165–194.
8. Ibid., 168.
9. Eric Berg, "The Lapses by Lincoln's Auditors," *New York Times*, December 28, 1989, D6.

13 Bank Robbers

1. "San Francisco Hearings Reveal S&L Fraud Rampant," *San Francisco Chronicle*, January 14, 1989.
2. Ibid.
3. Charles McCoy, Richard Schmitt, and Jeff Bailey, "Hall of Shame: Besides

S&L Owners, Host of Professionals Paved Way for Crisis," *Wall Street Journal*, November 2, 1990.
4. "San Francisco Hearings Reveal S&L Fraud Rampant."
5. Ron Wyden, "The First Line of Defense," *New Accountant*, December 1990, 15.
6. General Accounting Office, *CPA Audit Quality: Failures of CPA Audits to Identify and Report Significant Savings and Loan Problems*, AFMD-89-45, reprinted in *Journal of Accountancy* 167 (March 1989): 22.
7. Ibid., 30.
8. Ibid.
9. Lee Berton, "GAO Says Accountants Auditing Thrifts Are Hiding Behind Outdated Standards," *Wall Street Journal*, February 6, 1989.
10. Mary Malloy and Walter Primoff, "The S&L Crisis: Putting Things in Perspective," *CPA Journal* 59 (December 1989): 12.
11. Jerry Knight and Sharon Warren Walsh, "Panel Votes Higher S&L Capital Rule; Owners to Put Up More of Own Money," *Washington Post*, April 28, 1989.
12. General Accounting Office, *Failed Banks: Accounting and Auditing Reforms Urgently Needed*, AFMD-91-43, April 1991, 30.
13. Leonard Savoie and David Ricchuite, "Reports by Management: Voluntary or Mandatory?" *Journal of Accountancy* 151 (May 1981): 88.
14. The five associations comprising COSO were the American Accounting Association, American Institute of Certified Public Accountants, Financial Executives Institute, Institute of Internal Auditors, and Institute of Management Accountants.
15. "FDICIA Adds $20 Million to Accountants' Fees," *Accounting Today*, October 10, 1994.
16. Curtis Verschoor, "Internal Control Reporting: It's Here and Now," *Internal Auditor* 49 (June 1992): 39–42.
17. "Internal Control Audit Proposal Draws Fire and Praise," *Journal of Accountancy* 176 (October 1993): 20.
18. Ibid.
19. Dana Linden, "If Life Is Volatile, Account for It," *Forbes*, November 12, 1990, 114.
20. Ibid.
21. Kevin G. Salwen, "SEC Is Seeking Updated Rules for Accounting," *Wall Street Journal*, January 8, 1992.
22. Stephen H. Miller, "SEC Market Value Conference: Experts Urge Mark-to-Market," *Journal of Accountancy* 173 (January 1992): 13.
23. Ibid., 14.
24. Salwen, "SEC Is Seeking Updated Rules for Accounting."
25. Ibid.
26. Raymond V. O'Brien, "The Continuing Threat of Market Value Accounting," *Bottomline* 8 (November/December 1991): 6–7.
27. Financial Accounting Standards Board, SFAS No. 115, *Accounting for Certain Investments in Debt and Equity Securities*.
28. Financial Accounting Standards Board, SFAS No. 119, *Disclosure about Derivative Financial Instruments and Fair Value of Financial Instruments*.
29. Financial Accounting Standards Board, SFAS No. 91, *Accounting for Nonrefundable Fees and Costs Associated with Originating or Acquiring Loans and Initial Direct Costs of Leases*.
30. Robert A. Bartsch, William J. Read, and K. Raghunandan, "Accounting for Impaired Loans Under SFAS No. 114," *CPA Journal* 64 (July 1994): 48.

14 Auditors and Fraud

1. Commission on Auditors' Responsibilities, *Report, Conclusions, and Recommendations* (New York: American Institute of Certified Public Accountants, 1978), 31.
2. C.A. Moyer, "Early Developments in American Auditing," *Accounting Review* 26 (January 1951): 3.
3. Lawrence R. Dicksee's book *Auditing: A Practical Manual for Auditors* (London: Gee & Co., 1898) is described in Commission on Auditors' Responsibilities, *Report, Conclusions, and Recommendations* (1978), 33.
4. Robert H. Montgomery, *Auditing Theory and Practice* (New York: Ronald Press, 1912), quoted in R. Gene Brown, "Changing Audit Objectives and Techniques," *Accounting Review* 37 (October 1962): 699.
5. Robert H. Montgomery, *Auditing Theory and Practice*, 5th ed. (New York: Ronald Press, 1934), quoted in R. Gene Brown, "Changing Audit Objectives and Techniques," *Accounting Review* 37 (October 1962): 700.
6. Robert H. Montgomery, *Auditing Theory and Practice*, 6th ed. (New York: Ronald Press, 1940), quoted in R. Gene Brown, "Changing Audit Objectives and Techniques," *Accounting Review* 37 (October 1962): 700.
7. Robert H. Montgomery, *Auditing Theory and Practice*, 8th ed. (New York: Ronald Press, 1957) quoted in Commission on Auditors' Responsibilities, *Report, Conclusions, and Recommendations* (1978), 34.
8. D.D. Rae Smith, "Auditing: The Purpose and its Attainment," *The Accountant* (October 22, 1960): 525–529, quoted in Philip L. Defliese, "Auditor's Responsibility for Fraud Detection," *Journal of Accountancy* 114 (October 1962): 37.
9. American Institute of Accountants, *Verification of Financial Statements*, reprinted in the *Journal of Accountancy* 47 (May 1929): 324.
10. American Institute of Accountants, *Codification of Statements on Auditing Procedure* (New York: American Institute of Accountants, 1951), 12–13.
11. SAP No. 30, *Responsibilities and Functions of the Independent Auditor in the Examination of Financial Statements*, paragraph 5.
12. Frederick Andrews, "SEC Jolting Auditors Into a Broader Role in Fraud Detection," *Wall Street Journal*, July 12, 1974.
13. Arlene Hershman, "The War Over Corporate Fraud," *Dun's Review*, November 1974, 52.
14. George R. Catlett, "Relationship of Auditing Standards to Detection of Fraud," *CPA Journal* 45 (April 1975): 16.
15. Ibid., 17.
16. John J. Willingham, "Discussant's Response to Relationship of Auditing Standards to Detection of Fraud," *CPA Journal* 45 (April 1975): 20.
17. Commission on Auditors' Responsibilities, *Report, Conclusions, and Recommendations*, 31.
18. A.M.C. Morison, "The Role of the Reporting Accountant Today" II, *Accountancy* 82 (March 1971): 122.
19. Commission on Auditors' Responsibilities, *Report, Conclusions, and Recommendations*, 36.
20. Lee Berton and Bruce Ingersoll, "Dingell to Take Aim at Accountants, SEC in Hearings on Profession's Role as Watchdog," *Wall Street Journal*, February 19, 1985.
21. Douglas R. Carmichael, "Fraud and Illegal Acts: A New Look," *CPA Journal* 57 (February 1987): 95.
22. Bruce Ingersoll, "House Democrats Question SEC's Role in Guarding Against Audit Failures," *Wall Street Journal*, March 7, 1985.

23. Ibid.
24. Ibid.
25. Lee Berton, "Bill to Force Firms' Auditors to Report Fraud to Public Is Introduced," *Wall Street Journal*, May 23, 1986.
26. Gary Klott, "House Unit Bill Would Expand Role of Auditors," *New York Times*, May 23, 1986.
27. Berton, "Bill to Force Firms' Auditors to Report Fraud to Public Is Introduced."
28. Lee Berton and Daniel Akst, "CPAs May Soon Have to Report Fraud Earlier," *Wall Street Journal*, January 22, 1988.

15 ZZZZ Best

1. Daniel Akst, *Wonder Boy: Barry Minkow—The Kid Who Swindled Wall Street* (New York: Charles Scribner's Sons, 1990), 13.
2. Ibid., 153.
3. Ibid., 177.
4. Daniel Akst, "Behind 'Whiz Kid' Is a Trail of False Credit Card Billings," *Los Angeles Times*, May 22, 1987.
5. Securities and Exchange Commission, Accounting and Auditing Enforcement Release No. 312, *In the Matter of Samuel George Greenspan, CPA*, August 26, 1991.

16 Crazy Eddie

1. Joseph Wells, *Frankensteins of Fraud* (Austin, TX: Obsidian Publishing Company, 2000), 221.
2. Ibid., 221.
3. Ibid., 218.
4. Ibid., 253.

17 Closing the Gap

1. David Hilzenrath, "Auditors Face Scant Discipline," *Washington Post*, December 6, 2001.
2. James Traub, *Too Good to be True: The Outlandish Story of Wedtech* (New York: Doubleday, 1990).
3. National Committee on Fraudulent Financial Reporting, *Report of the National Commission on Fraudulent Financial Reporting* (1987), 31–48.
4. Ibid., 49–62.
5. Ibid., 13.
6. Dan M. Guy and Jerry D. Sullivan, "The Expectation Gap Auditing Standards," *Journal of Accountancy* 165 (April 1988): 8.
7. SAS No. 53, *The Auditor's Responsibility to Detect and Report Errors and Irregularities*, paragraph 5.
8. SAS No. 82, *Consideration of Fraud in a Financial Statement Audit.*

18 Auditors' Legal Liability

1. "The Auditor's Legal Liability," *Journal of Accountancy* 14 (July 1912): 55–57.
2. *Landell* v. *Lybrand et al.*, 264 Pa. 406 (1919).
3. *Ultramares* v. *Touche et al.*, 174 N.E. 441 (1931).
4. John Carey, *The Rise of the Accounting Profession, 1896–1939* (New York: American Institute of Certified Public Accountants, 1969), 192.

5. *Ernst & Ernst* v. *Hochfelder et al.*, 425 U.S. 185 (1976).
6. *Fischer* v. *Kletz*, 206 F. Supp. 180 (1967).
7. *Escott et al.* v. *ChrisBar Construction Corporation*, 283 F. Supp. 643 (1968).
8. Securities and Exchange Commission, Accounting Series Release No. 153, *In the Matter of Touche Ross & Co*, February 25, 1974.

19 Fund of Funds

1. John Train, *Famous Financial Fiascos* (New York: Clarkson N. Potter, 1994), 45.
2. "Bernie Cornfeld, Pyramid-selling King, Dies at 67," *Reuters News*, March 1, 1995.
3. *Fund of Funds* v. *Arthur Andersen*, 545 F. Supp. 1314, July 16, 1982.
4. Ibid.
5. Ibid.
6. Ibid.

20 MiniScribe

1. Kevin Moran, "MiniScribe Trial to Start in Galveston," *Houston Chronicle*, October 21, 1991.
2. Bruce Nichols, "Lawyers Can't Decide Who Really Won Case," *Dallas Morning News*, March 15, 1982.
3. "Coopers & Lybrand Settles Case: Judge Throws Out Fraud Verdict," *Houston Chronicle*, February 18, 1992.
4. Nichols, "Lawyers Can't Decide Who Really Won Case."
5. "Coopers & Lybrand Settles Case: Judge Throws Out Fraud Verdict."
6. Michael Allen, "MiniScribe's Wiles, Once a 'Dr. Fix-It,' Resigns Top Posts at Disk-Drive Maker," *Wall Street Journal*, February 23, 1989.
7. Andy Zipser, "MiniScribe's Investigators Determine That 'Massive Fraud' Was Perpetrated," *Wall Street Journal*, September 12, 1989.
8. Ibid.
9. Ibid.
10. Securities and Exchange Commission, Litigation Release No. 12942, *Securities and Exchange Commission* v. *Wiles et al.*, August 14, 1991.
11. Stanley Holmes, "MiniScribe Chairman's Fraud Trial Opens," *Rocky Mountain News*, July 12, 1994.
12. "MiniScribe Woes Became Joke," *Rocky Mountain News*, July 14, 1994.
13. John Accola, "Ex-MiniScribe Chairman Convicted," *Rocky Mountain News*, July 30, 1994.
14. Ibid.

21 Litigation Reform

1. Paul Gigot, "Big Fraud Verdict Against Andersen Shakes Up Accounting Profession," *Wall Street Journal*, February 3, 1982.
2. Ibid.
3. See, for example, Paul Geoghan, "Punitive Damages: A Storm Over the Accounting Profession," *Journal of Accountancy* 174 (July 1992): 46–49.
4. Thomas McCarroll, "Who's Counting?" *Time*, April 13, 1992.
5. Cook, Michael J., Ray J. Groves, Shaun F. O'Malley, Eugene M. Freedman, Jon C. Madonna, and Lawrence A. Weinbach. "The Liability Crisis in the United States: Impact on the Accounting Profession" (statement of position, August 6, 1992), 1.

6. Ibid., 6.
7. "Reformers Adopt a Two-pronged Attack," *World Accounting Report*, September 9, 1994.
8. Thou shalt not commit adultery.
9. Lee Berton and Joann S. Lublin, "Seeking Shelter: Partnership Structure Is Called into Question," *Wall Street Journal*, June 10, 1992.
10. M. Laurence Popofsky, "CPAs Win Big in Osborne Case," *Accounting Today*, February 1, 1993.
11. Ibid.
12. "Limit of Anti-racketeering Law Is Main Issue," *Wall Street Journal*, October 13, 1992.
13. Stuart Bass, "Supreme Court Limits RICO Liability for Accountants," *Commercial Law Journal* 98 (winter 1993): 458.

22 Auditor Independence

1. *United States* v. *Arthur Young & Co.*, 465 U.S. 805 (1984).
2. American Institute of Certified Public Accountants, *U.S. Auditing Standards*, AU Section 220.01.
3. Arthur Levitt, *Take on the Street* (New York: Pantheon Books, 2002), 118.
4. American Institute of Certified Public Accountants, *Code of Professional Conduct*, Section II, Rule 101.
5. American Institute of Certified Public Accountants, *Code of Professional Conduct*, Section I, Article IV.
6. John L. Carey, *Professional Ethics of Public Accounting* (New York: American Institute of Accountants, 1946), 7.
7. Commission on Auditors' Responsibilities, *Report, Conclusions, and Recommendations* (1978), 93.
8. The dialogue between Representative Lehman and Mr. Gladstone is quoted in Michael C. Knapp, *Contemporary Auditing: Real Issues and Cases*, 5th ed. (Cincinnati: South-Western College Publishing, 2005), 102–103.
9. Alison Leigh Cowan, "When Auditors Change Sides," *New York Times*, October 11, 1992.
10. A.P. Richardson, "The Accountant's True Sphere," *Journal of Accountancy* 40 (September 1925): 190–191.
11. George O. May, "Letter," *Journal of Accountancy* 40 (September 1925): 191.
12. Arthur E. Andersen, "The Accountant's Function as Business Advisor," *Journal of Accountancy* 41 (January 1926): 18–19.
13. Robert K. Mautz and Hussein A. Sharaf, *The Philosophy of Auditing* (Sarasota, FL: American Accounting Association, 1961), 223.
14. Abraham Briloff, "Our Profession's Jurassic Park," *CPA Journal* 64 (August 1994): 28.
15. Gary Previts, *The Scope of CPA Services* (New York: John Wiley & Sons, 1985), 94.
16. Securities and Exchange Commission, Accounting Series Release No. 304, *Relationships Between Registrants and Independent Accountants*, January 28, 1982.
17. Walter P. Schuetze, "A Mountain or a Molehill?" *Accounting Horizons* 8 (March 1994): 74.
18. Michael Schroeder and Elizabeth MacDonald, "SEC Plans New Board to Regulate Auditors," *Wall Street Journal*, May 21, 1997.

23 Waste Management

1. "The Flap Over Executive Pay," *Business Week*, May 6, 1991.
2. "Rooney Resigns Under Fire," Associated Press, February 18, 1997.
3. "No Doubt About It, Sunbeam's Dunlap Doesn't Want This Job," *Dow Jones Online News*, December 19, 1997.
4. Abraham Briloff, "Recycled Accounting: It Enhances Waste Management's Earnings," *Barron's*, August 6, 1990.
5. Julia Flynn, "Burying Trash in Big Holes—On the Balance Sheet," *Business Week*, May 11, 1992.
6. Securities and Exchange Commission, Accounting and Auditing Enforcement Release No. 1405, *In the Matter of Arthur Andersen, LLP*, June 19, 2001.
7. Ibid.
8. Ibid.
9. Securities and Exchange Commission, Litigation Release No. 17039, *SEC vs. Arthur Andersen, LLP*, June 19, 2001.
10. Securities and Exchange Commission, Litigation Release No. 17435, *SEC vs. Dean L. Buntrock et al.*, March 26, 2002.
11. Securities and Exchange Commission, Accounting and Auditing Enforcement Release No. 1405, *In the Matter of Arthur Andersen, LLP*, June 19, 2001.
12. Richard Melcher and Gary McWilliams, "Can Waste Management Climb Out of the Muck?" *Business Week*, March 23, 1998, 40.
13. Securities and Exchange Commission, Litigation Release No. 17435, *SEC vs. Dean L. Buntrock et al.*, March 26, 2001.

24 Sunbeam

1. Al Dunlap with Bob Andelman, *Mean Business: How I Save Bad Companies and Make Good Companies Great* (New York: Random House, 1996), 21.
2. Ibid., 21.
3. Ibid., xii.
4. John Byrne, *Chainsaw* (New York: HarperCollins Publishers, 1999), 180.
5. Jonathan Laing, "Dangerous Games: Did 'Chainsaw Al' Dunlap Manufacture Sunbeam's Earnings Last Year?" *Barron's*, June 8, 1998.
6. A "ditty bag" is a pouch used by military personnel to carry small personal items such as sewing implements and grooming items.
7. Byrne, *Chainsaw*, 167.
8. Securities and Exchange Commission, Accounting and Auditing Enforcement Release No. 1395, *SEC v. Albert J. Dunlap et al.*, May 15, 2001.
9. Byrne, *Chainsaw*, 361.
10. Ibid., 153.
11. Ibid., 157.
12. SEC, AAER No. 1395, *SEC v. Albert J. Dunlap et al.*

25 End of the Millennium

1. Laura S. Unger, "This Year's Proxy Season: Sunlight Shines on Auditor Independence and Executive Compensation" (speech, Center for Professional Education, Washington D.C., June 25, 2001).
2. Barry Melancon, "Accountants Need Clear, Modern Rules to Guide Them," *Business Week*, February 28, 2000, 13.

3. Arthur Levitt, *Take on the Street* (New York: Pantheon Books, 2002), 126.
4. Securities and Exchange Commission, *Proposed Rule: Revision of the Commission's Auditor Independence Requirement*, June, 27, 2000, section 2-01(b).
5. Levitt, *Take on the Street*, 128.
6. Ibid., 133.
7. Nanette Byrnes and Mike McNamee, "The SEC vs. CPAs: Suddenly, It's Hardball," *Business Week*, May 22, 2000, 49; Louis Lavelle, "Cozying Up to the Ref: Ernst's Role in Tough New SEC Rules Riles Rivals," *Business Week*, July 31, 2000.
8. Levitt, *Take on the Street*, 138.
9. Phyllis Plitch, "Investors Send 'Strong' Message in Disney's Auditor Vote," *Dow Jones News Service*, February 19, 2002.
10. "Grace Case Illustrates Earnings Management," *Wall Street Journal*, April 7, 1999, C1.
11. Arthur Levitt, "The Numbers Game" (speech, New York University Center for Law and Business, New York, NY, September 28, 1998).

26 Professionalism

1. John L. Carey, *Professional Ethics of Public Accounting* (New York, American Institute of Accountants, 1946), 13.
2. Mike Brewster, *Unaccountable: How the Accounting Profession Forfeited a Public Trust* (Hoboken, NJ: John Wiley & Sons, 2003), 61.
3. Matthew 6:24, Holy Bible, New International Version.
4. *Cooking the Books: What Every Accountant Should Know About Fraud*, VHS (Austin, TX: Association of Certified Fraud Examiners, 2005).
5. John L. Carey and William O. Doherty, *Ethical Standards of the Accounting Profession* (New York: American Institute of Certified Public Accountants, 1966), 47.
6. Philip B. Chenok with Adam Snyder, *Foundations for the Future: The AICPA from 1980–1995* (Stamford, CT: JAI Press), 58.
7. Sally Goll Beatty, "Deloitte Stops Pulling Punches in Assault on Consulting Rivals," *Wall Street Journal*, February 26, 1988.
8. Michael C. Knapp, *Contemporary Auditing: Real Issues and Cases*, 5th ed. (Cincinnati: South-Western College Publishing, 2004), 398.
9. Ibid., 400.
10. Ibid., 401.
11. John L. Carey, *Professional Ethics of Public Accounting* (New York: American Institute of Accountants, 1946), 107.
12. Lee Berton, "Total War: CPA Firms Diversify, Cut Fees, Steal Clients in Battle for Business," *Wall Street Journal*, September 20, 1985.
13. Lee Berton, "Audit Fees Fall as CPA Firms Jockey for Bids," *Wall Street Journal*, January 28, 1985.
14. National Commission on Fraudulent Financial Reporting, *Report of the National Commission on Fraudulent Financial Reporting* (1987), 56.
15. Mark Stevens, "No More White Shoes," *Business Month*, April 1988, 42.
16. Commission on Auditors' Responsibilities, *Report, Conclusions, and Recommendations* (1978), 179.
17. Tim Kelley and Loren Margheim, "The Impact of Time Budget Pressure, Personality, and Leadership Variables on Dysfunctional Auditor Behavior," *Auditing: A Journal of Practice and Theory* 9 (spring 1990): 21–42.
18. Robert K. Elliott, "The Future of Audits," *Journal of Accountancy* 178 (September 1994): 75–76.

19. Don M. Pallais and Sandra A. Suran, "Change or Die: The Need for Evolution in Auditing Practice," *Line Items* (June/July 1995): 12.
20. Michael Rosedale, "Is the AICPA's Vision Prehistoric?" *Practical Accountant* 33 (December 2000): 80.
21. Chris Quick, "The Rise and Fall of Cognitor," *The Times* (London), October 12, 2000.
22. Clar Rosso, "Reaching Critical Mass," *California CPA* 69 (June 2001): 24–30.
23. Jonathan D. Glater, "Risking Ridicule, Some Accountants Talk of Becoming Cognitors," *New York Times*, April 5, 2001.
24. Patricia V. Rivera, "Some CPAs Seek to Return Accounting Profession to Its Traditional Roles," *Knight Ridder*, May 20, 2001.
25. Quick, "The Rise and Fall of Cognitor."
26. Melody Peterson, "How the Andersens Turned Into the Bickersons," *New York Times*, March 15, 1998.
27. Barbara Ley Toffler with Jennifer Reingold, *Final Accounting* (New York: Broadway Books, 2003), 12.
28. Chenok, *Foundations for the Future: The AICPA from 1980–1995*, 91.
29. Stephen A. Zeff, "How the U.S. Accounting Profession Got Where It Is Today" II, *Accounting Horizons* 17 (December 2003): 268.
30. Floyd Norris, "Users and Abusers: Here's the Bottom Line on the Accounting Profession," *Barron's*, September 14, 1987.

27 Enron

1. Wendy Zellner, "Power Play," *Business Week*, February 12, 2001, 70.
2. *Fortune*, 1996–2001.
3. Harry Hunt III, "Power Players," *Fortune*, August 5, 1996, 95.
4. Wendy Zellner and Stephanie Anderson Frost, "The Fall of Enron," *Business Week*, December 17, 2001, 33.
5. *CFO: The Magazine for Senior Financial Executives*, October 1, 1999, 65.
6. Jonathan Weil, "Energy Traders Cite Gains, But Some Math Is Missing," *Wall Street Journal*, September 20, 2000.
7. Ibid.
8. Zellner, "Power Play," 72.
9. C. Bryson Hull, "Skilling Briefly Trades CEO Hat for Comedian Role," *Reuters News*, June 12, 2001.
10. Ibid.
11. William C. Powers, Raymond S. Troubh, and Herbert S. Winokur, *Report of the Special Investigative Committee of the Board of Directors of Enron Corporation*, February 1, 2002, 172.
12. Laura Goldberg, "Enron Posts Loss After Writedowns," *Houston Chronicle*, October 17, 2001.
13. Rebecca Smith and John R. Emshwiller, "Enron's CFO's Partnership Had Millions in Profit," *Wall Street Journal*, October 19, 2001.
14. Robert Manor, "Andersen Auditor Questioned Enron Account as Early as 1999," *Chicago Tribune*, April 3, 2002.
15. John R. Emshwiller and Gary McWilliams, "Enron's Fastow Testifies Skilling Approved Fraud," *Wall Street Journal*, March 8, 2006.
16. John R. Emshiller and Gary McWilliams, "As Enron Trial Heads Toward Jury, Defense Attacks 'Fictional' Case," *Wall Street Journal*, May 17, 2006.
17. Jesse Eisinger, "Lay's Defense Leans on His Optimism to Convince Jury He Was Truthful," *Wall Street Journal*, April 26, 2006.

18. John R. Emshwiller and Gary McWilliams, "Skilling Defends Enron, Himself," *Wall Street Journal*, April 11, 2006.
19. John R. Emshwiller and Gary McWilliams, "As Enron Trial Heads Toward Jury, Defense Attacks 'Fictional' Case," *Wall Street Journal*, May 17, 2006.
20. Gary McWilliams and John R. Emshwiller, "Enron Prosecutor Presses Jury for Convictions on All Counts," *Wall Street Journal*, May 16, 2006.
21. John R. Emshwiller, Gary McWilliams, and Ann Davis, "Lay, Skilling Are Convicted of Fraud," *Wall Street Journal*, May 26, 2006.
22. John R. Emshwiller, "Skilling Gets 24 Years in Prison," *Wall Street Journal*, October 24, 2006.

28 WorldCom

1. Michael Barrier, "One Right Path," *Internal Auditor* 60 (December 2003): 53.
2. *Time*, December 30, 2002.
3. Almar Latour and Shawn Young, "Ebbers Denies He Knew About WorldCom's Fraud," *Wall Street Journal*, March 1, 2005.
4. *CFO: The Magazine for Senior Financial Executives*, September 1998, 67–68.
5. Dennis Beresford, Nicholas Katzenbach, and C.B. Rogers, Jr., *Report of Investigation by the Special Investigative Committee of the Board of Directors of WorldCom Inc*, March 31, 2003, 13.
6. Amanda Ripley, "The Night Detective," *Time*, December 30, 2002, 47.
7. Susan Pulliam and Deborah Solomon, "Uncooking the Books: How Three Unlikely Sleuths Discovered Fraud at WorldCom," *Wall Street Journal*, October 30, 2002.
8. Ripley, "The Night Detective," 45.
9. Beresford *et al.*, *Report of Investigation by the Special Investigative Committee of the Board of Directors of WorldCom Inc.*, 226.
10. Melvin Dick, "Remarks of Melvin Dick," Testimony before the House Committee on Financial Services, July 8, 2002.
11. Beresford *et al.*, *Report of Investigation by the Special Investigative Committee of the Board of Directors of WorldCom Inc.*, 19.
12. Almar Latour and Shawn Young, "WorldCom's Sullivan Says He Told CEO of Problems," *Wall Street Journal*, February 9, 2005.
13. Almar Latour and Shawn Young, "Ebbers Denies He Knew About WorldCom's Fraud," *Wall Street Journal*, March 1, 2005.
14. Almar Latour, Shawn Young, and Li Yuan, "Ebbers Is Convicted in Massive Fraud," *Wall Street Journal*, March 16, 2005.
15. Dionne Searcey, "Ebbers Is Sentenced to 25 Years for $11 Billion WorldCom Fraud," *Wall Street Journal*, July 14, 2005.
16. Greg Farrell, "Sullivan Gets 5-Year Prison Sentence," *USA Today*, August 12, 2005.
17. Ibid.

29 The Perfect Storm

1. Barbara Ley Toffler with Jennifer Reingold, *Final Accounting* (New York: Broadway Books, 2003), 1.
2. Kurt Eichenwald, "Miscues, Missteps and the Fall of Andersen," *New York Times*, May 8, 2002.
3. "Bigger Than Enron," *Frontline*, directed by Marc Shaffer (Boston: WGBH, 2002).

4. Nicholas Kulish and John R. Wilke, "Called to Account: Indictment Puts Andersen's Fate on Line," *Wall Street Journal*, March 15, 2002.
5. Toffler and Reingold, *Final Accounting*, 4.
6. William Sternberg, "Accounting's Role in Enron Crash Erases Years of Trust," *USA Today*, February 22, 2002, A1.
7. Toffler and Reingold, *Final Accounting*, 217.
8. Alexei Barrionuevo and Jonathan Weil, "Duncan Knew Enron Papers Would Be Lost," *Wall Street Journal*, May 14, 2002.
9. Jonathan Weil, Alexei Barrionuevo, and Cassell Bryan-Low, "Auditor's Ruling: Andersen Win Lifts U.S. Enron Case," *Wall Street Journal*, June 17, 2002.
10. Cathy Booth Thomas, "Called to Account," *Time*, June 24, 2002, 52.
11. John C. Roper, "Government Won't Retry Andersen Criminal Case," *Houston Chronicle*, November 23, 2005.
12. Jonathan D. Glater and Alexei Barrionuevo, "Decision Rekindles Debate Over Andersen Indictment," *New York Times*, June 1, 2005.
13. David S. Hilzenrath, Jonathan Weisman, and Jim VandeHei, "How Congress Rode a 'Storm' to Corporate Reform," *Washington Post*, July 28, 2002.
14. Tom Hamburger, Greg Hitt, and Michael Schroeder, "WorldCom Case Boosts Congress in Reform Efforts," *Wall Street Journal*, June 27, 2002.
15. Stephen Labaton, "Chief of Big Pension Plan Is Choice for Accounting Board," *New York Times*, October 1, 2002.
16. Stephen Labaton, "SEC Chief Hedges on Accounting Regulator," *New York Times*, October 4, 2002.
17. Ibid.
18. Stephen Labatan, "Bitter Divide as Securities Panel Picks an Accounting Watchdog," *New York Times*, October 26, 2002.
19. Labaton, "SEC Chief Hedges on Accounting Regulator."
20. Michael Schroeder, "Regulator Under Fire: Pitt Launches SEC Probe of Himself," *Wall Street Journal*, November 1, 2002.
21. Carrie Johnson, "Fed Officer Chosen to Head Audit Panel," *Washington Post*, April 16, 2003.
22. Floyd Norris, "SEC Picks a Fed Banker to Lead Panel," *New York Times*, April 16, 2003.
23. Floyd Norris, "Federal Regulators Find Problems at 4 Big Auditors," *New York Times*, August 27, 2004.
24. Ibid.
25. Deborah Solomon, "Fraud Detector: SEC Sets a New Rule Aimed at Companies' Internal Controls," *Wall Street Journal*, May 28, 2003.
26. "Sox and Stocks," *Wall Street Journal*, April 19, 2005, A20.
27. Deborah Solomon and Cassell Bryan-Low, "Companies Complain About Cost of Corporate-Governance Rules," *Wall Street Journal*, February 10, 2004.
28. Del Jones, "S–Ox: Dragon or White Knight?" *USA Today*, October 20, 2003.
29. Nanette Byrnes, "Paying For the Sins of Enron," *Business Week*, February 11, 2002.
30. Floyd Norris, "A Crime So Large It Changed the Law," *New York Times*, July 14, 2005.

30 Conclusion

1. Dale Flesher and Tonya Flesher, "Ivar Kreuger's Contribution to U.S. Financial Reporting," *Accounting Review* 61 (July 1986): 429.
2. Joni J. Young, "Defining Auditors' Responsibilities," *Accounting Historians Journal* 24 (December 1997): 28.
3. I.F. Marcoson, "The Match King," *Saturday Evening Post*, October 12, 1929, 238.
4. Alan Rappeport, "Is the Auditor the CFO's Fool?" *CFO.com*, November 14, 2007.
5. Robert H. Montgomery, *Auditing Theory and Practice*, 6th ed. (New York: Ronald Press, 1940), quoted in Joni J. Young, "Defining Auditors' Responsibilities," *Accounting Historians Journal* 24 (December 1997): 30.
6. Securities and Exchange Commission, Accounting Series Release No. 19, *In the Matter of McKesson & Robbins, Inc.*, December 5, 1940.
7. John L. Carey, *The Rise of the Accounting Profession, 1896–1936* (New York: American Institute of Certified Public Accountants, 1969), 185.
8. Clay Shirky, "How Priceline Became a Real Business," *Wall Street Journal*, August 13, 2001, A12.
9. Ivy Xiying Zhang, "Economic Consequences of the Sarbanes–Oxley Act of 2002," *Journal of Accounting and Economics* 44 (September 2007): 74–115.
10. Flesher and Flesher, "Ivar Kreuger's Contribution to U.S. Financial Reporting," 429.

Sources

2 Out of darkness

"Annual Audit for the Equitable." *Journal of Accountancy* 1 (January 1906): 233–234.

Berle, Adolph A., and Gardiner C. Means. *The Modern Corporation and Private Property*. New York: Macmillan, 1932.

Brief, Richard. "Corporate Financial Reporting at the Turn of the Century." *Journal of Accountancy* 163 (May 1987): 142–157.

Carey, John. *The Rise of the Accounting Profession, 1896–1936*. New York: American Institute of Certified Public Accountants, 1969.

"Certified Public Accountants." *Fortune*, June 1932.

Flesher, Dale, Paul J. Miranti, and Gary John Previts. "The First Century of the CPA." *Journal of Accountancy* 182 (October 1996): 51–56.

Jereski, Laura. "You've Come a Long Way, Shareholder." *Forbes*, July 13, 1987.

Previts, Gary, and Barbara Merino. *A History of Accounting in America*. New York: John Wiley & Sons, 1979.

"The Reports of American Corporations." *Journal of Accountancy* 2 (October 1906): 458–459.

Ripley, William Z. "Stop, Look, Listen!" *Atlantic Monthly*, September 1926.

Ripley, William Z. *Main Street and Wall Street*. 1927. Reprinted Lawrence, KS: Scholars Book Company, 1972.

"Safeguarding Investment." *Journal of Accountancy* 27 (January 1919): 61–65.

Sterrett, J.E. "The Present Position and Probable Development of Accounting as a Profession." *Journal of Accountancy* 7 (February 1909): 265–273.

Wootton, Charles, and Carel Wolk. "The Development of 'The Big Eight' Accounting Firms in the United States, 1900 to 1990." *Accounting Historians Journal* 19 (June 1992): 1–27.

3 Ivar Kreuger

Churchill, Allen. *The Incredible Ivar Kreuger*. New York: Rinehart & Co., 1957.

Flesher, Dale, and Tonya Flesher. "Ivar Kreuger's Contribution to U.S. Financial Reporting." *Accounting Review* 61 (July 1986): 421–434.

"Ivar Kreuger III." *Fortune*, July 1933.

"Kreuger Books Are 'Grossly Wrong,' Some Assets False." *New York Times*, April 6, 1932.
"Kreuger's Defalcations Shown to Be $115 Million." *Barron's*, January 16, 1933.
"Kreuger's Suicide Depresses World Markets." *Barron's*, March 31, 1932.
"Market Sags Here on Kreuger Selling." *New York Times*, March 15, 1932.
"Monopolist." *Time*, October 28, 1929.
"More Sensational Kreuger Disclosures." *Barron's*, May 9, 1932.
Picton, John. "The Death of the World's Greatest Swindler." *Toronto Star*, August 21, 1988.
Wells, Joseph T. *Frankensteins of Fraud*. Austin, TX: Obsidian Publishing Company, 2000.

4 McKesson & Robbins

Berger, Meyer. "The Story of F.D. Coster (Musica): A Strange Human Record." *New York Times*, December 25, 1938.
Crossen, Cynthia. "A '30s Business Genius Fooled Bankers, Peers and Price Waterhouse." *Wall Street Journal*, November 6, 2002.
"Drug Mystery." *Time*, December 19, 1938.
Keats, Charles. *Magnificent Masquerade: The Strange Case of Dr. Coster and Mr. Musica*. New York: Funk & Wagnalls, 1964.
"Ledgers and Legends." *Newsweek*, January 2, 1939.
Wells, Joseph T. *Frankensteins of Fraud*. Austin, TX: Obsidian Publishing Company, 2000.

5 Into the Spotlight

"After Coster, Accounting Reform." *Business Week*, January 7, 1939.
Afterman, Allan B. *SEC Regulation of Public Companies*. Upper Saddle River, NJ: Prentice-Hall, 1995.
Austin, K.L. "Ivar Kreuger's Story in Light of Five Years." *New York Times*, March 7, 1937.
Carey, John L. *The Rise of the Accounting Profession, 1937–1969*. New York: American Institute of Certified Public Accountants, 1970.
Flesher, Dale and Tonya Flesher. "Ivar Kreuger's Contribution to U.S. Financial Reporting." *Accounting Review* 61 (July 1986): 421–434.
"Ivar Kreuger III." *Fortune*, July 1933.
Landis, James M. "The Legislative History of the Securities Act of 1933." *George Washington Law Review* 28 (October 1959): 29–49.
"Ledgers and Legends." *Newsweek*, January 2, 1939.
"Man Who Trapped Kreuger Describes Deals to Senators." *New York Times*, January 12, 1933.
"Musica Case Presages New Steps to Safeguard U.S. Investors." *Newsweek*, December 26, 1938.
Parrish, Michael E. *Securities Regulation and the New Deal*. New Haven: Yale University Press, 1970.

Securities and Exchange Commission. Accounting Series Release No. 19, *In the Matter of McKesson & Robbins*. December 5, 1940.
Skousen, K. Fred. *An Introduction to the SEC*. 5th ed. Cincinnati: South-Western College Publishing, 1991.
"The McKesson & Robbins Case." *The Journal of Accountancy* 67 (February 1939): 65–69.
Winkler, Max. "Playing With Matches." *The Nation*, May 25, 1932.

6 Generally Accepted Accounting Principles

"Asset Pooling Debate Heats Up." *Business Week*, October 26, 1968.
Blough, Carman. "The Need for Accounting Principles." *Accounting Review* 12 (March 1937): 30–37.
Briloff, Abraham J. "Dirty Pooling." *Barron's*, July 15, 1968.
Carey, John L. *The Rise of the Accounting Profession, 1937–1969*. New York: American Institute of Certified Public Accountants, 1970.
Cooper, William D., and Ida B. Robinson. "Who Should Formulate Accounting Principles? The Debate Within the SEC." *Journal of Accountancy* 163 (May 1987): 137–140.
Davidson, Sidney, and George Anderson. "The Development of Accounting and Auditing Standards." *Journal of Accountancy* 163 (May 1987): 110–127.
Hatfield, Henry Rand. "What Is the Matter With Accounting?" *Journal of Accountancy* 44 (October 1927): 267–279.
Seidman, J.A. "Pooling Must Go." *Barron's*, July 1, 1968.
Skousen, K. Fred. *An Introduction to the SEC*. 5th ed. Cincinnati: South-Western College Publishing, 1991.
"Some Hard New Rules for the Merger Game." *Business Week*, April 11, 1970.
"The Biggest, Wildest Merger Year Ever." *Fortune*, June 15, 1968.
Weis, William L., and David E. Tinius. "Luca Pacioli: Accounting's Renaissance Man." *Management Accounting* 73 (July 1991): 54–56.
Wise, T.A. "The Auditors Have Arrived." *Fortune*, November 1960.
Zeff, Stephen A. "Some Junctures in the Evolution of Establishing Accounting Principles in the U.S.A., 1917–1972." *Accounting Review* 59 (July 1984): 447–468.
Zeff, Stephen A. "The Evolution of U.S. GAAP, 1930–1973." *CPA Journal* 75 (January 2005): 18–27.

7 National Student Marketing

Abelson, Alan. "Up and Down Wall Street." *Barron's*, December 22, 1969.
Andrews, Frederick. "Fraud Trial of Peat Marwick Attracts Anxious Attention of Other Accountants." *Wall Street Journal*, October 29, 1974.
Barmash, Isador. "Troubles of Youth Concern Jolt the Industry." *New York Times*, March 8, 1970.
Knapp, Michael C. *Contemporary Auditing: Issues and Cases*. 3rd ed. Cincinnati: South-Western College Publishing, 1999.
Loving Jr., Rush. "How Cortes Randell Drained the Fountain of Youth." *Fortune*, April 1970.

McClintick, David. "National Student Marketing, Former Head Were Targets of Post Office Inquiries." *Wall Street Journal*, March 27, 1970.

McClintick, David. "Peat Marwick Partner Indicted Over Proxy Data." *Wall Street Journal*, January 18, 1974.

"National Student Says It Erred Over Deficit." *Wall Street Journal*, February 26, 1970

Olson, Wyatt. "Hustling for Models." *New Times Broward–Palm Beach*, September 6, 2001.

Securities and Exchange Commission. Accounting Series Release No. 173, *In the Matter of Peat, Marwick, Mitchell & Co.* July 2, 1975.

Tobias, Andrew. *The Funny Money Game*. London: Michael Joseph, 1972.

Walsh, Sharon Warren. "Cortes Randell Sets Up Shop All Over Again." *Washington Post*, October 12, 1987.

8 Equity Funding

Blundell, William. "A Scandal Unfolds." *Wall Street Journal*, April 2, 1973.

Dirks, Raymond, and Leonard Gross. *The Great Wall Street Scandal*. New York: McGraw-Hill, 1974.

Knapp, Michael C. *Contemporary Auditing: Real Issues and Cases*. 4th ed. Cincinnati: South-Western College Publishing, 2004.

Robertson, Wyndham. "Those Daring Young Con Men of Equity Funding." *Fortune*, August 1973.

Securities and Exchange Commission. Accounting Series Release No. 196, *In the Matter of Seidman & Seidman*. September 1, 1976.

Soble, Ronald, and Robert Dallos. *The Impossible Dream*. New York: G.P. Putnam's Sons, 1975.

Weinstein, Henry. "Goldblum Enters Equity Guilty Plea." *New York Times*, October 9, 1974.

Wells, Joseph T. *Frankensteins of Fraud*. Austin, TX: Obsidian Publishing Company, 2000.

Wright, Robert. "Twenty-two Indicted by U.S. in Equity Scandal." *New York Times*, November 2, 1973.

9 Déjà Vu

Allan, John H. "Accountants Get Report on Rules." *New York Times*, March 30, 1972.

Berton, Lee. "Frustrated CPAs: Accounting Body Fails in Attempts to Change Some Firms' Reporting." *Wall Street Journal*, January 8, 1969.

Commission on Auditors' Responsibilities. *Report, Conclusions, and Recommendations*. New York: American Institute of Certified Public Accountants, 1978.

Davidson, Sidney, and George Anderson. "The Development of Accounting and Auditing Standards." *Journal of Accountancy* 163 (May 1987): 110–127.

Jancura, Elise, and Fred Lilly. "SAS No. 3 and the Evaluation of Internal Control." *Journal of Accountancy* 143 (March 1977): 69–74.

Miller, Paul B.W., and Rodney J. Redding. *The FASB: The People, the Process, and the Politics*. 2nd ed. Homewood, IL: Richard D. Irwin, 1988.
Oelsner, Lesley. "Stans Pleads Guilty to Five Violations of Election Laws in Campaign of 1972." *New York Times*, March 13, 1975.
Olson, Wallace E. *The Accounting Profession: Years of Trial, 1969–1980*. New York: American Institute of Certified Public Accountants, 1982.
Rankin, Deborah. "Tough Senate Study on Auditing Practice Ends on Softer Note." *New York Times*, November 14, 1977.
Rickover, H.G. "The Accounting Establishment: Comments on the Metcalf Report." *Government Accountants Journal* 26 (fall 1977): 1–10.
Schroeder, Michael. "House Passes Curb On Expense Rules For Stock Options." *Wall Street Journal*, July 21, 2004.
U.S. Senate Committee on Government Operations. Subcommittee on Reports, Accounting and Management. *The Accounting Establishment: A Staff Study*. Washington, DC: Government Printing Office, 1976.
"Wheat Committee: Establishing Accounting Standards." *Journal of Accountancy* 163 (May 1987): 134–135.
Zeff, Stephen A. "Some Junctures in the Evolution of Establishing Accounting Principles in the U.S.A.: 1917–1972." *Accounting Review* 59 (July 1984): 447–468.

10 It's a Wonderful Life?

Eichler, Ned. *The Thrift Debacle*. Berkeley: University of California Press, 1989.
Mason, David L. *From Building and Loans to Bail-outs*. Cambridge and New York: Cambridge University Press, 2004.
Mills, Robert H. "Accounting Alchemy: It Turns S&L Red Ink Into Black." *Barron's*, May 31, 1982.
Tucker, James J., and Ahmad Salman. "Congress, Regulators, RAP, and the Savings and Loan Debacle." *CPA Journal* 64 (January 1994): 42–48.
White, Lawrence J. *The S&L Debacle*. New York: Oxford University Press, 1991.

11 ESM Government Securities

Brannigan, Martha. "Grant Thornton and Four Accountants Settle SEC Charges Tied to ESM." *Wall Street Journal*, October 17, 1986.
Brannigan, Martha. "Auditor's Downfall Shows Man Caught in Trap of His Own Making." *Wall Street Journal*, March 4, 1987.
Cary, Peter and Susan Sachs. "Founders of ESM Lived High." *Miami Herald*, March 31, 1985.
Dickerson, Brian. "The Lonely Death of Stephen Arky." *Miami Herald*, December 7, 1986.
Lyons, James. "How Many Hats Can Steve Arky Wear?" *American Lawyer* 7 (May 1985): 86–93.
Maggin, Donald. *Bankers, Builders, Knaves and Thieves: The $300 Million Scam at ESM*. Chicago: Contemporary Books, 1989.

Martinez, James. "Jury Holds ESM's Auditing Firm Liable for Preparing False Reports." *St. Petersburg Times*, November 7, 1986.

Rowe Jr., James. "Seventy S&Ls Are Shut in Ohio." *Washington Post*, March 16, 1985.

Sack, Robert, and Robert Tangreti. "ESM: Implications for the Profession." *Journal of Accountancy* 163 (April 1987): 94–100.

Sawyer, Kathy. "ESM Scandal Extinguished a Rising Star." *Washington Post*, July 28, 1985.

Securities and Exchange Commission. Litigation Release No. 11263, *SEC* v. *Thornton, et al.* October 16, 1986.

12 Lincoln Savings & Loan

Berg, Eric. "The Lapses by Lincoln's Auditors." *New York Times*, December 28, 1989.

Binstein, Michael, and Charles Bowden. *Trust Me: Charles Keating and the Missing Billions*. New York: Random House, 1993.

Erickson, Merle, Brian Mayhew, and William Felix, Jr. "Why Do Audits Fail? Evidence from Lincoln Savings and Loan." *Journal of Accounting Research* 38 (spring 2000): 165–194.

Hilder, David B., and John E. Yang. "Bank Board Appointee Has Close Ties to Thrift With Controversial Investment." *Wall Street Journal*, December 18, 1986.

Jefferson, David J. "Keating of American Continental Corp. Comes Out Fighting." *Wall Street Journal*, April 18, 1989.

Knapp, Michael C. *Contemporary Auditing: Real Issues and Cases*. 4th ed. Cincinnati: South Western College Publishing, 2001.

Mayer, Martin. *The Greatest-ever Bank Robbery*. New York: Charles Scribner's Sons, 1990.

Muller, Bill. "Chapter V: The Keating Five." *Arizona Republic*, October 3, 1999.

Thomas, Paulette, and Brooks Jackson. "Regulators Cite Delays and Phone Bugs in Examination, Seizure of Lincoln Savings & Loan." *Wall Street Journal*, October 27, 1989.

13 Bank Robbers

Bartsch, Robert A., William J. Read, and K. Raghunandan. "Accounting for Impaired Loans Under SFAS No. 114." *CPA Journal* 64 (July 1994): 48–51.

Berton, Lee. "GAO Says Accountants Auditing Thrifts Are Hiding Behind Outdated Standards." *Wall Street Journal*, February 6, 1989.

Calavita, Kitty, Henry N. Pontell, and Robert H. Tillman. *Big Money Crime: Fraud and Politics in the Savings and Loan Crisis*. Berkeley: University of California Press, 1997.

Cook, J. Michael, and Thomas P. Kelley. "Internal Accounting Control: A Matter of Law." *Journal of Accountancy* 147 (January 1979): 56–64.

Cushman Jr., John H. "Largest Recovery: Ernst & Young Accused of Failure to Discern Financial Troubles." *New York Times*, November 24, 1992.

Day, Kathleen. *S&L Hell: The People and the Politics Behind the $1 Trillion Savings and Loan Scandal*. New York: W.W. Norton & Co., 1993.

Eichler, Ned. *The Thrift Debacle*. Berkeley: University of California Press, 1989.

General Accounting Office. *CPA Audit Quality: Failures of CPA Audits to Identify and Report Significant Savings and Loan Problems*. AFMD-89-45, February 1989, reprinted in the *Journal of Accountancy* 167 (March 1989): 21–32.

General Accounting Office. *Thrift Failures: Costly Failures Resulted From Regulatory Violations and Unsafe Practices*. AFMD-89-62, June 1989.

General Accounting Office. *Failed Banks: Accounting and Auditing Reforms Urgently Needed*. AFMD-91-43, April 1991.

Knight, Jerry, and Sharon Warren Walsh, "Panel Votes Higher S&L Capital Rule; Owners to Put Up More of Own Money." *Washington Post*, April 28, 1989.

Linden, Dana Wechsler. "If Life Is Volatile, Account for It." *Forbes*, November 12, 1990.

Mason, David L. *From Buildings and Loans to Bail-outs*. Cambridge and New York: Cambridge University Press, 2004.

Malloy, Mary B., and Walter M. Primoff. "The S&L Crisis: Putting Things in Perspective." *CPA Journal* 59 (December 1989): 12–21.

McCoy, Charles, Richard Schmitt, and Jeff Bailey. "Hall of Shame: Besides S&L Owners, Host of Professionals Paved Way for Crisis." *Wall Street Journal*, November 2, 1990.

Miller, Stephen H. "SEC Market Value Conference: Experts Urge Mark-to-Market." *Journal of Accountancy* 173 (January 1992): 13–16.

Moraglio Joseph F., and James F. Green. "The FDIC Improvement Act: A Precedent for Expanded CPA Reporting?" *Journal of Accountancy* 173 (April 1992): 63–71.

Nash, Nathaniel C. "Saving-Unit Quarantine Is Proposed." *New York Times*, February 3, 1989.

Parks, James T. "FASB 115: It's Back to the Future for Market Value Accounting." *Journal of Accountancy* 176 (September 1993): 128–143.

Rosenblatt, Robert A. "GAO: Fraud May Have Had Big Role in S&L Failures." *Washington Post*, January 14, 1989.

Rosenblatt, Robert A. "GAO Estimates Final Cost of S&L Bailout at $480.9 Billion." *Los Angeles Times*, July 13, 1996.

Salwen, Kevin G. "SEC Is Seeking Updated Rules for Accounting." *Wall Street Journal*, January 8, 1992.

Savoie, Leonard M., and David N. Ricchiute. "Reports by Management: Voluntary or Mandatory?" *Journal of Accountancy* 151 (May 1981): 84–94.

Schmitt, Richard B., and Lee Berton. "Deloitte to Pay $312 Million to Settle U.S. Claims Related to S&L Failures." *Wall Street Journal*, March 15, 1994.

Swenson, Dan W., and Thomas E. Buttross. "A Return to the Past: Disclosing Market Values of Financial Instruments." *Journal of Accountancy* 175 (January 1993): 71–77.

Thomas, Paulette, and Thomas Ricks. "Tracing the Billions: Just What Happened to All That Money S&Ls Lost?" *Wall Street Journal*, November 5, 1990.

Thompson, James H., L. Murphy Smith, and Mary B. Throneberry. "SFAS 91 Changes Accounting Rules for Loan Fees and Costs." *CPA Journal* 58 (September 1988): 68–69.

Wallace, Wanda A. "Internal Control Reporting: 950 Negative Responses." *CPA Journal* 51 (January 1981): 33–38.

Wayne, Leslie. "Where Were the Accountants?" *New York Times*, March 12, 1989.

White, Lawrence J. "Mark-to-Market Accounting: A (Not So) Modest Proposal." *Financial Managers' Statement* 12 (January–February 1990): 27–32.

White, Lawrence J. *The S&L Debacle*. New York: Oxford University Press, 1991.

Wyden, Ron. "The First Line of Defense." *New Accountant*, December 1990.

14 Auditors and Fraud

Adelberg, Arthur H. "Auditing on the March: Ancient Times to the Twentieth Century." *Internal Auditor* 32 (November/December 1975): 35–47.

Andrews, Frederick. "SEC Jolting Auditors Into a Broader Role in Fraud Detection." *Wall Street Journal*, July 12, 1974.

Berton, Lee. "Bill to Force Firms' Outside Auditors to Report Fraud to Public Is Introduced." *Wall Street Journal*, May 23, 1986.

Berton, Lee, and Daniel Akst. "CPAs May Soon Have to Report Fraud Earlier." *Wall Street Journal*, January 22, 1988.

Berton, Lee, and Bruce Ingersoll. "Rep. Dingell to Take Aim at Accountants, SEC in Hearings on Profession's Role as Watchdog." *Wall Street Journal*, February 19, 1985.

Broockholdt, James L. "A Historical Perspective on the Auditor's Role: The Early Experience of the American Railroads." *Accounting Historians Journal* 10 (spring 1983): 69–85.

Brown, R. Gene. "Changing Audit Objectives and Techniques." *Accounting Review* 37 (October 1962): 696–703.

Carmichael, Douglas R. "What Is the Independent Auditor's Responsibility for the Detection of Fraud?" *Journal of Accountancy* 140 (November 1975): 76–79.

Carmichael, Douglas R. "Fraud and Illegal Acts—A New Look." *CPA Journal* 57 (February 1987): 94–96.

Catlett, George R. "Relationship of Auditing Standards to Detection of Fraud." *CPA Journal* 45 (April 1975): 13–18.

Commission on Auditors' Responsibilities. *Report, Conclusions, and Recommendations*. New York: American Institute of Certified Public Accountants, 1978.

Defliese, Philip L. "The 'New Look' at the Auditor's Responsibility for Fraud Detection." *Journal of Accountancy* 114 (October 1962): 36–44.

"Dingell Rebukes SEC on Its Disciplining of Accounting Firms." *Wall Street Journal*, February 21, 1985.

Grisdela, Cynthia S. "SEC to Oppose Bill That Forces Auditors to Report Possible Fraud by Their Clients." *Wall Street Journal*, June 20, 1986.

Hershman, Arlene. "The War Over Corporate Fraud." *Dun's Review*, November 1974.

Ingersoll, Bruce. "House Democrats Question SEC's Role in Guarding Against Audit Failures." *Wall Street Journal*, March 7, 1985.
Klott, Gary. "Auditors Face U.S. Scrutiny." *New York Times*, February 18, 1985.
Klott, Gary. "House Unit Bill Would Expand Role of Auditors." *New York Times*, May 23, 1986.
Morison, A.M.C. "The Role of the Reporting Accountant Today" II. *Accountancy* 82 (March 1971): 120–130.
Moyer, C.A. "Early Developments in American Auditing." *Accounting Review* 26 (January 1951): 3–8.
Stone, Williard E. "Antecedents of the Accounting Profession." *Accounting Review* 44 (April 1969): 284–291.
Willingham, John J. "Discussant's Response to Relationship of Auditing Standards to Detection of Fraud." *CPA Journal* 45 (April 1975): 18–21.
Young, Joni J. "Defining Auditors' Responsibilities." *Accounting Historians Journal* 24 (December 1997): 25–63.

15 ZZZZ Best

Akst, Daniel. "Behind 'Whiz Kid' Is a Trail of False Credit Card Billings." *Los Angeles Times*, May 22, 1987.
Akst, Daniel. *Wonder Boy: Barry Minkow—The Kid Who Swindled Wall Street*. New York: Charles Scribner's Sons, 1990.
Domanick, Joe. *Faking It in America: Barry Minkow and the Great ZZZZ Best Scam*. Chicago: Contemporary Books, 1989.
"Ernst & Young Not Liable in ZZZZ Best Case." *Journal of Accountancy* 172 (July 1991): 22.
Minkow, Barry. *Clean Sweep: The Inside Story of the ZZZZ Best Scam*. Nashville: Thomas Nelson Publishers, 1995.
Moll, Rob. "The Fraud Buster." *Christianity Today*, January 2005.
Rebello, Kathy. "Rise and Fall of ZZZZ Best." *USA Today*, July 13, 1987.
Savitz, Eric. "Born-again Barry." *Barron's*, May 19, 1997.
Securities and Exchange Commission. Accounting and Auditing Enforcement Release No. 312, *In the Matter of Samuel George Greenspan, CPA*. August 26, 1991.

16 Crazy Eddie

Belsky, Gary, and Phyllis Furman. "Calculated Madness: The Rise and Fall of Crazy Eddie Antar." *Crain's New York Business*, June 5, 1989.
Bryant, Adam. "Crazy Eddie's Chief Is Arrested in Israel." *New York Times*, June 25, 1992.
Cheney, Glenn. "How Crazy Was Crazy Eddie?" *Accounting Today*, October 26, 1998.
Lambert, Wade. "Crazy Eddie's Founder's Conviction in Stock Fraud Case Is Reversed." *Wall Street Journal*, April 13, 1995.
McMorris, Frances. "Crazy Eddie Inc.'s Antar Admits Guilt in Racketeering Conspiracy." *Wall Street Journal*, May 9, 1996.

Meier, Barry. "Crazy Eddie's Insane Odyssey." *New York Times*, July 19, 1992.
Pinder, Jeanne B. "Crazy Eddie Founder Guilty of Fraud." *New York Times*, July 21, 1993.
Queenan, Joe. "Positively Insane—The Absolutely Incredible Saga of Crazy Eddie." *Barron's*, June 13, 1988.
Securities and Exchange Commission. Accounting and Auditing Enforcement Release No. 247, *Securities and Exchange Commission v. Antar et al.* September 6, 1989.
Tannenbaum, Jeffrey. "Short Circuit: How Mounting Woes at Crazy Eddie Sank a Turnaround Effort." *Wall Street Journal*, July 10, 1989.
Wells, Joseph. *Frankensteins of Fraud*. Austin, TX: Obsidian Publishing Company, 2000.

17 Closing the Gap

Beasley, Mark S., Joseph V. Carcello, and Dana R. Hermanson. "Top 10 Audit Deficiencies." *Journal of Accountancy* 191 (April 2001): 63–66.
Carmichael, Douglas R. "The Auditor's New Guide to Errors, Irregularities and Illegal Acts." *Journal of Accountancy* 166 (September 1988): 40–46.
Committee of Sponsoring Organizations of the Treadway Commission (COSO). *Fraudulent Financial Reporting, 1987–1997: An Analysis of U.S. Companies* (1999).
Guy, Dan M., and Jerry D. Sullivan. "The Expectation Gap in Auditing Standards." *Journal of Accountancy* 165 (April 1988): 36–43.
Hilzenrath, David. "Auditors Face Scant Discipline." *Washington Post*, December 6, 2001.
Mancino, Jane. "The Auditor and Fraud." *Journal of Accountancy* 183 (April 1997): 32–36.
National Commission on Fraudulent Financial Reporting. *Report of the National Commission on Fraudulent Financial Reporting* (1987).

18 Auditors' Legal Liability

Carey, John L. *The Rise of the Accounting Profession, 1896–1936*. New York: American Institute of Certified Public Accountants, 1969.
Knapp, Michael C. *Contemporary Auditing: Real Issues and Cases*. 4th ed. Cincinnati: South-Western College Publishing, 2001.
Levy, Saul. *Accountants' Legal Responsibility*. New York: American Institute of Accountants, 1954.
Minow, Newton N. "Accountants' Liability and the Litigation Explosion." *Journal of Accountancy* 158 (September 1984): 70–79.
Olson, Wallace E. *The Accounting Profession: Years of Trial, 1969–1980*. New York: American Institute of Certified Public Accountants, 1982.
Reilly, David. "Micrel Says Deloitte Approved Options-Pricing Plan." *Wall Street Journal*, June 1, 2006.
Ruhnka, John, and Edward J. Gac. "RICO Claims Against CPAs." *CPA Journal* 57 (December 1987): 26–42.

Securities and Exchange Commission. Accounting Series Release No. 153, *In the Matter of Touche Ross & Co*. February 25, 1974.
"The Auditor's Legal Liability." *Journal of Accountancy* 14 (July 1912): 53–57.

19 Fund of Funds

Arenson, Karen. "Andersen Firm Is Found Guilty of Fraud." *New York Times*, November 5, 1981.
Cornfeld, Jessica. "My Father, the Playboy Who Could Never Have Enough Lovers." *Mail on Sunday* (London), June 29, 2003.
Dizard, John. "Fund of Funds: Its Long-suffering Shareholders Are Finally Cashing In." *Barron's*, February 1, 1982.
Fund of Funds v. *Arthur Andersen*. 545 F. Supp. 1314, July 16, 1982.
Gigot, Paul. "Big Fraud Verdict Against Andersen Shakes Up Accounting Profession." *Wall Street Journal*, February 3, 1982.
Knapp, Michael C. *Contemporary Auditing: Real Issues and Cases*. 4th ed. Cincinnati: South-Western College Publishing, 2001.
Raw, Charles. "Last of the Buccaneers—Bernie Cornfeld." the *Guardian*, March 2, 1995.
Train, John. *Famous Financial Fiascos*. New York: Clarkson N. Potter, 1994.

20 MiniScribe

Accola, John. "Ex-MiniScribe Chairman Convicted." *Rocky Mountain News*, July 30, 1994.
Allen, Michael. "MiniScribe's Wiles, Once a 'Dr. Fix-it,' Resigns Top Posts at Disk-drive Maker." *Wall Street Journal*, February 23, 1989.
Apodaca, Patrice. "Wiles Convicted of Fraud." *Los Angeles Times*, August 9, 1994.
Berton, Lee. "Numbers Game: How MiniScribe Got Its Auditor's Blessing on Questionable Sales." *Wall Street Journal*, May 14, 1992.
Drake, Philip, and John W. Peavy III. "Fundamental Analysis, Stock Prices, and the Demise of MiniScribe Corporation." *Journal of Portfolio Management* 21 (spring 1995): 68–73.
Harlan, Christi. "Jury Awards $550 Million in Damages to ex-Bondholders in MiniScribe Case." *Wall Street Journal*, February 5, 1992.
Harlan, Christi. "Coopers & Lybrand Agrees to Payment of $95 Million in the MiniScribe Case." *Wall Street Journal*, October 30, 1992.
Holmes, Stanley. "MiniScribe Chairman's Fraud Trial Opens." *Rocky Mountain News*, July 12, 1994.
Mamis, Robert and Steven Pearlstein. "Company Doctor Q.T. Wiles." *Inc.*, February 1988.
Miller, Michael. "Dr. Fix-it: Q.T. Wiles Revives Sick High-tech Firms With Strong Medicine." *Wall Street Journal*, June 23, 1986.
Moran, Kevin. "MiniScribe Trial to Start in Galveston." *Houston Chronicle*, October 21, 1991.
Nichols, Bruce. "Lawyers Can't Decide Who Really Won Case." *Dallas Morning News*, March 15, 1992.

Securities and Exchange Commission. Litigation Release No. 12942, *Securities and Exchange Commission v. Wiles et al.* August 14, 1991.
Zipser, Andy. "Cooking the Books: How Pressure to Raise Sales Led MiniScribe to Falsify Numbers." *Wall Street Journal*, September 11, 1989.
Zipser, Andy. "MiniScribe's Investigators Determine That 'Massive Fraud' Was Perpetrated." *Wall Street Journal*, September 12, 1989.

21 Litigation Reform

Bass, Stuart. "Supreme Court Limits RICO Liability for Accountants and Outside Professionals." *Commercial Law Journal* 98 (winter 1993): 452–463.
Berton, Lee. "Bad Numbers: Laventhol & Horwath, Beset by Litigation, Runs Into Hard Times." *Wall Street Journal*, May 17, 1990.
Berton, Lee, and Joann S. Lublin. "Seeking Shelter: Partnership Structure Is Called Into Question as Liability Risk Rises." *Wall Street Journal*, June 10, 1992.
Boyle, Edward J., and Fred N. Knopf. "The Private Securities Litigation Reform Act of 1995." *CPA Journal* 66 (April 1996): 44–47.
Cook, Michael J., Ray J. Groves, Shaun F. O'Malley, Eugene M. Freedman, Jon C. Madonna, and Lawrence A. Weinbach. "The Liability Crisis in the United States: Impact on the Accounting Profession" (statement of position, August 6, 1992).
Cowan, Alison Leigh. "Bankruptcy Filing by Laventhol." *New York Times*, November 22, 1990.
Gigot, Paul. "Big Fraud Verdict Against Andersen Shakes Up Accounting Profession." *Wall Street Journal*, February 3, 1982.
Hanson, Randall K., and Joanne W. Rockness. "Gaining a New Balance in the Courts." *Journal of Accountancy* 178 (August 1994): 40–44.
McCarroll, Thomas. "Who's Counting?" *Time*, April 13, 1992.
Popofsky, M. Laurence. "CPAs Win Big in Osborne Case." *Accounting Today*, February 1, 1993.
Taylor, Jeffrey. "Accountants' Campaign Contributions Are About to Pay Off in Legislation on Lawsuit Protection." *Wall Street Journal*, March 8, 1995.
Telberg, Rick. "Big 6 Race Into LLPs." *Accounting Today*, August 8, 1994.
Telberg, Rick. "Despite Reforms, New Liability Hazards Loom Ahead for CPAs." *Accounting Today*, May 22, 1995.

22 Auditor Independence

American Institute of Certified Public Accountants. *Final Report of the Ad Hoc Committee on Independence*, reprinted in *Journal of Accountancy* 128 (December 1969): 51–56.
Andersen, Arthur E. "The Accountant's Function as Business Advisor." *Journal of Accountancy* 41 (January 1926): 17–21.
Berton, Lee. "GAO Weighs Auditing Plan for Big Banks." *Wall Street Journal*, March 27, 1991.

Berton, Lee. "Accountants Expand Scope of Audit Work." *Wall Street Journal*, June 17, 1996.

Briloff, Abraham. "Our Profession's 'Jurassic Park.'" *CPA Journal* 64 (August 1994): 26–31.

Carey, John L. *Professional Ethics of Public Accounting*. New York: American Institute of Accountants, 1946.

Chenok, Philip B., with Adam Snyder. *Foundations for the Future: The AICPA from 1980 to 1995*. Stamford, CT: JAI Press, 2000.

Cowan, Alison Leigh. "When Auditors Change Sides." *New York Times*, October 11, 1992.

Cowan, Alison Leigh. "Seeking to Curb Auditor Job Hopping." *New York Times*, June 9, 1993.

Hayes, Thomas C. "Accountants Under Scrutiny: Consulting Jobs Called Risk to Independence." *New York Times*, June 25, 1979.

"Independence Standards Board Progress Report," *CPA Journal* 70 (May 2000): 8.

Levitt, Arthur. *Take on the Street*. New York: Pantheon Books, 2002.

Lowe, D. Jordan, and Kurt Pany. "Auditor Independence: The Performance of Consulting Engagements with Audit Clients." *Journal of Applied Business Research* 10 (winter 1994): 6–13.

MacDonald, Elizabeth. "Auditing Standards Board is Named Amid Concern by Business Executives." *Wall Street Journal*, June 18, 1997.

Mautz, Robert K., and Hussein A. Sharaf. *The Philosophy of Auditing*. Sarasota, FL: American Accounting Association, 1961.

May, George O. "Letter." *Journal of Accountancy* 40 (September 1925): 191.

Petersen, Melody. "SEC Staff Accuses KPMG Peat Marwick of Securities Violations." *New York Times*, December 5, 1997.

Previts, Gary John. *The Scope of CPA Services*. New York: John Wiley & Sons, 1985.

Richards, Bill. "Deloitte to Pay $65 Million in Bonneville Scandal." *Wall Street Journal*, April 24, 1996.

Richardson, A.P. "The Accountant's True Sphere." *Journal of Accountancy* 40 (September 1925): 190–191.

Salwen, Kevin G. "Ernst & Young Faces Lawsuit From the SEC." *Wall Street Journal*, June 14, 1991.

Schroeder, Michael, and Elizabeth MacDonald. "SEC Plans a New Board to Regulate Auditors." *Wall Street Journal*, May 21, 1997.

Schuetze, Walter P. "A Mountain or a Molehill?" *Accounting Horizons* 8 (March 1994): 69–75.

"SEC Affirms Independence Rules." *Accounting Today*, June 6, 1994.

Securities and Exchange Commission. Accounting Series Release No. 250, *Disclosure of Relationships with Independent Public Accountants*. June 29, 1978.

Securities and Exchange Commission. Accounting Series Release No. 264, *Relationships Between Registrants and Independent Accountants*. January 28, 1982.

Securities and Exchange Commission. *Staff Report on Auditor Independence*. Washington, DC: Government Printing Office. March 1994.

23 Waste Management

Bailey, Jeff. "Waste Management's LeMay Quits Posts, Clouding Future of Trash-hauling Firm." *Wall Street Journal*, October 30, 1997.
Bailey, Jeff. "Waste Management Inc. Takes Charges of $3.54 Billion, Restates Past Results." *Wall Street Journal*, February 25, 1998.
Blumenthal, Ralph. "Waste Hauler's Business Acts Faulted." *New York Times*, March 24, 1983.
Briloff, Abraham. "Recycled Accounting: It Enhances Waste Management's Earnings." *Barron's*, August 6, 1990.
Chakravarty, Subrata. "Dean Buntrock's Green Machine." *Forbes*, August 2, 1993.
Elkind, Peter. "Garbage In, Garbage Out." *Fortune*, May 25, 1998.
Flynn, Julia. "Burying Trash in Big Holes—On the Balance Sheet." *Business Week*, May 11, 1992.
Melcher, Richard, and Gary McWilliams. "Can Waste Management Climb Out of the Muck?" *Business Week*, March 23, 1998.
Miller, James. "Waste Management, Andersen Agree to Settle Holder Suits for $220 Million." *Wall Street Journal*, December 10, 1998.
Schroeder, Michael. "SEC Fines Arthur Andersen in Fraud Case." *Wall Street Journal*, June 20, 2001.
Securities and Exchange Commission. Accounting and Auditing Enforcement Release No. 1277, *In the Matter of Waste Management, Inc.*, June 21, 2000.
Securities and Exchange Commission. Accounting and Auditing Enforcement Release No. 1405. *In the Matter of Arthur Andersen, LLP*. June 19, 2001.
Securities and Exchange Commission. Litigation Release No. 17039, *SEC v. Arthur Andersen, LLP*. June 19, 2001.
Securities and Exchange Commission. Litigation Release No. 17435, *SEC v. Dean L. Buntrock et al.* March 26, 2002.

24 Sunbeam

Brannigan, Martha. "Sunbeam Slashes Its 1997 Earnings in Restatement." *Wall Street Journal*, October 21, 1998.
Byrne, John. *Chainsaw*. New York: HarperCollins Publishers, 1999.
Canedy, Dana. "Three Acquisitions by Sunbeam in Separate Deals." *New York Times*, March 3, 1998.
Dunlap, Albert, with Bob Andelman. *Mean Business: How I Save Bad Companies and Make Good Companies Great*. New York: Random House, 1996.
Greene, Kelly. "Dunlap Agrees to Settle Suit Over Sunbeam." *Wall Street Journal*, January 15, 2002.
Laing, Jonathan. "Dangerous Games: Did 'Chainsaw Al' Dunlap Manufacture Sunbeam's Earnings Last Year?" *Barron's*, June 8, 1998.
Lavelle, Louis. "Boy Next Door to 'Rambo in Pinstripes.'" *Sunday Record*, November 10, 1996.
Martinez, Amy. "Auditors Settle Sunbeam Suit; Investors to Get $110 Million." *Palm Beach Post*, May 2, 2001.
Norris, Floyd. "They Noticed the Fraud but Figured It Was Not Important." *New York Times*, May 18, 2001, C1.

Securities and Exchange Commission. Accounting and Auditing Enforcement Release No. 1393, *In the Matter of Sunbeam Corporation.* May 15, 2001.
Securities and Exchange Commission. Accounting and Auditing Enforcement Release No. 1395, *SEC v. Albert J. Dunlap et al.* May 15, 2001.
Securities and Exchange Commission. Accounting and Auditing Enforcement Release No. 1706, *In the Matter of Phillip E. Harlow, CPA.* January 27, 2003.

25 End of the Millennium

Byrnes, Nanette. and Mike McNamee. "The SEC vs. CPAs: Suddenly, It's Hardball." *Business Week*, May 22, 2000.
Lavelle, Louis. "Cozying Up to the Ref: Ernst's Role in Tough New SEC Rules Riles Rivals." *Business Week*, July 31, 2000.
Levitt, Arthur. "The Numbers Game." Speech at the New York University Center for Law and Business, New York, NY, September 28, 1998. Available at http://www.sec.gov/news/speech/speecharchive/1998/spch220.txt.
Levitt, Arthur. *Take on the Street.* Chicago: Pantheon Books, 2002.
McNamee, Mike. "How Levitt Won the Accounting Wars." *Business Week*, November 27, 2000.
Melancon, Barry. "Accountants Need Clear, Modern Rules to Guide Them." *Business Week*, February 28, 2000.
Moore, Pamela L. "This Scandal Changes Everything." *Business Week*, February 28, 2000.
Norris, Floyd. "Accounting Firm Is Said to Violate Rules Routinely." *New York Times*, January 7, 2000.
Norris, Floyd. "Rules That Only an Accountant Could Fail to Understand?" *New York Times*, January 8, 2000.
Plitch, Phyllis. "Investors Send 'Strong' Message in Disney's Auditor Vote." *Dow Jones News Service*, February 19, 2002.
Securities and Exchange Commission. *Proposed rule: Revision of the Commission's Auditor Independence Requirements*, June 27, 2000. Available at http://www.sec.gov/rules/proposed/34–42994.htm.
Securities and Exchange Commission. *Final Rule: Revision of the Commission's Auditor Independence Requirements*, February 5, 2001. Available at http://www.sec.gov/rules/final/33–7919.htm.
Sweeney, Paul. "Accounting for the Big Five Breakups." *Financial Executive*, October 2002.
Unger, Laura S. "This Year's Proxy Season: Sunlight Shines on Auditor Independence and Executive Compensation." Speech at the Center for Professional Education, Washington DC, June 25, 2001. Available at http://www.sec.gov/news/speech/spch502.htm.
Weil, Jonathan. "SEC Chief Calls Andersen Case 'Smoking Gun.'" *Wall Street Journal*, June 26, 2001.
Weirich, Thomas R., and Robert W. Rouse. "The New SEC Materiality Guidelines: When Are the Numbers Important Enough to Matter?" *Journal of Corporate Accounting and Finance* 11 (January/February 2000): 35–40.

26 Professionalism

Andreder, Steven S. "Profit or Loss? Price-cutting Is Hitting Accountants in the Bottom Line." *Barron's*, March 2, 1979.

Beatty, Sally Goll. "Deloitte Stops Pulling Punches in Assault on Consulting Rivals." *Wall Street Journal*, February 26, 1998.

Berton, Lee. "Audit Fees Fall as CPA Firms Jockey for Bids." *Wall Street Journal*, January 28, 1985.

Berton, Lee. "Total War: CPA Firms Diversity, Cut Fees, Steal Clients in Battle." *Wall Street Journal*, September 20, 1985.

Bialkin, Kenneth J. "Government Antitrust Enforcement and the Rules of Conduct." *Journal of Accountancy* 163 (May 1987): 105–109.

Carey, John L. *Professional Ethics of Public Accounting*. New York: American Institute of Accountants, 1946.

Carey, John L., and William O. Doherty. *Ethical Standards of the Accounting Profession*. New York: American Institute of Certified Public Accountants, 1966.

Elliott, Robert K. "The Future of Audits." *Journal of Accountancy* 178 (September 1994): 74–82.

Elliott, Robert K., and Don M. Pallais. "Are You Ready for New Assurance Services?" *Journal of Accountancy* 183 (June 1997): 47–51.

Glater, Jonathan D. "Risking Ridicule, Some Accountants Talk of Becoming Cognitors." *New York Times*, April 5, 2001.

Kelley, Tim, and Loren Margheim. "The Impact of Time Budget Pressure, Personality, and Leadership Variables on Dysfunctional Auditor Behavior." *Auditing: A Journal of Practice and Theory* 9 (spring 1990): 21–42.

Lantry, Terry. "Supreme Court Allows In-person Solicitations by CPAs." *CPA Journal* 63 (October 1993): 72–74.

Pallais, Don M., and Sandra A. Suran. "Change or Die: The Need for Evolution in Auditing Practice." *Line Items*, June/July 1995.

Peterson, Melody. "How the Andersens Turned Into the Bickersons." *New York Times*, March 15, 1998.

Quick, Chris. "The Rise and Fall of Cognitor." *The Times* (London), October 12, 2000.

Rosso, Clar. "Reaching Critical Mass." *California CPA* 69 (June 2001): 24–30.

Squires, Susan E., Cynthia J. Smith, Lorna McDougall, and William R. Yeack. *Inside Arthur Andersen: Shifting Values, Unexpected Consequences*. Upper Saddle River, NJ: FT Prentice Hall, 2003.

Stevens, Mark. "No More White Shoes." *Business Month*, April 1988.

Thomas, Tony. "Cognitor Drive Loses Backers." *Business Review Weekly*, October 20, 2000.

Toffler, Barbara Ley, with Jennifer Reingold. *Final Accounting: Ambition, Greed, and the Fall of Arthur Andersen*. New York: Broadway Books, 2003.

Trabert, Michael. "New Services in a Changing Environment." *Ohio CPA Journal* 58 (January 1999): 46–48.

Zeff, Stephen A. "How the U.S. Accounting Profession Got Where It Is Today: Part I." *Accounting Horizons* 17 (September 2003): 189–206.

Zeff, Stephen A. "How the U.S. Accounting Profession Got Where It Is Today: Part II." *Accounting Horizons* 17 (December 2003): 267–286.

27 Enron

Eichenwald, Kurt. *Conspiracy of Fools: A True Story*. New York: Broadway Books, 2005.

Eisinger, Jesse. "Lay's Defense Leans on His Optimism to Convince Jury He Was Truthful." *Wall Street Journal*, April 26, 2006.

Emshwiller, John R. "Skilling Gets 24 Years in Prison." *Wall Street Journal*, October 24, 2006.

Emshwiller, John R., and Ann Davis. "Untainted Enron Witness Watkins Helps Put Focus on Lay's Conduct." *Wall Street Journal*, March 16, 2006.

Emshwiller, John R., and Gary McWilliams. "Enron's Fastow Testifies Skilling Approved Fraud." *Wall Street Journal*, March 8, 2006.

Emshwiller, John R., and Gary McWilliams. "Skilling Defends Enron, Himself." *Wall Street Journal*, April 11, 2006.

Emshwiller, John R., and Gary McWilliams. "As Enron Trial Heads Toward Jury, Defense Attacks 'Fictional' Case." *Wall Street Journal*, May 17, 2006.

Emshwiller, John R., Gary McWilliams, and Ann Davis. "Lay, Skilling Are Convicted of Fraud." *Wall Street Journal*, May 26, 2006.

Emshwiller, John R., and Rebecca Smith. "Enron Slashes Profits Since 1997 by 20%." *Wall Street Journal*, November 9, 2001.

Emshwiller, John R., and Rebecca Smith. "Murky Waters: A Primer on Enron Partnerships." *Wall Street Journal*, January 21, 2002.

Goldberg, Laura. "Enron Posts Loss After Writedowns." *Houston Chronicle*, October 17, 2001.

Hilzenrath, David S. "Early Warnings of Trouble at Enron: Accounting Firm Found $51 Million in Problems, but Still Signed Off on Books." *Washington Post*, December 30, 2001.

Hull, C. Bryson. "Skilling Briefly Trades CEO Hat for Comedian Role." *Reuters News*, June 12, 2001.

Hunt III, Harry, "Power Players." *Fortune*, August 5, 1996.

Manor, Robert. "Enron Troubles Flagged in '99; Andersen Auditor Criticized Practices." *Chicago Tribune*, April 3, 2002.

McWilliams, Gary, and John E. Emshwiller. "Enron Prosecutor Presses Jury for Convictions on All Counts." *Wall Street Journal*, May 16, 2006.

Powers, William C., Raymond S. Troubh, and Herbert S. Winokur. *Report of the Special Investigative Committee of the Board of Directors of Enron Corporation*, February 1, 2002.

Preston, Robert, and Mike Koller. "Enron Surges into E-Markets." *InformationWeek*, November 6, 2000.

Rapoport, Nancy B., and Bala G. Dharan, eds. *Enron: Corporate Fiascos and Their Implications*. New York: Foundation Press, 2004.

Smith, Rebecca, and John R. Emshwiller. "Enron's CFO's Partnership Had Millions in Profit." *Wall Street Journal*, October 19, 2001.

Thomas, C. William. "The Rise and Fall of Enron." *Journal of Accountancy* 193 (April 2002): 41–48.

Weil, Jonathan. "Energy Traders Cite Gains, But Some Math Is Missing." *Wall Street Journal*, September 20, 2000.

Weil, Jonathan. "After Enron, Mark-to-Market Accounting Gets Scrutiny." *Wall Street Journal*, December 4, 2001.

Zellner, Wendy. "Power Play: Enron, the Nation's Largest Energy Merchant, Won't Let California Stand in its Way." *Business Week*, February 12, 2001.

Zellner, Wendy, and Stephanie Anderson Forest. "The Fall of Enron." *Business Week*, December 17, 2001.

28 WorldCom

Barrier, Michael. "One Right Path." *Internal Auditor* 60 (December 2003): 52–57.

Beresford, Dennis, Nicholas Katzenbach, and C.B. Rogers, Jr. *Report of the Investigation by the Special Investigative Committee of the Board of Directors of WorldCom*, March 31, 2003.

Bryan-Low, Cassell. "WorldCom's Auditors Took Shortcuts." *Wall Street Journal*, July 23, 2003.

Cooper, Cynthia. *Extraordinary Circumstances*. Hoboken, NJ: John Wiley & Sons, 2008.

Dick, Melvin. "Remarks of Melvin Dick." Testimony before the House Committee on Financial Services, July 8, 2002.

Farrell, Greg. "Sullivan Gets 5-Year Prison Sentence." *USA Today*, August 12, 2005.

Feder, Barnaby. "Team Leader for Andersen Had Years of Experience." *New York Times*, June 29, 2002.

Jeter, Lynne W. *Disconnected: Deceit and Betrayal at WorldCom*. Hoboken, NJ: John Wiley & Sons, 2003.

Latour, Almar. "Sullivan Calls Ebbers 'Hands On.'" *Wall Street Journal*, February 8, 2005.

Latour, Almar, and Shawn Young. "WorldCom's Sullivan Says He Told CEO of Problems." *Wall Street Journal*, February 9, 2005.

Latour, Almar, and Shawn Young. "Ebbers Denies He Knew About WorldCom's Fraud." *Wall Street Journal*, March 1, 2005.

Latour, Almar, Shawn Young, and Li Yuan. "Ebbers Is Convicted in Massive Fraud." *Wall Street Journal*, March 16, 2005.

Pulliam, Susan. "Over the Line: A Staffer Ordered to Commit Fraud Balked, Then Caved." *Wall Street Journal*, June 23, 2003.

Pulliam, Susan, and Deborah Solomon. "Uncooking the Books: How Three Unlikely Sleuths Discovered Fraud at WorldCom." *Wall Street Journal*, October 30, 2002.

Ripley, Amanda. "The Night Detective." *Time*, December 30, 2002.

Searcey, Dionne. "Ebbers Is Sentenced to 25 Years For $11 Billion WorldCom Fraud." *Wall Street Journal*, July 14, 2005.

Thornburgh, Dick. *First Interim Report of the Bankruptcy Court Examiner. In Re: WorldCom*, November 4, 2002.

Thornburgh, Dick. *Second Interim Report of the Bankruptcy Court Examiner. In Re: WorldCom*, June 9, 2003.

Zekany, Kay, Lucas Braun, and Zachary Warder. "Behind Closed Doors at WorldCom: 2001." *Issues in Accounting Education* 19 (February 2004): 101–117.

29 The Perfect Storm

Barrionuevo, Alexei, and Jonathan Weil. "Duncan Knew Enron Papers Would Be Lost." *Wall Street Journal*, May 14, 2002.
Barrionuevo, Alexei, and Jonathan Weil. "Andersen Defense Lawyer Is Stealing Show." *Wall Street Journal*, May 20, 2002.
Brevin, Jess. "Justices Overturn Criminal Verdict in Andersen Case." *Wall Street Journal*, June 1, 2005.
Brown, Ken, and Ianthe Jeanne Dugan. "Sad Account: Andersen's Fall From Grace Is a Tale of Greed and Miscues." *Wall Street Journal*, June 7, 2002.
Browning, E.S., and Jonathan Weil. "Burden of Doubt: Stocks Take a Beating as Accounting Worries Spread Beyond Enron." *Wall Street Journal*, January 30, 2002.
Byrnes, Nanette. "Paying for the Sins of Enron." *Business Week*, February 11, 2002.
Chakarun, Michael. "The Sarbanes–Oxley Act of 2002." *National Public Accountant* (October 2002): 6–9.
Glater, Jonathan D., and Alexei Barrionuevo. "Decision Rekindles Debate Over Andersen Indictment." *New York Times*, June 1, 2005.
Eichenwald, Kurt. "Miscues, Missteps and the Fall of Andersen." *New York Times*, May 8, 2002.
Hamburger, Tom, Greg Hitt, and Michael Schroeder. "WorldCom Case Boosts Congress in Reform Efforts." *Wall Street Journal*, June 27, 2002.
Hilzenrath, David S., Jonathan Weisman, and Jim VandeHei. "How Congress Rode a 'Storm' to Corporate Reform." *Washington Post*, July 28, 2002.
Johnson, Carrie. "Small Firms Exit Auditing." *Washington Post*, August 27, 2003.
Knowles, Francine. "Jurors Turned on Andersen: Six Initially Sided With Firm, Only to Change Their Minds." *Chicago Sun-Times*, June 17, 2002.
Kulish, Nicholas, and John R. Wilke. "Called to Account: Indictment Puts Andersen's Fate on Line." *Wall Street Journal*, March 15, 2002.
Labaton, Stephen. "Chief of Big Pension Plan Is Choice for Accounting Board." *New York Times*, October 1, 2002.
Labaton, Stephen. "SEC Chief Hedges on Accounting Regulator." *New York Times*, October 4, 2002.
Labaton, Stephen. "Bitter Divide as Securities Panel Picks an Accounting Watchdog." *New York Times*, October 26, 2002.
Labaton, Stephen, "Audit Overseer Cited Problems in Previous Post." *New York Times*, October 31, 2002.
Murray, Shailagh. "Bill Overhauling Audit Regulation Passes in Senate." *Wall Street Journal*, July 16, 2002.
Murray, Shailagh, and Michael Schroeder. "Governance Bill Has Major Consequences for Many." *Wall Street Journal*, July 26, 2002.
Norris, Floyd. "SEC Picks a Fed Banker to Lead Panel." *New York Times*, April 16, 2003.
Norris, Floyd. "Federal Regulators Find Problems at 4 Big Auditors." *New York Times*, August 27, 2004.
Norris, Floyd. "A Crime So Large It Changed the Law." *New York Times*, July 14, 2005.

Ramos, Michael. "Auditors' Responsibility for Fraud Detection." *Journal of Accountancy* 195 (January 2003): 28–36.
Reilly, David. "Internal-Control Help Becomes Less Costly." *Wall Street Journal*, April 19, 2006.
Roper, John C. "Government Won't Retry Andersen Criminal Case." *Houston Chronicle*, November 23, 2005.
Schroeder, Michael. "House, in Bipartisan Vote, Backs Moderate Accounting Overhaul." *Wall Street Journal*, April 25, 2002.
Shroeder, Michael. "Regulator Under Fire: As Pitt Launches SEC Probe of Himself, Criticism Mounts." *Wall Street Journal*, November 1, 2002.
Schroeder, Michael, and Tom Hamburger. "Accounting Reform Gets Big Lift As Senate Panel Backs New Board." *Wall Street Journal*, June 19, 2002.
Solomon, Deborah. "Fraud Detector: SEC Sets a New Rule Aimed at Companies' Internal Controls." *Wall Street Journal*, May 28, 2003.
Solomon, Ira, and Mark E. Peecher. "S–Ox 404: A Billion Here, a Billion There." *Wall Street Journal*, November 9, 2004.
Spinner, Jackie. "Sullied Accounting Firms Regaining Political Clout," *Washington Post*, May 12, 2002.
Thain, John. "S–Ox: Is the Price Too High?" *Wall Street Journal*, May 27, 2004.
Thomas, Cathy Booth. "Called to Account." *Time*, June 24, 2002.
Toffler, Barbara Ley, with Jennifer Reingold. *Final Accounting: Ambition, Greed, and the Fall of Arthur Andersen.* New York: Broadway Books, 2003.
Weil, Jonathan. "Auditing Firms Get Back to What They Do Best." *Wall Street Journal*, March 31, 2004.
Weil, Jonathan, Alexei Barrionuevo, and Cassell Bryan-Low. "Auditor's Ruling: Andersen Win Lifts U.S. Enron Case." *Wall Street Journal*, June 17, 2002.

Index